PRESENTED TO

THE PEOPLE OF JACKSON COUNTY

IN MEMORY OF

ALFRED S.V. CARPENTER
1881-1974

SHE CAN BRING US HOME

She Can Bring
Us Home

Dr. Dorothy Boulding Ferebee,
Civil Rights Pioneer

DIANE KIESEL

POTOMAC BOOKS
An imprint of the University of Nebraska Press

Library of Congress Cataloging-in-Publication Data
Kiesel, Diane.
She can bring us home: Dr. Dorothy Boulding
Ferebee, civil rights pioneer / Diane Kiesel.
pages cm
Includes bibliographical references and index.
ISBN 978-1-61234-505-5 (cloth: alk. paper)
ISBN 978-1-61234-758-5 (epub)
ISBN 978-1-61234-759-2 (mobi)
ISBN 978-1-61234-506-2 (pdf)
1. Ferebee, Dorothy Boulding, 1898?–1980.
2. African American civil rights workers—
Biography.   3. Women civil rights workers—
United States—Biography.   4. African American
physicians—Biography.   5. Women physicians—
United States—Biography.   6. Howard University—
Health Services—Biography.   7. National Council
of Negro Women—Biography.   8. African Americans—
Civil rights—History—20th century.   9. African
Americans—Social conditions—20th century.
10. African Americans—Health and hygiene—
History—20th century.   I. Title.
E185.97.F39K54 2015
323.092—dc23
[B]
2015002751

Set in Minion by Westchester Publishing Services

In Memory of
Dorothy Boulding Ferebee Jr. (1931–1950)
and Claude Thurston Ferebee II (1931–1981)

It was then that we initiated the first mobile health clinic in the country. . . . Those at home who thought we were down in Mississippi having a big time should have been there to see what difficulties we experienced. This was before the days that the WPA built decent roads in Mississippi. The roads were nothing but mud or shale and sand and rock—little rocks and gravel. And when we traveled we encountered nothing but dust. One couldn't see the car in front. No routes were marked, you didn't know where you were. But fortunately, there's been something about me that I can always come back from where I've been. So when the members of the team noticed that even without markings or signs, I could always get home, they made me the leader of the group. Because they said, "Wherever we've been, she can bring us home."
—Dr. Dorothy Boulding Ferebee

Describing her travels in 1935 as medical director of the Mississippi Health Project for the Black Women Oral History Project, December 28 and 31, 1979, Schlesinger Library on the History of Women in America, Radcliffe Institute, Harvard University, Cambridge MA

CONTENTS

ILLUSTRATIONS

PREFACE

Between 1977 and 1981 the Schlesinger Library on the History of Women in America, Radcliffe Institute for Advanced Study, recorded the memories of certain African American women, age seventy and older, which became known as the Black Women Oral History Project. Among the subjects was Dorothy Boulding Ferebee, who was interviewed at her home on December 28 and 31, 1979, by Merze Tate, a historian at Howard University. It was the most detailed interview she ever gave. The original tape is on file at Radcliffe, and copies of the official transcript of that interview are available at major research libraries around the country. The interviews were also published in book form in 1991.

I interviewed Ruth Edmonds Hill on August 2, 2011, who as Oral History coordinator for the library, supervised the Black Women Oral History Project. Ms. Hill said that each subject was given the opportunity once the interview was completed to review a transcript and make editorial changes. Unfortunately Dorothy was gravely ill when she granted the interview, and died before she was able to edit it. Therefore, the review and editing fell to her son, Dr. Claude Thurston Ferebee II, who was suffering from cancer and died a year after his mother's death, and to Dorothy's daughter-in-law, Carol Ferebee. In addition, Dr. Tate did her own editing and revising of those portions of the interview she thought were inaccurate or needed further clarification. I have listened to the tape and reviewed the edited transcript. The taped interview is rambling and repetitive. At times, Dorothy seemed confused about events in her life. Certain words and phrases have been changed in the official transcript, which is tighter and easier to understand than the original interview. The Schlesinger Library considers the edited transcript to be the official interview, and therefore, when I quote Dorothy from this interview, I am quoting from the official transcript. In my opinion the essential meaning of what she said was not altered by the editing process. But where there seems to be a problem with either Dorothy's memory or the editing, I have pointed it out.

The terminology for African Americans has changed repeatedly with the times. Words such as *colored* and *Negro*, now archaic, were once widely in use and are used in this book when appropriate for the narrative. Unfortunately, like all African Americans, Dorothy and her contemporaries were also subjected to vile racial epithets. Where necessary for historical accuracy, those words are also used.

ACKNOWLEDGMENTS

In her homage to librarians, *This Book Is Overdue*, Marilyn Johnson wrote, "They want to be of service. And they're not trying to sell us anything." I could not agree more. This book could not have been written without the help of many librarians, curators, and archivists. In recognition for all their dedication, hard work, and kindness, I'd like to thank David Smith, former senior librarian, New York Public Library; William Inge, Sargeant Memorial Room, Norfolk Public Library; Joellen ElBashir, Clifford Muse, Tewodros Abebe, Ida Jones, and Richard Jenkins, Moorland-Spingarn Research Center and the Howard University archives; Kenneth Chandler, National Park Service, Mary McLeod Bethune National Historic Site, National Archives for Black Women's History; Patrick Kerwin, Jennifer Brathvode, Joseph Jackson, Bruce Kirby, Lewis Wyman, and Jeffrey Flannery, Manuscript Reading Room at the Library of Congress; Mark Bartlett and Carolyn Waters, New York Society Library; Kelli Bogan, Colby-Sawyer College; Karen Green, New England Law School; Jason Wood, Simmons College; Meghan Lee-Parker, Richard Nixon Library and Birthplace; Dale Neighbors, Library of Virginia; Christopher Banks, Lyndon Baines Johnson Library and Museum; Virginia Lewick, Franklin D. Roosevelt Presidential Library and Museum; Yevgeniya Gribov, Girl Scouts of the USA; Ellen M. Shea and Ruth Edmonds Hill, Schlesinger Library on the History of Women in America, Radcliffe Institute; Amy LaVertu, Tufts University; Stephen E. Novak, Columbia University Medical Center, A. C. Long Health Sciences Library; Adrienne Sharpe, Beinecke Library, Yale University; Ashley Mattingly, National Archives and Records Administration; Crystal Finley, Bethune-Cookman College; Peter Weis, Northfield-Mount Hermon School; Rachel Saliba, Meg Rand, and Joy Jones, Tilton School; Kimberly Springle,

Charles Sumner Museum and Archives; Marta Crilly, City of Boston archives; Richard Baker, U.S. Army Historical Center, Carlisle, Pennsylvania; Christopher Harter, Amistad Research Center, Tulane; Debra Kimok, Benjamin Feinberg Library, Plattsburgh State University College; Steven G. Fullwood, Manuscripts, Archives, and Rare Books Division, Schomberg Center for Research in Black Culture, and Julia Jackson.

I thank James Ervin for permission to quote from the late Elsie Ervin's college paper on Rosier Dedwylder; Chris Chapman for permission to reprint the Lois Maillot Jones calendar drawing of Dorothy; and Leigh Montville of Conde Nast/Vogue for permission to use the stunning Irving Penn photograph of Dorothy that was published in *Vogue*. I thank Holly Shulman for sharing her insights about her mother, Polly Spiegel Cowan, and for allowing me to quote from her writings, and Professor James Forman Jr. of Yale for allowing me to quote from his late father's papers.

Despite the fact that Dorothy Ferebee would be more than 115 years old if she were alive, there are still people around who either knew her when or knew people in her life. I am indebted to several: John Beckley, William H. (Timmy) Johnson, Aurelia Roberts Brooks, Lynn French, William Lofton Jr., Vaughn Phillips, Rosier Dedwylder II, Susan Goodwillie Stedman, former DC Council member Charlene Drew Jarvis, Margo Dean Pinson, former congressman William Clay, Merle Moses Bowser, DeMaurice Moses, George Jones, Barrington Parker Jr., Anna Johnston Diggs Taylor, John Carter, Robert L. Harris Jr., and Christine Parker. I also would like to thank Sgt. Brent Kearney of the Montgomery County Police Department, Emily Jansen, Mildred Bond Roxborough, Alice Wyche Hurley, Peggy Canaday, Thayer Gallison IV, Bret Fikentscher, H. Jack Geiger, and Tom Ward.

Unfortunately, several people I interviewed have since passed away but I would like to acknowledge their help; DC Mayor Marion Barry, Dorothy Height, John Russell Eberhardt III, Mary Corinne (Candy) Murray, and Carolyn Wyche Martin Wilson.

Two sources have a special place in my heart because speaking with me required them to focus on difficult periods in the lives of their loved ones. I thank Iona Vargus, daughter of the late Madeline Dugger, and Nancy Simerly Schreiber, widow of Norburt Paul Schreiber. Their intelligence, insight, and honesty added an important dimension to this book.

Janice Ferebee provided me with introductions to family members, for which I am grateful. I thank W. Laurence Jones, Karen Paige Womack, and Dorothy L. Ferebee of National Public Radio for speaking with me.

Writing a book is an emotional roller-coaster of exhilaration, confidence, doubt, and despair—often in the same half hour. Friends tolerated my constant chatter about this book—did they *really care* that Dorothy wore Jean Nate cologne? Those with an editorial background were asked to put in their two cents. I thank dear friend Benjamin R. Shore, formerly of Copley Newspapers, a terrific editor and occasional researcher; and special confidante Heath Hardage Lee, also a University of Nebraska Press/Potomac author, who was my stalking horse in the publishing world, my shoulder to cry on, and my cherished friend. I could not have gotten through this multiyear marathon without her.

I want to thank David Davidson, always ready with sage counsel, and his daughters, Jennifer Davidson and Margaret Perillo, who hosted me on many research trips to Boston, and the Rev. Anne Skinner Piper. Laurie Goldstein was a trusted navigator on multiple field visits, including to the Mississippi Delta in July! Jeremy Korzenik and Laura Murray accompanied me on several Ferebee outings in and around Washington.

Many professional writers shared with me the benefit of their talent and experience: the late Laird Anderson, A'Lelia Bundles, Debby Applegate, Ellen Feldman, Nina Burleigh, Diane McWhorter, Harriet Washington, Debbie Z. Harlow, Michael Greenburg, Nick Kotz, Pamela Fessler, Gary Marmorstein, Robert Klara, Lee Lowenfish, James McGrath Morris, Thomas Ward, Anjulet Tucker, Susan L. Smith, Anne-Marie Taylor, and Beverly Palmer. I want to thank the Biographers' International Organization for all the support it has provided to me and other biographers.

Seattle media lawyer Judith Endejan gave me wise counsel and good friendship. Several academics and historians have my thanks for vetting certain chapters, saving me from faux pas large and small: Ann Short Chirhart, Fred Smith, Theodore McCord, and Cassandra Newby-Alexander.

I owe so much to my agent, Colleen Mohyde of the Doe Coover Agency, for her faith in me and this project. She read every word and gave me the benefit of her years of experience in publishing. I thank Elizabeth Demers, formerly of Potomac Books, my original editor, and Bridget Barry, who took over for her after Potomac became part of the University of Nebraska Press. She and Sabrina Ehmke Sergeant, her former assistant editor, left all the weak portions of this book on the cutting-room floor, which made all the best portions far better. The production team headed by Debbie Masi, including Judith Hoover as copy editor, was also excellent, as was the marketing and distribution group, Martyn Beeny, Tish Fobben, Sam Dorrance, and Rosemary Vestal.

I thank my mother, Helen Kiesel, and my sister, June Kiesel, for their love and support. And I thank Georges G. Lederman because he is patient, supportive, and I love him.

Finally this book could not have been written—or at least could not have been written very well—without the cooperation of Dorothy's family: her grandchildren, Todd Boulding Ferebee and Dorothy Ruth Ferebee, and Lisa Kleinman Ferebee, the widow of her late grandson, Claude Thurston Ferebee III. If I had a nickel for every time I called them with just one more question, I could retire. Besides the phone calls, emails, and visits, they gladly provided pictures and yellowed letters from their basements and attics and at my urging looked for more. Granddaughter Dorothy notarized countless letters so I could access school, military, FBI, and personnel records, as well as birth, death, and marriage certificates relating to her Ruffin, Boulding, and Ferebee ancestors. Moreover, they never interfered with my work, and when I asked them for their opinions, they responded with intelligence, candor, and grace. But after seven years even the long-suffering Ferebees had enough. As Todd put it so succinctly in an email in May 2014, six years after I met him, when I was *still* asking questions about his beloved "Gam," "Bring it on home darlin.'"

INTRODUCTION

Compassion, Cussedness, and Class

In her prime Dorothy Celeste Boulding Ferebee was the most recognizable African American woman in America. Had the time been less tainted by bigotry, she may have been the most recognizable woman in the country. But white America was not ready in the early twentieth century to embrace a pioneering woman of color. Long before Rosa Parks refused to move to the back of the bus in Montgomery, Alabama, and the young Reverend Dr. Martin Luther King Jr. led the boycott that followed, Dorothy Ferebee battled racism and gender bias. From the time she denounced lynching in a college essay in 1918 through her journey to Selma, Alabama, to champion voting rights in 1963 and beyond, she was on the cutting edge of major civil rights and women's equality issues.

Dorothy arrived in Washington DC during the Roaring Twenties with a diploma from Tufts Medical School in her hand, courage in her step, and big plans in her head. Her ostensible purpose for moving to DC was to begin an internship at the Freedmen's Hospital, which treated blacks, the only hospital that accepted her in the era of Jim Crow. That she became "a lady doctor" was in itself an amazing feat for an African American woman of her day. But this chosen child of the black elite had bigger ideas. She wanted to "uplift the race," as the expression went, while she rose professionally. On her family tree were lawyers, businessmen, politicians, and a judge. She set out to change the world and within five years of arriving in Washington was off to a running start.

If there is one word that captures the essence of Dorothy's greatness, it is *visionary*. She saw a future in which blacks and whites were equal, and she worked to bring it about. There was so much that needed to change, starting with the rigid segregation of the nation's capital. Poverty engulfed the city's black children, many of whom were left to fend for themselves while their mothers took care of white women's children. Because existing day care centers shut them out, Dorothy started a settlement house for African American children in 1930. She fought for reproductive rights; when the mere mention of the words *birth control* could land the speaker in jail, Dorothy, an obstetrician, advocated sex education for five-year-olds.

But it wasn't until she led a traveling medical clinic to the Mississippi cotton fields to bring health care to dirt poor sharecroppers during the Depression that she catapulted herself into the national spotlight. Each summer from 1935 until the start of World War II Dorothy directed the Mississippi Health Project with a team of hand-picked volunteer nurses sponsored by Alpha Kappa Alpha (AKA), the elite black sorority founded at Howard in 1908. They left comfortable homes to travel to the Mississippi Delta, where the humidity was a relentless stalker. The shade of the magnolia trees offered no respite, and the swaying front porch swings circulated more mosquitoes than air. They drove thousands of miles of unpaved roads through the Deep South with no public place to eat, sleep, or use the bathroom. It was tough, dangerous, and uncertain work.

The Mississippi Health Project would be a triumph for Dorothy and AKA, but it almost ended before it started. Dorothy underestimated the resistance of the white plantation owners who refused to allow laborers to leave their farm for checkups by a meddling "colored lady doctor." Undaunted, she improvised. She loaded cars with medical supplies and drove directly onto the cotton fields in the broiling sun to set up shop. When their cars got stuck in a ditch along an unpaved road—as was common—there was no AAA to tow them; the women got out in their silk stockings and high heels and pushed.

By the time gasoline rationing during World War II made it impossible to continue the long drive south, the Mississippi Health Project had treated fifteen thousand sharecroppers and their families.[1] The U.S. Public Health Service lauded it as one of the most successful volunteer public health programs in history.[2] Its legacy can be seen today as mobile vans affiliated with hospitals and clinics are routinely parked on city streets and in suburban shopping malls offering free mammograms, blood pressure screenings, and flu shots.

The Mississippi Health Project would make Dorothy famous in her day. Eleanor Roosevelt invited her to the White House; schools, churches, and civic groups wanted her to speak. *Reader's Digest*, with more than a million readers in 1940, published a feature about it, praising the "Negro college women who devote their summer vacations to a health project that is peculiarly effective and dramatic" and singling out Dorothy's leadership.[3] Her presence on a podium guaranteed a packed house. She became a recognizable figure in her impeccably tailored suits, veiled hats, seamed stockings, and the occasional corsage.

In 1939 she was elected president, or supreme basileus, of AKA. A decade later she reached professional nirvana, succeeding the iconic Mary McLeod Bethune to become the second president of the National Council of Negro Women, a powerful umbrella group of women's organizations. From this platform she had the ears of presidents, congressmen, business leaders, newpaper publishers, and international figures.

Aging did not stop Dorothy. More than thirty years after her work in Mississippi, when she could have retired to her cottage on the Jersey shore, she returned to the Deep South in 1963 to participate in a voter registration drive in Dallas County, Alabama, home of Selma. Of 15,115 blacks eligible to vote, just 242 were registered.[4]

At a standing-room-only rally in a Selma church, the audience was primed: they sang the mournful old Negro spirituals and the feisty new civil rights songs. With 750 locals, scores of national reporters, and a handful of undercover cops inside, Dorothy, by then an old pro at wooing an audience, took to the pulpit. With her exaggerated diction—a pastiche of Eleanor Roosevelt, Rose Kennedy, and the local elocution teacher—she gave an electrifying speech that prophetically championed expanding societal roles for women. By the time she sat down she had become a heroine for a new generation of civil rights warriors.

Her appearance that day only added to the Ferebee cachet; she had been a household name in the black press for years, her personal life fodder for the social pages. During her lifetime she would be photographed with Josephine Baker, Nelson Rockefeller, LBJ, Patricia Nixon, Mamie Eisenhower, Shirley Chisholm, and important civil rights leaders. As she aged and times changed, her work in the movement finally brought her recognition in the white press. The fashion photographer Irving Penn photographed her for *Vogue* magazine. "Charms birds off trees," the editors gushed.[5]

But ironically, as African Americans achieved the increased professional, economic, and political power for which Dorothy fought so hard, her relevance waned and her fame faded. She and her "uplift the race" philosophy became as woefully outdated as the veiled hats and floral corsages she continued to wear. When she died of congestive heart failure on September 14, 1980, her story for the most part died with her.

The headline in her *Washington Post* obituary read, "Dr. Dorothy Ferebee Dies: Fought for Rights of Women, Blacks."[6] She was described as a firebrand who descended from a slave family, overcame racism, and emerged as a medical pioneer and political powerhouse. But the real story is more complex—and more interesting.

Dorothy Boulding was born in Norfolk in 1898 to a prominent family of mixed racial heritage. Her grandfather, Richard Gault Leslie Paige, rose from slavery to the state legislature. Her great-uncle, George L. Ruffin, was the first black graduate of Harvard Law School; his wife was Josephine St. Pierre Ruffin, a crusading journalist and suffragette. Yet for all her fancy pedigree, her race and her gender presented huge challenges. Her description of her fate at Tufts Medical School, where she was among a handful of women who graduated in 1924, and one of the few African Americans, said it all. In an editorial about her published in the *Washington Post* after her death, she was quoted: "We women were always the last to get assignments. . . . And I? I was the last of the last because not only was I a woman, but a Negro, too."[7]

In 1930 she married a Howard colleague, Claude Thurston Ferebee, a dentist. They were the parents of picture-perfect twins, a boy and a girl. Movie star handsome, with the sculpted body of the track star he once was, Claude had an ego as big as his wife's. Like many vibrant women, Dorothy faced sharp criticism for her towering ambition in a way her equally ambitious husband did not. Her motivation for choosing the path less traveled was personal as well as political. She liked the attention; in fact she loved it. She left her children at boarding schools and her husband in the arms of other women while she aspired to a life of purpose. After twenty years of marriage to the great Dorothy Boulding Ferebee, they divorced and Claude married a much younger, less prominent woman.

Dorothy taught medicine at Howard and Tufts, ran the Howard student health clinic, and built a private obstetrical practice. She continued to make house calls well into her seventies, chauffeured by her adult grandchildren after her son considered her too old to drive (and too prone to flooring the gas pedal of her beloved Oldsmobile Cutlass). All the while she fought the good fight.

She could be controversial. Her support for birth control and abortion rights led to her intellectual flirtation with Margaret Sanger and the now discredited eugenics movement. Her involvement with progressives and leftists got her entangled with McCarthy-era witch hunters. The FBI kept tabs on her and the organizations and activities with which she was associated.

Little of this was known in her lifetime, partly because Dorothy was skillful at controlling her press image. When bad news knocked, she answered it with silence, platitudes, or outright lies before retreating to the next public event. She relied on these tactics when facing the most devastating blow of her life: the death of her only daughter. Dorothy Jr. died in February 1950 when she was just eighteen years old and her mother was at the height of her fame at the helm of the National Council of Negro Women. At her daughter's funeral, a near prostrate Dorothy was supported under one elbow by her husband and under the other by her son.[8] A little more than a month after her daughter was buried, she was back on the speaking circuit.[9]

Dorothy maintained until her own dying day that her daughter had succumbed to a sudden onset of pneumonia. But it is far more likely that Dorothy Jr. died from a botched abortion, all the more tragic because her mother could have performed it safely. Had the truth been known, it would have killed Dorothy's career. The death of their daughter ended the fiction Dorothy and Claude had fostered as the successful, high-powered couple. They divorced that summer. Although Claude outlived his ex-wife by nearly twenty years, she often told people he was dead. In her book *Too Heavy a Load: Black Women in Defense of Themselves, 1894–1994*, the Rutgers University historian Deborah Gray White writes that memoirs by African American women often read like "a list of accomplishments." She blames that one-dimensionality on the fact these women were wary of "putting their private lives and histories in the hands of a media that had for centuries stereotyped and slandered black women." Rather than allow themselves to be examined as individuals, the highest achievers saw themselves as representatives of their race. "They let their public see only what they wanted them to see. As far as their audience was concerned, the public was the private."[10] The unfortunate result is history that sometimes borders on hagiography and fails to capture the rich, nuanced lives of these trailblazers.

Thirty-five years after her death, as recognition of the African American contribution to history has grown, the significance of Dorothy Ferebee has grown too. On an individual level her story is that of a woman who inhabited the rarified world of the African American elite. She was the embodiment of what W. E. B. Du Bois heralded in his famous 1903 essay as "the Talented Tenth." These were the Negroes (to use the accepted, polite term of his Edwardian day) destined to lead "the Race" to the promised land of equality. In the broadest sense, Dorothy's story *is* the story of the racism and sexism imbedded in late-nineteenth- and much of twentieth-century American life and of the strength, bravery, and grace it took to transcend it. Her life coincided with the historical period when African Americans launched their long and bitter struggle for civil rights and with the time women fought for the fruits of suffrage. Dorothy Celeste Boulding Ferebee was both shaped by and helped shape these profound social changes.

Today Barack Obama is president of the United States, women serve in high positions in government and industry, laws exist against discrimination on the basis of race and gender, and it is hard to imagine the world into which Dorothy was born. In 2012, in a eulogy to Judge Robert L. Carter, another civil rights pioneer, Judge Barrington Parker Jr. of the U.S. Circuit Court of Appeals and the son of Marjorie Holloman Parker, who worked alongside Dorothy on the Mississippi Health Project, described how hard it was to change that world: "The struggle to arrive at this place has been long and difficult. The resistance to racial change in this country was far more determined than we care to remember and far more determined than most of us do remember. The achievements of that struggle are enormously impressive, but hardly conclusive. The changes we hasten to celebrate were by no means inevitable. But change came."[11]

Two days after the *Washington Post* ran Ferebee's obituary, the paper devoted a rare and precious eight inches on its editorial page to her. It lauded her "old-fashioned values" of "hard work, persistence and the pursuit of excellence" and summed her up perfectly: "It took more than a little courage to break down the barriers of sex and color. Dorothy Ferebee . . . knew how to do so with a marvelous blend of compassion, cussedness and class."[12]

Prologue

The posters went up in churches, on crepe myrtle trees, and along rotting walls of one-room schoolhouses all over the Mississippi Delta, addressed to the "colored people" of Bolivar County and written in large letters as if by a huckster announcing the arrival of the traveling circus: "Notice! Colored People! Everyone come to a Clinic for Health Advice." The anonymous author promised a genuine lady doctor from Washington DC, Dr. Dorothy Boulding Ferebee, and her staff of "trained colored assistants" who would treat the sick of their race. The Mississippi Health Project was coming to town.

Lord knows, the colored people of Bolivar County needed all the help they could get in the summer of 1936. While the rest of the population clawed their way out of the Great Depression that had engulfed the decade, blacks in the Delta still suffered the same miserable existence they always had, with no end in sight. Nearly a quarter of all African Americans in Mississippi were illiterate.[1] What little education was available in segregated schools in the Jim Crow South was abandoned during cotton-picking season so children as young as eight could work the fields.

Most African Americans in the Delta worked the land as tenant farmers or sharecroppers, akin to modern-day slavery. Entire families earned the grand sum of fifty dollars a year, sometimes less.[2] These farmworkers lived on the most fertile ground on earth, but their diet contained almost no fruits or vegetables because landowners refused to allow them to use the valuable acreage to cultivate small gardens. Wholesome foods weren't sold at the plantation commissary, the only store that would accept salaries of scrip. Dorothy found patients suffering from diseases that had not and should not have been seen in the United States of America since the nineteenth century. Pellagra and rickets were present, along with outbreaks of smallpox. Tuberculosis deaths were rampant and dysentery common. Thirty percent of the county's African American men suffered from long-term untreated syphilis.[3] Disease bearing mosquitoes swarmed the humid Delta, biting the ankles and necks of the workers in the fields and in their homes, which were nothing more than dilapidated shacks without window screens or, in some cases, front doors.

The health team battled more than disease. Belief in superstitions ran as deep as belief in the Baptist Church and Almighty God. Cut your child's lice-ridden hair and she'll never speak.[4] Chew horseradish to relieve hoarseness. Tea bags on the eyes will cure the common cold.[5] There was an abundance of ignorance and an absence of joy. Some mothers had no idea how old their children were. Others didn't know their own names, first or last. On seeing the children of the Delta, one of Dorothy's assistants wrote, "We had the opportunity again and again to strengthen our conclusion that children in Mississippi don't smile." She compared their little poker faces to the expressions on the faces of stockbrokers "regarding a 1929 Wall Street chart."[6]

There was little to smile about. In Mississippi racists ruled with impunity and long ropes; the state was the lynching capital of the country.[7] Between 1882 and 1927, 561 people were killed by lynch mobs there; 517 of them were black.[8] Merely looking a white man in the eye was enough of a reason for a black man to be hanged. Looking at a white woman was an even better reason. A black man accused of the capital offense of raping a white woman, either on the word of the victim or on a rumor, would be wise to pray for a quick arrest and conviction. At least he'd have a few weeks in a cell and a chance to see the preacher before his hanging. If acquitted he ran the risk of being dragged outside by a white mob and strung up on a sturdy branch of an oak tree in the courthouse square.

Blacks in the Deep South in the 1930s were prohibited from voting, eating in restaurants, or drinking at water fountains reserved for whites. Their children were barred from public parks and swimming pools. African Americans constituted 50 percent of the state of Mississippi and 75 percent of the eighty thousand residents of Bolivar County, but they had no role in mainstream life.[9] They crowded into shacks on plantations or into slums on the edge of towns. They sat in the back of the bus, if they could afford the fare, and had no chance at jobs providing a decent living. A black man called the white man "Sir," and the white man responded by calling him "Boy." Well into the 1950s the black NAACP attorney Robert Carter, who with Thurgood Marshall successfully argued *Brown v. Board of Education* in the U.S. Supreme Court, was not called "Mister" in a southern court of law; "Bob" was all the judge could manage.[10]

Fear was the dominant state for people then called "Negroes," "colored," or worse. It permeated every aspect of Delta life, including an act as simple as taking advantage of Dorothy's free medical care. For those few able to read the signs announcing her arrival and for those who had the signs read to them, retaliation by overseers for leaving the fields to visit the clinic was a worry.

For many of the tenant farmers and sharecroppers, some descended from slaves who once worked the same fields, Dorothy's clinic was the first health care available beyond cold compresses for fevers and homemade potions for ailing stomachs. Some of their children had never used a toothbrush and cried because their jaws ached from decay. So at night on the porches of their sagging shacks, sitting on old torn-up sofas damp from the leaden humidity, some parents agreed to take their children to the clinic whatever the repercussions. Others looked for spiritual guidance. On Sunday ladies in ill-fitting dresses trudged to church where the pastors, with the nascent sparks of the fire of future civil rights battles lighting their sermons, told them God had sent the Negro lady doctor to them, and visiting her was their divine right and duty. As the clinic's opening day approached, August 21, 1936, it was on everybody's mind and tongue.

As Dorothy and her volunteer aides made their final preparations for this, their second year of the Mississippi Health Project, their anxiety grew. Their sponsor, the prestigious Alpha Kappa Alpha sorority, whose members included the college-educated daughters of the African American elite, had asked its members for one thousand dollars to send Dorothy to neighboring Holmes County, Mississippi, for the first time in 1935.[11] The black press hailed their adventure as a triumph. In fact it had been tough going. The landowners pulled up the welcome mat as soon as Dorothy arrived, refusing to allow their workers near the medical team. It was not until she drove from farm to farm to explain she was there to provide health care, not organize a union or advocate for civil rights, that all but one owner relented. Even then the owners wouldn't let the workers off their land or out of their sight. Dorothy was forced to bring the clinic to the patients by setting up shop directly in the fields, under the watchful eyes of overseers.[12]

Now, a year later, in his office not far from the old whitewashed courthouse, Dr. Rosier Davis Dedwylder, chief health officer of Bolivar County, had his own headache over Dorothy's imminent arrival. It was Dedwylder who printed all those posters, stuck them everywhere he could, and made sure they got into the hands of the preachers.[13] He knew all about Holmes County the summer before. He felt both pity and awe for Dorothy when he received her letter telling him she wanted to try again, this time in Bolivar. He vowed to help.

Using memos and meetings he convinced Mississippi officials all the way to Jackson that the clinic was as beneficial for landowners as it was for the black sharecroppers. From his perspective, the arrival of the colored medical team was the best thing to happen to the county since FDR. Landowners who disagreed were too blinded by bigotry to realize that healthy field hands meant more profits, and allowing them to be treated by one of their own meant local white doctors did not have to deal with them. All Dedwylder had to do was make them see the light.

A longtime southerner and landowner himself, the fifty-eight-year-old Dedwylder lived on the Grove, one of the finest plantations in the Delta. With six hundred fertile acres producing King Cotton, he was a wealthy man. Before the Civil War, slaves had waited on his ancestors, and in the years since paid black servants worked in the great white house that crowned his property and sharecroppers plowed his land. Although the doctor's wife occasionally used what future generations discreetly called "the N word," the doctor early on shed whatever ingrained biases he may have had against the Negro. As a young physician before World War I, supported by Rockefeller brothers' funding, Dedwylder had engaged in research to stamp out yellow fever. His intellectual world extended well beyond the steamy streets of Cleveland, Mississippi.[14]

On the doctor's desk was the motto he aspired to live by: "Neither look up to the rich nor down to the poor."[15] Dedwylder dreaded leaving his office to grab a sandwich, and not simply because of the smothering heat. At the local luncheonette with his newspaper, as far away as he could get from the all-white clientele, he knew what they'd be whispering: "There goes the nigger lover."[16] Better to just pour another cup of coffee and add an extra sugar cube or two to curb his appetite.

On Monday, August 17, 1936, the entire country was parched; had a copy of the *New York Times* (with the out-of-town price of four cents) been on his desk, Dedwylder would have seen that even in New York City the thermometer hit 100 degrees. Given that Dorothy was likely to arrive in the middle of a heat wave, Dedwylder planned to be the first to invite her to his property for a tall glass of iced tea. Better yet, dinner. He'd make sure word got around. If that did not set an example for the other owners, nothing would.

Meanwhile, in Washington DC, where Dorothy lived, practiced medicine, and taught at Howard University, she was busily cajoling her husband, her friends, and the project volunteers to lend her their cars to carry the team and supplies one thousand miles into the Deep South. Before the New Deal public works projects were in full swing, Mississippi was so poor there were few miles of paved roads.[17] Beset by griping from car-owning volunteers over who would pay for repairs in the case of blown tires or broken axles, as well as last-minute cancellations from her medical team— some because their families feared for their lives—Dorothy was close to losing her mind. Tormented by similar nay-saying the year before as she prepared to leave for Holmes County, she boldly stated, "I am not discouraged, and I shall do all I can . . . single handed if necessary."[18]

But, as it turned out, she did not have to go alone. She and her health project team gathered in Washington on a hot July morning, loaded up their cars, and drove in a caravan into Mississippi—and history.

1 Push, Pluck, Prominence, and Merit

In a crumbling cardboard box of memorabilia gathering dust in her grand-daughter's attic is a sepia-tone picture of a young Dorothy Celeste Boulding, circa 1906. She wears a white pinafore, tights, and leather ankle boots—the uniform of privileged little girls—and a self-assured, almost smug expression. About the time the picture was taken, Dorothy had begun her backyard medical career. "I would nurse and rub the birds that fell out of trees, the dog that lost a fight," she recalled. Her mother and grandmother encouraged her dream of becoming a doctor every step of the way.[1]

Sometimes Dorothy claimed she was inspired to enter medicine after helping stuff and stitch the Thanksgiving turkey: "Stitches in the well-stuffed birds for baking were stitches in mending broken bones and open wounds—a considerable stretch of the imagination, but children have no brakes on theirs."[2] Given her lifelong aversion to the kitchen and her lack of culinary skill when she ventured into one, her wounded-bird story has more of the ring of truth.

Whatever led Dorothy to dream of becoming a doctor, it was unlikely a "colored girl" of her day would get her wish. In 1890 there were all of 909 black doctors in the United States—115 of them women. When she entered medical school in 1920, and Jim Crow had taken its toll the numbers of black women doctors in the nation had dwindled to sixty-five.[3]

But Dorothy was oblivious to barriers and fortunate enough to occupy a sliver of the universe inhabited by the successful black elite, the so-called Talented Tenth. The phrase was coined by NAACP founder W. E. B. Du Bois, who described the Talented Tenth as those upper-crust Negroes destined to lead the rest of the race out of its misery: "From the very first it has been the educated and intelligent of the Negro people that have led and elevated the mass."[4] Dorothy would cling to the philosophy of the Talented Tenth all her life.

The spoon in Dorothy Boulding's mouth at birth was solid silver. She was the youngest of three children born in Norfolk, Virginia, to the privileged Florence Cornelia Paige, called Flossie, and Benjamin Richard Boulding. Flossie's formidable father, Richard Gault Leslie Paige, known by his initials, R.G.L., began life a slave and ended it a wealthy businessman. In between he was elected to the Virginia legislature and fought fearlessly for his race.[5] On the floor of the General Assembly in 1880 he angrily (and futilely) demanded that the governor investigate a local lynching. His incendiary remarks were reported in the New York City papers.[6] Flossie's mother, Lillie Ruffin, was descended from the Boston Ruffins, a premier black family that included a judge, writers, lawyers, a professional musician, and one noisy suffragette.

In an oral history she gave shortly before she died of congestive heart failure Dorothy claimed her great-grandfather was Thomas Paige, a white governor of Virginia, but there was no such governor.[7] She may have been repeating family lore, or she may have been confused by her disease, which can cause extreme fatigue, or by high doses of digitalis, the standard drug for the condition, which also can cause confusion. There was a slave-owning Dr. Thomas Page (the "Page" surname is sometimes spelled with an "i") who lived in Norfolk before the Civil War, but whether the shared surname constituted parentage or merely ownership of her ancestors is unknown, assuming there is any family connection between Dr. Page and her grandfather.[8]

Dorothy's grandfather was one of four brothers, all of whom were born slaves. R.G.L. was born on May 31, 1846, and died from peritonitis on September 21, 1904.[9] He and his older brother, Thomas, who became a Norfolk business leader after the war, escaped slavery with the help of the Underground Railroad. Dorothy's grandfather was ten when he stowed away on a cargo ship bound for Philadelphia, where the local antislavery society arranged for him to go to Boston to join an aunt who had escaped earlier. To honor a Professor Lesley who assisted him on his perilous journey, R.G.L. took the man's name as one of his middle names, with a different spelling. In Boston he got lucky, living with his aunt under the roof of a pair of kind and generous abolitionists, the Harvard-educated lawyer George Hillard and his wife, Susan.[10] Hillard had been a law partner of Senator Charles Sumner, and his wife was active in the Underground Railroad along with the poet William Wadsworth Longfellow and others.[11]

Dorothy's grandfather was not the first black man to graduate from Harvard Law School, as she bragged. That honor belonged to his future brother-in-law, George Ruffin, who graduated in 1869 and married the famous suffragette, political journalist, and women's organizer, Josephine St. Pierre.[12] Ruffin became the first black judge in Massachusetts, a family connection of which Dorothy was very proud.[13] R.G.L. either apprenticed with a practicing lawyer—perhaps Hillard or Ruffin—or was self-taught and hung up a shingle once he returned to Norfolk. At other points in his life he was a craftsman, and Norfolk's assistant postmaster.[14]

While in Boston R.G.L. met the high-class Ruffins, probably in a pew at the Twelfth Baptist Church, an African American parish populated by many runaway slaves, and in 1868 married Judge Ruffin's baby sister, Lillie.[15] R.G.L. began amassing real estate, probably from his earnings as a craftsman. The first two of their nine children, including Dorothy's mother on December 19, 1871, were born in Massachusetts.[16] R.G.L. then moved his family back to Norfolk, where postwar political coalitions formed, making it possible for former slaves like him to hold political office.

Once in Norfolk, Lillie, and later, her daughter Flossie, were "club women," who were held in high esteem in the African American community in the nineteenth and early twentieth centuries. They joined forces with other like-minded ladies to help less fortunate families of color, filling the void occupied in more enlightened times by government agencies and paid social workers. In bustles, slender boots, and feathered hats they gathered in church basements to organize neighborhood improvement associations.

Florence Paige Boulding's power base was Norfolk's Grace Episcopal Church, home to black worshippers since 1883.[17] One of her "club woman" projects was to help find jobs for Negro teachers in Virginia's segregated schools.[18] Flossie also enjoyed singing in public, much as her daughter, Dorothy, would later enjoy speaking.[19]

Dorothy claimed not to know the day or year she was born. When the census taker came knocking on the family's door on June 1, 1900, someone told him little Dorothy was born in 1897.[20] When she was middle-aged and sought an appointment by the State Department as a public-health consultant in Europe, she said she was born in 1900.[21] She fibbed on her marriage license application, saying she was born in 1901, perhaps fooling her younger husband-to-be into thinking they were the same age, when she was really four years older.[22]

At the time Dorothy was born, Virginia had no registration requirements for the birth or death of anyone, black or white.[23] Dorothy said her "official" birthday, October 10, 1898, was one her father chose and was a source of disagreement between her parents.[24] It is hard to believe her educated, well-to-do mother and father did not know when their only daughter was born. Dorothy's claim that she was unsure about her birth date provided the cover she needed to pick the date that best suited the occasion.

There was no controversy about when Dorothy's two older brothers were born. Ruffin Paige Boulding was born on January 4, 1895; Benjamin Richard Boulding, named for his father and grandfather, was called Richard and was born on June 10, 1896.[25] Ruffin graduated from the prestigious law school at Howard University in 1925.[26] During those years of strict segregation in education, Howard was known as "the black Harvard."

Family fortune took a downward slide when Dorothy's wealthy grandfather died in 1904. It declined further with the early death in 1910 of her forty-two-year-old father and then went into a free fall when R.G.L.'s bereft widow, Lillie, died in 1913 and left the bulk of her estate to her favorite son, R.G.L. Jr., a lawyer known as Leslie. Lillie moped and mourned a full decade after her husband's death—to the point where it was listed as a secondary cause of her own death.[27] In his honor she erected a twelve-foot obelisk in the Norfolk cemetery he owned and where he and many family members were buried. It was only because Dorothy's brother Ruffin selflessly deferred his own schooling to finance her medical training that she got an education.

Brother Richard's station in life was less lofty. He worked as a laborer, ran a pool hall, and sold insurance. He was a steward at the whites-only Monticello Hotel and a bartender serving the white patrons of the Norfolk Yacht and Country Club. He was briefly employed at the Norfolk Naval Base and logged some time as a postman. At age forty-five he was a bachelor, still living at home in Norfolk with his widowed mother.[28]

Dorothy sanitized and upgraded Richard's professional life when speaking about him. The year before she died, in her interview for the Black Women Oral History Project, she said Richard graduated from Hampton Institute, the segregated trade school near Norfolk attended by her parents and Booker T. Washington that expanded to a full-scale accredited college. She also claimed he was a high school chemistry teacher who later had a stable career with the postal service.[29] None of that checks out.

When Richard died in February 1980, seven months before Dorothy, his obituary noted his forty-five-year career as a postman in Norfolk. Dorothy was his closest living relative and the likely source of the story.[30] He was hired as a temporary postal clerk in September 1943, probably to fill a wartime manpower shortage, but he resigned less than a year and a half later, after having racked up petty infractions like showing up late and going AWOL from his workstation.[31] Similarly when Dorothy's mother died in 1959 the headline of her obituary—the source of which was most certainly Dorothy—referred to Flossie as an "ex-teacher." Alumni records from Hampton Institute describe Flossie as "having taught," but she hardly had much of a classroom career. Year after year in Norfolk's city directories she was listed as a "domestic."[32]

Dorothy's father could have given her bragging rights, yet she rarely spoke of him. That may be because she hardly knew him; he died when she was only twelve, and she spent most of her childhood in Boston. Her most extensive reference to her father was to boast that she was the apple of his eye.[33] She heaped credit for her accomplishments on her mother, her grandmother, and her grandmother's sister, Emma, with whom she lived as a student in Boston. But Dorothy was a chip off the old man's block.

Benjamin Boulding was born in 1868 in either Crewe or Burkeville, Virginia, tiny towns about 110 miles west of Norfolk.[34] He was the oldest son of Benjamin Richard and Angelina Boulding.[35] Boulding would rank among the Talented Tenth, but his own parents were simple country folk. His father called himself a farmer; his wife of forty-six years was described in the 1900 census as a "wash woman."[36] Despite these modest beginnings, at the time of his death Dorothy's paternal grandfather owned thirty-five acres of land in Nottoway County that he left to his heirs.[37] Benjamin Boulding graduated in 1888 from Hampton Institute, and Flossie Paige graduated in 1892.[38] He became a school principal in the Nottoway County public schools, resigning in 1891 to work as a clerk for the U.S. Railway Mail Service, making one thousand dollars a year.[39] When the average annual wage for non–farm laborers was $480 a year, Boulding's princely salary placed him solidly in the upper middle class, particularly among members of his race.[40] By 1893 he was promoted to senior clerk in charge of all mail transported along a 208-mile stretch of the Southern Railway.[41] In Norfolk on December 27, 1893, he married Florence Cornelia Paige.[42] In anticipation of their marriage he plunked down two hundred dollars for a nice piece of property in Huntersville, part of Norfolk County.[43]

Like George Bailey in Frank Capra's Christmas chestnut, *It's a Wonderful Life*, Boulding was the neighborhood go-to guy for those of his race in need. When St. Vincent's, the local black hospital, burned to the ground it was Boulding who led the fund-raising drive to rebuild it.[44] When Norfolk's four thousand African American children—including his own—had no high school, it was Boulding who took up the battle to build one. He sat on the boards of segregated newspapers, banks, and savings and loans.[45] He was the director of a savings bank and was active in the National Negro Business League, started by Booker T. Washington in 1900.[46]

Reporters from the African American press wrote glowingly of Boulding, as they would one day of his daughter. They described him as a man of "push, pluck, prominence and merit" and took note of his "military carriage, which, added to a magnificent physique, [made] him a notable figure in any gathering."[47] Significantly, the same words could have been used to describe his daughter's future beaux.

Boulding's greatest claim to fame was the heroism he showed during the Southern Railway train wreck outside Danville, Virginia, on September 27, 1903. The incident was immortalized in the song "Wreck of the Old 97."[48] The four-car train, Number 97, was speeding southbound from New York to New Orleans when it jumped a seventy-five-foot trestle, killing nine of its sixteen crew members and seriously injuring the rest.[49] Sitting at his window at the postal station in Danville, Boulding suspected disaster when he heard the fire alarm. He ran out of the station and arrived at the wreck, where he took charge of rescuing the injured and salvaging the mail.[50] The *Richmond Planet* called him a "hero."[51]

The Norfolk that was home to Boulding and his family was a rapidly growing port three hundred miles by boat from New York City and one hundred miles southeast of Richmond. The population was 46,615 when Dorothy was born, 20,230 of whom were listed as Negro.[52] There were many educated, entrepreneurial blacks in Norfolk—like the Paiges and the Bouldings—who, as the nineteenth century wore on, were steadily being marginalized by the emergence of officially sanctioned segregation, commonly called Jim Crow after a character in a minstrel song, "Jump Jim Crow," that was routinely performed by white comedians in blackface.

Once federal troops and carpetbaggers pulled out of the South after the Civil War, the "Black Codes" sprang up, first in Mississippi in 1890 and then throughout the southern states like the boll weevil through a cotton crop. These were laws written to stop blacks from voting, serving on juries, or intermingling with whites. Virginia passed its own Black Code in 1902.[53]

Dorothy's grandfather went from being a legislator who made the laws to being just another black man oppressed by them. Prominent men of color were pushed out of elective office, professional positions, and mainstream life. Their race was their destiny, which they wore like an identity card, to the point where the names of persons of color were flagged by an asterisk in the official Norfolk city directory. But regardless of how far their standing slipped with the white community, the Bouldings remained on the top rung of the ladder among black families in Norfolk and held their heads high.

By February 1900, however, it all threatened to fall apart when Flossie filed for divorce.[54] The pending divorce answers at least one question about Dorothy's recollection of her childhood. When she was young she was sent to Boston to live with her mother's extended family. The excuse she gave was an unnamed health problem suffered by her mother: "My mother was very ill following my birth. Her illness was quite extended and my Great Aunt Emma was really the one who took charge."[55] But it was not Flossie's health that was ailing; it was her marriage.

Dorothy never described the mysterious health crisis that overtook her mother, adding to the dubiousness of her claim. Flossie's granddaughter, Dorothy Ruth Ferebee, a socially accepted single mother in the twenty-first century, overheard whispered conversations as a child to the effect that Flossie had provoked a marital breakup by taking a lover. Flossie finessed the situation by telling folks her husband was dead.[56] Verbally killing him off was a lesson her precocious daughter, Dorothy, learned well; it was the same tale she told after she divorced her own straying husband in 1950. Whatever illness Flossie suffered was cured because she managed to live well into her eighties, dying in 1959 at the Washington DC home of her then famous daughter.[57]

Other reasons may exist for Dorothy's Boston hiatus. A black girl with pie-in-the-sky dreams of becoming a doctor had no chance of realizing them in Virginia. The segregated school system of her day was inferior and would prepare her for little more than manual labor. In contrast, Boston established an elementary school for black children as early as 1820. By 1855 the city's public schools were integrated, which would not happen nationwide for another one hundred years.[58] Dorothy was enrolled in school in Boston in 1904 and lived on Beacon Hill. She stayed in Boston until 1908.[59]

It is unlikely the Bouldings' divorce was ever finalized. Flossie asked for alimony, and on March 5, 1900, Benjamin deeded the Huntersville rental property he had bought in 1893 to a trustee with instructions that his wife collect the rent as if she were a single woman.[60] Eventually their marriage improved and Dorothy returned to Norfolk. On November 26, 1906, Benjamin purchased a two-story brick house for $2,900 at 328 Bank Street (renumbered in 1913, as were all Norfolk streets, to 523 Bank).[61] By the time the Bouldings bought the house, the neighborhood was changing from white to black. It took a long time before all was forgiven between the couple, however. Not until June 23, 1909, did Flossie transfer back to her husband—for one dollar—the same parcel he gave her when she contemplated divorcing him.[62] A year later he was dead.[63] He died intestate, suggesting his death was sudden.

After she returned to Norfolk, Dorothy attended the Cumberland Street Colored School, its philosophy patterned after that of Booker Washington. The Gothic brick fortress, which opened in 1886, was heralded as a "monument of progress and enlightenment."[64] Dorothy bragged that she "won two gold medals for general excellence—one in 1910 and the other in 1911," while at Cumberland.[65] But on May 24, 1911, she was chosen to raise the flag of Virginia over the roof of the school to celebrate an exhibit of "manual training work."[66] It was all Great Aunt Emma had to hear; she insisted Dorothy be brought back to educational civilization in Boston.[67]

2 Among the Favored Few

In Boston Dorothy shed her childish Victorian pinafores and adopted the latest fashion craze: bloomers and middy blouses. In the summer she hit the rocky beaches of Quincy, Massachusetts, in her "bathing dress." She took up the banjo and started playing the piano. She blossomed on the school playing field, conquering track, the high jump, and field hockey with her usual determination to excel. And under the watchful, loving eye of tough but kind Great Aunt Emma, she sprinted ahead of everyone else inside the classroom too. She loved school so much her attendance was perfect.[1]

Dorothy's Boston home was a charming three-story, red-brick row house at 62 West Cedar Street on Beacon Hill, a few blocks from where her grandfather had been hidden by the Hillards. Her great-uncle by marriage, Henry Kenswil, a messenger for the Wabash Railroad, bought the place in 1904 by assuming the prior owner's five-thousand-dollar mortgage.[2] He lived there with his wife, Marie Louise, the baby of the Ruffins. She brought along the aging, unmarried remnants of her family: Great Aunt Emma, already sixty-five by the time Dorothy moved in, and their younger brother, Robert, then in his fifties.[3]

This branch of the Ruffin clan no longer held sway over Boston's social scene. They apparently suffered a financial downturn in the 1890s, forcing them to take in lodgers. Emma cleaned houses and Robert stitched together jobs as a janitor, a shipper for an optician, and a store clerk.[4]

As she would later help lift her race, young Dorothy aimed to lift her own diminished circumstances. Her Girls' High transcript reveals a child who needed a well-paying job once she graduated in 1915. She concentrated on practical courses in bookkeeping, typing, and civil service. Her major concession to pure academics was to study French, in which she earned nearly straight A's. Something caused Dorothy to change direction after graduation and set her sights on college, but she had failed to take the courses she needed to get in. To remedy her academic deficiencies, she remained at Girls' High an extra year and crammed in a punishing schedule filled with the prerequisites she had missed: algebra, trigonometry, ancient history, and more French.[5]

Dorothy entered Simmons College in the fall of 1916. Still demonstrating trepidation about her financial future she chose a medical-secretarial major, which trained her to be a doctor's receptionist after graduation. Simmons College was founded in 1899 as Simmons Female College by a Boston tailor, John Simmons. In the 1830's he had revolutionized the fashion industry by introducing off-the-rack suits.[6] He willed his fortune to the creation of a woman's college "for the purpose of teaching medicine, music, drawing, designing, telegraphy, and other branches of art, science, and industry best calculated to enable the scholars to acquire an independent livelihood."[7] It was the right spot for Dorothy. Losing her wealthy grandfather and her father at an early age taught her that the financial rug under a woman could be slippery. Her years at Simmons, 1916 to 1920, coincided in part with the Great War, further demonstrating that events beyond her control could have a profound impact on her life.

World War I erupted in Europe on June 28, 1914, with the assassination of Archduke Franz Ferdinand of Austria. Although reelected in 1916 on a peace platform, on the warm, rainy night of April 2, 1917, President Woodrow Wilson traveled from the White House to the Capitol to seek a declaration of war.[8] There he famously told a joint session of Congress, "The world must be made safe for democracy." Four days later the United States was at war.

The impact hit the Bouldings immediately. Men between the ages of twenty-one and thirty-one were required to register for the draft on June 5, 1917, and among the nine million who did was Dorothy's older brother, Ruffin.[9] Her brother Richard, just five days shy of his twenty-first birthday on registration day, was spared another year. He got even luckier, for the war was over before he was drafted. Ruffin entered the army even though his job as a stenographer at the Norfolk Navy Yard put bread and butter on his widowed mother's table. Dorothy said in her oral history that her brother served three years in the army, but he was in and out in about three months.[10]

Women flooded the workforce to replace the three million men in uniform. They operated machinery on factory floors, ran elevators in high-rise buildings, and delivered telegrams for Western Union.[11] From First Lady Edith Wilson, to the lady next door, women planted "victory gardens."[12] When Bernard Baruch, a Wall Street financier and the head of the War Production Board, urged women to use less material for their skirts so it could be saved for military uniforms, they shortened them.[13]

The war inspired Dorothy to do more than hike up her hemline. In her sophomore year she entered the civil rights arena. With war still raging, she challenged her government to live up to its rationale for entering the fighting abroad by confronting the lack of freedom afforded her race at home. In a powerful essay with the caustic title "Lynching as an Expression of Americanism," she used language as passionate (albeit with a few misspellings) as that used by her grandfather when *he* railed against lynching forty years before as a member of the Virginia legislature. She wrote:

> Lynching and Americanism! Does it not strike you that these two terms are singularly incongruous? They are incongruous—lamentably so—and have been for a great number of years; but I think that their incompatibility is all the more apparent now, than it has been before for the reason that America is just now allied to the cause of national and individual emancipation, of justic [*sic*] and freedom to the entire world, when, at the same time, her Americanism—her ideal of justice—and mercy meted out to all mankind—has been shamefully besmirched upon her own free soil.[14]

She was right. Although lynchings had fallen below their 1892 all-time high of 161 black victims, throughout the early twentieth century they continued at a reprehensible rate. Dorothy would have written this essay in either late 1917, when thirty-six blacks were lynched, or in 1918, when there were sixty black victims.[15]

The essay was published in the local newspaper under the headline "Colored Girl at Simmons Writes on Lynching."[16] Under the Espionage Act, passed on the eve of the war to prohibit "disloyal, profane, scurrilous, or abusive language" about the United States on pain of up to twenty years in prison, the essay arguably demonstrated sufficient disloyalty to warrant indictment and prosecution. Yet on this seminal occasion, as throughout her lifetime, Dorothy demonstrated a streak of fearlessness when it came to standing up for civil rights.

Dorothy's religious upbringing instilled in her the biblical idea that we are our brothers' keepers. "If the knowledge of such crimes is common to both the public and the government, and no voice, no pen, no hand is raised in protest against them, the sin swiftly settles upon the brow of every American citizen," she wrote.[17]

This was the political world Dorothy would inherit. But until she ventured into it, "Dot," as she was known at Simmons, wanted to enjoy life. She was a fun-loving jock, popular with her overwhelmingly white classmates (she was one of two black girls in the class of 1920), who viewed her with awe. "Would that we could be among the favored few, like Dot!" wrote the editors of the *Microcosm*, the Simmons's student yearbook in 1920. Recognizing their classmate's burning ambition (and demonstrating their own paltry professional aspirations), her peers wrote in a caption alongside her senior picture, "Is it not sufficient to be a clever secretary without aspiring to be a scientist? Who else but Dot could trace the course of the leucocytes and simultaneously learn the intricacies of the Edison rotary mimeograph!"[18]

Dorothy and her 166 graduating classmates filed into the Harvard Church in Brookline on June 14, 1920, for commencement.[19] They sweltered under their black caps and gowns with the temperature reaching 85 degrees, 20 degrees higher than normal.[20] Her proud mother traveled 471 miles from Norfolk to Boston to host a graduation party for her daughter. Flossie Boulding mailed out engraved invitations to a reception in Dorothy's honor on June 22, 1920, from eight to midnight, in Brattle Hall in Harvard Square.[21]

Dorothy waited until the eleventh hour to apply to medical school, perhaps fretting over how to pay for it. She submitted a one-page, handwritten application to the Tufts College Medical School on August 22, 1920, less than a month before school started.[22] Her application was approved on September 13, and an acceptance letter was mailed to her aunt's home. It was brief, to the point, and addressed, "Dear Sir": "I am glad to inform you that your credentials are sufficient for admission to the first year class of the Medical School. Registration is now going on and the classes commence the 16th of September." It was signed by Dr. Frank E. Haskins, school secretary.[23]

Getting into medical school in the 1920s was hardly the rigorous exercise it is today. Tufts advertised for students in a Boston medical journal. To be admitted required graduation from an approved high school and two years of college that included courses in chemistry, physics, biology, English, and French or German.[24] An applicant was required to provide his or her name, address, date and place of birth, and educational background and the name of a reference who could attest to the applicant's "good moral character."[25]

In September 1920 Dorothy traveled to 416 Huntington Avenue, site of the old Tufts Medical School and now part of Northeastern University, to register for classes. Ruffin Boulding probably gave her the $180 registration fee. From the day Tufts opened in 1893, it welcomed women; its first class of eighty medical students had fifty-seven men and twenty-three women.[26] There were 136 students in Dorothy's graduating class of 1924; seven were women. Four of these, including Dorothy, graduated cum laude.[27]

Dorothy worked hard in medical school. In the second year, 1921–22, she attended classes six days a week, including Saturdays until lunchtime.[28] Dorothy had found her calling. Her medical school grades were, for the most part, extraordinary. Whether she graduated first in her class, as she sometimes claimed and the press reported, is impossible to determine. No records indicating class rank survive, and 44 of the 136 students in the class graduated cum laude.[29]

Obviously popular with her classmates, Dorothy was selected class historian and took the podium at the senior banquet in the stately old Westminster Hotel in Boston's Copley Square on April 2, 1924. Her speech was printed in the Tufts Medical School yearbook, the *Caduceus*. Her remarks lacked the edgy appeal to the students' better angels that permeated her powerful Simmons essay on lynching. "How swiftly the days fade in the distance, when life is engaged and engrossed with increasing purpose!" she began.[30] One can appreciate the students' heroic struggle to stay awake after a large meal on a dismal night during a freak spring snowstorm as she recounted four years of med school in excruciating detail.[31]

Dorothy's peers on the yearbook had a high regard for one of their own; she was a staff contributor, and the speech got a rave review: "The combination of words and the ideas par excellence that Miss Boulding used in uttering the History of the Class held our attentions as well as our breath." Or maybe it was the booze. Dorothy's class graduated during Prohibition, but that hardly put a damper on the spirit—or spirits—that permeated the class banquet. It was advertised as a BYOB affair, and the young doctors had mastered chemistry well enough to create their own alcohol-laced concoctions that fueled a rollicking good time. Under raincoats and scarves and inside rubber boots most of the men wore tuxedos and dancing pumps, and the women were equally decked out. Dorothy was done up like a flapper, with her hair tucked under a broad, shiny headband fastened by a large flower at her temple.[32]

Dorothy went from dowdy schoolgirl to stylish young woman at Tufts. Perhaps her new sense of style was inspired by love. She was the object of the affections of a big man on campus, James Ernest "Ernie" Martin Jr., a star football player and graduate of the Tufts College Dental School, Class of 1921. He was on the small side, 162 pounds, in tip-top shape. Martin was handsome, with slicked-back wavy hair and round glasses, the height of Jazz Age fashion.[33]

Dot Boulding took a tremendous ribbing over her fling with the football star. Friends marveled at her ability to maintain her grade point average "despite her 'rush' from a certain well-known Tufts half-back who recently received his degree from the Dental School." In a blurb next to her senior picture they wrote, "Dot, we have wondered if your exceptional physical condition can be attributed to Ernie's coaching."[34]

Martin was much like Claude Thurston Ferebee, the man Dorothy married six years later. They were both dentists and active in the exclusive black fraternity, Alpha Phi Alpha. They were proud fellows, intent on excelling. They even resembled each other physically; both were handsome, lean, and compact, with exquisitely sculpted muscles developed on the athletic fields of the elite schools they attended. Claude Ferebee was a track star at Wilberforce College, and before being on the varsity football team at Tufts

Martin had been a four-letter man in track, field hockey, baseball, and football during his years at Boston Latin High School.[35]

Keeping scrapbooks was one of Dorothy's favorite lifelong hobbies. Only one small hint in her Tufts scrapbook reveals where Cupid's arrow might have struck. She saved an invitation to a formal hosted by Martin's fraternity on April 13, 1921, a few months before he graduated. The engraved invitation announced that dancing on that balmy Wednesday night was to begin at nine and keep going until three in the morning, demonstrating that Martin's aerobic stamina extended beyond the athletic field. The scrapbook includes her acceptance letter to medical school, copies of her grades, a picture of herself, the sheet music for "Thirty-Two Current Songs from the Book of Tufts Music," and her first business card, "Dorothy Celeste Boulding, MD."[36]

Her class schedule and Martin aside, Dorothy found the time to join the yearbook staff and participate in other extracurricular activities. She was rushed by the Zeta Phi fraternity and was asked to join in February 1922. Not surprisingly within a year was vice president of the local chapter.[37] Zeta Phi was a woman's group, despite being organized as a fraternity rather than sorority. It was formed at Tufts in 1909 "to promote friendship among physicians and medical students, loyalty to one another and the medical profession, and advancement in scientific work."[38] Dorothy said that while at Tufts in 1923 she joined Alpha Kappa Alpha, the elite African American women's sorority through which she would make history as the director of the Mississippi Health Project but she may have been mistaken about the year; the Boston AKA chapter was established in 1924.[39]

The romance between Dorothy and Martin did not survive long after their years at Tufts. After graduating, Martin practiced dentistry in Boston for at least three years, which would have coincided with the time he was dating Dorothy. Either in 1924, right after Dorothy left Boston, or in 1925 he married Bernice Hughes, a socialite from Baltimore and graduate of Bluefield State College, a segregated school in the West Virginia coal country.[40]

Following World War I, owing to increased black literacy and the proliferation of urban life, black newspaper circulation took off, until by the early 1940s there were weekly sales of 1.6 million copies.[41] Dorothy's Tufts scrapbook is filled with crumbling copies of the earliest newspaper stories about her. The articles, most from unnamed black papers, considered her a success symbol for her race. One touted her as proof "beyond a reasonable doubt [of] what a Colored girl can do if she be given the opportunity. . . . [She] makes us all feel proud of her and the colored youth of today."[42] Journalists described her as "charming," "vivacious," and "full of animation," which was most likely true enough. They reported that she had "the highest average of any student in the College for four years," which cannot be verified. This same newspaper claimed she scored no grade lower than 90, which was not true.[43] Whether the reporters made mistakes or she gilded the lily about her academic achievements or was such a fine example of African American womanhood that publishers took poetic license to showcase a stellar role model will never be known. The deification of Dorothy in the African American newspapers had begun.

In his groundbreaking book, *Black Bourgeoisie*, Howard University sociology professor E. Franklin Frazier was scathing in his assessment of the black press, accusing it of creating and perpetuating "the world of make believe" with its "exaggerations concerning the economic well-being and cultural achievements of Negroes, [and] its emphasis upon Negro 'society.' "[44] Be that as it may, this "world of make believe" became the foundation for Dorothy's future persona. In spite of the exaggerations, one thing was true: she stood out prominently "not as a Colored student, but as an exceptional student among students."[45]

Every prize, award, citation, and honor she ever achieved—and over the years there would be many—came as the result of hard work. Sometimes, though, she was overlooked just because she was a black woman. In her old age, when discussing her years at Tufts, she said ruefully that when it came to getting assignments, "I was the last of the last because not only was I a woman, but a Negro, too."[46]

Most galling for her was to have to watch as her white classmates, some academically inferior, walked away from Tufts with internship offers while she had none. Internship applications required photographs, and those with black faces were rejected. Numbers tell the story: there were 136 students in Dorothy's class; at least four appear to have been African Americans, and but by the spring of 1924 only one had secured an internship, even though Dorothy and another black student were about to graduate cum laude. Of the 132 known white students in the class, only nineteen had not found internships by graduation.[47]

The irony was that hospitals nationwide were begging for interns to fill empty slots. The American Medical Association determined that close to one thousand internships went unfilled when Dorothy could not find one that would take her.[48] So she did what she did best: she took a test, a civil service exam. She scored big and won an internship at Freedmen's, the historic black hospital in Washington DC.[49]

In 1924 Dorothy's doting mother again journeyed to Boston to enjoy what must have been one of the proudest moments of her life: seeing her precocious little girl graduate from medical school. Following graduation, after having spent nearly half her life in Boston, Dorothy gathered her belongings and jumped into a roadster her uncle bought her as a graduation gift.[50] It was quite a present, but the American economy was white hot in the mid-1920s. She never said which generous uncle bought her the car, but it was probably Leslie Paige, by then a lawyer in Norfolk for fifteen years. Dorothy floored the gas pedal and sped away to begin her new life in the nation's capital.

3 As If I Had Thrown a Bomb into the Room

The nation's capital between the wars was a sleepy, segregated southern town. Dorothy might have preferred to launch her career in Boston, but the internship in Washington was the only one she got. So she packed up and headed south, detouring to Norfolk to spend the summer after graduation with her family.

During what would be their last time together as a family, Ruffin and Dorothy could look forward to evenings sitting on the porch to catch up, while Ruffin puffed on his ever-present cigar. He had his own bragging rights, having just finished his second year at Howard's law school. From childhood, when they shared a friendly rivalry over which of them could memorize the most Psalms, Ruffin and Dorothy shared a lifelong bond.[1]

In the summer of 1924 Ruffin was twenty-nine. He was tall and solidly built, with hazel eyes and closely cropped black hair. He and his sister were two peas in a pod: smart and driven. "Diligence is the key to success" was the motto he chose to accompany his graduation photograph in the 1925 Howard yearbook.[2]

The skill with which Ruffin's fingers flew across the keys of a typewriter, obtained at the Norfolk Navy Yard, was instrumental in his early success in Oklahoma during the oil boom of the mid-1920s. Settling in Oklahoma may have seemed an odd choice for an African American lawyer. Native Americans had been slaveholders in Indian Territory, which became part of Oklahoma, though the relationships between the Indian masters and their slaves were supposedly better than those that existed between the white plantation owners and theirs. Ruffin's new boss, lawyer Buck Colbert

Franklin, descended from a slave owned by a Chickasaw Indian. When Indians were being cheated out of the ownership of their oil-rich land, they turned to Franklin, whom they trusted.[3] It was against this backdrop that Dorothy's brother arrived in Wewoka, Oklahoma, in 1925.

Wewoka, in the heart of Seminole country, sixty miles east of Oklahoma City and eighty-five miles south of Tulsa, was once a desolate trading post, but by 1930 there were 10,401 people living there, most of them speculators.[4] Franklin said Ruffin "was accomplished in shorthand and in taking dictation. He could do more in records and in research work on land titles than a dozen lawyers."[5]

They won or settled several lucrative cases. Back home everyone who read the *Norfolk Journal and Guide* knew Ruffin had hit it big: "Ruffin Boulding to Share in $25,000 Attorneys' Fee" was one of the headlines.[6] The successful Franklin-Boulding partnership lasted a little more than a year but caused a stir. "Possibly never before or since had two Oklahoma Negro lawyers created such excitement in so little time as Boulding and I had created in Wewoka, or been as successful in putting money in the pockets of Negroes and Indians," Franklin chortled in his autobiography.[7]

Ruffin won the heart of another Howard student, Julia Inez Wyche, a beauty from Charlotte, North Carolina, and one of the two most popular girls in the Class of 1915 at Howard University Teachers' College.[8] She earned a master's degree and taught in public schools in Virginia, Oklahoma, and North Carolina.[9] They married in North Carolina on August 11, 1927, and settled there.[10]

At the end of the summer Dorothy headed to Washington to begin her internship. Not long after she settled in, she scouted around for do-good projects she could sink her teeth into. She quickly made a name for herself speaking out on public health issues, a practice she continued for fifty years. Over time she spoke to school groups, women's clubs, college audiences, church members, medical societies, the U.S. Congress, and endless regional conferences of Alpha Kappa Alpha and the National Council of Negro Women. Each one of these speeches required research, writing, editing, and rewriting. The extensive penciled notes she left behind on yellow legal pads show how carefully she worked and reworked her thoughts. Then she typed them and edited again. These speeches are a window into what moved her: women's and children's health and nutrition, the elimination of poverty, easy access to birth control, the expansion of civil rights, and better educational opportunities for African Americans.

Dorothy had a gift for public speaking, even if she did suffer from a tinny voice and a hoity-toity style of delivery. It hardly mattered; every educated woman of her era spoke in the same stylized manner. Eleanor Roosevelt, Mary McLeod Bethune, Rose Kennedy, and Dorothy Boulding could have had the same elocution teacher. Dorothy was proud of the fact that she sounded like Mrs. Roosevelt. Her grandchildren did near-perfect imitations of her.

By 1928 Dorothy had moved to 821 Third Street SE, a home owned by a fifty-seven-year-old mailman, Charles Goodloe, and his forty-two-year-old wife, Blanche. Another boarder was a forty-year-old carpenter named Joseph Hall. They were black in an all-black neighborhood.[11] That was custom, not coincidence; Washington was strictly segregated.

Freedmen's Hospital was a few miles away at Fifth and W Streets NW, on the Howard University campus. The university, named after Gen. Otis Howard, a white hero of the Union Army in the Civil War, opened its medical school in 1868.[12] The school and the hospital were intertwined: all graduates of Howard University Medical School used Freedmen's as their clinical training ground.[13]

For nearly a century until 1965, when control was ceded to Howard University, Freedmen's Hospital was woefully underfunded. Until then, managed by various agencies of the federal government, its administrators routinely went hat in hand to Capitol Hill to beg for money. For thirty-five years, including part of the time Dorothy was affiliated with the hospital, that unhappy task fell to Dr. William Alonza Warfield, the surgeon in chief. In 1921, three years before Dorothy began her internship, Warfield complained to the U.S. secretary of the interior, then responsible for Freedmen's, "The physical condition of the hospital is not what it should be. The interior is in bad shape and in need of paint and other repairs. This situation is due to insufficient appropriations during the past few years and the mounting prices of all supplies."[14]

The contrast between Dorothy's privileged world in which she tooled around in a nice new car and that of the Negro patients at Freedmen's Hospital, most of them charity cases who passed through the hospital's peeling corridors, could not have been greater. A private hospital room at

Freedmen's was $2 a day, a bed in a ward $1.75, and a crib for a newborn 50 cents, but most of the patients could not afford it.[15] Despite these harsh realities, Washington was considered Mecca for African Americans. Jobs available for blacks in the government were menial—mopping the floors and emptying the wastebaskets in federal buildings—but they were steady, creating a solid African American working class. They spawned the need for a black professional class of doctors, lawyers, nurses, teachers, ministers, and undertakers. That class was Dorothy's world.

After the Civil War blacks had seats in Congress and in local government. The world's most famous former slave, Frederick Douglass, who was a close friend of Dorothy's Great Uncle George Ruffin, was Washington DC's recorder of deeds.[16] Blacks sat wherever they wanted on streetcars. They served on juries and taught at Howard. It was illegal to discriminate in restaurants, bars, or hotels.[17] But as the twentieth century approached, Jim Crow crawled into town, hampering not only those blacks already marginalized by poverty but upper-class blacks as well. Eventually segregation became so firmly entrenched that "by the turn of the century, not even Frederick Douglass could have dined in a downtown restaurant," historian David Levering Lewis noted wryly.[18]

When Dorothy arrived in 1924 her housing choices were limited. Restrictive real estate covenants kept blacks from living in desirable areas, even if they could afford homes there.[19] Segregation emphasized the divisive issue of skin color within Washington's African American community. Because of the social ostracism that accompanied being black in a racist world, some with light skin and Caucasian features chose to pass for white. It was such a common occurrence in Washington that the National Theatre hired a black bouncer to "spot and denounce intruders whose racial origins were undetectable by whites."[20] "It was a segregated city among blacks," Calvin Rolark Jr., an African American newspaper owner, once remarked. "The lighter-skinned blacks didn't associate with the darker blacks, and the Howard University blacks didn't associate with anyone."[21]

Dorothy's light skin, pedigree, educational advantages, and association with Howard placed her at the top of this caste pyramid. It was populated by a very small clique—or tribe, as they referred to themselves.[22] They pledged the same fraternities, supported the same charities, attended parties at each other's city homes in the winter, and vacationed at one another's country houses in the summer. They went to or worked at Howard University.

Dorothy had barely unpacked her bags when Robbie Lofton, the wife of her Howard colleague, obstetrician William Lofton, took her under her wing. The Loftons were social butterflies, and Robbie and Dorothy became inseparable.[23] There were ritual events in the upper-echelon black community and over time they participated in most of them; the annual Howard-Lincoln Thanksgiving Day football game, card parties at one another's homes, and dinner at segregated supper clubs. Dorothy's peer group kept on partying through the Depression and thirteen years of the Roosevelt administration.[24] But her sudden marriage in 1930, the birth of twins in 1931, the pressures of a demanding career, and her growing civic activism put a damper on Dorothy's socializing. As the 1920s melted into the 1930s, her name would appear less and less on the social pages and more and more in the news.

During her first year as an intern, Dorothy worked around the clock, rotating through the practice units at Freedmen's, treating patients under the eyes of experienced doctors, and answering emergency calls as part of the hospital's ambulance team. These calls brought her into contact with a depth of misery neither she nor other members of her social class had previously experienced. "I did a great deal of ambulance work, service which primarily took me to fights and to disruptive family life down in southeast Washington," she recalled. "Almost every Saturday night there was a big explosion or some kind of fight, and I came to know where the difficulties were." It was an eye-opener for this daughter of privilege. "I made up my mind while riding these ambulances . . . that we ought to do something about this."[25]

Dorothy survived her internship and was one of 107 applicants who sat for the DC medical licensing exam in 1925, nine of whom were women. She passed with a score of nearly 88 percent and was granted the privilege of practicing medicine under District of Columbia Medical License Number 584, which she held under her maiden name until four years into her marriage.[26]

Three months after she passed the exam, Dorothy was appointed assistant obstetrician at Freedmen's Hospital.[27] In 1927 she became a clinical instructor in obstetrics at Howard University Medical School, a position she would hold until 1940.[28] Despite the physical condition of Howard, the teaching post was an honor; until 1950 half of the African American physicians in the United States were educated there.[29]

In 1926 Mordecai Wyatt Johnson, a Baptist preacher with no doctorate and just two years of college teaching experience, was elected the first black president of Howard.[30] Dorothy cultivated the impressive but often imperious and difficult Johnson as a mentor and lifelong friend. She was one of a handful of speakers at his funeral service in 1976.[31] She would conscript his wife, Anna Ethelyn Gardner Johnson, into helping her with do-good projects. Johnson, his wife, and their five children lived on the eighty-nine-acre Howard campus in a three-story Victorian mansion. At least two of the Johnson children—William Howard, known as Timmy, and Anna Faith—played on the lawn with Dorothy's twins and their best friend, John Beckley, the son of a Howard physician and medical school professor.[32]

Increased responsibilities at Howard did not stop her from dedicating herself to the kind of social welfare work her mother and grandmother had engaged in. One of her early speaking engagements was before the Women's Co-operative Civic League in Baltimore on February 28, 1928, presenting the topic "Sex Education for the Adolescent." Shortly before the program the president of the group sent a note to Dorothy to express her dismay at the title. She asked if they could "eliminate 'sex' in the subject," suggesting the word *biology* take its place.[33] Whether Dorothy toned down the title is unknown, but even if she did, she did not soften her message. On the dais she urged parents to teach sex education to their five-year-olds.[34]

Whenever Dorothy climbed on her soapbox, sexuality, birth control, and abortion were among her favorite subjects. As late as 1917 Margaret Sanger, with whom Dorothy would align herself in the birth control movement, went to jail in New York for telling women how and where to obtain contraceptives.[35] Dorothy supported liberal access to contraception long before the rest of the medical establishment did; the American Medical Association did not endorse birth control until 1937.[36]

Dorothy's interest in reproductive issues injected her into the eugenics debate. In the 1920s eugenics was a respectable discipline. Esteemed scientists, presidents Theodore Roosevelt, Woodrow Wilson, and Herbert Hoover and Supreme Court justices Oliver Wendell Holmes and Louis

Brandeis supported eugenics. "It promoted enlightened parenthood and raising healthy children, and also, in its darker side, supported involuntary sterilization—all in the name of improving heredity," wrote Jean H. Baker in her biography of Sanger.[37] As late as 1932 twenty-seven states mandated sterilizing the feebleminded and the insane. In some states criminals could be subjected to involuntary sterilization.[38] At the Civic League talk Dorothy reportedly "urged women to seek for themselves mates of the highest type in order that the best possible heritage might be handed down to posterity."[39] It was advice she took herself.

Sex education and child health were her niche in the early days. She spoke at a DC Conference on Social Hygiene and Juvenile Delinquency in 1929, on "Sex Education of the Child."[40] That same year, while serving as physician to the DC juvenile court, she gave a lunchtime lecture to the Washington Council of Social Workers at the Phyllis Wheatley YWCA on "The Health of the Problem Child."[41]

In 1930, while working as a part-time clinical instructor in obstetrics, making four hundred dollars a year, she was hired as physician to the Howard University women students for another $1,200.[42] Each student was assessed a yearly two-dollar "student health fee" to pay for her services.[43] She kept office hours on campus each weekday morning from nine until noon.[44]

Dorothy's first big social-welfare project, the Southeast Settlement House, was the foundation for her formidable reputation. She started it in 1929, and it survived well beyond her death in 1980. Although not without its problems—from its early financial difficulties to later claims of mismanagement, having nothing to do with Dorothy—the Southeast Settlement was the embodiment of her altruistic vision to improve the lives of the District's underprivileged black youngsters.[45]

The story Dorothy told about the birth of the Southeast Settlement may have been apocryphal. She said that in 1929 she was in her office when she received a phone call from the local police precinct. A black boy was in custody for stealing a quart of milk from a white woman's porch. The frightened child, fearing he was going to jail, invoked Dr. Boulding's name.[46] Dorothy drove to the precinct, where she encountered a sobbing little boy. When she told the story to the *Washington Post* in 1978, she called him "Georgie."[47] In the oral history she gave a year later, she called him

"Johnny."[48] Whatever his name and whether he existed, the story she told about him is heartbreaking.

The boy lived across the street from her. His mother was a cleaning lady who left him and his baby brother in the care of a neighbor while she worked from dawn until sundown. On the day Georgie (or Johnny) was arrested, the neighbor was sick and sent them home, where the cupboard was bare. The boy stole a bottle of milk for his brother and was caught.

Dorothy was livid. "Do you mean to tell me that you would arrest a little boy who's trying to help his baby brother who's hungry, and there isn't anything in the icebox?" The desk sergeant released the boy only after Dorothy slapped seventeen cents on the counter for the milk. "And then it occurred to me, there's something wrong with this town. Any time a child goes hungry, and the mother has to work and leave a child home like this, we need some place for children," she said.[49]

A six-room, vacant house at the corner of Third and G Streets SE beckoned. Dorothy thought the empty house would be ideal for a day care center. She spoke with the realtor, who offered to rent the house to her for seventeen dollars a month or sell it for two thousand. "We don't have that money," she told him. "Do you expect to be given it?" he asked. "No," she replied. "We expect you to come down."[50]

It was Dorothy's first campaign, and it demonstrated her determination. In less than a year she had organized the Washington Welfare Association to raise money. The association secured the property, hired staff, bought furnishings, and opened for business. And in Dorothy's telling of the story many years later, the end justified the means. Early on, Dorothy paid a call on Lydia Burklin, director of Friendship House, an all-white day care center in the neighborhood where Dorothy hoped to open her own settlement. She claimed she shocked Burklin by saying, "We want to have a day care center and I understand you have one here. May I bring my Negro children?"[51]

In her wildest dreams Dorothy could not have thought Friendship House would acquiesce. She said Burklin "got red behind the gills, and replied, 'This house is for white children only.'" Nonetheless Burklin invited her to make her pitch at an upcoming meeting of the Friendship House board.[52] Getting a chance to speak to the board was Dorothy's real goal, assuming the encounter with Burklin is true.

Dorothy went to the meeting, dusted off the story of the boy and the stolen milk, and renewed her request to bring black children to Friendship House. "It was as if I had thrown a bomb into the room," she said. "Everybody began to speak. 'Oh no, we couldn't do that.'" So she slyly switched tactics and asked for money. "Well, will you help us? We are thinking of trying to get a house right around the corner from you." There was a sigh of relief and a round of donations.[53]

Dorothy's timing was impeccable; when she spoke to the board of Friendship House, Burklin was already worried about the social work needs of the neighborhood's growing black population. As early as March 19, 1929, the Friendship House board had discussed the impact of "the increasing colored population of the neighborhood."[54] A month later Burklin drafted a letter to the president of the board noting that changing demographics made it crucial to "start some work among the people of the colored race." She proposed a meeting of African American social workers, the new director of the Community Chest, and the Friendship House board to address the issue.[55] This might have been the meeting Dorothy attended.

In another example of good timing, when Dorothy was starting her settlement, Washington was organizing its first Community Chest under the direction of Elwood Street, a white social welfare organizer from Ohio. The Community Chest provided a means to manage local fund-raising by allowing donors to give to one entity, which distributed the money to approved charities. Dorothy later said Street invited her to attend a Community Chest board meeting immediately upon meeting her because he respected her mettle. She also said the board, filled with businessmen, handed her five thousand dollars without so much as blinking an eye.[56] This was an exaggeration; it was not until she had assembled a board of directors and demonstrated that she was capable of raising start-up money that her organization was added to the list of Community Chest charities eligible for funding. This took until early 1930, and with the Community Chest tightening its belt like the rest of America following the stock market crash, it gave her only $3,804.[57]

Southeast Settlement House kept Dorothy occupied for most of 1929, although she continued her other activities. For an honorarium of eighty dollars, she went to West Virginia by train on July 18, staying through July 25 to lecture about health to girls attending an annual YWCA conference.[58]

And she kept up with her active social life, hosting her annual spring dance with Robbie Lofton in early June that year.[59]

Had she found time to visit her mother in Norfolk that summer, she might have browsed through the local *Journal and Guide* for the latest news. If she had flipped to page 4 of the September 7 issue she would have seen a picture of a drop-dead handsome man with light, smooth skin, penetrating eyes, and a serious expression. He was described as the "brilliant" recent graduate of an Ivy League college, Columbia University in New York City, "where he was vice president of his class." According to the article, he was en route to Washington to become an instructor at Howard's dental school. His name was Dr. Claude Thurston Ferebee.[60]

4 The Count

While Dorothy worked tirelessly at the end of the 1920s to secure her settlement house, Claude Thurston Ferebee, movie-star handsome and popular man about town, was enjoying the Harlem Renaissance. At no other time and place in history was it as exhilarating to be young and black and living in New York City.

African Americans in Harlem, a three-square-mile enclave of upper Manhattan, were defining their own culture through black writers, artists, and musicians and setting the standard for intrepid white visitors who wanted to think of themselves as avant-garde. Claude was in the thick of it, living in a row house at 203 West 138th Street, at the end of a stretch of buff-colored brick houses. The homes were beautiful, with staircases rising from the street, wrought-iron handrails, recessed doors with curved arches, and terra cotta edging around the large windows.

When Claude arrived in New York City to attend dental school at Columbia University in 1924 there were nearly 200,000 blacks in Harlem, from West 110th Street to West 155th Street, making it the world's largest community of color.[1] To the sophisticates of Jazz Age Harlem Claude was fresh off the farm, the "beautiful, spacious and unprejudiced campus of Wilberforce University" in Wilberforce, Ohio, a tiny college town fifty miles from the state capital, Columbus.[2] Founded before the Civil War and named for the eighteenth-century abolitionist William Wilberforce, it was the country's first private black college.[3] Claude Ferebee at Wilberforce could have been Ernie Martin at Tufts. He was a star athlete in terrific shape. In his junior year he was on the track team, at one meet winning the 100-yard, 220-yard, and 440-yard dashes. He was team captain his senior year.[4] He also enjoyed archery, golf, tennis, and fencing. The only sport at which he did not excel was swimming; while in the army a fellow officer tried to teach him to float, but he sank like a stone.[5] Off the athletic field he was something of a Renaissance man; he belonged to the French Club, the Dramatics Club, the elite Alpha Phi Alpha fraternity, and the NAACP. He tutored fellow students in physics. His nickname at Wilberforce was "the Count," possibly after the debonair Count Basie.[6]

As a student he had a whimsical, imaginative side, and he nurtured his artistic streak. "Claude T. Ferebee distinguished himself as one of our best caricaturists," wrote the historian for the Class of 1923 in the *Wilberforcean*, the student yearbook.[7] His delicate pen-and-ink drawings graced many of the yearbook's pages. Claude graduated in 1923 with a bachelor of science degree but nourished dreams of making a living as an artist.[8]

After graduation Claude returned to his Norfolk home to spend the summer with his family before heading off to art school in Chicago.[9] By the 1920s there were almost ninety thousand African Americans living in the Norfolk area, or about 40 percent of the population.[10] Claude and Dorothy did not know each other, even though they lived less than two miles apart. She was three and a half years older, and most of her childhood was spent in Boston. Claude also left Norfolk for part of his education, attending Wilberforce Academy, a prep school affiliated with the college, from which he graduated in 1919.[11]

Claude was born on April 8, 1901, to Charles Ferebee and Nannie Jordan.[12] He was the oldest of three siblings; his middle sister, Maxine Lucetta, was born on March 12, 1903, and his baby sister, Constance Marguerite, was born much later, on July 26, 1912.[13] Their parents came from Norfolk. Charles was born on March 31, 1875, and Nannie on May 10, 1878.[14] They were married on June 20, 1900, at St. John's AME Church in Norfolk.[15]

Charles Ferebee attended Norfolk Mission College, a glorified high school at a time when there was no high school for blacks in the city. He worked as a mailman for thirty-six years. From his initial employment on July 1, 1904, through his reluctant mandatory retirement on March 31, 1940, he was an exemplary worker. He routinely earned citations for "perfect punctuality" and near-perfect employee evaluations.[16] After retiring from the post office, he worked for seven years in the advertising department of Norfolk's *Journal and Guide*. He had eclectic interests; he played the cello in the church orchestra and sang in its choir and in the local Phil-harmonic Glee Club.[17]

Oddly, when Claude was an old man he was disdainful of his father's singing and cello playing, saying such activities were "sissy."[18] Yet as a teenager he seemed only too happy to emulate his father by participating in music-related activities. He was a member of a choir, the Junior Men-delssohn Clef Club.[19] During World War II he put his musical background to good use wooing his mistress—behind Dorothy's back—in letters addressed to her as "My Concerto."[20]

Nannie Jordan Ferebee was a housewife and church lady. She did not hail from the Talented Tenth. She was one of at least twelve children of John Jordan, a barber, and his wife, Hannah Waller Jordan, who took in wash.[21] Nonetheless Nannie's own three children found their way into Norfolk's Negro ruling class and by extension onto its social calendar. Maxine was one of the founders in Norfolk in 1928 of the Moles, an African American women's social and service club that grew into a national organization.[22] Constance played in local theater productions and had a beautiful alto singing voice.[23]

Charles Ferebee's steady job at the post office and some shrewd land deals enabled him to be a good provider. In 1903 he purchased an empty lot for just $260, and in 1908 he built a house on it, numbered 1281 Bolton Street.[24] In 1922 he got a deal on a lot on Chapel Street, for which he paid only $175. Four years later, after he built a home on it, which became 708 Chapel, the land was worth $1,000 and the house, $2,400.[25]

The Chapel Street home would be the site of family parties, weddings, dances, and neighborhood celebrations for the many years it remained in the Ferebee family. The cedar-shingled house was two stories high with a small front yard and a porch. It had a large living room with a brick fireplace and a staircase with a long wooden banister that invited sliding. Besides the living room, the first floor had a dining room, kitchen, pantry, bath-room, and boiler room with radiators that would creak, pop, and gurgle as hot-water heat flowed through them in the winter. The boiler room was the territory belonging to Snowball, a tough, white street cat that ruled the neighborhood. Upstairs were three bedrooms and a bathroom.[26] In 1968, after their parents were dead, the Ferebee siblings sold the Chapel Street house.[27]

Whether Claude ever made it to art school is unknown. There is a lost year between when he graduated from college and when he entered dental school. Perhaps that was when he realized he would never be able to earn a living as an artist.[28] But he pursued art as an avocation for the rest of his life; the watercolors he painted while in the Far East during World War II ended up on the walls of his bachelor pad after he broke up with Dorothy in the late 1940s.[29]

Claude entered Columbia University Dental School on September 24, 1924.[30] He struggled there—it took him five years to get through the four-year program—perhaps because he was not much of a student, not much of a student of dentistry, or distracted by Harlem's high life. There were many temptations; every night was like New Year's Eve. Prohibition was a technicality; liquor flowed like water. Beautiful café-au-lait chorus girls populated the nightclubs.

With all that was going on around him, no wonder Claude's mind was rarely on his studies. He was making inroads of his own into the New York social scene. He was active in Alpha Phi Alpha, the elite black fraternity founded at Cornell in 1906. It beckoned the men of the Talented Tenth to perform the public service that would bring distinction to the race.[31] While at Columbia he was linked to Miss K. Vogelsang, whom he took to the Wilberforce Yuletide dinner-dance in January 1929.[32] Kathleen F. Vogelsang was a dressmaker who lived with her parents and was a fixture at Harlem parties in the 1920s and 1930s. She remained single on the New York social circuit long after Claude and Dorothy married.[33]

Given how poorly Claude performed in dental school, it is not a stretch to conclude that his heart was not in drilling teeth, other than as a way to earn a good living. His first-year courses included anatomy, histology (the microscopic study of cells), and metallurgy, specifically the making of dental fillings. He was great at making false teeth, perhaps because doing so required a bit of artistry. But he flunked histology, which meant he had to retake the final exam the following September.[34] The rules at the Columbia dental school were clear: any student who failed a course could retake the final, but if he failed it the second time, he had to repeat the entire year. No student was permitted to languish in the four-year program for more than five years.[35]

The second year he ended up no better off than the first. He flunked biochemistry, then flunked the retest, which resulted in his having to repeat the entire academic year. During the encore of his second year, he failed bacteriology but managed to salvage his dental career by earning a C on the repeat exam. His third year (which was really his fourth) was lackluster, but at least he passed his courses. His grades improved during his fifth and final year; perhaps he had come to terms with his professional future.[36]

Claude graduated as a doctor of dental surgery on June 4, 1929, in a class of twenty-four men.[37] On June 29 he received his New York State dental license.[38] Less than five months later the stock market would crash, signaling the end of the decade of prosperity and the beginning of the Great Depression. Had anyone been listening to more than the jazz in Harlem, it would have been clear the good times were already over. "Black Harlem had become a community in crisis," wrote Jonathan Gill, "leading the nation in poverty, crime, overcrowding, unemployment, juvenile delinquency, malnutrition, and infant and maternal mortality." By the end of the 1920s Central Harlem was close to 100 percent black. Bad economic times meant whites had no extra cash to spend in Harlem. The end of Prohibition in 1933, coupled with the economic downturn, caused many Harlem nightclubs to close. Increased crime scared those few whites who still had money from making the trek above 125th Street.[39]

By then Claude was long gone, lured to Washington by a young hotshot, Dr. Arnold Donowa, who had big plans for breathing life into Howard's moribund dental program. Donowa sacked the part-time dentists who populated the Howard faculty and brought aboard a handful of young professionals like Claude to help him build a Class A dental school.[40] They were both in for a big surprise.

5　Petunia Ticklebritches

Howard Dental School had at most nineteen students when Claude arrived in October 1929.[1] Throughout the years he was associated with Howard he taught classes in crown and bridge technique to upperclassmen.[2] He later added periodontia (the study of gum disease) and metallurgy to his teaching repertoire.[3]

Meanwhile Dorothy was teaching obstetrics while delivering babies at expectant mothers' homes—where most births still took place—for thirty-five dollars a delivery.[4] As a clinical instructor, her post was part time, allowing her to focus on her private practice, which, like everything else in Washington, was segregated. Rare was the occasion when a white person sought treatment from a black doctor.[5]

Soon Dorothy's and Claude's paths crossed. Cupid's arrow did not strike directly at Dorothy's heart in her version of how they met. Her description of their first encounter sounds as exciting as one of her Washington Welfare Association board meetings: "After I was appointed to the Howard University Health Service in 1929, I met professors and instructors in different areas of the university. One was Dr. Claude Ferebee."[6]

Dorothy's chronology was a little off. She was not appointed to the University Health Service until September 25, 1930—more than two months after she married Claude. She was given the part-time post of physician to the university's 1,106 women students at a salary of $1,200 a year. Earlier in 1930, her teaching stipend was raised from $100 to $400 a year.[7] Her post with the university health service put Dorothy on the cutting edge of a nationwide trend. Fueled by the influenza epidemic of 1918–19, which hit the college-age population hard, colleges and universities upgraded how they responded to student health needs by hiring on-campus doctors. As it became the norm to give incoming students full physical examinations, it was considered inappropriate in that modest era to have male doctors examine female students.[8]

Seeing Dorothy at a faculty meeting, Claude was quickly smitten. "He appeared to be impressed with what I was trying to do, not only in the Health Service, but at Southeast House. We became good friends, interested in each other's professional activities and spent more and more time together."[9] Her prissy, matter-of-fact description of their romance explains in part why her grandchildren teasingly called her "Petunia Ticklebritches."[10] "One evening he said, 'You know, I think we ought to open up offices together.' So that was the nature of the courtship of Ferebee and Boulding," she recalled, leaving out the part about his lean athletic body, his smooth café-au-lait complexion, his sexy smile, the twinkle in his eyes, and the buttery smooth sound of Norfolk in his voice.[11]

For a woman with a healthy ego, Dorothy sold herself short. Her professional activities and racial uplift work were impressive, but young Dorothy Boulding had intelligent eyes, a delightful smile, near-perfect facial bone structure, and a sense of style. She was charming and smart—and could even play the ukulele. She loved parties and socializing; no doubt she could dance the Charleston, the Bunny Hug, the Shimmy, or the Black Bottom as well as any other Roaring Twenties gal. Dorothy was a catch, and it is not likely that the only thing that attracted Claude was her résumé. By the spring of 1930 they were very much a couple.

Dorothy remained involved in every aspect of Southeast House, which was set to open on April 22, 1930. She personally signed off on hiring Marion Grace Conover, an attorney and social worker from Boston, as executive director at a salary of $1,800 a year, more than Dorothy was earning at Howard.[12] As an ominous harbinger of their future, Dorothy and Claude continued to maintain separate lives, despite their growing affection. Still the suave bachelor, Claude continued to zip up to Harlem with friends. It is a mystery why they did not proudly return home to marry in the local church or at least in the Ferebee living room, the site of many of the family's important events. Instead, on July 2, 1930, they eloped to West Chester, Pennsylvania, a suburb of Philadelphia. The same day they applied for a marriage license—with Dorothy, almost thirty-two, claiming to be the same age as her twenty-nine-year-old groom—they were married by the local justice of the peace.[13]

Their quickie marriage begs the obvious question as to whether theirs was a shotgun wedding. But their twins were born on August 8, 1931, thirteen months after their marriage.[14] There is one slender and intriguing thread of evidence to suggest the marriage may have been a necessity; a possible miscarriage in October 1930.

Shortly after the 1930 school year began, a cryptic item appeared in the *Hilltop*, the Howard student newspaper. Under the headline "Dr. Boulding to Resume Duties," the article reads, "During the week of October 20, Dr. Boulding, physician to the women of Howard, was absent from her office because of injuries received in a recent accident."[15] The length of her convalescence, its timing during what would have been around the time of the risky first trimester, and the lack of detail about the "accident" raises suspicions, particularly in light of the lifetime of misinformation Dorothy provided about personal matters large and small.

Dorothy was no prude about sex, at least when it came to talking about or teaching it. But she was a highly respected and respectable woman. An unwed pregnancy would have brought dishonor to their families, although given the times, it would have fallen harder on the Bouldings. One cannot imagine that Howard would have permitted her to continue to be a physician and role model to its women students. Nor would she have been able to continue her high-profile public service work. If she were single and pregnant, abortion or a fast marriage were her only options. Given that she was pushing thirty-two at a time when the median age for a woman at her first marriage was twenty-one, she may have thought marriage was the better choice.[16]

Another reason they may have eloped, having nothing to do with pregnancy, might have been her future mother-in-law's dislike of her. Nannie Ferebee tried to throw cold water on the romance, telling her son that Dorothy would put her career ahead him, which turned out to be prophetic.[17]

Whatever acted as the catalyst for their elopement, immediately afterward the newlyweds hopped into their black roadster, which they nicknamed "Buddie," to honeymoon at the Virginia seashore with two other couples.[18] It did not bode well that they chose to interrupt their first days of marital bliss to keep speaking engagements of no great importance, his before a dental convention and hers at a black college.

The unexpected marriage of Dorothy Boulding and Claude Ferebee caught their social circle off guard. "Dr. Claude Ferebee surprised Harlem last week by arriving on Wednesday, with Mrs. Ferebee, better known as Dr. Dorothy Bolden [sic], of Washington," announced the society columnist for the *Afro-American* in Baltimore.[19] The local Norfolk newspaper sent a reporter scurrying around Claude's dental convention to find out whether the rumors that the couple had married were true.[20]

While readers may have been stunned over the unexpected wedding, Claude and Dorothy took it in stride. Within weeks of their marriage, Claude was back in New York—solo—where he spent the summer of 1930 putting his New York dental license to good use practicing with Dr. Thomas H. Walters at 60 West 129th Street in Harlem.[21] It was great training; Walters would run the department of oral surgery at Harlem Hospital for more than forty years.[22] Claude did not return to Washington, his new bride, or Howard University until the fall.[23] In no apparent hurry to get home, he took a side trip in early September to Indianapolis to attend another dental convention. "Of course," reported the *Afro-American*, "Dr. Ferebee took in the Tennis Tournament and Chicago while in the Middle West."[24]

Dorothy, meanwhile, embarked on her new life as a married woman and her old life as a workaholic. She cranked up the publicity machine about Southeast House. She made sure to make a pitch to Dr. W. E. B. Du Bois for an article about it in the NAACP magazine, the *Crisis*.[25] After their marriage Claude moved into Dorothy's southeast Washington apartment, where they remained until early 1931.[26] Dorothy must have felt uncomfortable under the heavy burden of carrying twins, but that did not deter her from a busy professional life. In February 1931 she was one of fifty African American doctors at the White House Conference on Child Health, held at the Willard Hotel in Washington.[27] In April she traveled to Baltimore to speak at a program for National Negro Health Week, sponsored by the local YWCA.[28] She and Claude visited friends in New York City in May.[29]

The year the twins were born, 1931, was a rough one everywhere. On March 25 one of history's most infamous injustices against African Americans unfolded as nine young men were accused of raping two white women while riding a freight train through Alabama. The Scottsboro Boys, named after the town where they were arrested, would spend years in jail facing the death penalty while their case became a cause célèbre. Nearly 16 percent of the civilian labor force was out of work.[30] Dorothy was lucky to have a job. She worked full time until a month before the children were born and kept going part time right up until she was ready to deliver.[31]

It was a scorcher in the nation's capital the first week of August 1931, with no relief in sight. The Saturday before the twins were born, the city's high temperature was 83 degrees, and as the week wore on it only got hotter.[32] By August 3 the mercury hovered around 100. The heat sent fourteen people to the hospital, and shoppers collapsed in the street.[33] The only places offering respite from the relentless heat and humidity were the movie theaters and, ironically, the hospitals, where Dorothy would find herself by the end of the week as she entered labor.

On Saturday, August 8, 1931, the heat and humidity exploded and the temperature reached 102 degrees in Washington—an unimaginable level of discomfort for a woman in labor.[34] At one o'clock in the morning Dorothy gave birth to a boy, Claude Thurston Ferebee II. After another half hour of labor, his sister, Dorothy Boulding Ferebee Jr., arrived.[35] A boy for Claude, a girl for Dorothy. "No controversy," Dorothy said bluntly, many years later. Sadly there was already trouble in Paradise. Before learning she was pregnant with twins, Dorothy hoped her unborn child would be a boy "because that would please my husband. You see, he was becoming more and more resentful of everything that I was doing as a woman," she said, "because what I attempted seemed to turn to gold, and his effort was turning to mud."[36]

It was a harsh assessment of a man whose professional achievements, by any measure, were impressive. It begs the question as to whether she would have considered any man her equal. From the hindsight of old age she claimed her marriage fell apart fast, but at the time she gave birth to the twins the couple seemingly still had many happy years ahead of them. The arrival of little Claude and Dorothy Junior—the boy known as "Thurston," and nicknamed Buzzy by his father (nobody knows why) and the girl called Dolly—made the pages of the *Journal and Guide* in Norfolk, the *Chicago Defender*, and the *Afro-American* in Baltimore.[37] Dorothy's mother swooped into Washington to be by her daughter's side, as she would whenever she was needed.[38]

Poor Dorothy appeared exhausted ten weeks after giving birth. In a picture from October 1931 that she included in her honeymoon photo album, she is in Potomac Park near the Tidal Basin on a sunny autumn day, holding her adorable newborns. The babies are swaddled in a white blanket and sleeping snugly next to one another in little matching sweaters and berets. Dorothy is not herself. She appears thin, and her usually well-coiffed hair is messily pushed away from her face.

At that moment Dorothy seemed to be having trouble doing it all. Her face told the story she and countless other women faced during most of the twentieth century as they were forced to choose between competing responsibilities as mothers and professionals. In her case the choice was more profound as she struggled to maintain a high-powered career, nurture two babies, soothe a jealous husband's giant ego, and crusade for justice for her race and gender. She would accomplish much in her lifetime, but even the amazing Dorothy Boulding Ferebee would learn she could not to do it all.

6 Everything Was Precise

Within two years of their marriage, the Ferebees rented a three-story brick row house at 1809 2nd Street NW, not far from Howard, that served as their home and the joint medical and dental practice that Claude had suggested while they were courting.[1] From the day they opened their offices, Dorothy and Claude struggled with their fundamentally incompatible and competitive natures. "He had beautiful equipment, because he had fine ideas of having only the best," Dorothy recalled. "I was able to get along almost with a stethoscope and a blood pressure machine, without fancy medical equipment and material. But he had the most modern dental equipment, with all the instruments that he required, and everything was precise, had to be precise."[2] Claude was so exacting he would never permit any of his children or grandchildren to eat a snack in any of his fine cars.[3]

Dorothy credited Claude with being "a skillful dentist" but said his dream of launching a phenomenally successful practice to turn his Howard colleagues green with envy did not materialize. "The fact that I became busier and perhaps had a larger group of patients, that didn't set too well with him."[4]

All that survives of Dorothy's patient records are a few scribbled entries in stenographers' notebooks. But it is hard to understand how she could have had a thriving practice, given her teaching and staff obligations at the hospital and the university and her involvement with Southeast House and other social welfare activities. Plus she was the mother of two small children.

Dorothy said she devoted "a great deal of time" to her children, although she qualified that by adding "as much as I possibly could between seeing people in my office and the requirements at Howard University."[5] Years later some of the twins' friends would see it differently. From their vantage point, Dorothy never seemed to be home, the adult Ferebees never seemed to be together, and the twins seemed to spend a lot of time in the company of other families or at boarding schools. But of course it was Dorothy, not Claude, who was faced with unpleasant choices about balancing home and family.

After the Ferebees moved to 2nd Street, Florence Boulding joined them once again, perhaps to lend a hand with the children.[6] Besides helping her increasingly busy daughter, Mama Boulding might have been avoiding trouble back home. In 1934 her sister, Emma, and her brother-in-law, Edward Crocker, were killed in a head-on car collision.[7] That same year her brother, Leslie Paige, the lawyer-son to whom Lillie Paige left most of her money, was indicted for bilking a client's estate. He was released on a $1,500 bond guaranteed by his brother, Warren, in the event Leslie failed to return to court.[8] The story was all over town and must have been humiliating for the family. After five trials—three that resulted in hung juries and one in a mistrial—Leslie was finally convicted in 1936 and sentenced to a year in prison.[9]

Besides help from her mother, Dorothy had paid servants, as did others at Howard, from President Mordecai W. Johnson on down through the rest of the faculty. The "colored" maid was a common sight in the homes of Washington's African American elite.[10] The Ferebees had a Miss Green, called "Geen" by the twins. Dorothy credited Miss Green with doing "everything she could to make life happier and easier for me. She not only cooked and did the housework, but she looked after the children."[11] The fact Miss Green was on hand gave Dorothy peace of mind. When the infant son of Col. Charles Lindbergh was kidnapped from his nursery window in Hopewell, New Jersey, on March 1, 1932, less than a year after her twins were born, it was front-page news around the world, and few mothers rested easily again. Miss Green also provided loving stability for little Buzzy and Dolly in a family where the adults were always on the go.

Dorothy said she was around enough to routinely read her children bedtime stories, even if it meant her patients had to cool their heels in her waiting room downstairs. The twins were exacting taskmasters, like their father. If she tried to edit the fairy tale to get back to work, she "was called to time on it."[12]

By the time Dorothy and Claude opened their practices, the Depression was beating down on the populace and Franklin Roosevelt had not yet appeared in shining armor to save the day. Dorothy asserted in her oral history that her husband became jobless around this time, but that is wrong. She said he was fired by the man who hired him, Arnold Donowa, the dean of the dental school. As she recalled, her egotistical husband "wanted the world to know he was good. He didn't have the kind of disposition that allowed people to accept him on a basis that would make them admire him." Dorothy said Claude and the dean "were very soon at odds and Donowa dismissed him." Claude was so livid about his firing, she claimed, that he wanted his wife to sever her ties with Howard too: "He felt that this gave me more prestige than he enjoyed. He had lost his university status when Dean Donowa put him out." After a while "he began to say that he didn't see why I wanted to remain at Howard University; he wasn't there, why should I continue?"[13]

But it was Dean Donowa, not Claude Ferebee, who was dismissed from Howard in 1931 in a political power play that is not entirely clear; Claude remained at the school until June 1936, when his contract was not renewed for what were said to be financial reasons. In a lukewarm endorsement of Claude, President Mordecai Johnson said at the time, "Dr. Ferebee was not reappointed. Several very fine people are being discontinued.... The fact that a number of teachers have not been re-employed should not necessarily be construed as indicating that their work has not been entirely satisfactory."[14] Claude claimed he chose to leave.[15]

What happened to the Ferebees professionally at Howard in the 1930s is murky, and in their dotage neither one remembered it clearly. At the time it was believed they *both* got fired, either as casualties of the Depression or as delayed fallout from the Donowa departure. In the campaign of 1932 Franklin Roosevelt promised to cut federal spending. As president he signed the Economy Act into law in early 1933, which cut federal employees' salaries by 15 percent.[16] Because Howard was under federal control, its payroll was cut. Dorothy worked there until April 11, 1933, when the Board of Trustees voted to discontinue her services as physician to the women students, under the guise of cost savings.[17] There was no discussion at that meeting about firing Claude.

The trustees' meeting was top secret, but leaks to the press were inevitable. Whether those leaks dripped accurate information is questionable, but soon after the April 11 meeting, a media firestorm erupted. Without referring to him by name, the *Afro-American* newspaper of Baltimore reported that the administration asked Claude to take over as dean and he refused. "It is not strange, therefore, that the instructor who absolutely refused to play into the hands of the administration, and was manly enough to refuse the deanship when it was proffered him, should now be among the proscribed." And "to make the blow 100 percent efficient, the wife of Dr. Ferebee, who has been the lady resident physician of the university, has also been advised to go in peace and sin no more."[18]

Whether the *Afro-American* article pressured the trustees into reassessing its decision to fire Claude or the paper had it wrong in the first place is unknown. But at a special trustees' meeting after the article appeared all employees of the dental school were reappointed. The trustees reiterated the university policy of cutting salaries rather than firing employees.[19] For some reason Claude still had a job and Dorothy did not.

Firing Dorothy meant reverting to the practice of having a male doctor examine female students, which caused some parents to have fits.[20] Women students were unhappy too. Led by Rietta May Hines, president of a group called the Women's League, they sent an open letter to Mordecai Johnson on May 2, 1933, asking that Dorothy be reinstated. As reported in Norfolk's *New Journal and Guide*, the students said they had high regard for Dorothy's "qualifications and personality."[21]

Despite the protests, Dorothy was not rehired. Another article in the *New Journal and Guide* on June 17, 1933, reported that her firing had infuriated the alumni of the law school as well. The Howard University Law Alumni Association issued ten resolutions lambasting everything from Dorothy's firing to the rise of Hitler. Further, Howard's Board of Trustees president Abraham Flexner, the author of an infamous report that had resulted in closing most black medical schools twenty years earlier as inadequate, was drawn into the debacle. He responded rudely to a female student (presumably Rietta May Hines), who requested that the board rescind Dorothy's firing. The students "went on record as being violently opposed to the dismissal of Dr. Ferebee on ground of economy and condemning 'the discourteous, uncivil and ungentlemanly tone,' of a letter written by Dr. Abraham Flexner to a woman student, who had protested the dismissal of Dr. Ferebee."[22]

Although she has been dead thirty-five years, the school refuses to release details about Dorothy's employment beyond what is available in the board minutes, so why the university did not cut her salary rather than fire her is not known. But the university catalogues indicate she was gone, and there is no reference to any female doctor at the health service for the 1933–34 school year.[23] Her sole remaining connection to Howard—until she was hired much later to help run the entire University Health Service—was as a part-time clinical instructor in obstetrics at the medical school for four hundred dollars a year.[24]

When he was in his eighties, Claude told his oldest grandson, Claude Thurston Ferebee III, that he left Howard in solidarity with Dean Donowa. But the dean left five years before Claude, making that claim suspect. Claude said he resigned because he was sick of the "political upheavals in the university, especially with Mordecai Johnson and the dental faculty. . . . We decided we would stand by our dean and our principles" and go.[25] Perhaps Claude simmered for years over the firing of Dean Donowa, and after his anger reached a boiling point he left.

In the near term the Ferebees drowned their sorrows by attending the annual What Good Are We dance in the spring of 1933.[26] It was an elaborate dress ball. The 1933 event, which attracted hundreds of the black bourgeoisie from up and down the East Coast, was "prettier and gayer than in former years."[27]

Before the year was out, on December 11, 1933, Claude joined the U.S. Army Reserve as a first lieutenant.[28] In between the wars this meant little more than donning a uniform for a few weeks each summer and performing some quasi-military duty. But it also meant he was a candidate for active duty in what then may have seemed the very unlikely event of another major war.

As the decade wore on, Dorothy continued to oversee Southeast House, which always seemed on the brink of financial disaster. She ducked the bills as best she could. She got a letter from the General Heating Company seeking an overdue payment of $285 for the heat bill for Southeast House. It claimed, "We called the attention of this bill to someone who answered the telephone at the above address some time ago."[29] As the address was Dorothy's home, she had obviously decided to ignore it.

But despite its financial troubles, by 1932 Southeast House was nothing short of a miracle. There were mothers' clubs to encourage homemaking projects and a Junior Dressmakers Club where poor teenage girls could make themselves nice clothes. There were vocational classes for boys and Boy Scout troop meetings. Children's theater and art classes were run by a professional actor and artist. A medical school intern taught youngsters about sex. There was a library club, a nursery school, and free daily lunches. Public school teachers were on hand to supervise safe play in the summer.[30] And the neighborhood had Dorothy to thank for it.

Dorothy left her own children in the good hands of Dorothy Waring Howard, who founded the Garden of Children nursery school in a three-story brick row house at 1728 S Street NW. The Garden of Children, Washington's first private nursery school for blacks, opened in 1929 with fewer than a dozen children, including Howard's own two-year-old daughter, Carolyn. Although she was married to a prominent dermatologist, Dr. William J. Howard, everyone called her "Miss Howard."[31]

The school became another rite of passage for the children of Washington's African American ruling class, many of whom worked at Howard. It closed in 1961, falling victim to stricter city building codes for preschools and financial difficulties.[32] "They were delighted to go to the school and she [Miss Howard] was efficient with them," Dorothy recalled.[33] But for being forced to eat tapioca pudding, which some of them loathed ("We were told to think of all the children who didn't have anything to eat," said Aurelia Roberts Brooks, who was Dorothy Ferebee Jr.'s close friend and a Garden of Children alumna), the toddlers loved it there and adored Miss Howard.[34] A creative teacher, she staged little theatrical productions starring her students. The Ferebee twins were featured in one play as bunny rabbits.[35]

At the end of the school year Miss Howard and her husband tossed some of the children into their car for a picnic at the old Peirce Mill, an 1829 stone gristmill at the entrance to Washington's 1,755-acre Rock Creek Park. It was a popular event, attracting the students' families and alumni.[36] "We all jostled around to get a window seat so that we could dangle our arms out as he drove through the fords," recalled Brooks, "to see how wet we could get our hands and arms. There were always at least three of us piled on top of each other, reaching out of the window as we approached the fords—no seat belts in those days. If you were wet to the elbow, you were ecstatic. On those trips, the next best thing was catching tadpoles in the creek."[37]

The Ferebee twins could have been child models, solidifying Dorothy's theories about eugenics and demonstrating how wisely she had chosen her handsome mate. Blessed with their parents' genes, they were beautiful children who were the picture of prosperity in a decade of want. They were always identically and splendidly dressed in the height of childhood fashion. Photographs captured the twins happy with the world and with each other, smiling, laughing, holding hands, or hugging. Dorothy preserved these Kodak moments in her scrapbook, penciling in cute captions in which she called the twins her "bunnies" or "field mice." Occasionally more elaborate artwork accompanied these pictures—a delicate flower for May 1933, a snowfall for January 27, 1934, and a sunburst for July 1934—suggesting that the talented hand of Claude was involved. The Ferebees clearly adored their children. And despite Claude's later claims to the contrary, he and Dorothy appear to have adored one another too.

At this early stage of their marriage Dorothy Ferebee was not a household name. The Southeast House was new, and the Mississippi Health Project was several years into the future. Dorothy and Claude were on equal footing in their careers, and Claude was on more solid ground at Howard than she was. If his professional jealousy was one of the reasons the marriage disintegrated, there was nothing for him to be jealous about in the early 1930s.

Meanwhile, across the country events were evolving that changed all that. In Oakland, California, in 1933, the Jubilee Harmonizers, a girls' choir from the impoverished Saints' Industrial and Literary School in Lexington, Mississippi, performed to raise money for the down-at-the-heels institution. Ida Louise Jackson, the new president of Alpha Kappa Alpha, was in the audience.[38] The girl's quintet tugged at Jackson's heartstrings with stories of working as child laborers on farms in Mississippi and Alabama.[39]

Ida Jackson was born in 1902, one of eight children of a Vicksburg, Mississippi farmer and his wife. She educated herself into the middle class and obtained a master's degree from the University of California at Berkeley in

1923 and became the first black teacher in the Oakland public school district.[40] She viewed education as a religion, having had it drummed into her head by her father, who never finished high school, that an education was "the one thing that the white man can't take from you."[41] She might have thought the white man could not take musical training away either, because she played the piano, the pipe-organ, and the saxophone.[42] In 1921 Jackson founded the first AKA chapter in the West.[43] Having uplifted herself, she believed it was her duty to help others.

Saints' Industrial was a religious school founded in 1917 by members of the Church of God in Christ, the oldest and largest black Pentecostal denomination in the country. The religion was premised on a lot of no's, as in no card playing, no secular music, no parties. Like many religious-affiliated schools in the South, Saints' was established to educate illiterate, rural black children because Mississippi officials had no interest in doing so. These schools shared a common problem: they were always broke. One way to raise money was to send the school choir on the road. The Jubilee Harmonizers were known nationwide; in 1938 they even performed for Franklin and Eleanor Roosevelt at the White House.[44]

Saints' Industrial School was in the heart of the Mississippi cotton fields where the children of the farmworkers lived in desperate poverty. But black students fared poorly all over Mississippi. A full 63 percent of the state's black teachers did not have high school diplomas, never mind college degrees, and more than 25 percent had no education beyond the eighth grade.[45] Jackson, who had not returned to her Mississippi home in fifteen years, decided it was time to investigate. She visited Lexington over Christmas break in 1933.[46]

Her trip confirmed what Saints' Industrial School director Arenia Mallory and the Jubilee Harmonizers had told her. She returned to California fired up to start a teacher training institute using Saints' Industrial as the headquarters. When asked in her old age why she did it, she responded, "Who else would be crazy enough to go there?" Jackson, whose youthful militancy earned her the nickname "Emma Goldman" after the early twentieth-century anarchist, was looking for a meaningful public service experience for AKA.[47]

She put out feelers for volunteers for the Mississippi teaching project and selected six. Before they left California they shipped 1,228 books to

Lexington, many of them in such poor condition they were on their way to the garbage. Then Jackson and her volunteers piled into a Plymouth, filled the rumble seat with more books, a radio, and their tennis racquets. Before arriving on the campus of the fundamentalist school, they bowed to religious modesty by changing from shorts and sleeveless dresses into long-sleeved outfits, complete with stockings, despite the unbearable heat and humidity. "Cosmetics would be replaced by the maidenly blush of Mother Nature," Jackson wrote.[48]

Once in Lexington, battling "heat, dust, mosquitoes, and attendant evils, plus having to wear long sleeves in so hot a climate," Jackson realized that lack of trained teachers was the least of the problems in Mississippi. Many people had no decent food or health care. Without meeting those basic needs, it would be futile to attempt to institute a teacher education program. After she returned from Mississippi, Jackson suggested that AKA take on an even bigger public service program.[49] She envisioned it would address the most fundamental health needs of the rural poor and create a groundswell of national attention for the sorority. Enter Dorothy Ferebee.

7 We Went, We Saw, We Were Stunned

Not until Gen. Dwight D. Eisenhower plotted the invasion of Normandy in World War II would there be as much planning as that done by Alpha Kappa Alpha to set up the Mississippi Health Project. The supreme allied commanders were Ida Jackson and Dorothy Ferebee. Dorothy took Ida's inspiration and turned it into one of the most successful volunteer social welfare projects in history.

En route to New York City to the 1934 Boule, AKA's annual convention, Jackson detoured to Washington to attend a banquet in her honor hosted by Dorothy's local sorority chapter and to join the Roosevelts in lighting the National Christmas Tree.[1] While there she stayed with Norma Boyd, an AKA founder, and talked nonstop about the need for a sorority-run health project in the Mississippi Delta. Because Dorothy was a doctor and Southeast Settlement had cemented her local reputation, Boyd introduced the two.[2] When Ida Jackson, the tall, radical activist with the sweet smile from California, met the imperious, elegant Dorothy Ferebee from Washington, they clicked. It so happened that the day they met Dorothy was waiting for an obstetrical patient to deliver. While the uncomfortable mother-to-be struggled all night in labor, Dorothy, Ida, and Norma stayed up brainstorming about what would come to be known as the Mississippi Health Project. Before the sun came up, Dorothy agreed to be its medical director.[3]

With Southeast House a reality and her marriage rocky, she was ripe for a new challenge. Ida left for the Boule with a game plan for the health project that her new friend had prepared. She wrote Dorothy on January

21, 1935, "When I realize that as busy as you are you had taken the time to outline a technical program as well as sense the need for creating an atmosphere for the acceptance of the thing we wish to do, I almost wept and said, 'Here's a soror who loves her work and her fellowman!'"[4]

Alpha Kappa Alpha was founded at Howard University in 1908 by nine coeds and went national in 1913. It had two thousand members in 125 college and alumnae chapters by the time the health project plans were under way.[5] Its motto was "By Culture and By Merit," and it came to be known for its social activism.[6] In 1918 the sorority initiated an annual boule, or membership meeting.[7] Its educated members adopted pretentious Greek titles for its officers; the leader of the organization was the supreme basileus. Dorothy joined the Epsilon Chapter of AKA at Tufts and the Xi Omega graduate chapter after she moved to Washington.[8]

Dorothy was not among the 405 sorors who attended the 1934 Boule in New York. On Friday, December 28, 1934, Supreme Basileus Ida Jackson proposed that AKA "promote or assist in the promotion of some service project." That vague suggestion was fleshed out by Dorothy's blueprint for a traveling health clinic. The goal, Dorothy wrote, was to "carry medical service, its instruction and understanding, to a community where public health work has been greatly neglected." In case there was any doubt of the need, she pounded home the problems of little Lexington: "There are thousands of illiterates in this backwoods town, who, besides having no medical care, have no idea what it is, or what to do about their plight." There was "a fairly general failure on the part of the public authorities to recognize the situation as one of grave local and national importance." She concluded, "It does seem to me that Alpha Kappa Alpha could undertake no more humane project than that of a medical field service." AKA's health committee "heartily" endorsed the plan, immediately establishing an ad hoc project committee, headed by Dorothy, to get it going. Each soror was asked to kick in one dollar to pay for it.[9]

Dorothy did not exaggerate the need for the Mississippi Health Project. In 1930 whites could expect to live to age sixty, but blacks could expect to be dead at forty-eight.[10] In Mississippi in 1934 blacks died from diseases that whites survived: pulmonary tuberculosis killed 847 blacks, compared to 272 whites; venereal diseases left 243 blacks dead, compared to 35 whites.

That year 43 blacks and 23 whites died of typhoid; 234 blacks and 84 whites died of whooping cough; 1,007 blacks and 774 whites of kidney disease.[11]

Holmes County in the Mississippi Hill Country, where Lexington was located, had its own problems. At 752 square miles, it was the largest county in the state, with 40,200 residents, 76 percent of whom were black.[12] The soil was rich and the people who worked it poor. In 1925, 90 percent of the land was plowed by tenant farmers and sharecroppers, 94 percent of whom were black, many the offspring of slaves.[13]

All of Mississippi had its share of health problems. The smallpox vaccine had existed since 1796 but between 1930 and 1932, there were nearly two thousand cases of the disease in the state. The health needs of the black majority population were overwhelming. Black infant mortality was sixty-one per one thousand births compared to forty-four for whites. Holmes County residents suffered from TB, scarlet fever, typhoid, and dysentery. Midwives attended 95 percent of all black births and county health officials ridiculed them as "old, ignorant, superstitious women."[14]

From the moment she met Ida in December 1934 until she led a multicar caravan into the Deep South on July 5, 1935, Dorothy charmed, begged, or bullied key people to support the AKA clinic. Together they raised money, selected staff, arranged transportation to Mississippi, obtained medical supplies, secured the blessing of state and local—meaning white—officials, and tried to convince landowners to let their sharecroppers participate. "The Duty of Every AKA Woman," Dorothy wrote to the sorors, was to "get behind the Health Committee with moral and financial support. She can do this best by talking about the project wherever she goes, thus creating a national interest in the work while doing a good press agent job."[15]

And so the Mississippi Health Project began, fueled by a stream of letters from Ida to Dorothy and back again and to anyone else they thought could help. Ida had a better inkling of what was in store for them, having spent the previous summer in Lexington with Arenia Mallory. "The school and town as I told you is behind time," she wrote to Dorothy on the eve of their journey to the South. "Miss Mallory is *very* sensitive about 'not belonging'—I think you know what I mean for we Sorors can make other people feel they had no right to be born if we so desire." She warned Dorothy to tread lightly. "She is *afraid* she wont [sic] get recognition in this *Health Project*," Ida continued.[16]

Arenia Mallory was born in 1904 in Jacksonville, Illinois. Her father had been in a traveling circus and in vaudeville, and her mother played the Italian concert harp.[17] One of her brothers, Eddie Mallory, also known as "Pretty Boy," would count among his four wives the actress and blues singer Ethel Waters.[18] Arenia was a talented musician who was "born again" at seventeen, when she claimed to have gotten knocked unconscious by the Holy Ghost at a revival meeting.[19] Consequently she yearned to be a missionary in Africa; perhaps running the Saints' Industrial School in the impoverished Deep South satisfied that urge.[20]

Mallory's pugilistic encounter with the Holy Ghost precipitated a lifetime of religious devotion. When Saints' needed a new brick building in 1931, she said God instructed her to go to New York City with the Jubilee Harmonizers to raise money for it.[21] Mallory was something of a paradox; a born-again Christian who was married multiple times. Although she was obviously dedicated to her school, it was always broke while she wore a fur coat. On a visit to New York City in 1949 her three-strand pearl necklace worth two thousand dollars was stolen.[22]

Dorothy, Ida, and Arenia would work together off and on for years, always for the common good of uplifting the quality of African American life, yet the three of them often seemed to be at odds. It is unclear what bothered Ida about Arenia; with Dorothy and Arenia it might have been something as simple as Arenia's insecurity. Dorothy was more attractive, sure of herself, a trait racist southern whites might have called "uppity," a label Dorothy would have worn as a badge of honor. Unlike Arenia, Dorothy had no fears others would steal credit that was due her or that she did not belong.

Dorothy quickly discovered that the sorors were enthused about the *idea* of a Mississippi Health Project but weren't clamoring to give up their summer vacations to sweat alongside her in the cotton fields. But there was at least one over-eager volunteer. Nurse Mary E. Williams was ready to sign on the dotted line immediately; she participated for five of the seven summers the project was conducted. In her early letters to Dorothy and Ida, in which she claimed credit for thinking up the idea, there were hints that she could become a problem.

Williams was a stylish woman given to wearing her hats cocked at a dramatic angle.[23] She was also a serious woman, having graduated from Hampton Institute and the Richmond Hospital Medical Training School for nurses.[24] In the wake of the worst flood in American history, when torrential rains caused the Mississippi River to overflow in 1927, leaving one million people homeless, Mary Williams was one of two women named to the Colored Advisory Commission, chaired by Robert Russa Moton, head of the Tuskegee Institute, to investigate reports that black flood victims had been forced into slave labor, denied food, and held at gunpoint in refugee camps.[25]

Williams helped create a settlement house in New Orleans in 1927, and by 1935 she was the director of the Tuskegee Institute's health center and local American Red Cross activities.[26] Despite her stellar credentials and her good works, however, she was decidedly odd. She inundated Ida and Dorothy with bizarre letters littered with typographical errors in which she claimed credit for the Mississippi Health Project, dropped nasty slurs, and made wildly inappropriate promises to bequeath money to Dorothy's twins though she never met them and did not even know their names. She also complained of depression.

In her initial letter to Ida, written on February 6, 1935, she took credit for the idea for a traveling health clinic and said the White House was interested. She claimed to have written to Eleanor Roosevelt about it. "When I conceived of the idea I did not know you had same in mind."[27] In a second letter she asked to meet with Ida and Dorothy in Washington to discuss her idea further and wanted train fare to get there.[28] Ida politely but firmly replied that she had no time or money to attend the meeting.[29]

Shifting her campaign to Dorothy, she wrote to her on March 7, and again hinted that the sorority had stolen her thunder, but nonetheless offered her help.[30] Her many letters to Dorothy and others about the project show her to be erratic, suspicious, jealous, and divisive.

Five days after Mary Williams's opening salvo, she sent Dorothy another letter in which she offered to leave two life insurance policies worth two thousand dollars each to her twins. She also tried to get sixty dollars out of Dorothy that she couldn't get from Ida for railroad fare from Tuskegee to Washington to discuss the project.[31] On March 18 she suggested that

Dorothy give a heads-up about AKA's plans to Mississippi's health officials and local doctors: "I know the south better than you. . . . Unless the doctors down this part of the south KNOW that you are NOT going to start something to take thier [sic] practice away from them. . . . you are NOT going to succeed."[32]

But Dorothy was ahead of her, having contacted Roscoe C. Brown, director of the National Negro Health Movement at the U.S. Public Health Service. He suggested she write to Dr. Felix Underwood, the Mississippi state health officer, and Mary D. Osborne, the state's associate director of child hygiene. He also told her to reach out to Holmes County health officials "and set forth in a comprehensive manner the origin of the proposed project, its objective, and what assistance in finance and personnel the Sorority sponsoring the project can contribute to its operation."[33]

After consulting with the white director of the Holmes County Health Department, Dr. C. J. Vaughn, Dorothy decided to concentrate on inoculating the county's black children against diphtheria and smallpox.[34] With the five hundred dollars she earmarked for medical vaccines, Vaughn told her, she could expect to immunize 3,333 children. He also tried to dispel her misguided notion that sharecroppers could drop in on her clinic in Lexington the way paying patients visited her medical office in Washington. There was no transportation for poor black mothers and their children in rural Mississippi.[35] It was a warning Dorothy may not have believed, which forced her to have to improvise once she got there.

Vaughn's description of life for African Americans in Holmes County did not begin to touch on the reality of their misery. In the 1920s the night-riding, sheet-wearing, cross-burning Ku Klux Klan was in its prime. In 1925 in Mississippi, there were 93,040 members of the Klan and sixty-six reported lynchings in the state; all but two of the victims were black. "No state was more severe in terms of lynching than Mississippi, which holds the record for the highest number of lynching victims in the United States from 1865 to 1965, at more than 500 out of at least 5,000 victims since reconstruction," wrote Julius E. Thompson in his study, *Lynchings in Mississippi: A History, 1865–1965*. Lynching victims were usually accused of sexually assaulting white women, but that was often a ruse. Blacks who refused to be cowed and demanded voting rights, organized workers, or became even moderately prosperous were targets. Because blacks were the majority population of Mississippi until 1930, white racists felt it necessary to keep them in their place.[36] Lynching was a successful intimidation tool; between 1890 and 1964 there were just twenty-six registered black voters in Holmes County.[37]

Dorothy knew this. Yet with all the letters that passed among the sorors in preparation for their journey to the Deep South, none alluded to fear that they could be in danger. Perhaps they were in denial, but the unspoken thought must have crossed their minds that they could have been killed.

The sorority earmarked one thousand dollars for the Mississippi Health Project.[38] The budget Dorothy drew up relied on the $1,000 appropriation, a $250 gift from her own chapter, a $50 credit from Saints' Industrial School, and a contribution of $18.85 from Norma Boyd, who had introduced her to Ida Jackson. That the project was able to get started on so little is a testament to the labor of love it was.

Guarding the purse strings like a lioness was AKA founder Ethel Hedgeman, later Ethel Hedgeman Lyle. She was a stern taskmaster who verbally swatted Dorothy and Ida for their failure to follow her exacting protocols. On April 1 Dorothy wrote to Lyle seeking a loan against the one thousand dollars they hoped to raise from donations. Lyle waited seven weeks to reply, leaving Dorothy increasingly anxious about whether they would have money to begin.[39] When she finally contacted Dorothy, she claimed to be unable to open up the AKA coffer without a direct order from Ida. She wrote: "I was sure you had communicated with our Basileus, who might have told you that I have *no power* to pay out money without a direct order from her.[40]

This drove Ida crazy. "Imagine my disgust," she wrote to Dorothy weeks before they were scheduled to leave, "when I received a wire from Ethel Lyle Friday saying my letter was not clear and to send her authorization for payment of $1000 to the Health Comm."[41] When the check finally arrived, Dorothy was diplomatic: "On behalf of the committee, may I again thank you for all you have done. We hope that the final report of all our activities will be so stimulating that no soror can hesitate in quickly reimbursing the treasury for its generous loan."[42]

Meanwhile, hoping to secure the government's blessing, Dorothy dashed off letters to Frances Perkins, FDR's secretary of labor and the first woman cabinet member, and to the surgeon general of the United States, offering to meet with them before she left for Mississippi. She shored up her credentials by passing on letters touting the project from Senator Byron Patton (Pat) Harrison of Mississippi, and Congressman Will M. Whittington of Greenwood.[43] There is no indication that Perkins or the surgeon general took her up on her offer, nor is it apparent how she got the legislators on board.

In the midst of Dorothy's frantic preparations, Mary Williams reared her strange head again. Mary had asked Dorothy to write to her supervisor and to the president of the Tuskegee Institute to get her a leave of absence to participate. She also tried to get Dorothy to convince Tuskegee to pay her salary and travel expenses.[44] She demonstrated a bigoted, paranoid streak, describing Tuskegee's new president, Dr. Frederick D. Patterson, as "a good friend of mine . . . and we are VERY friendly, [but] you can never tell when a darkey will change on you."[45]

Dorothy wrote a polite letter to Patterson requesting that he grant Mary a leave, but she kept quiet about whether she should collect a salary for it.[46] He offered to give Mary a leave provided AKA pay for the trip.[47]

Dorothy left little to chance. In a letter to Arenia Mallory dated June 22, she asked that an area at the Saints' school be set aside to serve as a headquarters and offered to pay to screen a porch to use as a clinic. She also asked whether she could expect electricity—Ida had warned her that Lexington was backward—and inquired about the cost of their room and board. Arenia responded by telegram promising ice, electricity, "three wholesome meals," daily laundry, and maid service for $4.50 a person per week. She also gave permission to have the porch screened; it would cost sixty-five dollars.[48]

As they were about to leave, Ida sent Dorothy a handwritten letter expressing her appreciation: "I think God has wonderfully blessed me, in that he pointed you out to Direct and plan this most important part of the work of the Sorority—the greatest thing ever done. You're great and we are justly proud of you."[49]

Dorothy summoned the stamina for a few last-minute public appearances. She spoke to a group called the Mississippi Society at the 12th Street Branch of the YWCA in Washington on May 9 and asked the audience to donate a camera so the volunteers could record the project for posterity.[50] She went to the AKA regional conference in Philadelphia in June to give a talk titled "Improving the Social Status of the Race," which surely included a pitch for the trip. In the audience was a Philadelphia soror, Ruth A. Scott, a large, ungainly, and rather masculine-looking woman who would become Dorothy's closest friend, spurring suspicions on the part of some—who had no proof—that they were lovers.[51] Dorothy finally took a night off on a Friday in May to go to the Lincoln Colonnade with Claude and six hundred other revelers to attend one of their favorite events, the What Good Are We dance. Among the guests were Dorothy's old friends the Loftons.[52]

At last they were good to go. Ida planned to leave from Oakland by car on June 22 and pick up Marion Carter, a teacher, in Memphis and another teacher in Nashville. The initial plan was to start the teacher training program on July 1, a week before Dorothy was slated to arrive. Ida confessed that she was exhausted and suffering from hay fever. "I fear your first patient will be your Soror," she wrote Dorothy before she left.[53]

The clinic would begin on Monday, July 8, 1935, and end Friday, August 16. Almost forty-five years later Dorothy was still smarting at the treatment she claimed she received from the station master or a ticket agent at Union Station in Washington. In her oral history she said her plan had been to take the train to Mississippi, but when she went to the station in June to buy seventeen tickets the agent refused to sell them to her. "He said, 'Seventeen tickets will take up all the space we have in those special cars'—he wouldn't say Jim Crow cars, you know, the special cars," she recounted. "'And going up and down the line, if you take seventeen, we'll have no space for our other niggers'—he forgot himself there and called them niggers."[54]

Dorothy's story raises questions, for in retrospect it seems odd that the women considered such a ludicrous plan. They were aware that once the train traveled south of Washington DC the cars would be segregated. Furthermore it is unclear how they would have transported all their medical supplies. And why wouldn't the station master have taken cash on the barrel and filled the Jim Crow car with Dorothy's team rather than keep seats open for other African Americans who may or may not have showed up to fill them?

The first time Dorothy appears to have mentioned the Jim Crow incident was in a 1976 issue of the official sorority magazine, *Ivy Leaf*, a retrospective edition about AKA's finest moments. She repeated the story in her oral history interview four years later. In the 1976 article she wrote, "Ugly racial discrimination upset well structured travel plans to bring on July 1, 1935 the first staff members from around the nation to Washington, DC from where as a group they would entrain to Lexington, Mississippi." She called the setback "a great blow to our pride" that "created a devastating and terrifying situation." To remedy the problem "emergency calls went out to all staffers to bring to Washington, their own cars or those they could borrow."[55] In response, she claimed, eight cars arrived in Washington to get the job done, but this seems like too many. Only twelve AKA volunteers went to Mississippi in 1935. A contemporary newspaper article reported, "Four autos were used for the traveling clinic."[56]

Dorothy also might have alluded to the Jim Crow incident in an earlier interview with Dr. Count D. Gibson in 1967. Gibson, who was the chair of the department of preventive medicine at her alma mater, Tufts, had been recruited by a Harvard physician, H. Jack Geiger, to develop community health centers in the South.[57] Gibson knew Dorothy had been to Mississippi in the 1930s and sought her input. In a memo from Gibson to Geiger about his interview with Dorothy, he wrote, "They drove their vehicles down from the North, thus avoiding the segregated trains."[58]

There seems to be nothing in the letters from the participants in the Mississippi Health Project about an unexpected snag in buying train tickets due to a racist ticket-seller. As early as June 5, Dorothy planned to drive south. In a letter to Ida, in which she described putting the finishing touches on their travel plans, Dorothy wrote: "The only other travelling expense to me is $100, which I shall not use for a railroad ticket, but for road expense for my car, as I intend to take 3 girls with me [one of whom was Claude's baby sister, Connie, perhaps sent by him to keep an eye on things]."[59] On June 27 Dorothy wrote to Elsie Cain, "We, eight of us, are leaving Washington early (5 or 6) Friday morning, July 5, going direct to Richmond. . . . You will travel with me in my car."[60] Other letters sent in the summer of 1935 can be read either way. Mary Williams wrote on June 15 suggesting that Dorothy come to her house in Alabama (how, it does not say) with Dr. Zenobia Gilpin of Richmond, and that the three of them drive to Lexington in Mary's "lovely Plymouth car."[61] And, on July 1, Williams sent another letter to Dorothy reiterating her suggestion they drive down together. "It's much better than riding on the train," she added.[62]

Dorothy and Ida were forced into the Jim Crow car from Richmond to Washington for a meeting with Mrs. Roosevelt on New Year's Eve 1935 and complained about it to her. But they said nothing about having been faced with similar discrimination on their way to Mississippi. This is puzzling, given that the express purpose of the meeting with the first lady was to discuss the health project in detail. It is possible that by the time she wrote the 1976 article, when she was seventy-eight and already ill with congestive heart failure, Dorothy had confused the two events.

When Dorothy submitted that article to the *Ivy Leaf*, she asked that it not be cut or edited: "I did not want it to be just a report or recital of a medical clinic activity. Rather I wanted to present it as an interpretation of the why, the how, the flavor, the mood, the total dynamics of a saga of the will and determination of Alpha Kappa Alpha women—a view and understanding not yet available or comprehended by our young sorors and pledges."[63] Perhaps she decided to take a little poetic license with the truth and add the story about the racist station master to capture "the flavor, the mood" of her "saga."

Dorothy was hit with a huge blow on the eve of their journey. Zenobia Gilpin, the other doctor, backed out, leaving Dorothy as the sole physician on the project.[64] "Lord, what a head ache I have had just trying to get people to say yes," she lamented in a letter to Ida. "And now Zee (Gilpin) turns up with a changed mind. Unless the Health Department there can carry on to a large extent, I shall be in a very difficult spot. However, I am not discouraged, and shall do all I can in the time I have to put it over, single handed if necessary. . . . I leave weary but courageously."[65]

A dozen women made their way to Mississippi in 1935. Besides Dorothy and Mary Williams, the only volunteers with health care experience were Ella Payne, a dietician with a master's degree from the University of Kansas, and Genevieve Mayle, a graduate nurse. Ida ostensibly came to lead the teaching program, assisted by Ruth Handy, who held a master's degree from Columbia University, and Marion Carter. They, too, ended up acting as nurses. Dorothy's twenty-year-old sister-in-law, Connie Ferebee, and a woman named Elsie Cain were brought along to act as secretarial assistants. Irma Barbour, a Howard University student, Nell Jackson, who was Ida's niece and a student at the University of California studying French, and

Alice Avery, who had a degree in art, came to help too.[66] Four of the volunteers—Mayle, Avery, Barbour, and Nell—were not members of AKA.[67]

Looking back from the twenty-first century of superhighways, central air-conditioning, jet travel, and laws against racial discrimination, it is tempting to underestimate the strength and bravery of Dorothy and the women who went with her to Mississippi. Given the kudos it brought Dorothy and the sorority, it is equally tempting to accuse them of undertaking the project because of how it would enhance their reputations. But in 1935 they had no idea how it would all turn out.

The sun rose at 4:48 on the morning of July 5, 1935; the temperature reached close to 90 degrees in Washington and got steadily hotter farther south.[68] It was hardly an ideal day to begin an 830-mile road trip. Cars were not air-conditioned, and decent middle-class women did not leave the house without wearing dresses, silk stockings, and girdles. Dorothy loaded up her husband's car with medical supplies, three passengers, and their luggage. Ever the field marshal, she dictated what the women could bring: one suitcase filled with white smocks and cool cotton dresses.[69]

Dorothy drove straight to Bennett College in Greensboro, North Carolina, some 247 miles southwest from Washington, past Charlottesville, Lynchburg, Roanoke, and Danville in Virginia. Perhaps it was on this trip that she earned her lifelong reputation for driving with a "granite" foot. She had considered leaving for Lexington a day earlier, but Claude had vetoed the idea. He did not want his wife and sister traveling by car in heavy July 4th holiday traffic.[70] His concerns were real; twenty-seven people were killed in car crashes on the holiday that year.[71]

The travelers were forced to stay at black colleges or in the homes of friends or sorority sisters along the route because Jim Crow went well beyond the railroads to include hotels and restaurants. After a good night's sleep at Bennett College, they soldiered on to Atlanta on Saturday, another punishing 306 miles. A heat wave continued to bake most of the country. On Sunday they drove 119 miles to Tuskegee Institute in Alabama to meet Mary Williams, whose "lovely Plymouth car" joined the caravan. By driving her own car Dorothy spared herself having to listen to Mary take credit for the health project or promise to leave her money to her twins for the remaining 257 miles to Lexington.[72]

The roads were unlike any they were used to: gravel and mud, held together by "dilapidated bridges [that would] perilously sway under the weight" of the cars, Dorothy wrote in her draft of a report for the sorority.[73] The clinic was scheduled to start on Monday, July 8, but given the state she was in when she arrived, no work would be accomplished that day. Anticipating that would be the case, she wrote ahead to Arenia Mallory, asking her to "use all your influence to hace [sic] as many children under the age of seven at the clinic on Tuesday morning at 9 as possible."[74] After months of planning, last-minute setbacks, and four days of driving, Dorothy thought she would be ready for anything when the clinic opened that Tuesday. But nothing could prepare her for the grinding ignorance, poverty, and health problems she encountered there. As she wrote later, "We went, we saw, we were stunned!"[75]

8 Stupid, Vacant, and Void of Hope

After the Mississippi Health Project team returned home, and for years afterward, they basked in the glory of their success, which by any measure was stunning. The stories they told were consistently upbeat, but behind the scenes, what could go wrong in 1935 did. The Holmes County landowners were hostile and suspicious, the sharecroppers were ignorant and scared, and some sorors who promised to help were more talk than action. The volunteers had to contend with Arenia Mallory's difficult nature, and there were petty disagreements among the participants.

Dorothy arranged the clinic schedule to coincide with the summer lay-by, that period between chopping the cotton and picking it.[1] Yet it became immediately clear Dr. Vaughn was right. At sunrise on Tuesday, July 9, after a four-day power drive, Dorothy woke up refreshed and ready to open the clinic doors. She was more than a little surprised when only a handful of patients trickled in.[2]

Dr. Vaughn's warning that patients could not travel to the clinic was true, but poverty wasn't the only obstacle. They were bound to the "place" (the plantation was called the "place" in Mississippi) by their "jailors," the plantation owners.[3] The landowners were wary of allowing visits to a health clinic run by Negro strangers who, for all they knew, were more interested in agitating than inoculating. "To our astonishment, 13 owners refused our services, and forbade their sharecropping families to leave the plantations to attend any one of the 5 proposed clinics," Dorothy wrote years later. Only one was willing to cooperate.[4]

"So here we are, in Mississippi, with all the materials and drugs that we had bought, all of the things necessary for the health of young children, and we couldn't use them because the plantation owners would not allow the Negroes to come to us. So we had a consultation and agreed, 'Well, if they can't come to us, we'll go to them,'" Dorothy recalled.[5]

With Dr. Vaughn in tow, Dorothy, Ida, and Ruth Handy drove from place to place to pay friendly calls on the recalcitrant landowners. All but one relented, but there was a condition: the sharecroppers were not allowed to leave the plantation, so the project team had to come to them.[6] Suddenly, getting shut out of the Jim Crow railroad car looked like divine intervention. With the vehicles they used to get to Mississippi, Dorothy's team could take the show on the road. The first casualty was the summer school. The teachers—Ida Jackson, Marion Carter, and Ruth Handy—were now "volunteer" heath aides; there was no other way to get the job done.

The days were long and hard, starting before dawn and continuing into the evening. Rather than sip coffee in those calm moments at sunrise before the clinic opened, the volunteers used that precious time to warm up their cars and load them with vaccines, sheets, registration forms, needles, and uniforms. They made a quick trip to the local ice house for ice to preserve the vaccines, and they were good to go.[7]

The vehicles formed history's first mobile health delivery system as their drivers fanned out through the broiling countryside, logging hundreds of miles each day. There were mishaps, documented in Dorothy's scrapbook. "Stuck in the mud—a frequent occurrence," was the caption she wrote beneath a picture of the health team pushing a car.[8] Along the side of the road they saw disturbing scenes; convicts wearing striped prison uniforms doing hard labor on chain gangs and horses so skinny their ribs were showing.[9]

Once they reached the day's destination farm, they parked under a tree in the cotton field or next to an old school or crumbling church and set up a clinic. Behind the wheel in the lead car, Dorothy saw not a picturesque antebellum *Gone with the Wind* landscape filled with white-columned mansions but the grinding poverty of one-room shacks, some without screens or front doors. Within their crumbling walls they often housed ten to fifteen family members.

Two types of nonlanded farmers worked the fields: tenants and sharecroppers. Tenant farmers paid a landowner for the right to grow crops on a patch of land; theoretically at least, they had some cash. Sharecroppers, poorer and usually black, had nothing but their sweat. They worked the land with the promise of "sharing" the resulting crops with the landlord. If there was flood, drought, blight, or just falling prices, sharecroppers ended up with a share of nothing.[10]

The sharecropper was often paid in scrip that had value only at the owner's commissary. If a sharecropper was over his head in debt, the landowner paid his bills and then "owned" him until he worked it off. Even if the sharecropper were debt-free, he still had to pay the landowner for seeds and supplies. Accounts were tallied on settlement day, which came once a year. If the sharecropper had anything left, he was enticed to blow it all by the car dealers who parked their shiny vehicles along the road outside the plantations. One car dealer was able to sell nineteen cars on a single settlement day at the Delta & Pine Land Plantation in Bolivar County, where Dorothy visited in 1936.[11]

Cotton sold at eighty-three cents a pound at the end of the Civil War, but was going for five cents a pound in 1932. By that time, 10 percent of the farms in the Delta were in foreclosure.[12] To get every nickel out of the land, owners were not about to set aside acreage for sharecroppers to grow vegetables for their own consumption. Sharecroppers had only whatever food was on sale at the plantation's commissary, at a markup as high as 100 percent.[13] Skinny, sickly, barefoot children stared from the sagging porches wearing rags. Dorothy wrote, "Diseased, deformed, aged and wizened all too soon, [they] return no smiles to one's eager gaze." The adults were even more depressing; Dorothy described their faces as "stupid, vacant and void of hope." She thought they all looked drugged.[14]

Dorothy led the automobile caravan over the dirt roads of Holmes County and would continue to do so year after year. Her colleagues came to trust her sense of direction after it became clear that following their own instincts led to ditches and dead-ends. "When we traveled we encountered nothing but dust. One couldn't see the car in front," Dorothy explained years later.

No routes were marked, you didn't know where you were. But fortunately, there's something about me that I can always come back from where I've been. So when the members of the team noticed that even without markings or signs, I could always get home, they made me the leader of the procession. . . . Because they said, "Where ever we've been, she can bring us home." It was because I have a knack of recognizing a certain tree stump, or a certain rock, or a certain object that stands out, assuring me, "This is the way I came."[15]

Each day one or two of the workers (including Ella Payne, who hated driving the unpaved Mississippi back roads) stayed behind to act as clerical worker and car mechanic. They filled the gas tanks, checked the water gauges, and inspected the tires. The tires of Ruth Handy's poor Ford, which she had driven from New York, regularly attracted nails as they drove over the "cross-at-your-own-risk" bridges.[16]

At each location the volunteers set up clinics from scratch. They hung clothes lines between trees and placed sheets over them to create privacy.[17] As many as eight hundred sharecroppers and their families lived on each plantation. Once they got the okay from the owners, they came to the clinic in the morning on foot, in cars, and in horse-drawn wagons. They didn't stop coming until nightfall.

The sharecroppers wanted health care, but some were wary. As parents lined up with their whining children for vaccinations, the plantation overseers sat close by on fidgety horses with guns in their belts and leather whips in their boots. They wanted to hear what their workers were telling Dorothy. "Apparently there was a strong belief among the landowners that this colored woman doctor and her staff were outside agitators who might use the pretext of free health care to agitate their workers," wrote Professor Tom Ward in an article for the *Journal of Mississippi History*.[18]

There were other obstacles. Many of the mothers had their own "medicines." To ward off disease in their children they placed bags of grasshoppers' nests around their tiny necks. To encourage the growth of healthy teeth they put buzzards' feathers around their necks, too.[19] Ignorance was pervasive. Some mothers struggled with simple questions from Ida and Ruth Handy, who were keeping the records. Child's name? "Fat Back.'" Date of birth? "She was born around cotton picking time."[20] Hanging back, curious yet cautious, were dirt-poor whites. Their children could have benefited from Dorothy's services, but they did not dare step forward and ask; the taboos against racial mixing were just too great.[21]

Even while injecting vaccines into little arms, Dorothy's headaches continued. Though she had planned the work schedule as a round-robin, with rotating teams relieving the initial participants, her prophecy to Ida proved to be accurate; she ended up doing the work herself. On July 9 Bessie Patterson of Maryland, scheduled to serve on the second team, wrote to complain of the hardships she faced. Her father had driven into a telephone pole, damaging the car in which she had planned to travel as well as the pole. She wanted an all-expense-paid trip, including car repairs if needed. Patterson reminded Dorothy, as if she did not know, "Twenty-two hundred miles is a long distance and there is apt to be a great deal of wear and tear upon a car."[22] Dorothy wrote back saying thanks, but no thanks. Sensing early on that she would not get the reinforcements she needed, she secured local help and worked double shifts, which allowed her to shut down by July 23, half the scheduled time.[23]

Later, in discussing Dorothy's decision to cut the clinic short, Ida said, "Three weeks were all she could give away from those adorable twins and a 'choice' husband."[24] But sadly there is no evidence the Ferebee household was clamoring for Dorothy's return. The entire time she was in Mississippi—unless she destroyed them before her death—there were no letters from her husband asking after her welfare and no scribbled notes from her five-year-old twins saying they missed their mommy.

The Mississippi Health Project volunteers trudged home after three weeks, having endured twenty-one days of relentless heat, 5,324 miles of driving over the country's worst roads, swarms of mosquitoes, and periodic temper tantrums.[25]

They were greeted like conquering heroes when they arrived home. The AKA historian Marjorie Holloman Parker wrote, "The first Mississippi Health Project not only had an electrifying effect on the social consciousness of members of Alpha Kappa Alpha but it also gave the general public a new awareness of cooperative community service."[26] Unfortunately this "electrifying effect" did not give the sorors enough of a jolt to make them want to dig into their wallets. By the end of the year the sorority had collected only $194.05 toward the $1,000 the treasury had advanced for the project.[27]

Yet the Mississippi Health Project became known as one of AKA's finest hours. In 1995 Susan L. Smith observed in her book *Sick and Tired of Being Sick and Tired* that Dorothy's Mississippi adventure was significant well beyond the field of public health. In Smith's view, the project not only "epitomized black women's volunteer health organizing, which had originated among club women at the turn of the century," but served as "the advance guard of a future army of activists who would seek to transform the South in the coming years."[28]

Steering the post-project publicity effort was almost as arduous as driving over unpaved Mississippi roads. It required Dorothy to be more politic than ever. No good would come of the world knowing that by the last day tempers had flared to the point that even the unflappable Dorothy Ferebee had crumpled up in tears. Instead stories trumpeted, "More than 2,500 Negro children were immunized in two weeks in Lexington, Mississippi by twelve volunteer workers" (*Negro Star* in Wichita, Kansas), and a wire service piece that reported, "A sordid story of almost unbelievable conditions existing in rural Mississippi was revealed to Xi Omega chapter of Alpha Kappa Alpha sorority by Dr. Dorothy Boulding-Ferebee here recently."[29] African American newspapers in New York, Pittsburgh, and Atlanta touted Dorothy's work.

There were no stories about in-fighting among the volunteers, but letters among the volunteers that passed around afterward made reference to it. Dorothy and Ida feared that Arenia Mallory intended to use her connection to the health project as a fund-raising opportunity for the Saints' Industrial School, and it irked them. Arenia also seemed to want to sow the seeds of divisiveness. Dorothy heard through the grapevine that Arenia (whom the volunteers derided behind her back as "Madam Queen") was spreading the story that Dorothy was making Ida jealous by taking too much credit for the project's success. Dorothy denied it, but she did not want the credit going to Arenia. It galled her that Arenia was visiting churches to talk about AKA's health project as if she were a central part of it. "I knew that after all she wasn't interested in the personal sacrifices of the women who went, but that she saw a wonderful opportunity to trade in on the work of Alpha Kappa Alpha Sorority and to boost her school," Dorothy complained. "And she is resting comfortably on the laurels of AKA," she observed."[30]

Given her professed aversion to watching Arenia claim credit, it is hard to understand why Dorothy accepted an invitation from Arenia to share a church podium where the project would be discussed. Once there she held her nose, thanked Arenia for her hospitality in Holmes County, and finished with a half-hearted pitch for money to modernize Arenia's woeful school. Much to Dorothy's horror Arenia told her she had set up a meeting with Eleanor Roosevelt. Dorothy asked to tag along, telling Ida, "I thought that the only way to know what the devil is doing, is to stand beside him and not let him out of your sight."[31] This did not sit well with Ida. She wrote to Dorothy, "I understand that Madam Queen plans on getting an interview [with the first lady] and expects to spread it on about the Project. . . . I can see no reason why you should accompany the *Saints* group for an interview regarding the Project—I trust you will . . . allow the Committee as well as the Basileus to be a part of the group that is seeking or will have an interview with the First Lady!"[32]

Dorothy herself wrote to Eleanor Roosevelt on December 2, 1935, requesting an audience.[33] In response she and Ida were invited to meet with the first lady at 4:30 in the afternoon on New Year's Eve.[34] The invitation was a major coup, putting Dorothy on par with her three-year-old twins, who had snared a visit with Mrs. Roosevelt back in May 1935. Back then, they had posed on the south steps of the White House with her and other children. The picture was wired to newspapers around the country. It even appeared in the venerable *New York Times*.[35] The twins' presence at the White House coincided with National Child Health Day and was surely engineered by their ambitious mother.

The invitation from the first lady helped to smooth the bumps in Dorothy's relationship with Ida. Like soldiers in the trenches during wartime, their experience in Mississippi brought out the best and worst in them. Ida was imperious and often referred to herself in the third person by her title, Supreme Basileus. In a story she wrote about the project for the sorority magazine, the *Ivy Leaf*, she took a swipe at Dorothy's sister-in-law, Constance Ferebee, calling her "petulant."[36] That comment ruffled the feathers of other participants. "I suppose you noticed the crack Ida made concerning Connie," Marion Carter wrote to Dorothy.[37] One can only wonder why Ida would write such a mean-spirited thing about the sister-in-law of the heart and soul of the project. Yet anxious to foster good public relations, Ida also wrote in the sorority magazine, "I think one of the greatest tributes that can be paid the group, was the apparent joy and pleasure they got in serving and the absolute lack of friction within the group. During these four weeks, there were many times when the heat,

dust, and problems of many kinds, all lent themselves to disagreement—
but never was there a cross word exchanged."[38] Marion Carter could not
contain herself. "My! didn't we all get along—'but never was there a cross
word exchanged,'" she wrote Dorothy, dripping with sarcasm after reading
the article.[39]

While the participants in the health project were sorting out their summer and thinking about 1936, in New York two dozen women were meeting,
including one representing AKA, to chart a new course: an umbrella organization of organizations of black women that would grow to be the powerful
National Council of Negro Women. At a lunch meeting on December 5,
1935, at the YWCA on 137th Street, Mary McLeod Bethune, president of
Bethune-Cookman College, an administrator of the New Deal's National
Youth Administration and a confidante of Eleanor Roosevelt, was making
a pitch for this new group. A few of those present were skeptical, but by
the end of the three-and-a-half-hour meeting Bethune had the blueprint
for the National Council of Negro Women, an organization that Dorothy
would lead one day.[40]

The AKA Boule was set for December 27–30 in Richmond, Virginia.[41]
Freak weather conditions prevailed. On Christmas Eve the country fell
under a cold snap, the mercury in Washington hit a low of 15 degrees, and
snow was predicted.[42] Temperatures reached only the 20s as the women
made their way to Richmond on the 26th.[43] Forecasters were predicting
more snow in Washington and the surrounding areas on Saturday, December 28. The cold weather forced even the hearty women of AKA inside at
Virginia Union University, site of the meeting, ensuring that most were
around on Saturday afternoon to hear Dorothy's report on the Mississippi
Health Project. She "took the convention by storm," according to one
attendee.[44]

Dorothy's report was part rallying cry, part campaign speech that set
the stage for her election as supreme basileus four years later. Despite the
relief measures enacted by the Roosevelt administration, she told the audience, "very little has been done for the health of the black folk in the far
south." Blacks had been left out of the Depression-era recovery because of
"local race prejudice and discrimination" as well as "the deplorable lack
of initiative and organization among the Negroes themselves, many of
whom are still waiting for donations from benefactors or hoping in vain

that their own leaders, the special advisers and experts, will accomplish something for them." She continued, "We could do little about the preju- dice, but we felt we could do something about the organization of Negroes to help Negroes. We could start to till the soil most ready for our cultivation." She urged her sisters to join her in fighting to uplift the race, demonstrating the vast demographic difference between AKA and the sharecropper popu- lation. "Negroes—everywhere and with no exceptions—must go down, side by side with the humblest, blackest, 'distorted and soul-quenched' Negro serf and elevate him by actual contact." Sorors who answered her call would show racists a thing or two: "It will permit those who hold the whip hand in these areas to see that the Negro race is as variegated as any other race of human beings. They will see a type of Negro vastly different from those whom they already know—one that is ready and well qualified to aid—willingly—the less fortunate members of the race."[45]

The next morning, while the sorors exchanged goodbyes, Dorothy and Ida dashed to the train station to board the train in time for their 4:30 meeting with Mrs. Roosevelt. Once again the weather failed to cooperate. A storm from Alabama made its way north on December 29, dumping a foot of snow in the Carolinas, eight inches in Virginia's Shenandoah Valley, and seven inches in the nation's capital, blocking roads and snarling traf- fic.[46] The train crawled. "Consequently you can understand the frame of mind and the thoughts that were uppermost in the mind of your Basileus," wrote Ida for the *Ivy Leaf.* To make matters worse, they were stuck on the Jim Crow car.[47]

It was growing dark by the time Dorothy and Ida hurried to their appointment with the first lady. The bright lights on the national Christmas tree illuminated Lafayette Park, across the street from the White House. Because of the importance of this meeting, the women were dressed in their winter finery. For Dorothy, that would have meant at least one item of fur.[48]

Although New Year's Eve 1935 would be a raucous, all-night celebration in the nation's capital, the economy having improved sufficiently to give the weary populace something to party about, the Roosevelts had no plans to join the festivities. The first family intended to hunker down in the White House, enjoying the company of just a few close friends; Secretary of the Treasury Henry Morgenthau and his family were coming by at eight to quietly celebrate the arrival of 1936.[49]

At exactly 4:28 Dorothy and Ida rushed up to the While House visitors' entrance on Pennsylvania Avenue, invitation in hand. Mrs. Roosevelt had very few public appointments that day. She noted in her calendar a "Miss Ferebee" and a "Miss Jackson" and in parentheses reminded herself that her guests were "colored."[50] Dorothy and Ida were escorted to the Red Room on the first floor of the White House. Mrs. Roosevelt entered through one of the room's six doors. The guests bowed and were seated.[51]

Dorothy introduced Ida, following protocol as Ida was AKA's leader but also implying Dorothy may have been acquainted with Mrs. Roosevelt, perhaps having met her when the twins went to the White House in May. The trio talked beneath the life-size oil painting of Uncle Teddy Roosevelt, the nation's twenty-sixth president. The first lady had blocked out a half hour on her schedule for the meeting, although the black newspapers later reported they spoke for a full hour.[52] How long the session really lasted is unknown; it was not recorded, nor did the White House issue a transcript, photograph, or press release. But even getting five minutes of Eleanor Roosevelt's time was nothing short of a miracle. Constant demands were made of the influential first lady by those who hoped to use her to funnel messages to the president.

At the meeting Ida asserted that money appropriated for projects in the South "should benefit the Negro as well as others."[53] She implied that nothing would change until more blacks were hired to fill high-level government jobs.[54] Mrs. Roosevelt suggested that federal public works' money might be available for future health projects if the volunteer workers were on relief. But women like Ida and Dorothy would not be on relief. As an alternative, the first lady said, AKA could continue to run the project itself and seek clerical and other nonprofessional assistants who were eligible for government assistance.[55]

What the sharecroppers of Mississippi really needed was for the federal government to pick up the entire tab for their health care. But over the life of the Mississippi Health Project AKA was never able to convince any government entity—federal, state, or local—to take it over and keep it going.[56]

The conversation with Mrs. Roosevelt included discussion of Dorothy and Ida's Jim Crow experience from Richmond that day but no mention of a similar incident at Union Station prior to leaving for Mississippi. As they sought the meeting to discuss the health project, it seems odd that this incident, so vividly remembered by Dorothy forty-five years later, would not have come up.

For all the Mississippi Health Project did for the downtrodden share-croppers, Alpha Kappa Alpha, and Dorothy's reputation, it was almost ended the year it began. After the summer of 1935 Dorothy and her husband were done with it. "I am awfully afraid I am out of it for next year, as my husband feels the strain on top of a very full year was too much for me," she wrote to Ida in October. "I feel so too but won't admit it to him," she added.[57]

Claude had a practical reason to wash his hands of his wife's Mississippi adventure: the trip had destroyed the family car. "Dragging six women with their luggage to Mississippi was a little short of suicide for it," Dorothy told Ida. Claude must have blown his own gasket at the sight of his beloved "Buddie," the honeymoon car, after Dorothy finished with it. But she described his reaction more delicately: "My poor husband was heart broken when the mechanics took it down. Well, such is life, I suppose."[58]

9 As the Moonlight Turned Barn Roofs to Silver

Wild horses could not have kept Dorothy away from Mississippi in 1936 after headlines like "Sorority Makes Phenomenal Gains with Health Project in Miss. During Last Year" and a face-to-face meeting with the first lady.[1] She was the symbol of the Mississippi Health Project and in nationwide demand as a speaker. She pasted into her scrapbook dozens of articles about the project and made a handwritten list of the cities where they appeared; Philadelphia, Richmond, Pittsburgh, New York, Chicago, Washington DC, Norfolk, Nashville, Oklahoma City, San Antonio.[2]

"She is eagerly awaited everywhere," her sorority sisters gushed.[3] "I cannot say too much for your Mississippi health project," wrote Dr. M. O. Bousfield of the Julius Rosenwald Fund, the philanthropy for black education.[4] Mississippi's senator Byron Patton (Pat) Harrison urged the U.S. Public Health Service to cooperate "in this unselfish program."[5] Her success catapulted her into the presidency of Xi Omega, the local AKA chapter. Her husband may not have been so impressed; there was still the matter of the car. It is not likely she convinced Claude to relinquish their new one for a second ruinous trip down south. In 1936 she relied on a young male driver from Washington, David J. Brown, and probably made the journey in his automobile.[6]

Dorothy was having the time of her life. In a letter to an AKA soror, in language more relaxed than she used behind the podium, she called herself a "globe trotter since I got mixed up in this here Sorority doings!" From March through early May 1936 she was on the road. She intended to bring along her five-year-old twins, leaving them with a soror named Marita in

Chicago. In her letter asking for babysitting help she wrote, "I'd rather that my own kids didn't go to the dogs while I'm trying to save the world!"[7]

She told Ida in October 1935 that she was finished with Mississippi, but by January 1936 she was already scouting a new location for the upcoming summer and, through soror Florence O. Alexander, who was in charge of Mississippi's black public schools, came up with Bolivar County, in the heart of the Delta where the all-black town of Mound Bayou was located.[8] Anything to get away from Madame Queen.

Named for South America's liberator, Simón Bolívar, the county was settled in 1836 by planters attracted to the rich soil and the Deep South location, far away from pesky abolitionists making trouble in the border states. Harsh slave labor was used to tame the land. Of its 10,471 residents in 1860, 9,226 were slaves. When Dorothy arrived in Bolivar, the population had peaked at 71,051, and about 73 percent was black.[9] It was also populated by an excess of "useless and worthless" stray dogs, "roaming and biting at will," leaving the locals vulnerable to rabies. The county's largest city was Cleveland, with a population of 3,800. There was no industry; it was solely the land of King Cotton, including the world's largest cotton farm, the Delta and Pine Land Company, with sixty square miles of fields. It was as backward as any area Dorothy could find in Mississippi, and its residents suffered from unconscionable rates of malaria and tuberculosis. There were only thirty-six doctors in the entire county. The houses of the poor had no screens, bathrooms, or electricity.[10]

But Bolivar County it would be. On March 31 Dorothy wrote to the state health officer, Dr. Felix J. Underwood, to tell him the sorority wanted to come to Bolivar. Two weeks later the Mississippi Board of Health approved, and she was informed that Dr. Rosier Dedwylder, director of the Bolivar County Department of Health, would be waiting for her.[11]

Dorothy's experience in 1936 was a far cry from the one in the previous summer, owing to her move to Mound Bayou and Dr. Dedwylder. Initially she thought he was cool to her, but Ida remembered him as being "surprisingly cooperative."[12] When he learned that Dorothy was coming, Dedwylder wrote, "I am glad to say we will welcome representatives from your organization and will cooperate with you in rendering service to our colored people."[13] Whether his early coolness was real or imagined, he and Dorothy quickly warmed to each other. Later he praised the Mississippi Health Project as "the best conducted health service offered by any volunteer organization in the country."[14]

The press attention inspired new volunteers in 1936,[15] but the second-year staff was lean—only eight women participated—and better organized. They were in and out of the county between August 21 and September 2. Dorothy's goal was to inoculate three thousand children against smallpox and diphtheria and possibly include treatment for malaria.[16] She wasted no time futilely enticing patients to a central location but instead established six satellite sites, all within a forty-mile radius of headquarters at the Bolivar County Training School for black children in Mound Bayou.

Dorothy had some old and new faces along for the 836-mile ride to Bolivar. Besides Ida, the erratic Mary Williams, the unlucky driver Ruth Handy, and her sister-in-law Connie Ferebee, there were two nurses from Freedmen's Hospital, Bessie Cobbs and Melissa Blair. One visit to Mississippi was enough for them; neither ever returned. Another welcome addition was young Marjorie Holloman from Washington, an AKA member who had just graduated magna cum laude from Miner's Teachers' College.[17] The chic, smart, and literary Holloman would come to serve as the amanuensis of their travels, participating in the Mississippi Health Project for the next four summers and capturing details of the experience with a writer's eye and a professional's pen. Years later President Richard Nixon rewarded her Republican political activism by appointing her to the DC Council. She later married Barrington Parker, whose career was also shaped by Nixon, who gave him a lifetime appointment to the federal district court in 1969.[18]

On August 17, 1936, Dorothy crammed into a car with Marjorie Holloman, Constance Ferebee, the two nurses from Freedmen's, and driver David Brown. They left at dawn, driving the picturesque Skyline Drive along the Blue Ridge Mountains and stopping in Roanoke, Virginia, 240 miles from Washington. On day 2 they drove 260 miles to Knoxville, Tennessee, to a home found for them by an AKA sister. That night at Yankee Stadium thirty-five thousand fans watched former heavyweight champ Jack Sharkey battle Joe Louis, "the Brown Bomber." Louis was the greatest black boxer since Jack Johnston punched his way into the twentieth century.

When Louis knocked out Sharkey seven minutes after the opening bell, African Americans around the country listening on the radio, including those in Knoxville, went crazy with delight. Dorothy and Marjorie joined the throngs in an impromptu street celebration.[19]

From Knoxville, Dorothy's driver pushed 180 miles to Nashville, where they spent the night at Fisk University. The next day the southern heat enveloped them. Temperatures were in the 90s.[20] They continued through Memphis until they reached Mississippi, where they encountered dust, dust, and more dust.[21] At times it was so thick that despite the soaring heat they were forced to drive with the car windows rolled up, their six sweaty bodies stuck to one another.[22] Meanwhile Ida and Ruth Handy were driving in from California through Texas. At some point Mary Williams joined them so they could all reach Mound Bayou by August 20, the day the clinic was to open.[23]

Three weeks before Dorothy arrived, Bolivar County celebrated its centennial as only a community in the Jim Crow South could: by ignoring the sensibilities of its black majority population. On August 6, a sunny day with the temperature a comfortable 80 degrees, a string of bands, floats, and cars made its way to the athletic field at the all-white Delta State Teachers College. There the Imperial Bolivar pageant was performed for five thousand spectators. Local white belles wore antebellum ball gowns and young white men marched in Confederate uniforms while black men pretended they were the slaves who had chopped down the forests one hundred years earlier. The Confederate flag was flying. To top off the show, the Ku Klux Klan paraded around with a flaming cross.[24]

Dorothy's appearance in all-black Mound Bayou was highly anticipated and very welcome. About eight thousand people lived in the farm area surrounding the town, and another two thousand resided in the city.[25] Founded in 1887 by former slaves of the family of Confederate president Jefferson Davis, Mound Bayou was built on the premise of black autonomy. Public officials and employees from its mayor to its schoolteachers, postmaster, and utility company workers were persons of color.[26]

The residents were proud of Mound Bayou's infrastructure and independence. It had a modern school for eight hundred students, with fifteen teachers and a principal boasting a Tuskegee education.[27] Most important, the town had no jail; there was no need for one because it was a peaceful, friendly, crime-free place. In 1936 it had gone more than a dozen years without a homicide.[28] That was about to change, however. During the years Dorothy stayed in Mound Bayou, a scandal would explode involving the city founder Isaiah Montgomery's family and her local host, a prominent Mound Bayou politician named Eugene P. Booze.

Isaiah Montgomery, the former slave who founded the town with his cousin, was local royalty. By 1912 he was worth $200,000 ($4.8 million in today's dollars).[29] He had been dead a dozen years by 1936.[30] He left a sizable estate, a beautiful home, and two sets of twin daughters. One of these daughters, Mary Montgomery, married Booze, and they moved into the Montgomery mansion, much to the chagrin of the other sisters. Booze was the administrator of their father's estate. One of his sisters-in-law, Estelle Montgomery, sued him, claiming he was "looting" it and "permitting white people to get control of much of it."[31] The smoldering family feud exploded in 1927, when Estelle alleged that Eugene and Mary, as well as the town postmaster and his wife, and Mayor Benjamin Green Jr., son of Mound Bayou's cofounder, had conspired to kill her father by serving him poison tea. Montgomery's official cause of death was listed as the flu.[32]

The accused perpetrators were arrested. Suddenly Mound Bayou needed a few jail cells. Ten days later a justice of the peace dismissed the case for lack of evidence.[33] That should have been the end of it, but in 1933 Booze and his sister-in-law got into a fight in the ancestral home; and she either jumped or was thrown out the window.[34] She survived and moved to St. Louis, periodically returning to torment Booze. In 1938 he obtained a court order barring her from his home.[35] Because Estelle was out of the house, Booze had room for the entire AKA Mississippi Health Project under his roof in the summer of 1938.

In 1939 Estelle would violate the court order by returning to Booze's house. He called the police, and Estelle was shot to death by a pair of white police officers known locally for their brutality.[36] The tragedy would play out a month later, in November 1939, when Booze was shot to death in his car in downtown Mound Bayou by an unknown assailant.[37]

But in the summer of 1936 Booze could only offer Dorothy accommodations in local homes for one dollar a day each, including a bed, "wholesome meals and a laundress."[38] Booze and Dedwylder drove all over Bolivar County posting signs about the Mississippi Health Project on trees, on church bulletin boards, and on the side of Mound Bayou's school. Booze arranged a town meeting for Dorothy's first night to tout the clinic.[39]

The key figure waiting for Dorothy was Dr. Rosier Davis Dedwylder, or "Dr. Ded." Born in Alabama in 1883, for twenty-eight years until he died on February 20, 1948, following a heart attack, Dedwylder ran the Bolivar County Department of Health true to the motto that sat on his desk: "Neither look up to the rich nor down to the poor."[40] This wealthy white cotton farmer from a proud slaveholding Confederate family dedicated his professional life to saving the health of the downtrodden, regardless of their skin color. Consequently some of the diehard Rebels, clinging to their lost Southern Cause seventy years after the end of the Civil War, had no use for him.[41]

Dr. Ded earned his medical degree from the University of Alabama and did graduate work at Tulane, finishing around 1907.[42] During the early twentieth century he worked in Rockefeller Foundation campaigns against hookworm and malaria, expanding his world beyond rural Mississippi.[43] Early in his career he loaded his medical supplies into a saddle bag to make house calls on the back of Jim, his Tennessee Walking Horse, a favorite breed of country doctors because of its smooth gait and ability to travel great distances.[44] In the 1920s Dr. Ded switched to a Model-T with a caduceus of Mercury on the driver's side door, the physician's symbol of wisdom and speed. He drove around Bolivar to inoculate the population against diphtheria and to screen porches to ward off malaria-spreading mosquitoes. It was a losing battle against not only the roads and the dreaded mosquito but the intractable ignorance; he would no sooner convince a landlord to screen the door of a tenant farmer's shack than the tenant would tear a huge hole in it so the cat could roam in and out.[45]

As a child Dedwylder read *Gray's Anatomy* before he was able to pronounce the words in it. He grew to be a handsome man of medium build with dark hair and gray eyes. Something of a good-ol' boy, he liked his liquor and his pack of fighting pit bulls. He was close to forty in 1919 when he married Mary Ruby Tyrone, a public health nurse. He called her Ruby; she called him Dr. Dedwylder. She contracted tuberculosis, gave birth to their first son in a TB sanitarium, returned to Bolivar, and, to everyone's surprise, recovered at their plantation, the Grove, outside Cleveland.[46]

Well-to-do southern whites "heavily relied on black laborers to cook their food, wash their clothes, chop their cotton, tend to their children, and maintain their property," writes Sharon D. Wright Austin in *The Transformation of Plantation Politics*.[47] The Dedwylders were no exception. Dorothy Ferebee and the Mississippi Health Project volunteers were the first blacks not employed by the Dedwylders to be invited to eat at their dining room table. The gesture made a great impression on Dedwylder's children, his black employees, and the white planters in the neighborhood, which may have been his goal. Doors opened for Dorothy because of it.[48]

Dorothy's clinics offered expanded services that summer. The volunteers inoculated children under seven against diphtheria and smallpox and, for the first time, treated both adults and children suffering from malaria. At the Bolivar County Training School in Mound Bayou they hosted evening lectures on child nutrition, personal hygiene, and well-baby care.[49] By the time the two weeks were up, the Mississippi Health Project had treated an astounding 3,500 patients, nearly 250 a day.[50]

Unlike the year before, Dorothy hit the ground running in Bolivar. On Friday and Saturday, August 21 and 22, at the Bolivar Training School she treated 350 children and adults who came on foot, in cars, or in horse-drawn wagons.[51] It was unbearably hot; a regional heat wave pushed temperatures close to 90 degrees. By Saturday cloud cover and the threat of showers made it feel cooler.[52]

The volunteers spread out in two cars. The morning bell to wake the sharecroppers and signal the start of the workday went off at the crack of dawn, but the clinics did not get started until eight. The volunteers worked in the middle of a broiling cotton field, which could get as hot as 100 degrees. They brought scales, measures, cards, ink, towels, sterilizers, aprons, cameras, dry ice, and their own drinking water.[53]

They divided the county into quadrants. On Monday and Tuesday, August 24 and 25, Dorothy and the volunteers took the clinic directly onto cotton fields twenty-two miles south of Mound Bayou in Shaw, on the border with Sunflower County.[54] Plantation owners from Shaw and Cleveland sent their workers to the clinic by the truckload.[55] After they were finished there the volunteers traveled twenty-eight miles to Busey. On Thursday, August 27, they opened the clinic in Pace, the central point in the county, nineteen miles to the southwest of Mound Bayou. Friday and Saturday, August 28 and 29, were the busiest days. The volunteers had the longest drive on each of those days: thirty-nine miles one way to the Delta and Pine Land Company in Scott, near Lake Bolivar in the southern part of the county.[56] There they treated five hundred patients in the relentless heat.[57] Sundays were not days of rest. The first Sunday the volunteers put on their best dresses and visited the rural churches to drum up business.[58] The second Sunday, after working so hard in Scott, they reopened the clinic at the county training school. On Monday, August 31, they traveled sixteen miles northwest to Perthshire, and on Tuesday they went another sixteen miles north to a town named, aptly or not, Alligator.[59]

Once the volunteers set up, Ruth Handy, in a colorful bandana to protect against the burning sun, and Ida interviewed each adult about the family's medical history.[60] After the interviews, Dorothy, Nurse Holmes, Mary Williams, and other volunteers took over. "This may sound like simple routine unless you realize or can believe that there are a number of children who are afraid to stand on a scale. It was here that the crying began," wrote Marjorie Holloman. The little ones howled the moment their arms were swabbed with cotton balls soaked in warm, soapy water. One look at the needle in Dorothy's hand and the screaming intensified.[61] Holloman got a big "surprise" when a hysterical child hell-bent on not getting stuck with a needle gave her a "ferocious bite" on the hand.[62]

They saw polio victims and young girls with goiters, an unsightly swelling of the thyroid gland in the neck, signifying iodine deficiency. Dorothy observed "hundreds of children covered with sores, many with open lesions, lame and partially blind from syphilis and gonorrhea; many malformed children, [and] babies with rickets due to improper diet."[63]

There were 1,500 tenant and sharecropper families working on the Delta and Pine Land plantation, which opened its own on-site hospital after the post–World War I influenza pandemic that decimated the worker population in the area. Workers not only paid the cost of their own health care out of the pittance they earned, but were assessed for the cost of the construction and maintenance of the facility.[64] Dorothy and the team were treated to generous lunches and fresh-brewed iced tea that hit the spot, courtesy of the company's president, Oscar Goodbar Johnston, who had been a prominent lawyer before he took over the company. Johnston held outrageous ideas about race, exemplifing the attitudes Dedwylder, the Mississippi Health Project team, and the farmworkers had to endure. Johnston was a firm believer in white supremacy; the races should be segregated, office-holding should be limited to members of the white race, and if he had his druthers, black farmworkers would not be employed on his property. But, pragmatist that he was, he recognized he had no choice—the overwhelming majority of available sharecroppers and tenant farmers were African American.[65]

Dorothy and Marjorie Holloman did not think all that highly of his hospital. To ensure infant and maternal health, women tenant farmers were encouraged to deliver at the Delta and Pine hospital. But when the Mississippi Health Project volunteers toured the women's ward, Holloman was shaken to see no signs of any bassinettes or cribs where babies were being delivered. Despite the hospital's inadequacies, Dorothy wrote in her year-end report, "There has been an awakening in the South that is slowly breaking the death-like grip of prejudice and ignorance. . . . [A] hopeful sign is the efforts at hospitalization found on Delta Pine Plantation in Scott, Mississippi. There are many objectionable and questionable features but the fact that there is a place where sharecroppers may be housed and receive treatment and care, however inadequate, is a greater evidence of humantarism [sic] than we found on any other plantation."[66]

Better evidence of "an awakening in the South" could be found at the cooperative farm founded by Sherwood Eddy, an official in the national YMCA, and Sam Franklin, a devotee of Eddy's and a one-time Presbyterian missionary to Japan.[67] Their enterprise, the Delta Cooperative Farm, near Hillhouse, Mississippi, was the rare place where white and black sharecropper families worked side by side.[68] The farm was not on AKA's itinerary in 1936; it was brand new and off the beaten trail. Dorothy and the volunteers paid a social call, leaving behind unused vaccines and the promise of a visit the following summer.[69]

The 1936 health project went over the estimated budget by $162.67.[70] After two arduous weeks Dorothy and her colleagues packed up their cars, said their good-byes, and pulled out of Mound Bayou just after midnight on September 2. They were bone-tired but deeply satisfied with how much they had accomplished in just two weeks.[71]

Marjorie Holloman was pensive in the backseat of the car, pressing her head against the door frame and taking in what little air she could through the open window as they headed out of Mound Bayou on the hot, still night. Reflecting on their time in Mississippi, she took some notes, which she later typed up with a few spelling or typing mistakes here and there: "The last scene, a picture to always remember as the moonlight turned barn roofs to silver and the stillness seemed to wisper [sic] the still mamoth [sic] needs of the Negroes of the South."[72]

10 Tell Claude Ferebee to Keep His Shirt On

Two summers in Mississippi put Dorothy on a dizzying climb up the AKA ladder. Her name was floated as the next supreme basileus, a position for which candidates campaigned vigorously, which Dorothy denied doing, despite her nonstop, coast-to-coast speaking schedule at sorority events.[1] At the 1936 Boule in Louisville, Kentucky, she was nominated from the floor to lead the sorority, but declined on the spot. The honor went to Margaret Bowen Davis, a New Orleans school principal who hopped aboard the health project bandwagon and joined Dorothy for two years in Mississippi.[2] But after Dorothy's triumph in the Delta in 1936, it didn't matter who was AKA president; all eyes were on her.

The sorors worshiped Dorothy; they paid attention to what she said and buzzed about how she looked. She turned heads in a shimmery cocktail dress at a tea dance during the Boule, warranting mention in the AKA magazine.[3] Now pushing forty, although she did not admit it even to her own husband, Dorothy was at the height of her attractiveness. She was perfectly coiffed; her clothing was tailored, stylish, and expensive-looking; and her signature accessories—button earrings, large lapel pins or corsages, plus a splash of Jean Nate—complimented her outfits. She planned those ensembles as carefully as she planned the health project, making lists of what she planned to wear for sorority events. Although never svelte, she was never flabby. She was solid with large breasts and, at 5′7½″, tall for her time, with sculpted cheek bones, a straight nose, and café-au-lait-colored skin.

By 1936 the cotton field clinics were here to stay. The Mississippi Health Project had become what Ida dreamed it would: an institution representing the best ideals of the sorority. For Dorothy the project was practically a full-time, year-round job, overshadowing her other roles as physician, community activist, wife, and mother.

Dorothy still worked on other pet projects, particularly Southeast House. In the fall of 1937 Southeast House had six hundred children enrolled and had outgrown its six-room space at 301 G Street SE that Dorothy had struggled so hard to buy. Now she had her eye on Friendship House at 324 Virginia Avenue SE, which by refusing to admit black youngsters in 1929 had ignited Dorothy's fire to start her own settlement. It was a gorgeous twenty-room, three-story mansion built in 1800, surrounded by a playground, tennis courts, and gardens.[4] By the end of the 1930s it was time for Friendship House to move; the neighborhood was rapidly shedding its remaining white population.[5]

Dorothy threw herself into the campaign to raise ten thousand dollars to buy Friendship House. She went right to the top, dashing off a letter to the White House to ask Eleanor Roosevelt for money: "The children of Southeast House remember with great delight the huge Easter eggs you have sent them on several occasions. We are now hoping with equal joy that you will share in our effort to secure new and larger quarters."[6] The first lady got tens of thousands of letters each year; to ensure her "personal appeal" did not get lost among them, Dorothy sent hers along with another letter to the first lady's personal secretary, Malvina T. Scheider, with a reminder of their 1935 New Year's Eve meeting in the Red Room.[7]

The letter found its way to Mrs. Roosevelt, who considered it seriously. She scribbled a note to Scheider with instructions to contact Clarence Pickett of the American Friends Service Committee for guidance: "Ask Mr. Pickett what he knows about this. If he thinks good and a $10,000 goal sufficient would he advise giving $1,000."[8] Pickett, a Quaker minister, was the executive secretary of the committee and an informal advisor to presidents Hoover, Roosevelt, Truman, and Kennedy. Eleanor Roosevelt said, "I always try to do the things Clarence asks because I have great trust in his judgment"—so much so that she routinely gave him her earnings from her radio broadcasts to support his good works.[9]

Pickett forwarded the first lady's query to Richard Hurst Hill, executive secretary to the president of Howard University. Hill responded that the board of Southeast House was "one of the most responsible" in the city, but "the cost of such undertaking has been miserably understated. It is more likely that the project will approach $18,000 before it is completed. You would be amazed to understand the megre [*sic*] sum necessary for our people to swing an enterprise."[10] And nobody could do more on less money than Dorothy.

Pickett gave the thumbs up to Mrs. Roosevelt, who drafted a four-line letter to Dorothy on December 7, 1937: "My dear Dr. Ferebee: I have looked into the Southeast Community House situation and will try to give something toward the new house if I get a radio contract this winter."[11] The letter was sent, but there wasn't any money in the envelope. Perhaps Mrs. Roosevelt did not secure another radio contract, or maybe other charities commanded her attention.

On March 19, 1938, Southeast House moved into its new home, but as predicted by Richard Hill, its governing board was already struggling to dig out of the debt incurred to buy it. Dorothy again looked to Mrs. Roosevelt. "We have had a hope since your last letter that Southeast House would be fortunate in having part in the sharing of your generosity," she wrote, again asking for money.[12] This letter went into the White House files, and Mrs. Roosevelt neither responded nor donated to Dorothy's cause.[13]

A month before Southeast House relocated, Dorothy was elected to the racially mixed board of the DC Community Chest, which was duty noted by the *Washington Post* in one of the few early stories published about her in the white press.[14] Her Community Chest position was the news peg the Baltimore *Afro-American* used to publish "Meet Your Neighbor," a puff piece: "Although she is a housewife and mother of twins, Neighbor Dorothy Ferebee carries on a lucrative medical practice and finds time for social uplift work."[15] The housewife label was clearly a fiction; Dorothy's family headed for the door whenever she headed for the kitchen, and her cleaning skills weren't much either. She was a packrat whose home was filled with clutter.

In 1938, when Dorothy was president of the local Xi Omega AKA chapter, she helped the sorority's founder, Norma Boyd, start the Non-Partisan Lobby for Economic and Democratic Rights. Dorothy was also a member of the Lobby's legislative committee. Boyd, who had also been president of the Xi Omega chapter and had introduced Dorothy to Ida Jackson four years earlier, recognized that it was time to make AKA's voice heard on

Capitol Hill.[16] The Non-Partisan Lobby, later renamed the National Non-Partisan Council on Public Affairs, signaled that the role of the elite Negro club woman was moving from social work to social change. Similarly the National Council of Negro Women (NCNW), founded by Mary McLeod Bethune (Dorothy's patient), fostered political involvement as the way to combat racial inequality. Among the stated purposes of the NCNW were these: "To educate, encourage and effect the participation of Negro women in civic, political, economic and educational activities and institutions."[17]

The most important relationship of Dorothy's professional life, her association with Mary Bethune, was solidifying at this time. Bethune was close to Eleanor Roosevelt, who allowed her to invite prominent black women leaders, including Dorothy, to the White House for a historic conference to assess how black women and children were faring under the New Deal.[18]

As the 1930s drew to a close, so did the Ferebee marriage, although Dorothy and Claude kept up appearances until the death of their daughter in 1950. They hardly fooled anyone; tongues wagged about their imminent split years before their divorce.[19]

Claude's association with Howard ended with the 1936 academic year. Afterward he concentrated on his dental practice at his state-of-the-art home office, where he kept an eye on the twins, who enjoyed playing together on the front porch. Around this time Claude became president of the Robert T. Freeman Dental Society, a professional organization named for DC's first black dentist.[20] He was the also president of the Wilberforce Alumni in Washington.[21] Social engagements for the couple sometimes meant Dorothy was front and center and Claude was in the background. At a reception at Howard for the well-known artist Lois Mailou Jones attended by three hundred guests in the winter of 1937, Dorothy was in the receiving line while Claude was left to mingle among the guests.[22]

Through his involvement with the dental society, Claude injected himself into the contentious debate over the role African American dentists would play in World War II. Months before Pearl Harbor, he lobbied hard for more black officers in the dental corps. The army brass did not take kindly to his efforts and saw him as an opportunist. In a meeting at the War Department in 1941, Brig. Gen. Leigh Fairbank, head of the Army Dental Corps, remarked, "Dr. C. Thurston Ferebee [should] keep his shirt on and press for the general inclusion of Negro dentists and not be so concerned about himself."[23]

Claude eventually had enough of not being the king in his own castle. He began making noises about moving back to New York City, which was *his* town, not Dorothy's, and in 1940 he was spotted in Manhattan on weekends and holidays without his wife.[24] But while they remained in Washington, life was good to the Ferebees, as it was to many in their professional peer group. The Depression made money tight for many families, but not so in the Ferebee home. With a doctor and dentist in the house, Dorothy had furs, Claude had cars, and the children had expensive matching outfits from the Twin Shop.

Meanwhile poverty continued unabated in the Delta. By the third year the team was ready to head to Mississippi in 1937, Dorothy had it down pat. "The Health Project has become efficiently departmentalized while the addition of new services has enhanced its technical value," she wrote in the *Ivy Leaf*.[25] For the first time she did not have to bear the brunt of the medical work alone. She was joined in 1937 by Dr. Thelma Coffey, an obstetrician from New Orleans; Dr. Mary Crutchfield Wright, a dentist from Cambridge, Massachusetts, who, like Dorothy, had studied at Tufts; and Mildred Wood, a nurse with Howard's student health service. Ever faithful Mary Williams was also back.[26]

Dr. Wright's dental clinic was immensely popular and would remain a central component of the project until the end. Adults and children waited patiently in long lines in the broiling sun to sit in her traveling, collapsible dental chair and open their mouths wide. Wright set it up on any available porch or under any shade tree and treated cavities and abscessed teeth while curious friends and neighbors of the patients stood by, flinching and cringing as they watched. Wright pulled as many as sixty teeth a day.[27] Any child who braved her drill got to pick a brightly colored toothbrush as a present, an exotic gift that was a first for some.[28]

There were thirteen volunteers in 1937, including Dorothy. Herman Washington, a sociologist from Xavier College in New Orleans, participated to gather and analyze information in a more uniform, professional manner from the clinic patients. He was assisted by Melva Price of New York City, Portia Nickens of New Rochelle, Mae Rhodes of New Orleans, and Audrey Augustine, a social worker from Brooklyn. Supreme Basileus Margaret

Davis Bowen joined the group, and Marjorie Holloman, the youngest member, returned. Newcomer Irene Baxter of Philadelphia proved adept at weighing and measuring patients. Dorothy spent every dime of the $2,250 AKA appropriation, going over budget by $37.19.[29]

Missing from Mississippi in 1937 was the project's matriarch, Ida Jackson.[30] Dorothy's sister-in-law, Connie Ferebee, did not return either; she pursued other interests. In 1938 she did postgraduate work at Boston University, and in 1939 she and her sister, Maxine, spent the summer there.[31]

In 1937 the sorority set up clinics at sixteen makeshift locations and treated 1,500 families.[32] The mission that summer was altered to one of "intensification of individual service, as opposed to numerical coverage."[33] Among Dorothy's stops that summer and for the rest of the decade was the Delta Cooperative Farm, near the town of Hillhouse in Bolivar County, where she had paid only a social call the year before.

The Delta Cooperative Farm was spawned by the unintended consequences of a New Deal program that paid farmers to take acreage out of production. The government subsidies were supposed to be shared with tenants who lived on the farms, but unscrupulous landowners evicted them, pocketed the subsidies, and hired day laborers at fifty to seventy-five cents a day. Tenants from Arkansas, having been tossed off their farms because of this scheme, organized the multi-racial Southern Tenant Farmers' Union. This did not sit well with landowners, and by early 1935 union members were "invited" to leave Arkansas through threats, beatings, and murder.[34]

Sherwood Eddy and his protégé, Sam H. Franklin, along with the Christian philosopher Reinhold Niebuhr and others, founded the Delta Cooperative Farm to provide a place for the Southern Tenant Farmers' Union refugees.[35] The Mississippi historian Fred C. Smith called it "an unstable blend of principles drawn from Jesus and Marx." In March 1936 Eddy bought 2,138 acres in Bolivar County for $17,500 as a home for the Delta Cooperative Farm.[36] By August 1936 thirty-one families—twelve white and nineteen black—were living there.[37] The farm provided residents with an improved standard of living, healthier diets, and more schooling. Wide-eyed college students flocked to it to volunteer to babysit, build houses, chop cotton, and cook.[38] Eleanor Roosevelt was intrigued by it.[39] When Dorothy and AKA volunteers showed up in the summer of 1937 they were also enchanted. They signed the guest register and couldn't heap enough praise on the place. Herman Washington could barely contain himself. "Practical ideals such as this will save the world from itself," he wrote. Melva Price offered best wishes: "May this be the beginning of the new order for which generations have longed." For her part, Dorothy was more subdued, writing, "We wish you much success in this most interesting enterprise."[40] The Mississippi Health Project would operate at the Delta Cooperative Farm for three summers, although by 1938 the novelty of being on the site had worn off; their guestbook entries were confined to their signatures.[41]

After Dorothy was elected supreme basileus in 1939 and pulled in many directions beyond the Mississippi Health Project, Alpha Kappa Alpha considered making the traveling health project a year-round endeavor.[42] Ida Jackson suggested they partner with Sam Franklin to build a permanent health facility at the Delta Cooperative Farm.[43]

But the Eddy-Franklin cooperative farming venture would not last long enough for that. A confluence of factors did it in. A plan to diversify crops failed because the farm's soil was good for nothing but cotton. Its financial strength rested largely on the shoulders of philanthropists. The good-ol' boys with whom Dr. Dedwylder had to contend for years were none too happy with the integrated social experiment going on under their noses.[44]

Besides lack of money and no lack of community hostility, life was none too rosy on the farm. Sam Franklin's top-down management style ruffled feathers, and for all the talk of postracial nirvana, the black and white tenants did not get along. Eventually the Delta Cooperative was sold and its founders focused their attention on a second farm, the 2,880-acre Providence Cooperative Farm in Holmes County, which they had purchased in 1938.[45] The Mississippi Health Project would make the Providence Farm its working headquarters in the summer of 1942, the last time it operated in the state.[46]

Dorothy visited Bolivar County again in 1938. At Dedwylder's suggestion she scheduled the clinics to coincide with the "lay-by" season, July 20 through August 4, the time between chopping cotton and picking it, which allowed them to treat entire families rather than just the children.[47]

There was no problem securing comfortable accommodations in 1938. With his annoying sister-in-law finally out of his house and his hair, thanks to a court order barring her from having any contact with him, Eugene Booze had plenty of room for the AKA entourage at his mansion. Reading between the lines of a cryptic letter he wrote to Dorothy, Booze seemed to be referring to his feud with his wife's sister by noting that in the past "certain obstacles prevented" him from being able to accommodate all the volunteers. Now Booze offered to "take care of the entire party in the Montgomery residence, upon the same terms as agreed upon last year, in the event you wish to have the party together." Much had changed since the volunteers roughed it at Arenia Mallory's school. At Booze's home they would enjoy a housekeeper, a laundress, a two-car garage, hot and cold running water, and a bathroom on each floor for the grand total of $1.50 a day per person.[48]

But little had changed for the Delta sharecroppers. Families with as many as eight to ten children and their parents and grandparents still lived in tiny unscreened shacks without plumbing. Some families were lucky enough to have nearby outdoor privies; others relieved themselves in the woods. Everyone age five and over worked in the fields. Some tenants were charged ten dollars an acre to rent land the owner had bought for two dollars an acre.[49] The extent of the gouging of powerless sharecroppers and tenant farmers is shocking in light of the cost of living. Dorothy's volunteers paid seventy-nine cents for breakfast for four, about twenty-two cents a gallon for gasoline, and a nickel for sodas while traveling to Mississippi in 1938.[50]

The work the volunteers accomplished in 1938 was phenomenal. In three weeks they set up at twenty-four clinics, where they treated 4,150 patients, including 2,800 children. They took 1,839 blood tests and diagnosed 475 cases of syphilis. They treated pellagra, eye infections, and recurrent malaria. At the dental clinic, teeth were filled and pulled.[51] Dorothy added lectures about hygiene at the start of each clinic day, the price to be paid for free medical care.[52]

Dorothy wasn't the only Ferebee away from home in the summer of 1938. As a first lieutenant in the Officers' Reserve Corps, Claude worked as a dental surgeon at Fort Howard. Clearly quiet war training had already begun, even though Hitler's troops were still eight months from marching into Prague. From July 10 through 21 Claude and six other officers ran a training camp for 250 black servicemen on the Chesapeake Bay, near Baltimore.[53] Because Dorothy had to be on the road no later than July 16 to open the clinic on the 20th, the twins presumably were left in the care of

Miss Green or Dorothy's mother. By the end of the summer of 1938, four years without a vacation caught up with the seemingly invincible Dorothy Ferebee; she spent a month flat on her back in bed with an undisclosed illness, an event she called "an interminable incarceration." In describing her ailment to Melva Price, she wrote, "Somehow (as if I don't know why) the bottom completely dropped out of me leaving me prostrate."[54]

Even from her sickbed Dorothy gave orders and assignments for the annual report due at the 1938 Boule: "No one of the previous issues has done what I should like so much to see—historical completeness, dignified presentation of accomplishments and evaluations done with clarity and directness."[55] The final product includes several pictures of Dorothy, with captions, including one drawing blood from a young woman and another holding a baby in her lap. She is dressed in a white uniform and matching button earrings.[56] Accessorized in the middle of nowhere!

By 1938 the sorors were contemplating the legacy of the Mississippi Health Project. Marjorie Holloman wrote an article for the *Ivy Leaf* about its significance beyond delivering medical care: "The Project is a unique effort in this day, whose light will shine brighter with the passing of time."[57]

It was also high time to honor Dorothy for her four summers of sacrifice. The sorority wanted to buy her something in recognition of "her untiring and splendid work" in Mississippi. Irma Clark of Chicago suggested a new medical bag.[58] Among Dorothy's effects at her death was a well-worn, weather-beaten black doctor's bag, which might have been her gift from AKA. At the Detroit Boule that winter, some three hundred sorors braved single-digit temperatures to travel to the midwestern city to discuss AKA business, with the funding for the health project and Boyd's lobbying unit at the top of the list.[59]

In Detroit a luncheon was hosted in Dorothy's honor.[60] Midway into the four-day Boule, snow started falling and the entire nation was locked in a deep freeze, but that didn't stop the sorors from braving the weather to dance the night away with the Alpha Phi Alpha fraternity brothers and loosen up at a members-only cocktail reception. The women went sightseeing in and around Detroit and attended a concert given by honorary soror Marian Anderson.[61]

Alpha Kappa Alpha became closely involved with Anderson and a seminal moment in the civil rights movement: the concert on Easter

Sunday in 1939 when Anderson was refused permission to sing at Constitution Hall, owned by the Daughters of the American Revolution, which had a "white artists only" policy.[62] The DAR's intransigence riled high-level officials of the NAACP, newspaper editors, AKA, the NCNW, Interior Secretary Harold Ickes, and Eleanor Roosevelt. Protesters formed the Marian Anderson Citizens Committee; its supporters included fifty organizations, among them AKA.[63] Mrs. Roosevelt resigned her membership in the DAR. This was not a fight the dignified Anderson went looking for. She would later write in her autobiography, "I did not feel that I was designed for hand-to-hand combat."[64]

After every attempt to secure concert space failed, the NAACP's Walter White dreamed up the idea of an open-air concert at the Lincoln Memorial. Secretary Ickes, the official caretaker of the nation's public lands and monuments, agreed, and President Roosevelt gave his blessing. On a cold Easter Sunday Anderson famously stood in a full-length fur coat before the nineteen-foot marble statue of a seated Abraham Lincoln and sang "My Country, 'Tis of Thee," to a shivering audience of seventy-five thousand, many of whom had waited patiently all day for the 5 o'clock concert to begin.[65] Dorothy Ferebee was among them.[66] She and Anderson would continue to cross paths, and in the 1960s they would be appointed by President Kennedy to the Food for Peace Council.[67]

By the summer following the Anderson concert, the Mississippi Health Project was so much a part of the landscape that not even the whip-toting plantation overseers bothered to show up.[68] And while she would have had no way of knowing it, 1939 was the last year Dorothy would be the houseguest of Eugene Booze. In November he would be gunned down on the street as he entered his car in downtown Mound Bayou. Officers found twenty-six bullet holes in Booze's car and five spent shell casings nearby.[69] His murder was never solved.

The clinic emphasized nutrition in 1939. The bad eating habits of the sharecroppers were only partly due to poverty; some of them simply did not want to eat their peas. Dorothy dubbed this new emphasis "dietotherapy" and sold the federal government on the idea of supplying food samples for cooking demonstrations.[70] It was one of the few times over the life of the health project that Dorothy got government help.[71] The Federal Surplus Commodities Corporation, under the control of Agriculture

Secretary Henry Wallace, donated the food. Although she had hoped the food giveaways would continue and expand, the government did not provide surplus food to the sharecroppers beyond what she needed for the summer cooking demonstrations.[72]

As the years went on, Dorothy got better at figuring out how to get the sharecroppers to eat what was good for them. Like mothers everywhere trying to get their children to eat, Dorothy tricked them. What was an everyday diet seemed exotic and unappetizing to them "because even though they had chickens on the plantation, they were never allowed to cook a chicken," she said. Nutritionist Ella Payne joined the health project in 1940, carting her heavy cast iron pot, colorful food posters, and recipe box all over Bolivar County. By the time Dorothy treated patients' ailments and the teachers recorded their vital statistics and lectured about healthy living, half the day was shot and they were starving. Ella would then cook up healthy foods in her trusty pot, enticing them to come over and have a sample. "Because they were then so hungry, they would eat most anything." Dorothy said.[73]

In 1939 Dorothy again participated in a conference organized by Mary Bethune on racial problems. In describing the conference-goers, a reporter wrote: "A youthful and attractive face and a becoming costume these days, it seems, is the badge of an alert and militant attitude towards serious issues affecting the race." Dorothy's "costume" was a stylish "green wool tunic dress."[74]

Dorothy's growing prominence brought her to the attention of Congressman Martin Dies, who dragged her through the mud because of her tangential connection to the American League for Peace and Democracy, which had protested the DAR's treatment of Marian Anderson. It was a group the right wing branded a communist front.[75] The League was formed in September 1933 by pacifists alarmed by the growing fascist menace in Europe and grew to several million members, some belonging to the American Communist Party.[76] Representative Dies was a Dixiecrat from Texas who presided over the House Special Committee to Investigate Un-American Activities, a precursor to the infamous House Un-American Activities Committee.[77] Journalist David Brinkley considered Dies "one of the great buffoons of his time."[78] After deciding the League was crawling with communists, the Dies Committee released the names of 538 of its members employed by the federal government to pressure them to resign from the group or to pressure the government into firing them.[79]

As a member of the League and a government employee at Howard, Dorothy was among those whose names were released. The Roosevelt administration paid the committee no mind.[80] Her connection with the group, however tangential, was the subject of an FBI investigation in 1941–42 that turned up nothing. According to bureau files, the investigation uncovered "no evidence of Community Party Membership on the part of Ferebee, and numerous individuals recommended her as to character and loyalty."[81]

At the end of the summer of 1939, Dorothy needed a break. She and Claude traveled to Harlem, making a rare public appearance together. In August they attended an afternoon reception (Dorothy gussied up for the event) at the Savoy Ballroom at 140th Street and Lenox Avenue to participate in the Ladies' Auxiliary of the National Medical Association.[82] One week later, no one was in the mood for frivolity. Before dawn on September 1, 1939, German troops marched into Poland, igniting World War II. The next night Great Britain demanded that Hitler cease all military action and withdraw. On September 3, after Hitler ignored the order, Britain and France declared war on Germany.

For a while life in the United States went on as usual. Dorothy returned to the Boston home of her girlhood to participate in the AKA Boule at Christmas 1939, where she was elected supreme basileus. This time she wanted the job. The slate of candidates for leadership was presented to the Boule on Friday afternoon, December 29. It was Dorothy versus Edna Over Gray for the top spot.[83] Gray was a Baltimore schoolteacher long involved with AKA.[84] Dorothy beat her by just twenty votes, 149 to 129, surprisingly close given how incessantly Dorothy had traveled to AKA chapters around the country and how much national name recognition she had earned through the health project.[85] Contemporary news accounts ignored the closeness of the vote and viewed the election as a glowing referendum on Dorothy and her work. Her hometown paper observed, "After appropriating $2,000 for the continuance of its famed Mississippi Health Project, the Alpha Kappa Alpha sorority, holding its grand annual boule here during the Christmas holidays expressed further approval of the manner in which their health project had been operated by electing its director, Dr. Dorothy Boulding Ferebee, to the office of supreme basileus."[86]

The Ferebees were great supporters of FDR. On January 19, 1941, the president, having been elected to an unprecedented third term, was feted at an inaugural gala at Constitution Hall attended by fewer than twenty African-American supporters. The next night a special musical event featuring black artists for black guests was presented in a government auditorium. Dorothy and Claude were on the entertainment committee that planned the segregated program, which led to scathing criticism in at least one Negro newspaper. "The usual segregation practiced in the nation's capital . . . was not lessened one whit by the majesty of the occasion," reported the Cleveland *Call and Post.* "Serving on the Jim Crow entertainment committee were the Negro pets of the administration, their wives and friends."[87]

As the storm clouds burst over Europe, Claude served as the point man for the Preparedness Committee of the National Dental Association, through which he sought to get dentists commissioned as officers in what was sure to be a wartime service.[88] Finally, on March 4, 1941, Uncle Sam called to active duty First Lt. Claude Thurston Ferebee of the U.S. Army Reserve. He was assigned to the 318th Medical Battalion, which was attached to the 93rd Infantry Division, Army National Guard units of "colored" soldiers with white commanders. Lieutenant Ferebee would fix the decayed teeth of black men in uniform. In just a few short months he would be promoted to captain at a salary of $240 a month.[89] Captain Ferebee's first duty station was Fort Devens, Massachusetts.[90] It would be a brief and memorable stay that would ignite his own war with his wife.

11 Madeline, My Concerto

In the last year of pre–World War II peace in the United States, Claude spent New Year's Eve 1940 partying in New York City while Dorothy presided over the AKA Boule in Kansas City and their eight-year-old twins were left in the care of who knows who in Washington.[1] In Kansas Dorothy pledged that the sorority would be "dedicated to the making of a democratic America in which racial hatred will have no place."[2]

When she became supreme basileus, the focus of Dorothy's professional life shifted. By the end of 1940 the sorority had 2,830 members who were either students at top colleges or graduates working as teachers, school administrators, nurses, or government workers. Among them was a smattering of doctors, lawyers, journalists, and businesswomen.[3] This sophisticated constituency expected Dorothy to run the sorority like a well-organized CEO. She relished her new position that required her to be everywhere, all the time. Rarely did she turn down a request to make a speech, join a committee, participate in a program, or accept an award. She was off to so many places, so often, that her neighbors dubbed her "Go-to-Meeting Ferebee." The nickname was not intended as a compliment.[4]

After 1940 Dorothy and Mary Bethune had become the most visible, powerful African American women in America. In deference to her hard-earned expertise in public health matters acquired after five summers in Mississippi, in March 1940 Dorothy was invited to testify before Congress on the Wagner-George National Hospital bill. Democratic senators Robert F. Wagner of New York and Walter George of Georgia had introduced legislation to provide ten million dollars for hospitals in remote corners of the country.[5] The question was how much of that money, if any, would go toward the construction of hospitals for African Americans.

Dorothy was all business as she marched up the stairs of the Capitol on a balmy 60-degree day in a dark suit with a chic black wide-brimmed hat, white blouse, black leather gloves, and matching bag and shoes.[6] At her side were Dr. Paul Cornely, director of public health at Howard University, and Thomasina Walker Johnson, the lobbyist for AKA's Non-Partisan Council on Public Affairs.[7] Dorothy urged Congress not to bypass rural communities populated by poor black sharecroppers.[8] But despite the prodding of AKA and other African American organizations, the hospital bill never became law.

After her congressional testimony, Dorothy lugged her movie projector up to Philadelphia, where, on a Saturday in early April, Ruth Scott introduced her to the AKA chapter at the University of Pennsylvania. There, in honor of Negro Health Week, Dorothy narrated the movie she had made the previous summer about her work in Mississippi.[9] National Negro Health Week was started in 1915 by Booker Washington, who was worried about the brief life expectancy of his people. The week was taken very seriously by African American doctors.[10] Eventually the program was taken over by the U.S. Public Health Service and phased out in 1951.[11]

At the end of April Dorothy joined delegates at the third annual meeting of the National Negro Congress, a short-lived lefty organization that gave the FBI another professed reason for investigating her.[12] The meeting in Washington was called to order with a gavel made by students from Hampton Institute from the wood of a slave ship. It was a racially and culturally diverse group that sought fairness for labor and blacks.[13]

During the first year of her term as supreme basileus, Dorothy visited AKA chapters in more than twenty cities, while keeping her hand in other pots.[14] She was vice president of the Medical Chirurigical Society of DC, an executive committee member of the DC Community Chest, and a member of the advisory committee on vocational education of the board of education for the still-segregated DC public schools.[15] Between June 18 and 23 she attended the Thirty-first Annual Conference of the NAACP in Philadelphia, where she presided over a session titled "What NAACP Branches Can Do about Health."[16] Earlier that month she attended an AKA chapter meeting in Norfolk where her sister-in-law, Connie Ferebee, hosted a linen shower for the Mississippi Health Project.[17] Dorothy's relationship with

Claude's sisters and later, their children, was always good, even after she and Claude broke up.

Sometimes Dorothy and AKA were used as window dressing. She was asked to join the National Committee for the Participation of Negroes in the "American Common" at the New York World's Fair of 1940, better known as "Negro Week." In retrospect, setting aside a "Negro Week" to honor a segment of the population that in 1940 was marginalized because of skin color, denied basic human rights by the government, and terrorized with impunity in the South seems at best hypocritical. This was particularly so in that throughout the life of the Fair, blacks were denied decent on-site employment opportunities.[18] The American Labor Party complained to the Fair's president Grover Whalen because only forty out of more than two thousand available jobs at the Fair went to blacks.[19]

The 1940 health project opened on July 8 with conferences at the county health department in Cleveland, Mississippi. It operated for two weeks in Bolivar County, focusing on nutrition and hygiene. Ruth Scott joined that summer and provided practical assistance. Every day she picked a dirty child out of the crowd of clinic patients, peeled off his clothes, and plopped him in a tub of soapy water. As Dorothy described it, Ruth "deftly soothed and calmed many frightened children who were rewarded at the end of the bath with a new outfit, from skin out."[20] It was also the first year of Ella Payne's popular cooking demonstrations.

Throughout the years of the health project, Bolivar County's middle- and upper-class white women were well aware of what AKA was up to in their backyard and they watched in silence. That changed in 1940, when liberal white church women reached out to Dorothy to launch a discussion about race. The result was an unprecedented meeting in Mississippi between local women and the health project volunteers.

Katherine Gardner, the associate secretary for the Federal Council of the Churches of Christ in America, a consortium of thirty-three mainline Protestant denominations later called the National Council of Churches, had been aware of the project. In 1937 she wrote to Ida Jackson, expressing her desire that the project get publicity in a church newspaper. "So many white people have the feeling that Negroes do not care much about the masses of their race that I should like them to appreciate this sacrificial piece of work done by your sorority."[21]

A few years later Gardner visited the Delta Cooperative Farm.[22] Like Dorothy's volunteers in 1937, she was bowled over by it. She again reached out to Jackson, proposing a meeting between the white Methodist Women of the Northern Mississippi Conference and the volunteers. Ida promptly forwarded the suggestion to Dorothy, who offered to meet with the women to "exchange ideas and suggestions for improving health conditions and race relations in that section of the country." Dorothy wrote, "I feel the good will contribution as well as that of better understanding is one of the most needed services at this moment, an intangible gift, to be sure, but one of the most valuable." On the afternoon they wrapped up the clinic, Dorothy and the volunteers filed into the Bolivar County Court House in Cleveland, wearing their newly washed, starched, and pressed white uniforms. A few local black women showed up too. Following custom, the white women found seats on one side of the courtroom, and the black women took seats behind them. Dorothy put a stop to that, telling the audience that if they were going to work together, they needed to "be" together, and so AKA women took seats among the white ladies. To everyone's surprise, the white women didn't move, Dorothy didn't get run out of town on a rail, and talks began. One AKA volunteer, Ella Payne, wrote a paper about the meeting for an education class at Howard in 1942 that was probably sanitized. "The discussion became very tense, but fortunately no one became unduly excited," Payne wrote.[23]

It was a start and it resulted in at least some change in Bolivar County. A second meeting was held in the summer of 1941, with a larger audience and, according to Ida Jackson, a "more friendly attitude." The result of the sessions was a new recreational facility for Negro boys in an old school building in Cleveland. Although the center was segregated, a biracial board of directors was established to oversee it, an unheard-of arrangement in pre–World War II Mississippi.[24]

The 1940 health project gave Dorothy national exposure. J. D. Ratcliff wrote a feature article, "Cotton Field Clinic," for the September 1940 issue of *Survey Graphic*, a small but influential journal appealing to readers with a social conscience. It was reprinted in the *Reader's Digest*.[25] "This is a cottonfield clinic," Ratcliff wrote, "vaguely a social engagement, but more particularly a gathering of poor people come to seek that elusive thing, good health, which they hope the 'doctor women' will give them." "The impact of their effort is profound," he asserted, crediting it with treating 14,500 children, encouraging adult sharecroppers to engage in better health habits, and inspiring local efforts to build a badly needed black hospital.[26]

Dorothy returned to Washington at the end of the summer, but not for long. She was the guest speaker at the Charleston, West Virginia, branch of the NAACP on October 13, and two weeks later she was honored along with Dr. Virginia Alexander, the new physician to the women students of Howard (Dorothy's old job that had been eliminated during the Depression), by the Pennsylvania Institute of Negro Health in Philadelphia.[27] Alexander was a graduate of the University of Pennsylvania and a scholarship student at the Women's Medical College of Philadelphia. She received a master's degree in public health from Yale in 1937 and during World War II would serve the government as a public health doctor in the coal and iron mines of Alabama.[28] Both women received Golden Scroll awards, Dorothy for her work in Mississippi and Virginia for her research activities and for establishing a private hospital for convalescing maternity patients.[29]

On the Friday before leaving town to retrieve her Golden Scroll, Dorothy joined Mary Bethune and the NCNW in Washington at its annual conference at the U.S. Department of Labor, after which she donned her fur coat and joined a procession of similarly cloaked women to march up Pennsylvania Avenue to the White House for a meeting with Mrs. Roosevelt. Fur coats were utterly unnecessary for anything other than a show of status; large lavender and yellow dahlias were still in bloom in the White House garden on the day of the reception.[30]

Mrs. Roosevelt was waiting for her four hundred guests in the East Room, dressed in a simple brown wool dress with long sleeves and a high neckline. She wore a gold chain around her neck and two huge diamond rings on her left hand. The ladies sipped coffee and tea while they chatted with the first lady.[31]

Dorothy was becoming more involved with the increasingly influential NCNW. By 1940 she was on the executive board and also served as a vice president.[32] The following year she was named chair of the NCNW's national committee on family planning.[33] She used her position as a bully pulpit for birth control. In a speech at the Waldorf Astoria Hotel in New York in early 1942 for the Birth Control Federation of America, the precursor to Planned Parenthood, she blamed a lack of family planning for crime, illness, and poverty.[34] In April 1942 she traveled to Chicago to deliver a speech titled "Planned Parenthood as a Public Health Measure for the Negro Race."[35]

Through the NCNW Dorothy was more visible than ever. The NCNW had a larger reach than AKA. Run by the well-connected Mary Bethune, it was a good fit for Dorothy's grand ambitions; the organization claimed to represent the interests of a half-million African American women in 1940.[36] Whether Dorothy yet saw herself as the heiress apparent to Bethune is unclear. As Bethune's personal physician, Dorothy was certainly her confidante. But Bethune was surrounded by smart, ambitious women; she consciously cultivated them, referring to them as her "daughters." Dorothy would have to elbow those rivals aside if she wanted to take over. Such a contest seemed a long way off. Although the original NCNW by-laws called for the election of new officers every two years, as the founder of the group Bethune could be president as long as she wanted.

At the NCNW annual conference, like everywhere else in 1940, war was at the front of everyone's mind. The NCNW adopted a three-point program; it called for the integration of blacks into all branches of the service, asked that black reserve officers—one of whom was Dorothy's husband—be called up for duty, and sought assurances that ROTC units at black colleges would be trained for combat duty.[37]

Claude was also pestering the War Department to enlarge the number of black medical officers. He wasn't doing it just for self-recognition or to compete with his wife; he was representing the interests of the black medical community that sought opportunities for black doctors and dentists to serve their country as officers. He had his work cut out for him. In 1940 Secretary of War Henry Stimson said, "Colored troops do very well under white officers but every time we try to lift them a little bit beyond where they can go, disaster and confusion follows."[38] Casting aside the moral arguments against segregation in the military, the policy made no sense from administrative or economic standpoints either. To the extent soldiers were separated by race, extra (and expensive) layers of bureaucracy were required. Separate training facilities had to be set up as "Negro" facilities, and institutions to meet their needs, such as hospitals, recreation centers, and officers clubs, had to be duplicated to avoid race mixing. Internal memos and letters about mobilization show the complexity of the problem. Anticipating twenty-five thousand black enlistees in 1941, William Hastie, the civilian aide to the Secretary of War in charge of issues involving black soldiers, wrote to the surgeon general, "I understand . . . that Negro officers are to be assigned as physicians and dentists for all Negro regiments. . . . If so, what steps are being taken toward that end?"[39]

To get into the Army Medical Corps as a first lieutenant, the entry-level rank, one had to be a male graduate of an acceptable U.S. or Canadian medical school, complete a one-year internship at an approved hospital, and be no older than thirty-two. The candidate had to pass a written test and be physically fit for military service.[40] As point man for the National Dental Association, Claude sent letters to members on December 20, 1940, alerting potential draftees to notify him so he could help get them appointments as medical officers: "Seven colored dentists are needed at once. Your promptness in answering will assure me of your interest and will prevent your being placed in any other but a medical service in the Armed Forces."[41]

Even the War Department recognized the unfairness of the limited opportunities for black dentists. General Fairbank met with Dean Hastie's assistant, Truman K. Gibson Jr., on January 27, 1941. It was the same meeting in which the general had suggested Claude keep his shirt on. Gibson wrote a detailed memorandum about the meeting in which he reported that Fairbank conceded "the policy and plans as announced are harsh and inequitable and should be changed to admit Negroes into the Reserve Dental Corps, particularly the applicants who are subject to draft." Fairbank thought the army would need at least sixty black dental officers once war was declared. But the general wasn't calling the shots, and all he could do was go up the chain of command, make his wishes known, and hope for the best.[42]

Claude was a patriotic man; until his dying day he carried himself like a soldier and kept his body in trim, fighting form. He raised and lowered the American flag each night on a pole in front of his home in White Plains, New York.[43] But his tenure in the army was stormy. He was harshly critical of how Uncle Sam treated blacks, and once he was stationed in the South Pacific he served as a backchannel conduit to the NAACP in its efforts to investigate and expose racial injustice in the wartime army.

Claude Ferebee was called to active duty on March 3, 1941.[44] He was attached to the 318th Medical Corps of the 366th Infantry, which was all black with the exception of the top commanders. Claude was shipped to

Fort Devens, Massachusetts, and in June 1941 was sent to the Medical Field Service School at Carlisle Barracks, Pennsylvania, for a month of special training.[45] While he was participating in training, Dorothy traveled to Pennsylvania to visit him.[46] Claude returned to Fort Devens at the end of training and on August 8, 1941, was promoted to captain.[47]

While Claude was occupied with the military in the summer of 1941, Dorothy managed to get herself so overextended that she could not stay in Mississippi for the duration of the health project. AKA's seventh summer clinic was scheduled for three weeks, from July 7 through 29. Nine volunteers were slated to go with Dorothy, among them Ida, Mary Wright, Ruth Scott, Ella Payne, and Marion Carter. Initially, Dorothy had every intention of getting the clinic up and running. "Unfortunately, I shall not be able to stay the full term this year, as I must go on to several other cities on business for the sorority," she alerted Dr. Dedwylder in mid-June. "However, I will get them started, and see that everything goes well," she promised.[48]

But then Dorothy agreed to be the guest speaker at AKA's Far Western Regional Conference in Los Angeles, scheduled for the same time she was supposed to be firing up the health project. Worse, she did not break the bad news to Ida until July 6, the day before the 1941 clinics were supposed to open. Dorothy was a hit at the conference, where she delivered an "outstanding address."[49] Meanwhile Ida was left to scramble around Mississippi to find a doctor to *do* the work of the AKA, irritating her to no end and possibly contributing to her conclusion it was time to call it quits.

That winter Ida could not resist letting the sorority know Dorothy had left her high and dry in Mississippi. At the annual Boule that year, she reported: "Because of Soror Ferebee's commitment to serve as guest speaker at the Far Western Regional Conference, I was told by her on July 6 that I was to take charge of the Clinics, opening next morning; she would leave immediately for California." Ida pointed out that in prior years "the type of clinic, the staff, medicines and budget had been decided upon by Soror Ferebee," and she recounted her desperate efforts to fix the mess Dorothy had left her. She managed to find eight local doctors willing to lend a hand—two of whom charged the sorority a fee.[50]

Ida continued to carp about Dorothy, complaining in a letter to one soror, "Last year I landed in Mississippi and found myself left in charge of the Project with neither Doctor or [*sic*] Nurse. I had to make the contacts necessary to secure help."[51] Ida was well-known for her sharp tongue, and Dorothy was not the only soror who had suffered its sting over the years. "What a relief your little explosion must have given you!" remarked AKA founder Ethel Lyle after Ida blew up at her for some transgression or other.[52] Dr. Edna Griffin, who replaced Dorothy as the physician on the health project in 1942, was blunt with Ida: "At times you approah [sic] one with such a repulsive, critical attitude that I fear it impossible to not respond likewise."[53]

In 1941 Dorothy shocked the sorors by turning down the opportunity to continue as AKA supreme basileus another year. At the Boule in Philadelphia, Norma Boyd insisted the sorority should not switch leaders on the eve of war and while trying to keep the health project and the Non-Partisan Council going. Even an appeal to her patriotism didn't work; Dorothy was unmoved when urged to emulate FDR by breaking precedent and accepting a third term. Her decision to step down took AKA by such surprise that the directorate had not even arranged to buy her the traditional parting gift—a string of pearls. During a moment at the Boule when Dorothy was out of the room, an ad hoc committee led by Ruth Scott was appointed with a mandate to secure a necklace for her.[54]

With Claude called to active duty, Dorothy was, in essence, a single mother. Her children turned ten that August, and she may have felt pressure to spend more time with them. In a newspaper interview in May 1941, besides talking about her extensive travels for AKA, she waxed eloquent about life's simpler pleasures. She described how much she liked roller-skating with the twins and taking them to sporting events. She discussed the joys she found in making her scrapbooks—with several in the works at once—and in collecting small metal dogs. She claimed to be fond of cooking and housecleaning.[55] While she was doing what she could to hold the remnants of her family together, Claude was behaving like a single man with no ties.

Claude's first stop in the army, Fort Devens in northern Massachusetts, was 428 miles by car from Washington. Named after Charles Devens, a Civil War general, it went from being a sleepy prewar army reception center to a boomtown. By the fall of 1941 sixty-five thousand troops were stationed there.[56] Fort Devens could have passed for a New England college campus or a suburban country club. There were baseball and softball diamonds, basketball courts, horseshoe courts, and a sports arena suitable for boxing, volleyball, and wrestling. There was a library with a large selection of books and magazines, including *Life, Look, Redbook,* the *New Yorker, Atlantic Monthly, Newsweek, Time,* and the *Fort Devens Digest.* Leading African American newspapers were also available.

Soldiers could use their spare time for Bible study or French lessons. The musically talented could play in a military band or dance orchestra or sing in a glee club. On weekends the recreation staff sponsored dances, movies, card parties, Ping-Pong tournaments, bingo games, and talent nights. With a weekend pass, soldiers could go to nearby art galleries, churches, and community centers, or they could remain on base and, depending on their rank, hang out at the Officers' Club or the Servicemen's Lounge.[57] All of these activities were coordinated by a social staff living on base, one of whom was Madeline Dugger, a widow who promptly stole Captain Ferebee's heart.

Madeline Mabray Kountze Dugger was the forty-four-year-old senior hostess at the service club at Fort Devens.[58] For young GIs away from home for the first time, or seasoned officers about to lead men into battle, Madeline Dugger was their wartime fantasy. In their minds, she might be their first or, God forbid, last fling.

The "hostess" title was misleading; it was not a euphemism for party girl or prostitute, but a legitimate position for a responsible, respectable woman like Madeline. She was a paid civilian employee of the War Department; the military considered this work essential for the morale of the troops. Madeline was well-qualified, if not overqualified, for the post.[59] Back in 1931, when her husband was still alive and she was raising their six children, she somehow found the time and energy to earn a law degree from the Portia Law School in Boston, which later became New England School of Law. Her graduation was significant enough to warrant headlines in the local newspaper: "Mother of Six Gets LLB Degree at Portia Law School."[60]

Madeline arrived at Fort Devens on October 13, 1941. The job required her to leave her children at home and live in a cottage on base.[61] Within five short months she and Captain Ferebee were such an "item" that the base commander, Col. West Hamilton, had a heart-to-heart with her to remind her that Claude was a married man.

Each was ripe for the experience. Raising six children alone was no picnic, and Madeline was hoping to fall in love and remarry. Claude and Dorothy were two ships that passed in the night—and had been for years. Although Madeline tried to pass it off as a friendship, she and Claude fell hard for each other. Claude called her his "Darling," his "Concerto," and his "Beloved." In long letters to her he described himself as "your perfect lover—your husband—your protector."[62] The relationship was full of the joy and intimacy he and Dorothy had long since stopped having time for—if they ever did. You "made me live again," he told her.[63]

Somewhat recklessly they went out in public. When Claude could score a car and some gasoline—no easy feat in wartime—he drove Madeline home to West Medford, thirty miles from Fort Devens, where they ate together, slept together, and even interacted with Madeline's children. Her youngest child was a girl about Dorothy Jr.'s age. "I liked him. He was kind of a handsome man and he was nice to my mother," recalled that daughter, Dr. Ione Dugger Vargus, more than seventy years later.[64]

The widow Dugger was not a beautiful woman; her daughter described her as "nice looking," but even she admitted Dorothy was more attractive.[65] Madeline was built a lot like Dorothy, though, about 5'8" tall, weighing anywhere from 160 to 175 pounds. She had a medium-brown complexion. Like Dorothy, she had a polished Boston accent and was well-spoken. She would speak out against racial injustice in the military, leading the government to maintain a file about her activities, harmless as they were.

Claude and Madeline acted like people in love. They went swimming together at nearby Mirror Lake in the afternoon and bowling together in Fitchburg in the evening.[66] He bought her corsages and birthday presents. They relished small pleasures: eating custard pie and ice-cream and sharing news about their children.[67] Claude intervened when Madeline had issues with her son. "I'll come to see the young man—try to persuade him to look at things differently and to be a source of pleasure and not worry to so fine a Mother," he wrote.[68] Their intimacy knew no bounds; he used his surgical skills to nick whiteheads from her face and offered to repair her teeth.[69] They had "their" songs: the Andrew Sisters' weepie "I'll Pray for You" and "Moonlight Cocktail" by the Glenn Miller Orchestra.[70]

There was also a deep, strong, sexual attraction. "So, be sweet and love me; I'll miss you these few hours of your absence," Claude wrote to Madeline after having just seen her. "I pull my sheets up and snuggle deep in a pillow— much like that one on the farther corner of your Devens Castle—but whose fragrance is not that which I knew there."[71] Claude was clearly a new man— revitalized, he said. At least until Dorothy showed up at Fort Devens on Sunday, March 8, 1942, to put the kibosh on the affair.[72]

12 The Skipper

With self-confidence bordering on hubris, Claude Ferebee aspired to be a brigadier general.[1] It may have been his way of competing with Dorothy in their perpetual game of Can You Top This? His career plans could have been considered slightly delusional given that there was but one African American with that rank in the entire military at the time, Benjamin O. Davis.[2] And his goal was hampered by his own actions; by the time he expressed it to a newspaper reporter, Claude was in the crosshairs of an outraged Fort Devens colonel over his affair with Madeline Dugger.

Claude, who prided himself on shrewdness and self-discipline, could not have exhibited worse judgment if he tried. As a captain he was a role model to other African American servicemen. When he commenced the affair the Ferebees were a very public couple. In the hands of skilled syndicated gossip writers like Charlie Cherokee, who wrote the "National Grapevine" column, or Toki Schalk, who wrote "Toki Types about People Here and There," news of a love triangle involving Dorothy, the dashing Captain Ferebee, and a widowed social hostess on the military base where he was stationed would have exploded in the black press like the 1940 blitzkrieg over London.

Given there seemed to be less than six degrees of separation among the Talented Tenth, Claude's dalliance seems especially foolish. Dorothy and Colonel Hamilton, commander of Fort Devens, went way back; they were among the three African Americans on the board of trustees of the DC Community Chest in the 1920s.[3] Hamilton caught wind of the potential public relations nightmare on March 8, 1942, right after Dorothy showed up on base, twins in tow, to plant the flag on her straying husband. Her visit set in motion a series of events that threw cold water on the lovebirds and was the beginning of the end of the Ferebee marriage. Four days after Dorothy left, Hamilton sat down with Madeline to tell her to get hold of herself. With the United States at war the colonel did not need the headache of a Ferebee-Dugger affair.

Madeline was rattled. "Just a line to thank you for your talk this afternoon and to assure you that you need worry no more about Dr. Ferebee visiting me evenings," she scribbled on 366th Infantry stationery to Colonel Hamilton on March 12, 1942. "I have told him definitely that he is not to come to see me." She also said she encouraged Claude to mend fences with his wife. "As for Dorothy,—I have told him many times to go back and make up with her. I told him that just last Sunday when she was here."[4]

Whether Madeline ever sent the letter is another story. An unsigned two-page draft that petered out in midsentence was left among her personal papers. After she died, her daughter, Ione Dugger Vargus boxed it up and shipped it off with her mother's other letters and personal papers— unread—to the National Archives of Black Women's History in Washington. Regardless of whether the letter found its way into Colonel Hamilton's hands, most of it wasn't true. The affair between Captain Ferebee and the Widow Dugger was a two-way street, and it continued well after he was shipped 2,500 miles away to Fort Huachuca in Arizona in June 1942.

Even if she was hoping to one day marry her handsome captain (which her daughter never believed was the case), as a single mother Madeline desperately needed her job and had little choice but to bend to Hamilton's wishes, or at least make him think she had. There is no evidence that he ever spoke to Claude about the affair, but Claude knew he had confronted Madeline. "I don't blame the colonel," Claude wrote to Madeline, perhaps under the impression it was Dorothy's doing.[5] Hamilton might have decided against berating Claude because he was about to be shipped out to Arizona anyway.

Madeline worried the affair would damage her reputation with Hamilton. "I think too much of you and [the] faith and trust you had in me for me to do anything to make you lose that faith—and I appreciate the fact that you are trying to help me," she wrote to the colonel. Then she played the widow card: "Being a widow, alone in the world, with the heavy responsibilities that I have, is hard. I have had a hard time since my husband died—very hard."[6]

She did not exaggerate; fate had dealt her a rough hand. But she was one tough cookie. Madeline Kountze married Edward Dugger on October 29, 1917.[7] In 1939, not long after putting herself through law school, Madeline's husband, a decorated lieutenant colonel in World War I, died at the Boston Veterans Hospital following a long battle with heart and kidney disease. His death left her in circumstances that might have caused a woman of lesser substance to fall apart. The late Lt. Col. Dugger had $2.18 in the pocket of his coat at the hospital when he died, and his estate was not worth much more.[8]

Bill collectors hounded the grieving widow. After leaving the military, Edward Dugger worked at the post office from 1924 until his death on March 5, 1939. He was into the postal credit union for $375.39. "This sum may be remitted at your convenience," Madeline was informed.[9] The New England Telephone and Telegraph Co. threatened to shut off service because she failed to pay a $3.08 bill.[10]

Nothing demonstrates the extent of the sexism and racism embedded in 1940s society like Madeline's predicament following her husband's death. The year before he died Madeline was active in the NAACP and helped run the local chapter's fund-raising drive.[11] Her organizational skills were so impressive that the Republican Party recruited her to gather signatures for its candidate for district attorney in 1938, and she was selected as a delegate to the state GOP convention that year.[12] But Madeline could not get a permanent job sorting mail at the post office because the local postmaster did not believe in hiring women.[13] The fact that she was an African American shut her out of most professional jobs.

Madeline fought Uncle Sam for a widow's pension, insisting that her husband's death was the result of latent war injuries. She also badgered political contacts for a job at the post office. When neither tactic worked, the resourceful Madeline wrote to the Roosevelts for help. In a letter to the president, drafted in April 1939, she wrote that her husband "was in several major engagements in France during which he was very sick and has never been well since he returned." She begged FDR to issue an executive order directing the local postmaster to hire her.[14] It is yet another letter she may never have sent given that several versions of it were among her papers at her death.

A year later, still without a job at the post office, she did mail a letter to Eleanor Roosevelt. "Knowing how strongly you believe in Justice I am writing to ask you if you will see that it is obtained in my case," she wrote. She reiterated that she was a war widow receiving "no pension or help from the government." She was not seeking a handout. "I have been on the Post Office Civil Service List for fourteen years . . . and cannot get appointed because I am a woman."[15] Mrs. Roosevelt's social correspondence officer, Ralph W. Magee, responded, "I am sure Mrs. Roosevelt would be very sorry to hear of your difficulties in obtaining an appointment. Unfortunately, there is nothing she could do personally to help you, as she never interferes with the administrative affairs of a government department."[16]

Having run out of options, Madeline filled out an application on May 16, 1941, to be the senior hostess at Fort Devens. She had performed similar unpaid duties as an officer's wife during World War I.[17] She was interviewed in August and hired to begin work in October at an annual salary of $2,300 (about $35,800 in today's dollars). She remained with the War Department until early 1946, when she was let go because of postwar downsizing.[18] She continued to work for the federal government in various jobs until her mandatory retirement in 1967.[19]

Within weeks of Dorothy's visit, the clandestine couple continued where they had left off. "I'll miss you these few hours of your absence," Claude wrote Madeline on April 1, 1942, intimating that they had just parted. In the same note he pledged to see her as soon as possible: "Look for me to meet you but don't be disappointed if I don't—as you know the circumstances."[20] Perhaps Dorothy's visit inspired a little caution in the couple, or stricter surveillance by the colonel.

Extramarital affairs hardly raise eyebrows today, and such romances were hush-hush but not uncommon during World War II. Spouses were separated for years at a time, not knowing whether they would ever see one another again. Madeline was surrounded by men at Fort Devens and, as a single woman, was free to date any of them. Although she knew Claude had a wife, he assured her he was attempting to extricate himself from the marriage, which seems to have been true. She did not share the fact that he was married with her daughter, who was only eleven and did not have the slightest idea her mother's beau had a wife.[21]

Madeline's relationship with Claude was special. Nobody knows what Claude did with her many letters to him, so the description of their romance comes exclusively from his melodramatic musings. His letters reflect a man who was intelligent, proud, pompous, petulant, and occasionally corny. Less than a dozen of these letters survive, but they paint a vivid picture of an unhappily married man over the moon with his new love. Some of the words are blacked out—perhaps by modest Madeline's pen—lest prying eyes discover the real nature of their "friendship." "Remember your promise, and our prayers—together. Tell me . . ." The sentence that follows, ending with a question mark, is blacked out.[22]

Besides exuding passion, Claude's letters communicate a sense of comfort. He *liked* her and liked being with her. Resting in her arms or sitting next to her in the car, Claude Ferebee was not Mr. Dorothy Boulding Ferebee; he was his own man. Although Madeline was not his intellectual inferior, she was not as professionally accomplished as he or Dorothy, and though she had given birth to six children, she may have been less experienced when it came to sex. Her contorted efforts to paint their love as a friendship point to how uncomfortable she was in the role of "the other woman."

In June 1942, on the eve of being shipped out west, Claude apparently told Madeline his mother had confronted him about the affair. Nannie Ferebee may have learned of it from her son, or perhaps an angry Dorothy spilled the beans. To gloss over matters, Madeline wrote to Nannie: "I am a mother, and I would not have any mother least of all Claude's mother, unhappy over anything to which I may have been an innocent party. . . . Since your son decided to call upon me, there have been untrue rumors circulated regarding us. I want you to know that we are simply very good friends." Her excuse for the relationship was that she thought his marriage was over: "I would not have let him call upon me at all if he had not told me that he and Dorothy were separated long *before* he met me. I would never come between husband and wife." Madeline took pains to assure Claude's mother that she was an upstanding, church-going woman who "always taught in the Sunday School."[23]

As unhappy as Claude might have been, he and Dorothy were not separated in any official sense prior to his meeting Madeline. He may have *told* Madeline he was separated, as married men have told mistresses for aeons. Or Madeline might have been stretching the truth to make herself look better in the eyes of Claude's mother. Regardless, one cannot help but feel for Madeline, who apparently loved Claude deeply. In her letter to Nannie, she said, "Do not worry over the fact that your son likes me, because it is a wholesome liking. I do not encourage him, but occasionally he does drop down to visit me. I guess he likes to get away from camp once in a while."[24]

In fact, Claude's letters to Madeline hardly demonstrate a "wholesome liking." They show that the situation with Dorothy was hardly resolved: "Never let anyone say—that others will entice me not to think of you or love you—I think you understand what I mean. If I could write what I'm thinking, and let you have it straight, down to earth talking—we would take planes tonight and meet near the Mississippi and enfold each in the other's arms—in loves [sic] greatest embrace."[25]

Later, when Madeline got tired of messing around with a married man and Claude feared he was losing her, he tried to convince her that he was ending his marriage. One letter suggests Madeline may have accused him of being more attached to his wife than he let on. "I am not emotionally torn—there were no goodbyes simply—au revoir—or so long. See you later," he insisted. As to his divorce: "The case is still pending. I'm changing lawyers for a very definite reason—and my selection is being made in New York."[26] There is no way to confirm this; matrimonial records in New York are sealed for one hundred years.[27] But he could not have sued Dorothy for divorce in that state, as his new attorney would have told him. The only ground for divorce in New York at the time was adultery, and Dorothy was not the one cheating.

The irony, of course, is that for all of his griping about Dorothy—"As a kid I had a happy life—would I could recover and begin where I made my fatal mistake in 1929," he wrote to Madeline—Claude and Dorothy were very much alike, perhaps too much.[28] They were smart, ambitious, proud, and fearless. They inspired awe, respect, and no small amount of jealousy from their peers. Yet those same qualities, admired in a man, were viewed by Claude and the sexist society in which they lived as flaws in Dorothy's character.

Madeline was not much different from Dorothy; she was educated, passionate about racial equality, and brave. After she was promoted in 1944 to direct the service club at Camp Myles Standish in Taunton, Massachusetts, she was not afraid to speak out about the army's dismal treatment of black soldiers. The army was none too happy with her either, as evidenced by the fact investigators were watching her and keeping reports. In one she was described as "a potential agitator of disturbances in and around

Service Club #4, through her determination to seize every opportunity to complain of discrimination against the negro."[29]

Separating was torture for Madeline and Claude. Immediately after they parted, their letters flew back and forth across the country.[30] "How we never know the fate of our lives until something catastrophic happens as my being torn away from you," Claude wrote once he arrived in Arizona.[31] "You didn't know that I turned around and came back to your vicinity and almost came in again before I really put my foot down on the accelerator and moved away for real—did you?" he wrote.[32]

En route from Massachusetts to Arizona, Claude took a detour to Norfolk to visit his parents and sisters.[33] He also stopped off in Washington, telling Madeline he did so to "straighten out some matters, to remind them again of my change of heart—that I desired a divorce."[34] Years later Dorothy provided a different version of their breakup, saying their divorce was clean and quick. As soon as he asked for one, which she said did not happen until after their daughter's death in 1950, she was only too happy to oblige: "Since this was his desire, I said, 'It is my pleasure to give you your freedom.' Thus, in a very calm fashion, we were divorced."[35]

Claude and Madeline continued to correspond until at least 1944, but not long after Claude was transferred to Arizona in 1942, the reality of their situation hit Madeline.[36] She may have been unnerved by an item in the "Washington Social Notes" column in the July 25, 1942, *Chicago Defender*: "Dr. Dorothy Boulding Ferebee, physician, and children, joined her husband, Dr. Thurston Ferebee, dentist . . . recently and motored with him to Fort Huachuca, Ariz. where he has been transferred to the 93rd Division."

Madeline's friends and family were a chorus of naysayers about Claude's sincerity. She no longer knew what to believe. Claude had a lot of explaining to do about the little cross-country trip he, Dorothy, and the children took in July. He said it was Dorothy's idea. "I knew when she brought the subject up that there existed ulterior motives," he wrote, suggesting that her goal was "to attempt to impress her friends and theirs and the entire East at large." He said that "she was advised against taking the trip."[37]

He said he wanted a divorce but complained that nobody believed him. "To the world—and you—this does not seem to be the fact," he wrote. Yet any objective reading of the same letter shows he was dragging his feet.

"I am attempting to give my children their share of the fatherly protection they need, and I want to keep their love and respect," he wrote on September 22, 1942. "To proceed with caution is a lesson I learned the hard way, and have now to regret at leisure."[38]

Dorothy may have been doing some foot dragging of her own. It was she who sought the divorce, but not until nearly a decade later. In the matrimonial action she filed against Claude on July 26, 1950, in the Cook County, Illinois, Domestic Relations Court, Dorothy swore he deserted her without cause on or about July 15, 1942, and that they never again lived together as husband and wife. Something must have happened on that date; most likely Claude's confession about the Madeline affair. This undercuts Dorothy's assertion that he did not ask for a divorce until after their daughter's death, a request she granted quickly and "with pleasure."

Whether for love or social appearances, Dorothy tenaciously clung to Claude. Calling herself a widow, as she did after they broke up, may speak to the fact that her status as a divorcée made her uncomfortable. But between 1942 and 1950 there was little Claude could do about getting out of his marriage if his wife did not consent. Unilateral divorce did not exist until 1969, when California's governor Ronald Reagan signed the nation's first no-fault divorce law. Until then an unhappy spouse without grounds—like Claude—was stuck. And even with three thousand miles between them, Claude could not quite get away from Dorothy. Her fame had reached the point that she was Miss October on a calendar of prominent women published by the National Council of Negro Women in 1942, based on stunning sketches by the well-known artist Lois Mailou Jones. It surely hung on the walls of any one of a number of segregated government facilities Claude entered that year.

Once Claude arrived in Arizona and Madeline pulled back emotionally, he grew suspicious. "Above all things I realize you want to get married no matter what you say. . . . The jibes have gotten you. You can't take them and you have fallen for someone else. You could at least tell me yourself. . . . You took things in your own hands, thinking that nothing would come of our love, and there were other[s] more easily available. Am I wrong?" he asked in a letter on August 7, 1942.[39] But Claude was sending his own mixed signals; a passive-aggressive invitation to Madeline to end the affair mixed with a little self-pity:

Now that there is so much uncertainty with you, and your family is hurt, you are hurt and all your friends are talking to you . . . perhaps you better go on enjoy yourself, and pity me. . . .

This—you need not accept as a break off—unless you must be free. I'm not one to hamper another if I can't do more about it at the moment.[40]

Still, contact between the lovers continued, although the later letters to "Madeline darling" were filled with more news and fewer declarations of passion. In November 1943, he wrote, "Last month I inserted in my field dental clinic—263 partial dentures and 16 full upper and lowers. The dental laboratory bill for [the] desert training center was 78,000 dollars for Sept. alone."[41] The situation at home, he wrote, was "about the same."[42]

The affair upended everyone's lives. Even steadfast Dorothy was rattled by it. Although her name was synonymous with the Mississippi Health Project, she opted out of its eighth and final year in 1942, in Holmes County on the Providence Cooperative Farm. She was replaced by Dr. Edna L. Griffin of Pasadena, California. Participating in the clinic would have prevented her from being able to follow Claude to Fort Huachuca that summer.

Fort Huachuca was the end of the earth as far as the African American soldiers stationed there were concerned, which may have been the reason the War Department sent them there in the first place. "Everything wrong with the army's treatment of black soldiers converged on this big training facility," wrote Truman K. Gibson Jr., the civilian aide to the secretary of war in World War II. "It was ground zero for the collision of the conflicting demands of a war to save democracy and American society's commitment to segregation."[43]

Claude was part of the 318th Medical Battalion and as such was attached to the 93rd Infantry, at the hospital in Fort Huachuca, which like everything else there, was segregated. There were "separate hospitals, officers' clubs, civilian quarters, and other facilities—and the most corrosive of all, the entrenched rule that no white officer could serve under a black officer," wrote Gibson.[44] Claude's letters to Madeline complained of discrimination. "These white officers don't give a hoot about Negro advancement," he wrote as soon as he arrived in Arizona.[45]

Eventually the 92nd Infantry was sent from Huachuca to Italy, and the 93rd was shipped to the South Pacific. By the time they were shipped out, the war was nearly over, which should come as no surprise given that the War Department did everything it could to avoid using African American soldiers in battle.[46]

Arriving in Guadalcanal in early 1944, the 93rd was split up and its members apportioned to various Pacific islands for the remainder of the war.[47] Claude was stationed on the Molucca Islands, also known as the "Spice Islands," in Indonesia, on Mindanao in the Philippines, and on Morotai Island, also in Indonesia.[48] Natural beauty aside, he moaned that the area was "hot as blazes" and impossibly rainy.[49]

As a high-ranking dental officer Claude worked hard, and, whether due to a dearth of available officers or because his supervisor was transferred and the post left vacant until later filled by a white officer, he worked two jobs.[50] To relieve boredom and relax, he put together what he called "Field Manual One Dash One," a series of pictures of pinup girls; his own version of a Dorothy scrapbook.[51]

The rest of the 93rd Infantry Division was divvied up and parceled out throughout the South Pacific for support duties. In the division's "Combat Narrative" supplied by the army, the soldiers' work was described as "fatigue details at docks, warehouses, and supply dumps," establishing "outposts," supplying "stevedore crews," and constructing "fortifications." In other words, black men were assigned to manual labor and janitorial work.[52] Members of the 93rd faced criticism after they allegedly cut and ran from a beachhead in Bougainville, the easternmost island of Papua New Guinea.[53] This allegation led indirectly to Claude's fast friendship with the NAACP's executive secretary Walter White.

White obtained credentials as a correspondent for the *New York Post* and used them to spend ten days in the South Pacific. He concluded that the alleged display of cowardice at Bougainville, if it happened at all, could not have involved the 93rd because the invasion took place in the fall and winter of 1943, and the 93rd did not arrive in Bougainville until April 1944.[54] General MacArthur labeled White "a troublemaker and menace to the war effort."[55]

The army's policy of dumping white officers on the 93rd rather than promoting black ones from within had a profound impact on the morale of the African American officers in the division, including Claude, who had hoped to be promoted to major. On July 26, 1945, the officers of the 93rd Infantry wrote a letter to Walter White, decrying the unfairness of the army's method of filling key vacancies and asking that he intercede with the War Department: "The Senior Medical and Dental Officers of our race have not been given the ordinary privilege of assuming leadership in either of the Division Medical Staff vacancies."[56]

White wrote to Maj. Gen. Harry H. Johnson, commander of the 93rd Infantry, focusing primarily on Claude: "I am . . . informed that the suggestion was made to you that Captain Ferebee be promoted to Major and made Division Dental Surgeon. . . . I am further informed that you . . . refused to accept this suggestion. Subsequently, a white Major was sent from the States to become Division Dental Surgeon."[57]

Walter Francis White was a blond-haired, blue-eyed African American. He passed for Caucasian when he had to, such as in 1918, when he investigated lynchings.[58] White and Claude bonded in the South Pacific. They had nicknames for each other; Claude was the "Skipper," and White was the "Bossman."[59]

White arrived in Guam two days after Christmas 1944 and mingled with the men of the 93rd Infantry.[60] He and Claude shared a wild ambulance ride to the airport, with Claude careening down the back roads of New Guinea and White cowering in the passenger seat. Claude took many photos of White, including silly ones in which the NAACP chief is harrumphing over the typewriter in his tent and washing in the officers' shower.[61] Claude built a model ship for White's son, and entrusted White to hold for safekeeping another hand-made ship for Thurston.[62]

In 1945 Claude felt close enough to White to clue him in on his unhappy marriage and to take a few swipes at Dorothy. The organizing conference of the United Nations was scheduled to take place in San Francisco. Dorothy attended, not as a delegate but as Mary Bethune's personal physician. "I understand there are no colored delegates to the San Francisco Conference, only advisors," Claude wrote to White in May 1945. "Mrs. Bethune has selected, D.B.F. MD as her personal physician for the trip. I was so informed from Ogden Utah today. Some Stuff, eh?"[63] White also attended the conference. Later Claude wrote, "I'm sure, from reports, you had a time in San Francisco. I also understand there was a personal physician worked in on the deal? Some stuff."[64] For his part, White remained neutral in the war between the Ferebees. He obviously appreciated Dorothy's prominence and knew they would cross paths in the long fight for civil rights.

World War II ended on August 10, 1945, when Japan announced it intended to unconditionally surrender after the United States dropped atomic bombs on Hiroshima and Nagasaki. "Well, it's over, even over here," Claude wrote to White. Claude was still smarting over not getting promoted. "It seems that one of my brother dental officers has been making things uncomfortable for me behind my back, thinking or hoping to get the sought after job." Nonetheless, Claude was grateful that White had tried to help. "It is just to mince words that you must know I greatly appreciate your efforts and action." Claude's fantasy about becoming a brigadier general was over. He had his fill of the army, calling himself and his fellow black officers "racial prisoners of war."[65]

Before the war ended, Claude was awarded the Bronze Star. His citation reads, "For meritorious achievement in support of military operations against the enemy at Stirling Island, Treasury Group, British Solomon Islands, Hollandia, Dutch New Guinea, and Morotai, Netherlands East Indies from 27 October 1944, to August 1945."[66]

In his soul-searching as to what to do next, Claude considered his options, none of which included a life with Dorothy and their twins. He gave a passing thought about moving to Michigan or California but asked White for his help resettling in New York: "In case you are in a position to look around, try to locate a dental office site—in a building for me—since I expect to be established thereabouts." In a clear reference to Washington, he added, "I'm not interested in segregated districts. I want to be a free citizen."[67]

By February 1946 Claude was back in the States at Camp Beale in California, north of Sacramento. Technically he did not become a "free citizen" again until June 23, 1946, but his informal separation from military life began on February 19 because he had accumulated four months of unused vacation time. He got in his car, possibly the same one he nearly ruined when he got sand in the break lining from squiring Madeline around the beaches of Massachusetts, and drove 2,964 miles to Washington. When he left the army for good, he took nearly $2,000 with him, of which $1,144 was back pay.[68]

Once in Washington, he did not stay long. His association with Howard University had ended years earlier, his children were about to head off to fancy New England boarding schools, and the thought of fixing teeth in the same space where his estranged wife had her practice, even if she seemed to spend little time there, was unappealing. He packed up and moved to New York.[69] In his wildest dreams he could not have imagined that Dorothy would pull up stakes and follow him.

FIG. 1. (*left*) Dorothy's maternal grandfather, Richard Gault Leslie Paige, in his official photo as a member of the Virginia General Assembly during Reconstruction. (Photo by C. R. Rees & Co. Library of Virginia.)

FIG. 2. (*below*) Dorothy's maternal grandmother, Lillie Ruffin Paige, who once graced the finest Boston drawing rooms. This may have been her *carte de visite*. It was probably taken shortly after the Civil War. (Worden Photography Studio. Courtesy of Lisa Ferebee.)

FIG 3. (*above*) Dorothy's immedi-
ate family, circa 1900: her mother,
Florence (Flossie) Cornelia Paige
Boulding; her brothers, Benjamin
Richard Boulding and Ruffin Paige
Boulding; and Dorothy on the
knee of her doting father, Benja-
min Richard Boulding. (Photo by
Freeman Studio. Courtesy of Lisa
Ferebee.)

FIG. 4. (*right*) Dorothy as a little
girl around the time she practiced
her budding medical skills by
setting the broken wings of birds.
Even then, she was self-assured.
(Photo by Jefferson Studio. Courtesy of Dorothy Ruth Ferebee.)

FIG. 5. Dorothy Celeste Boulding, probably around the time she graduated from Simmons College, Class of 1920. (Photo by J. E. Purdy & Co. Courtesy of Lisa Ferebee.)

FIG. 6. (*above*) James Ernie
Martin, Dorothy's first serious
beau, on the 1916 Colby College
football team, standing second
from the end on the right.
(Cleveland Colby Colgate
Archives, Colby-Sawyer College.)

FIG. 7. (*right*) Handsome Dr.
Claude Thurston Ferebee in
June 1929, on the day he gradu-
ated (finally!) from the dental
school at Columbia University.
(Courtesy of Lisa Ferebee.)

FIG. 8. (*right*) Although neither ever seemed able to admit it; as a young couple, the Ferebees were very much in love. Here, Claude and Dorothy have eyes only for each other on their honeymoon in Buckroe Beach, Virginia, July 1930. (Courtesy of Lisa Ferebee.)

FIG. 9. (*below*) Dorothy and Claude visit Virginia State College in May 1931. Notice how artfully she hides the fact that she is pregnant with twins and just three months away from delivering. (Courtesy of Lisa Ferebee.)

FIG. 10. An obviously exhausted Dorothy in the fall of 1931 with her twins, Claude Thurston Ferebee II, called "Thurston" or "Buzzy," and his sister, Dorothy Boulding Ferebee Jr., "Dolly." In a sign the honeymoon was already over, Dorothy said she gave birth to a boy and girl—one for her husband and one for herself—so there would be no controversy. (Courtesy of Lisa Ferebee.)

FIG. 11. Dorothy, with her toddler twins in front of her home in May 1933 looking far more chipper than she did immediately following their birth. (Courtesy of Lisa Ferebee.)

FIG. 12. The Ferebee twins play in front of their father's beloved car. Nicknamed, "Buddie," it took the Ferebees on their honeymoon. Dorothy would run it into the ground in Mississippi soon after this picture was taken. (Courtesy of Lisa Ferebee.)

FIG. 13. The Ferebee twins, Dolly (sixth from the left) and Buzzy (next to her, seventh from the left), as the bunnies Flopsy and Mopsy in a Garden of Children theatrical production of *The Tale of Peter Rabbit*. Dolly's best friend, Aurelia Roberts Brooks, playing a vegetable, is second from the end, wearing a pained expression along with her costume. (Photo by Scurlock Studio. Records, Archives Center, National Museum of American History, Smithsonian Institution. Courtesy of Aurelia Roberts Brooks.)

FIG. 14. (*right*) Dorothy, in one of the many hats she adored, stands proudly before the home and medical office she once shared with her husband at 1809 2nd St. NW in Washington. Today it is on a walking tour of notable African American sites. (Courtesy of Lisa Ferebee.)

FIG. 15. (*below*) Dorothy and her medical team stuck in the mud in Mississippi. For seven summers the members of the Mississippi Health Project endured heat, humidity, insects, ignorance, bad roads, poverty, pervasive disease, and rampant racism to bring desperately needed health care to Delta sharecroppers and tenant farmers. (Moorland-Spingarn Research Center, Howard University, Ferebee Scrapbook, Box 183-30.)

FIG. 16. A young Dr. Rosier Davis Dedwylder making house calls to sick patients on Jim, his Tennessee Walking Horse. The Bolivar County health director and Mississippi plantation owner opened his heart, mind, and home to Dorothy and the Mississippi Health Project volunteers, paving the way for their acceptance on plantations around the county in 1936. (Courtesy of Dr. Rosier D. Dedwylder II.)

FIG. 17. Dorothy in an undated photo, probably from the late 1930s or early 1940s, demonstrating her undying love of fashion. (Courtesy of Dorothy Ruth Ferebee.)

. PHYSICIAN .

DOROTHY BOULDING FEREBEE *has achieved distinction given to few American women in the field of medicine. As an honor graduate of both Simmons and Tufts Medical College, she came to Washington, D.C. to enter practice after appointment to the staff of Freedman's Hospital. Her social vision inspired the founding of the Southeast Settlement House in the Nation's Capital, and lead ultimately to the crowning achievement of her career, the direction she has given for seven years to the Alpha Kappa Alpha Sorority Health Project in Mississippi, the first volunteer medical service to sharecropping families in the country. A busy person in private life, Dr. Ferebee is wife of Captain C. Thurston Ferebee (a Regimental Dental Surgeon in the U.S. Army) and mother of a twin son and daughter. Her contribution to social hygiene and health organizations combines in services to the Board of Directors of the Social Hygiene Society of the District and membership on the Executive Committee of the National Maternal and Child Health Council.*

FIG. 18. Dorothy as Miss October 1942 in a calendar featuring prominent black women. Her portrait was painted by the noted African American artist Lois Maillot Jones. (Courtesy of Moorland-Spingarn Research Center, Howard University.)

FIG. 19. (*above*) Claude's "Concerto," Madeline K. Dugger, at her desk at the service club for black soldiers in Fort Devens, Massachusetts, during the second world war. The calendar behind her reads January 1944, by which time her hot affair with Dorothy's husband had cooled. (National Park Service, Mary McLeod Bethune NHS, National Archives for Black Women's History, Dugger Papers, Fort Devens/Camp Miles Standish Series, Photographs and Albums Series 1, Subseries 3-2003.)

FIG. 20. (*opposite*) Dr. Claude Thurston Ferebee in uniform after he was released from the U.S. Army in 1946. There is an oak leaf insignia on his shoulder, indicating the rank of major, but his cap is plain, signifying he was a captain. Whether he was promoted after his release from active duty while in the U.S. Army Reserve could not be confirmed. (Photo by Scurlock Studio. Records, Archives Center, National Museum of American History, Smithsonian Institution. Courtesy of Dorothy Ruth Ferebee.)

FIG. 21. Dorothy leads the way up the Capitol steps as part of an NCNW delegation lobbying a congressman, November 15, 1946. (NPS, NABWH, Records of the NCNW, Series 14-1221.)

FIG. 22. The Ferebee family poses at the Altaraz School in Great Barrington, Massa-chusetts, where the twins had a brief and undistinguished academic career. The picture was taken in 1946, by which time the Ferebee marriage existed in name only. (Courtesy of Lisa Ferebee and Simmons College Archives.)

FIG. 23. (*above*) Dorothy Ferebee Jr. as princess in the Court of the May Queen at the Northfield School for Girls in 1949. The radiantly beautiful seventeen-year-old is slightly to the right knee of the queen, wearing a dress that is slipping from her shoulder. Within the year she will be dead. (Photo by Clifford Scofield. Courtesy of Northfield-Mount Hermon Archives.)

FIG. 24. (*right*) Thurston's 1949 graduation photo from the Tilton School. He finished near the bottom of his class academically, but he had a good time. (Courtesy of Tilton School.)

FIG. 25. (*above*) Dorothy in a black lace dress with a white corsage at the retirement dinner for NCNW founder and legend, Mary McLeod Bethune, November 1949. Dorothy had just been elected her successor as president council in a hotly contested race. Bethune, next to Dorothy, wears the Haitian Medal of Honor and Merit. On Bethune's right is Vivian Carter Mason (NCNW president from 1953 to 1957). Dorothy Height (NCNW president from 1957 until her death in 2010) is at the far right of the photo, her dress strikingly similar to Dorothy's. (Photo by Fred Harris. NPS, NABWH, Records of the NCNW, Series 14-0056.)

FIG. 26. (*left*) Portrait of Dorothy, circa 1950, while president of the National Council of Negro Women and one of the most influential women in America. (Photo by Harris & Ewing. NPS, NABWH, Records of the NCNW, Series 14-0489.)

FIG. 27. (*opposite*) Undated picture of Thurston and his bride-to-be, Carol Phillips, whom he married in 1951. Carol was a sweet and gentle soul; everyone loved her. (Courtesy of Lisa Ferebee.)

FIG. 28. (*above*) Two months after being elected NCNW president, Dorothy joins civil rights leaders in calling on President Truman during Emergency Mobilization Week, January 15–17, 1950, in an effort to move his stalled civil rights package. Dorothy is in the front row in a long fur coat. The impatient president barely heard them out during their visit, telling them their beef was with Congress, not him. (Photo by Harris & Ewing. Courtesy of Dorothy Ruth Ferebee.)

FIG. 29. (*above*) Dorothy sits between Josephine Baker and an unidentified woman in the back seat of a convertible on a motorcade through the streets of Washington DC, surrounded by an adoring crowd in June 1951. The Jo Baker concert helped fill the coffers of the financially struggling NCNW. (Photo by Fred Harris. NPS, NABWH, Records of the NCNW, Series 14-0164.)

FIG. 30. (*opposite*) Dorothy greets Josephine Baker on stage for the NCNW Concert, June 1951. Photo by Fred Harris. (NPS, NABWH, Records of the NCNW, Series 14-0172.)

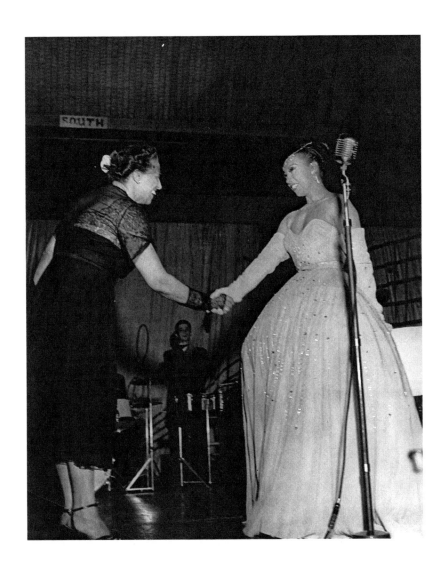

FIG. 31. (*opposite top*) Dorothy (first row, second from left), joins Mary McLeod Bethune and others with First Lady Mamie Eisenhower. (NPS, NABWH, Records of the NCNW, Series 14-0338.)

FIG. 32. (*opposite bottom*) President Johnson wishes Dorothy farewell after a luncheon on October 24, 1967, for the president of the Republic of Cameroon. (Photo by Yoichi Okamoto. Lyndon Baines Johnson Library and Museum, Austin TX.)

FIG. 33. (*above*) Portrait of Dorothy that appeared in *Vogue*'s May 1969 issue, taken by the iconic photographer Irving Penn. (Dorothy Boulding Ferebee, New York, 1969, © Condé Nast.)

FIG. 34. (*opposite top*) Dorothy and officials of the NCNW enjoy afternoon tea with First Lady Patricia Nixon after the unveiling of the Mary Bethune statue in Washington DC's Lincoln Park, July 1974. Dorothy is to the right of Mrs. Nixon in the photo. (Photo by Jack Kightlinger. Richard Nixon Library and Birthplace, Yorba Linda, California.)

FIG. 35. (*opposite bottom*) Dorothy greets future New York governor and U.S. vice president Nelson Rockefeller at the NCNW's International Night celebration in November 1953. The man in the turban is unknown. (Photo by Pease. NPS, NABWH, Records of the NCNW, Series 14-1104.)

FIG. 36. (*above*) Dorothy in her role as national vice president of the Girl Scouts of the United States of America, in her uniform designed by Mainbocher. (Reprinted with permission from the Girl Scouts of the USA.)

FIG. 37. (*opposite top*) An aging Dorothy and others participating in the Bethune Memorial unveiling ceremony in Lincoln Park in Washington DC on July 10, 1974. She is next to Andrew Young, who is second from right. (Photo by Sultan Salahuddin. NPS, NABWH, Records of the NCNW, Series 14-3075.)

FIG. 38. (*opposite bottom*) Dorothy, approaching eighty years old and ill, at the launching of the Bethune Collection on Black Women's Organizations, July 11, 1976. She wears the symbol of International Women's Year around her neck. (NPS, NABWH, Records of the NCNW, Series 14-0422.)

FIG. 39. (*above*) Dorothy Jr.'s sad, lonely, and untended grave at the Mount Hope Cemetery in Hastings-on-Hudson, New York. (Photo by Diane Kiesel.)

FIG. 40. (*opposite*) The twelve-foot obelisk placed over the grave of Dorothy's grandfather R. G. L. Paige by his grieving widow, Lillie. Dorothy's mother is buried nearby, and after her death on September 14, 1980, Dorothy's ashes were scattered there by her oldest grandson, Claude Thurston Ferebee III. (Photo by Diane Kiesel.)

FIG. 41. (*above*) Claude with his great-grandsons in the late 1980s, the children of Claude Thurston Ferebee III and Lisa Kleinman Ferebee, at Claude's home in White Plains, New York. On the left is Charles Andrew and on the right is Claude Thurston IV. Already close to ninety years old when this picture was taken, Claude still weighed what he did when he was a captain in the army during World War II. (Photo by Claude Thurston Ferebee III. Courtesy of Lisa Ferebee.)

13 Some Stuff

While Claude was away in the army, Dorothy was left behind to adjust to the changes. As the war began, five thousand new federal employees a month poured into Washington. Women—mostly young and exclusively white—flocked to the nation's capital in search of jobs as government typists, filing clerks, and telephone operators, in part to help the war effort and in part to seek adventure. The city population exploded from 621,000 in 1930 to more than a million in 1941.[1]

After Pearl Harbor the brightly illuminated dome of the U.S. Capitol was turned off and not turned on again until May 8, 1945, the night the war ended in Europe. Even the pomp and circumstance of an inauguration was absent when FDR took the oath of office for his fourth term. Instead of a swearing-in ceremony at the Capitol followed by a lengthy inspirational inaugural speech, the president's final term began on the bitter cold Saturday of January 20, 1945, with a fifteen-minute ceremony on the South Portico of the White House. Dorothy was among the 1,800 shivering guests who stood in the snow, watching.[2] President Roosevelt, dressed in a business suit, gave a 557-word speech, shook a few hands in a receiving line, and called it a day.[3] From there Dorothy rushed up to the NCNW headquarters to host an open house to celebrate the inauguration.[4]

Life was radically altered at 1809 2nd Street NW. Dorothy had to manage the twins, a medical practice, her responsibilities at Howard University, and her civic obligations while nursing her broken heart and injured pride. She, her children, and her mother suffered large and small deprivations, like everyone else.[5] Her taxes went up and the quantity of food in her kitchen went down, especially sugar, although she and her family could eat chicken, chicken, and more chicken—one of the few food items not rationed—until they were ready to cluck.[6]

Gasoline rationing started on the East Coast in May 1942. Most drivers were limited to five gallons a week, but those who could demonstrate a need for more could get it.[7] This finished off what remained of the Mississippi Health Project. Although AKA might have been able to show a medical necessity for extra gasoline, it was pointless. If one of the medical team's tires blew out on the rocky Mississippi roads there was no rubber to replace it.

By the end of the summer of 1941 the idea of a permanent AKA health clinic in the Delta was percolating. Sam Franklin, still involved with Sherwood Eddy's Providence Cooperative Farm, showed up in Washington in the fall of 1941 "urging" Dorothy to consider setting up shop there.[8] Early in 1942 Dorothy and Ida met in Chicago with Franklin and others to discuss the feasibility of a joint health venture. "In times of democracy's peril we have democracy's opportunity," Franklin told the group. The opportunity he heard knocking was for AKA to establish a permanent clinic at the Providence Cooperative Farm. He wanted AKA to fork over $1,500 a year for two years to erect a clinic building and another $600 to buy a fluoroscope to screen workers for tuberculosis. In exchange, he offered to place the director of the AKA Health Project on the Providence Farm board and to name the clinic after the sorority. He also offered living space at a nominal cost for AKA members who wanted to come to Holmes County in 1942 for a final year of the mobile clinic and volunteered to host it at Providence Farm to cut down on travel in light of gas rationing.[9]

The sorority paid for the fluoroscope and went to Providence in 1942, but Dorothy did not participate.[10] The joint venture never got off the ground. In April 1943 Ida sent a letter to AKA members to sell them on it but she failed to appreciate the concerns of AKA lawyers. "Although the Directorate is to have legal investigation, we believe that no legal obstruction will be found," she wrote to the sorors.[11] But in September 1943, when AKA representatives again met in Chicago with a representative of the Providence Farm board and an AKA attorney, and Dorothy was not there, the lawyer promptly threw cold water on the proposal. Practically speaking, a single AKA vote on the board would hold no power over how the sorority's money would be spent. Nothing in the farm's charter allowed for an on-site health care facility. And if the cooperative went under, AKA's investment would be lost. Consequently the AKA lawyer advised against it.[12] At the next Boule, in 1946 in Los Angeles, the sorority vetoed the idea. Supreme Basileus Beulah Whitby made it official: "The Mississippi Health Project has been regarded as temporarily discontinued until the War emergencies and the Boule could determine what next steps should be taken with reference to it."[13]

When all was said and done, the Mississippi Health Project was Dorothy Ferebee, Ida Jackson, and AKA's shining hour. The sorority's tireless work in one of the worst parts of the country, at one of the worst times in history, brought health care to fifteen thousand of the nation's poorest and most powerless.[14] It is fitting that the epitaph for the health project should have been written by Marjorie Holloman. In her book about Alpha Kappa Alpha, published more than fifty years after the cotton field clinics had closed forever, she wrote:

> The pilgrimages to Mississippi anticipated by nearly thirty years the "Freedom Schools" and "Witness of Presence" in the "long hot summer" of 1964. As public health gains importance as the major problem in human rehabilitation, it is very heartening to remember that Alpha Kappa Alpha was in the vanguard of those who, recognizing that better health is one factor in the social and economic progress of the nation, also believe in personal, direct involvement for the attainment of goals.[15]

The end of the health project coincided with the end of Dorothy's family life as she knew it. But despite her marriage having erupted like a volcano, she put on her game face for friends and family, including Claude's family. She was matron of honor at sister-in-law Maxine Ferebee's wedding to John Burrell of Columbus, Ohio, over the Christmas holidays in 1942–43, transporting herself and the twins to Norfolk, despite gasoline shortages. Wartime deprivations did not prevent the Ferebees from cheerfully decorating the house on Chapel Street for the happy occasion with white carnations, chrysanthemums, narcissus, and a glowing candelabra. Dorothy, wearing a brown crepe and wool dress accented with aqua jewelry, stood next to the bride. Young Connie Ferebee, the maid of honor, was on the other side of her big sister, in a wool dress in a soft shade of ashes of roses.[16] Claude did not show up in Norfolk to congratulate the new bride and groom until June, when he was granted leave.[17]

Dorothy's passion remained her work. In October 1941 the NCNW became the first national women's group to endorse contraception. Dorothy chaired the NCNW Committee on Family Planning. It passed a resolution "which aims to aid each family to have *all* the children it can support and afford, but no more—to insure better health, greater security and happiness for all."[18]

Dorothy's strong support of contraception was taken out of context and served to haunt her for years to come as she was accused—unjustly—of supporting Negro genocide. In an unfortunate choice of words, she told a Planned Parenthood conference in Chicago in 1942 that family planning was "a vital key to the elimination of human waste."[19] The "waste" she referred to was the unnecessary deaths of mothers and babies due to poverty, poor prenatal care, and ignorance about spacing children. It was a stock speech in which she urged the use of birth control by *everyone*, not just African Americans. On January 29, 1942, at an annual meeting in New York City of the Birth Control Federation of America, which later became Planned Parenthood, she said:

Negro mothers die at twice the rate of the white mothers; Negro babies die at 2½ times the rate of white babies; Negro children show a 50% higher death rate. Out of the one-quarter million Negro live births annually, 22,000 babies die before their first birthday, while an additional 18,000 are born dead, raising the total annual loss to 40,000 infants. . . .

As a nation, we cannot afford to overlook any factor which may be vital to the lives and welfare of the mothers and babies of this country. One signally important factor is Family Planning. Certainly it is not the whole answer to all the health and economic problems of the Negro people, yet pregnancy spacing will do much towards general welfare improvement, and is a major step towards health and happiness for a greater number of people. . . .

Those of us who believe that the benefits of Family Planning, as a vital key to the elimination of human waste, must reach all groups of the population, also believe that a double effort must be made to extend this program as a public health measure to Negroes whose need is proportionately greater than other groups.[20]

Nothing in Dorothy's speech on that or any other day suggests she endorsed birth control as a means of eliminating damaged Negro fetuses or phasing out the black race. Her overarching goal was to uplift the race, not eliminate it. Nonetheless she took some heat. "Catholics were horrified when Dr. Dorothy Ferebee (AKA) publicly advocated birth-control for Negro masses," wrote the *Chicago Defender* columnist Charlie Cherokee.[21]

The ideological debate over a woman's right to control her sexuality has been going strong since Margaret Sanger was arrested in 1914 for mailing copies of her magazine, the *Woman Rebel*, which included birth control information. Ten days after Sanger opened the country's first birth control clinic in Brooklyn in 1916, the police shut it down. She was arrested, tried, and convicted. There is no doubt that Sanger, a woman Dorothy knew and admired, flirted with eugenics, a field that had not yet been discredited by the horrors of the Holocaust. But Sanger parted company with those who thought the "better stock" of the population should have more babies and the "feebleminded" should have fewer. She thought *all* women should be able to control their reproduction. "Women were aware that they could not continue to produce high-quality babies if they had a large family. That was why middle-class women used contraception and poor women demanded it," wrote Carole R. McCann in her 1994 book, *Birth Control Politics in the United States.*[22]

What was true was the existence of a racial disconnect between whites and blacks over family planning. Dorothy was aware that some African American women suspected birth control was a way for whites to foist "race suicide" on them and that some feared birth control would impair their sexual function. White family planning activists considered those concerns "the irrational fears of a backward race," wrote McCann. However, in minimizing those fears, white birth control supporters were being "willfully blind to the contours of racial history that made such fears rational."[23]

Dorothy was in good company among the members of her race when it came to her support of birth control. In 1943 Planned Parenthood's Division of Negro Service endorsed contraceptives for the nation's 13 million blacks. Sanger formed a National Negro Advisory Council to assist Planned Parenthood in an educational campaign about family planning and contraception in the black community. Among the members of that council were Dorothy, Dr. Paul Cornely of Howard, Walter White, Dr. M. O. Bousfield, Mary Church Terrell, W. E. B. Du Bois, sociologist E. Franklin Frazier, journalist Claude Barnett, and the Reverend Adam Clayton Powell Jr.[24]

Even a high-status woman like Dorothy was not immune from race discrimination. After inviting her to speak at the annual Planned Parenthood meeting in 1942, Florence Rose, Sanger's assistant, tried to reserve a room for her at either New York's Shelton Hotel or the Waldorf-Astoria. In a letter to Sanger, Rose related, "I ran up smack against the fact that they won't accept a Negro! . . . They suggested I tell her that 'no space' was available." Sanger's sister, Nan, saved the day by allowing Dorothy to stay in her apartment while she took a hotel room. More potential embarrassment lurked. Another staffer contacted Planned Parenthood's board member Dr. Richard N. Pierson "to ask if Dr. Ferebee should receive an invitation to the Reception preceding the Dinner, and happened to mention to Dr. Pierson that Dr. Ferebee was so light in color, and Dr. Pierson, God bless him, replied in heat: 'I don't care if she's as black as the Ace of Spades! She comes, and I'll be honored to have her sit right next to me!' "[25]

Besides her civic activities, Dorothy was rehired at the Howard University Health Clinic in 1941, working as a part-time assistant to Dr. Cornely. She would hold the post until 1949, when she became the acting medical director of the health service, eventually becoming director and remaining so until her retirement in 1968. Until she became a full-time employee, she earned about three thousand dollars a year (equal to about $28,900 today) to supplement income from the private practice she ran out of her home, where standard charges for an office visit were two dollars and for a house call three dollars.[26]

Dorothy increased her involvement with the NCNW. She became a contributing editor for the NCNW house organ, the *Aframerican Woman's Journal*.[27] Her growing prominence within the NCNW hierarchy put her front and center in the media spotlight. She was in Portland, Maine, on June 3, 1944, for the launching of the first Liberty Ship bearing the name of a black woman, the *Harriet Tubman*, named for the fearless leader of the Underground Railroad. Dorothy may have felt a special connection to the occasion given her ancestors' escape from slavery with the help of the railroad's conductors. The NCNW pledged to raise two million dollars by selling war bonds to pay for the ship, which gave it naming rights.[28] The government built 2,711 of these ships during the war. Franklin Roosevelt called them "ugly ducklings," but they were reliable workhorses that ferried men and supplies across the ocean.[29] How the ship looked wasn't important; the fact that the NCNW could name one was yet another sign Bethune's organization was becoming increasingly influential.

The beautiful, sunny June day of the launch was dulled by the absence of Bethune, who had been hospitalized for asthma. But the NCNW rear guard—Dorothy, Vivian Carter Mason, Jeanetta Welch Brown, and Mary Church Terrell—were there to represent their ailing founder.[30] In a prepared speech at a luncheon following the launch, Dorothy called Harriet Tubman "a challenge to all American Womanhood." As always, Dorothy implored women to be their best selves long before labels like "women's liberation," "feminism," or "womanism" existed: "We have the importantly dual task of holding the resources on the home front and of guiding the country through this turbulent period."[31]

Mixed with Dorothy's indefatigable energy and good intentions was her desire to be noticed by her heroine, Eleanor Roosevelt. She could not resist sending the first lady a quick note: "I just thought you would be interested in knowing our approach to the christening of the 'S.S. Harriet Tubman.' Experiences like this are heartening!" She included a copy of her speech and a newspaper clipping about the event.[32] Mrs. Roosevelt sent a polite thank you through her secretary.[33]

In August 1944 diplomats met at Dumbarton Oaks in Washington to outline a plan for world peace through the creation of the United Nations. FDR and Secretary of State Edward R. Stettinius Jr. chose a seven-member delegation to the first UN Conference in San Francisco, on April 25, 1945. One woman was chosen, but there were no blacks.[34] On April 12, 1945, just three months after his fourth inauguration, FDR died of a massive stroke at his vacation cottage in Warm Springs, Georgia. The first official decision made by President Harry S. Truman was to announce that the UN Conference would go on as planned.[35]

There was intense lobbying on the part of the NCNW to send a black representative to the Conference.[36] Dorothy recalled Bethune being chosen as a delegate, but she was incorrect;[37] Bethune was a "consultant" with no power other than persuasion. The State Department selected a number of consultants representing various special interest groups. The NAACP lobbied to be included, and Walter White, Du Bois, and Bethune were chosen to represent the group.[38]

Dorothy attended the conference, courtesy of Bethune, who insisted she be allowed to go along as her personal physician. Dorothy had been treating Bethune, who was not a healthy woman, since 1940.[39] Bethune was certainly no taller than 5'4" and was heavy, with high blood pressure, asthma, and swollen ankles that were probably indicative of looming heart failure. She was not an easy patient, as Dorothy found out the hard way. In a letter to a Chicago doctor who also had treated Bethune, Dorothy wrote, "In spite of your very strict diet instructions, she now carries 164 pounds. The explanation of it came this morning when she confessed that she has been 'stealing' sweets, cakes and little delicacies which some of her admirers have been smuggling into her. I assure you that this situation will be corrected."[40]

Whether Bethune needed a personal physician along for the ride to San Francisco is open to question. In a speech to a church group in California, Bethune insisted she did: "I could not have come here without her."[41] The Pittsburgh Courier reported the arrangement more irreverently: "Dr. Dorothy Boulding Ferebee also along to see that La Bethune metabols okay."[42] Beyond taking care of Bethune's health needs, Dorothy also served as her secretary at the conference.[43]

Dorothy boarded the Golden Arrow, which pulled out of Union Station in Washington at 10:50 on Thursday night, April 19, 1945, for the three-and-a-half-day trip to San Francisco, via Chicago, where she changed trains and met up with Bethune. In her excitement she forgot her briefcase and spent her first few hours aboard the train scrounging around for paper.[44] She scored a small notebook (how or from whom, she did not say), about the size of a steno pad, and used it to create a 152-page record of her trip.

The Golden Arrow arrived in Chicago on April 20 at 5:20 in the afternoon, an hour late, necessitating a mad dash to catch up with "Mrs. Bethune," as Dorothy referred to her in her diary, despite the fact that they were NCNW colleagues with a longtime doctor-patient relationship. They boarded a special reserved State Department train for the conference-goers. On Saturday, April 21, after a late and hearty breakfast of fruit, cream of wheat, ham, five eggs, muffins, and coffee, she read Psalm 91.[45]

Bethune also recorded the journey. In a letter addressed to "My dear Children" and intended for her staff in Washington, she described a decadent few days with Dorothy: "We have been in our negligees since Friday night, lolling in and out of bed, reading, resting, eating. The food is luscious—abundant and beautifully prepared. The waiters are outdoing themselves bringing not only all we order but everything we don't."[46]

At eight in the morning on Sunday, April 22, the train stopped briefly at Ogden, Utah, where Dorothy found the weather "cold & sunny and altogether invigorating." Stepping off the train, she popped a letter in the mail to Claude to tell him she and Bethune were headed to the UN extravaganza. It reached him in the South Pacific on May 1, prompting his letter to Walter White in which he commented, "some stuff, eh?" about his wife's trip. The letter may have signaled that Dorothy loved her husband more than she let on, or it may have been her way of rubbing his nose in her latest professional triumph.

That night the Bethune train suite became a salon for the few blacks on board, including White, Du Bois, and executives from the *Chicago Defender*. "Everyone is much excited over the history making aspect of this great SF parley," Dorothy wrote.[47] This journal entry, confirming the appearance of White and Du Bois at the gathering two days after the train left Chicago, calls into question the veracity of a charge Bethune reportedly made: that once she boarded the train in Chicago she did not interact with either of the men again.[48]

Whatever bonhomie existed among the NAACP consultants that night was short-lived anyway; they lobbed charges and countercharges at one another during the conference. Bethune accused the NAACP men of elbowing her out of the way for press attention. White sniffed that the only reason she was chosen to be a consultant in the first place was because she was a friend of Eleanor Roosevelt and that she had no loyalty to the NAACP.[49] A *San Francisco News* columnist, P. L. Prattis wrote, "Squabble, squabble, squabble—white folks squabbling among themselves privately and colored folks hiring halls to air their squabbles."[50]

First thing Monday morning, April 23, the train pulled into Oakland, across the bay from San Francisco. Ferries waited to take the weary travelers on a twenty-minute ride across the water, where an honor guard of soldiers, sailors, and marines awaited them. "The whole city, teeming with activity and people, is gay under bunting and national flags atop every building of importance," Dorothy wrote. She and Bethune stayed at the Madam C. J. Walker House at 2066 Pine Street, a white three-story building with steps leading up from the street that were so steep, it's a wonder Bethune was able to negotiate them.[51] The Walker House was established by the millionaire entrepreneur who launched a hair-growing enterprise. It was a place where African American women, new to San Francisco, could find clean, safe, welcoming lodging.[52] It was illegal in California for hotels to refuse to rent rooms to black guests, but choice rooms were scooped up fast during the conference, with the likes of Nelson Rockefeller enjoying the luxury of the St. Francis and Secretary of State Stettinius staying at the elegant Fairmont.[53]

At night there were theatrical productions, parties, and dinners. Bethune and White buried the hatchet long enough on April 29 to attend a tea at the home of the regional NAACP director that included Dorothy and her good friends, Howard University president Mordecai Johnson and his wife, Anna Ethelyn.[54]

At 4:30 in the afternoon on April 25, in a driving rainstorm, the world's first UN Conference opened inside the ornate San Francisco Opera House. A military honor guard marched up the center aisle beneath the gold sunburst chandelier, past the 3,500 red plush seats. Dorothy sat in row CC, seat 14 beside her patient at all times during the plenary sessions.[55]

There was a moment of silence, a tribute to Roosevelt, and a radio greeting from President Truman.[56] Work began in earnest the next day, April 26. The UN Conference provided Dorothy with an unparalleled opportunity to learn, observe history in the making, and get close to Bethune without having any rivals tugging at her elbow. If she did want to succeed the NCNW president someday, the conference was her chance to break out of the pack and show Bethune her mettle.

It was a star-studded event. Delegates from forty-six nations attended, as did Nelson Rockefeller, then an assistant secretary of state, Adlai Stevenson, Alger Hiss, and the journalist Walter Lippmann.[57] Future president John F. Kennedy reported on the event for the Hearst newspaper chain.[58] Dorothy rubbed elbows with luminaries like Vyacheslav Molotov, the Soviet foreign minister for whom the Molotov cocktail was named.[59] Her notes, on every facet of the conference, show her fascination with Jawaharlal Nehru's sister, Madame V. L. Pandit, leader of the Congress Party in India, who wore "a beautiful black taffeta sari striped horizontally in silver threads and bordered top and bottom. . . . She speaks flawless English, smokes endless cigarettes and converses in a low-pitched, beautiful voice."[60] When a speaker gave remarks in French, as several of them did, Dorothy took notes in French, demonstrating a surprising level of proficiency in a language she had not formally studied since she attended Simmons College twenty-five years earlier.

Dorothy would always remember where she was at exactly 5:45 in the evening, Pacific Standard Time, on Friday, April 28, when two of the delegates caused pandemonium in the Opera House by holding up a newspaper with a foot-high headline: "Nazi's Quit." "The audience clapped, shouted, cameras clicked and diplomats shook hands. Molotov rose to quiet the house," Dorothy recorded in her journal. She and Bethune were still in San Francisco for V-E Day on May 8, which she called "the magnificent day of unconditional surrender." She rejoiced in the fact the Capitol dome and the Statue of Liberty would be illuminated for the first time since the bombing of Pearl Harbor, but she made no mention in her journal that her husband was still in harm's way in the South Pacific, where the war would continue for another three months.[61]

After the war Claude returned to Washington long enough to remove his once state-of-the-art dental office equipment. "He pulled up stakes, moved his furniture and equipment—moved everything—to New York, and left me there in the house on Second Street with the empty area where his dental office had been," Dorothy recalled. Although the forlorn space with its outlines of her husband's missing furniture must have been a harsh reminder of the failure of her marriage, she said she paid it no mind. "I didn't allow this to disturb me, because the children were here and required my attention and spare time."[62]

Claude lost no time building a new life for himself. He set up a bachelor pad in Harlem and covered the walls of his apartment with watercolors he had painted in the South Pacific. He also displayed his old fencing mask and foils as decorative art; in a feature story in the New York Amsterdam News in 1949, he said he hoped to find time to take up the sport again. The reporters noted incorrectly that Claude "was made Battalion Dental Surgeon of the 93rd Infantry Division's 318th Medical Battalion with the rank of major."[63]

Captain Ferebee desperately wanted to be Major Ferebee, but pervasive racial bigotry in the military got in the way. As late as 1945 White intervened with the commander of the 93rd to get Captain Claude Ferebee promoted, but to no avail.[64] His separation papers from the army, compiled on February 19, 1946, at Camp Beale, California, indicate he was still a captain when he was discharged from active duty.[65] Yet for the rest of his life, Claude's children and grandchildren referred to him (usually behind his back when he was being particularly rigid) as "the Major." In a photograph taken after the war, he wears the gold oak leaf insignia of a major but does not have the same regulation leaf cluster insignia on his hat, adding to the mystery. His grandchildren were under the impression that he became a major in the army reserve after the war, but efforts to confirm that through Claude's available military records were not successful.

Life in postwar Harlem was vastly different from what it had been during the heady Harlem Renaissance. "When Harlem's soldiers came home from World War II, they found their neighborhoods in ruins, with heroin stalking the avenues," wrote Jonathan Gill in his history of Harlem. "By any measure—poverty, racism, joblessness, health, education or simply the sight of block after block of burned-out, boarded-up buildings—the Negro Mecca increasingly seemed beyond redemption."[66] It was against this backdrop that in the summer of 1946 Claude opened a dental office at 745 St. Nicholas Avenue in a four-story brick townhouse. It was convenient to patients, being smack up against the 145th Street subway station. There was no sign now of Madeline Dugger or any other steady woman in his life, including Dorothy. In the same 1949 newspaper profile in which he is identified as a major, Claude is described as the father of eighteen-year-old twins but not as the husband of one of the most prominent women in the country.[67]

Although a married man until 1950, Claude was openly stepping out. In March 1949 he ventured downtown to Hunter College on Manhattan's tony Upper East Side to listen to the Howard University Choir. At his side was Bobbie Branche, the manager of the national office of the NAACP. Branche was an energetic, popular woman with a beautiful wardrobe who was often featured in the social columns of the black newspapers.[68] Although she never married, she was never at a loss for the company of interesting, accomplished men. "A man like Claude Ferebee was a good example," said former NAACP field secretary Mildred Bond Roxborough, who knew them both.[69]

Not long after Claude left Washington, Dorothy, too, moved to New York City. In February 1948 she bought a house at 114–15 176th Street in the chic Addisleigh Park section of St. Albans, Queens, for $7,927. Although still married, she purchased the home in her own name.[70] Why she decamped for New York when her professional life and community service activities were all in Washington is unclear; other than to follow Claude, there is no rational explanation.

Dorothy had stellar neighbors. Baseball great Jackie Robinson, who integrated Major League Baseball and made history when he joined the Brooklyn Dodgers in 1947, and his wife, Rachel, lived nearby, as did Lena Horne, Count Basie, and Ella Fitzgerald.[71] Dorothy's house was a large, lovely, two-and-a-half-story 1920s Tudor Revival, made of cement stucco.[72] Her relocation to St. Albans, in which she included her ever-present mother, could have been part of a grand plan to reunite with Claude. If so, it was a pipe dream. J. Russell Eberhardt, one of their son's best friends, described the Ferebee home with both Ferebees in it as "two generals in one house."[73] Word on the street was the marriage was over.[74] In 1950 their relationship would implode; the catalyst was an event so awful neither one of them ever could have imagined it.

14 Every Bone in the Body

Uplifting the race began at home. Dorothy's twins met Eleanor Roosevelt when they were four. They were members of the exclusive Jack and Jill Club, an invitation-only club for privileged black children.[1] There, Dolly participated in a fund-raising drive to feed Chinese orphans during World War II, while her brother avoided doing anything involving the group.[2]

Just as upper-class whites in the postwar years made sure their offspring had all the social advantages, black doctors, lawyers, and college professors wanted their kids to have the best. Although the twins' friends sometimes painted Dorothy as an absentee parent, when it came to launching her children on the road to success, she approached the task with gusto. She enrolled them in the "right" schools and introduced them to the "right" friends. When Dolly was still in pigtails her mother set her sights on Mordecai Johnson's son, William "Timmy" Johnson, as the ideal husband for her daughter. "I was attracted to her," admitted Johnson, sixty years after Dolly's death. But with Dolly and Timmy as close as brother and sister, it is understandable why the relationship was never to be. Johnson remembered Dorothy and his own mother as the equivalent of modern-day "soccer moms" who "made sure we were doing something all the time."[3]

That "something" included developing their intellectual skills. Dorothy constantly drilled her children on their multiplication tables. "Three times two," Dorothy would shout over her shoulder, half-paying attention to the road while roaring up to Annapolis in the Oldsmobile. When one of the twins shouted "Six," she would yell back, "Times eight" and if "Forty-eight" came from the backseat, she would keep pushing. The game occupied them until the twins were safely deposited for the summer at the red clapboard house in Highland Beach rented by the Beckleys. Thanks to his mother's incessant testing on all subjects, "Thurston could list every bone in the body," recalled Timmy Johnson.[4]

Dorothy wanted the twins to be well-rounded individuals. Dolly took ballet lessons; learned to swim, sail, and water-ski at Highland Beach; rode horses, played tennis, and joined her mother and brother on the ice at the skating rink. She wore adorable, hand-made Halloween costumes, perhaps stitched by her father, given Claude's skill with an embroidery needle. One Halloween Dolly went Trick-or-Treating as a fairy queen, and on another as an American Indian girl. Buzzy loved downhill skiing, singing, and photography.

Their mother also addressed the twins' spiritual needs. She and the children regularly attended mass at St. Mary's Episcopal Church in Foggy Bottom, Washington's first black Episcopal church, dating back to 1867 and today a National Historic Landmark.[5] Dorothy would worship there her entire life.

But beyond acting as the architect of the twins' futures, there is a question about how involved Dorothy was in their day-to-day lives. "Dr. Dorothy Ferebee was all about her career. The kids were always dropped off somewhere," remembered Aurelia Roberts Brooks, one of Dolly's closest friends. "Dolly spent most of her time growing up in my house." Brooks described Claude as the baby-sitter and house-husband. "I have vivid memories of him on the front porch, wearing jodhpurs. He was so handsome and as sweet and kind a man as could be."[6]

Claude was no less a stickler than his wife for putting the children through rigorous mental exercises in his fine cars, at one point a gray Hudson. "Dr. Doctor Ferebee," as Claude was called by his children's friends (Dorothy was "Mrs. Doctor"), "believed in talking about ideas, not gossip or things," recalled John Beckley.[7]

Timmy Johnson's and John Beckley's families were also straight out of the Talented Tenth. Mordecai Johnson was president of Howard University for thirty-four years.[8] Timmy, academically gifted, was a Howard-educated engineer who would spend his professional life at NASA. Mordecai's daughter, Anna Faith, attended prep school with Dolly. All three Beckley boys ran with the Ferebee children. The oldest, Edgar, was born in 1928 and became an engineer; John was born in 1930 and trained as a pharmacist; the youngest, Charles, was born in 1932 and worked in government. Their father, Dr. Edgar R. Beckley, was on the medical school faculty with Dorothy. His wife, Howard graduate Dorothy Pelham Beckley, was a teacher; her mother was Gabrielle Lattimore, a white concert pianist from England who attended Oberlin College. Their maternal grandfather was Robert Pelham, a Howard-educated lawyer who was the powerful editor of DC's premier black newspaper, the *Washington Tribune*. Pelham's other daughter was Sara Pelham Speaks, a New York lawyer who ran against Adam Clayton Powell on both the Republican and Democratic tickets during his first race for Congress in 1944.[9]

From his branch on this eclectic family tree, John Beckley struggled with his own demons. He had a successful career as a pharmacist and later became a sculptor. There was a strong streak of nonconformity running through him, which what may have led him to Champlain College rather than Princeton, toward which his good grades and his guidance counselors were pointing him.[10] Once he got to Champlain, one of a number of non-selective colleges slapped together after the war to accommodate returning GIs, he wasted time playing pool and the bongos and being the local bad boy. He was hardly the best role model for Thurston, who enjoyed being the life of the party and idolized Beckley. Years later Thurston, Beckley, Johnson, and two other friends, Sammy Singleton, also from their neighborhood, and Russ Eberhardt, a police detective from New York, formed their own clique, "the Filthy Five." Like Frank Sinatra's legendary Rat Pack of hipster movie stars who lived on the edge, the Five were Talented Tenth guys who worked hard and partied hard.

After graduating from Dorothy Howard's Garden of Children, the twins went to the Lucretia Mott School at 4th and W Streets NW, named after the nineteenth-century Quaker abolitionist and women's rights' activist.[11] Given its proximity to the university, Mott's student body was populated by the children of Howard professors, dropped off by their parents on their way to work. Classes were offered up to the sixth grade, after which the twins went to Banneker Junior High on Euclid Street between Georgia and Sherman Avenues NW. They stayed until the end of their freshman year in June 1945. The school was named for Benjamin Banneker, an eighteenth-century free black man who was a self-educated astronomer and one of the surveyors of the land that would become Washington DC.[12]

For all their parents' tutoring, the twins were not the strongest students, although Dolly showed promise. She had a lovely singing voice, got straight A's in music, and aspired to perform on stage. Like their father, both twins had aptitude for drawing.[13] Unlike his sister, Thurston's marks at Banneker were nothing to write home about; he got B's in music and physical education, C's in Latin and math, and a D in science.[14]

Most summers, especially when they were teenagers, the twins and their friends congregated at Highland Beach. The forty acres of land along the Chesapeake Bay, less than an hour from Washington, had been purchased in 1893 by the son of Frederick Douglass, who built a home there and named it Twin Oaks. Before long it lured weary black professionals from the nation's capital and became known as a summer playground for the African American elite.[15] Highland Beach was where John Beckley played cards with Thurgood Marshall and his aunt Sara when he was eleven. It was where he dated Joan Bunche, the daughter of Ralph Bunche, a United Nations undersecretary and Nobel Prize winner. It was at Highland Beach where Edgar Beckley taught Aurelia Roberts to drive in his father's 1936 black Ford. Thurston Ferebee met and fell in love with Carol Phillips, who once had been Timmy Johnson's heartthrob, at Highland Beach.[16] Thurston and Carol would marry in 1951.

The beach could have been dubbed "the Howard University summer annex." Dr. Montague Cobb, head of the anatomy department, taught Beckley to row a boat on the bay there. Dr. Carnot Evans of the medical school faculty taught the kids to water-ski. Dr. Robert C. McMurdock from the dental school had croquet matches on his lawn. Dr. Charles Drew, a professor of surgery and a surgeon at Freedmen's Hospital, famous for inventing a method of preserving blood plasma, vacationed in the area.[17] Charlene Drew Jarvis, his daughter, loved her summers there. "The place made us feel special," she said. "It insulated us against the racial discrimination."[18]

Attending boarding school was on the established path for many of the children of Washington's African American elite, but Dolly did not want to travel that route. Aurelia Roberts Brooks said Dolly protested against going, but Dorothy insisted on it as there was no one at home to supervise them.[19] Thurston, on the other hand, was excited about boarding school. The boys in his crowd were going, and he wanted to be among them.[20]

Sending the children away to school appealed to both parents. Claude bristled at the discriminatory treatment and the segregation that permeated Washington life, and Dorothy agreed: "We were both anxious to get them out of the city." So, in typical fashion, she set about conducting an in-depth investigation of the most prestigious prep schools. "I studied all the educational material that I could gather and found a school to my liking."[21] She wrote a letter on Dolly's behalf to the headmaster of the Northfield School for Girls in May 1945, but the class for the 1945–46 school year was already filled.[22] Dorothy went to Plan B: she deposited the twins in the Altaraz School in western Massachusetts, run by Dr. Isaac M. Altaraz, known for an unorthodox approach to education called "character training,"[23] which required frequent rest periods and less rigidity in the school curricula. It included dance programs for restless children, public speaking for children who interrupted their teachers, leadership clubs for delinquents, and puppet-making for class clowns.[24]

The Altaraz School had to have been Dorothy's idea; one cannot imagine Captain Ferebee having faith in an educational system that relied on more rest and fewer rules. The Altaraz program did not work for the Ferebee children, who clearly needed more structure. Although Dorothy would puff her children's academic achievements in her oral history, saying, "They both did very well," that was not so.[25] The twins could not grasp Latin, and without Dorothy around to drill numbers into their heads, they could not fathom algebra either. Neither completed the requirements necessary to receive final grades in Latin II and Algebra II.[26]

They had barely settled into Altaraz when Dorothy renewed her efforts to get them into the prestigious Northfield/Mount Hermon school. This time Dolly played the dutiful daughter. She wrote a valiant letter to the director of Northfield in December 1945 asking to be admitted to the junior class, perhaps with her mother dictating over her shoulder. In beautiful script Dolly wrote, "My purpose in life is to become a doctor like my mother and I know Northfield will teach me to study and to concentrate so that my college career will be successfull [sic] and my studies easier to grasp."[27]

The Northfield Seminary for Young Ladies opened in 1879. The nearby Mount Hermon School for Boys opened in 1881.[28] The schools merged in 1971.[29] Nestled in bucolic western Massachusetts, the gorgeous Northfield campus, which sat on the eastern bank of the Connecticut River, was straight out of a Hollywood movie set. From its earliest days Northfield and Mount Hermon had multiracial student bodies.[30]

In February 1946 Dorothy was in full-court press mode with the admissions committee. She enlisted Dorothy Height, then on staff at the national YWCA and a Mary Bethune protégée, and E. A. Christian, rector of St. Mary's Episcopal Church, for recommendations.[31] On the afternoon of April 3, 1946, Dorothy and her daughter arrived at Northfield for a meeting.[32] They were absolutely charming. A faculty member wrote:

D. F. a bright-eyed, slight and eager little Negro girl, came with her fine-looking doctor mother. Both were dressed with taste, seemed to be people of intellectual interests. Mrs. or Dr. (medical) Ferebee is a Simmons graduate who took her medical training at Tufts. Her husband is a dentist. . . . To me she seemed like an integrated person of intelligence, judgments & good-will. D. wants to go to college, possibly to Calif. & then on to medical school. She likes to study & likes to sing. Would fit in well to our life here, I'm sure.[33]

Dorothy plunked down a ten-dollar deposit toward her daughter's tuition and room and board, which cost anywhere from $550 to $800 a year, depending on a girl's financial circumstances. (Today tuition at Northfield/Mount Hermon costs approximately $50,000 a year.)[34] Although Dorothy and Claude were still married when their daughter applied to Northfield on January 25, 1946, Dorothy told the school she would be solely responsible for her daughter's bills.[35]

There were 514 students at Northfield the year Dolly entered, a handful of them African Americans.[36] Mira B. Wilson, the Northfield principal at the time, referred to the few "colored students" on campus as "a real asset." She observed that "only one family . . . has withdrawn its daughter's application for entrance on seeing colored girls on our campus." That being said, even for an enlightened school Northfield reflected its time. Black girls were assigned to room together and, as noted by Wilson in a journal article, "it [was] customary for them to be invited for the social occasions between our two schools by colored boys."[37]

In short order, perhaps because she never wanted to be there in the first place, Dolly went off the academic rails at Northfield, never earning another A for the rest of her high school career. The school focused heavily on religion; Bible study was part of the curriculum. "The school was very conservative with religious chapel services every day," recalled U.S. District Judge Anna Diggs Taylor, who went to Northfield with Dolly.[38] Unlike her mother and Uncle Ruffin, who could rattle off the Psalms like the days of the week, Dolly stumbled through Bible class with C's and D's. She got D's in modern European history and a D in geometry.[39] Forced to repeat the half-year of Latin she never finished at Altaraz and doing poorly in geometry, she was not promoted to the senior class at the end of the 1947 school year.[40] Aurelia Roberts Brooks thought sending Dolly to boarding school was "a disaster. When she came home from school, she crossed her legs and showed me how she learned to smoke."[41]

When Dolly returned to school in the fall of 1947, it was with both parents in tow.[42] It didn't help. No matter how much pressure Dorothy and Claude put on their daughter, she still had no aptitude for the rigors of Northfield. Dolly muddled through another two years. But Northfield wasn't a total debacle. Known as "Dotty" on campus, she was popular. This was hardly surprising; during her short life Dolly was considered by those who knew her to be a sweet, kind, and gentle soul. Under her senior picture in *Highlights*, the Northfield yearbook, was this description: "Versatile . . . warm singing voice . . . dancing feet . . . joyous heart . . . sweet perfumes . . . exotic jewelry . . . lollypops . . . hordes of correspondents . . . 'Hi girl' . . . faultless complexion . . . tip-tilted nose . . . tales well told . . . carefree and sweet . . . Dotty."[43]

"She was a little overweight, a little buxom, but quite beautiful," recalled Judge Taylor. The Northfield girls did not have much chance to make contact with boys outside of occasional school dances with Mount Hermon, five miles down the road. Taylor remembered Dorothy Junior— "We didn't call her Dolly then"—being quite popular with the few boys who were in the picture.[44]

Dolly excelled in anything musical at Northfield. She sang in an elite campus singing group and played an instrument in a quartet. She was a graceful dancer. In the May 1949 "Tree Day" festivities, a spring tradition on campus, she performed a dance solo to Jacob Gade's tango "Jalousie" as her mother watched.[45] The school principal later called Dolly's performance "the loveliest we have ever had."[46]

Dorothy had hoped to deposit Buzzy at Mount Hermon, where he could have kept watch over his sister, but he ended up at Tilton. Perhaps he wanted to be near Beckley, and Dorothy figured if Tilton was good enough for Dr. Edgar Beckley's son, it was good enough for hers.[47] Tilton was ninety-five miles up the road from Northfield. It was founded in 1845 as a coed high school, closely connected to the Methodist Church. In 1939 it became a school for boys. The campus centered around Tilton Hall, the mansion where Maj. Charles Tilton, the town's and school's namesake, lived after returning from the California Gold Rush.[48] Like Northfield, the school was exclusive and expensive. Tuition and room and board was $975 a year when Thurston enrolled, and the year he graduated it had gone up to $1,200. (Today it costs $49,750 a year to be educated at Tilton.)[49] There was no segregation within the walls of Tilton, even back in 1946. The African American student population was small, a half-dozen out of about 150 boys who attended. Unlike at Northfield, there was no effort to assign rooms according to skin color.[50]

Thurston's grades at Tilton were abysmal. During the 1946–47 school year he was forced to repeat Latin II and Algebra II because, like his sister, he had not completed those courses at Altaraz. The second time around he flunked them both. Repeating his junior year did not help; he flunked chemistry in the first semester. His senior year was no better; he flunked French—the language in which his mother could write like a native twenty-five years after she had studied it—but managed to get a C– on the French makeup exam.[51]

While at Tilton, Thurston and Beckley had plenty of fun. They attended dances at the local high school (and got tossed out of a few) and in church basements around town. They took advantage of their central New Hampshire location to go skiing in the winter. If they felt like shooting pool, they took a taxi to Franklin, New Hampshire, about three miles away. If they felt like bowling, they went nine miles up the road to a bowling alley in Laconia. If they had a few bucks burning holes in their pockets they took a train to Boston for the weekend.[52]

Thurston gained a reputation as a "hail-fellow-well-met" at prep school, which stuck with him all his life. John Beckley blamed racism as much as anything else: "Here is a society that tells you at every turn you're nothing.

So why do you want to do anything but have a good time?"[53] The caption under Thurston's senior picture in *The Tower*, where he is referred to by his childhood nickname, Buzzy, largely reflects that philosophy: " 'Be-Bop' crazy . . . the Bronx is where his flame is burning . . . a smile for one and all . . . future dentist . . . 'You crack me up!' "[54]

Thurston was a good-looking young man. He was thin, with wavy brown hair, a medium-to-light complexion and dark, dreamy eyes. Unlike Dolly, who had her father's turned-up nose, his was longer and straighter, like Dorothy's, and his lips were like hers. In pictures in the Tilton yearbook Thurston looks frailer and younger than his classmates, even though he remained at the school an additional year. In adulthood his full height would be just over six feet and his weight would balloon to 250 pounds.

During the years the twins were at prep school Dorothy traveled extensively. In August 1947 she was the featured speaker at the annual convention of the National Medical Association in Los Angeles.[55] She joined Mary Bethune and Mordecai Johnson and others at a dinner at the Waldorf-Astoria in New York to honor Ralph Bunche in May 1949.[56] Wearing a black gown with a gold-dotted net bolero jacket over her shoulders, she joined the 5,300 guests who danced at Harry Truman's integrated inaugural ball on January 20, 1949, at the National Guard Armory in Washington.[57]

Thurston graduated from Tilton on Sunday, June 5, 1949. Temperatures all over New England were fair and warm.[58] From an academic standpoint the boarding school adventure was hardly a success for either Ferebee child. Thurston was ranked seventy-seven out of a class of eighty-five.[59] Dolly, who graduated from Northfield the following day, was also near the bottom of her class.[60]

Washington was no longer their home. Their father was ensconced in Harlem and their mother and grandmother were living in Dorothy's huge house in St. Albans. The St. Albans house became a coming-of-age playground for Thurston, Dolly, and their friends. There was a bedroom in the attic where Dolly and Beckley engaged in a few rudimentary romantic encounters. "She had a crush on me; I dated her, we went to a dance, to a movie," Beckley recalled. But their teenage sexual fumbling was not something Beckley bragged about. Like all of Thurston's friends, he respected Dolly. "She was a nice girl."[61]

Dorothy regularly commuted between New York and Washington, although on July 15, 1949, she was granted a medical license in New York. She opened an office in her home, as she had in Washington, advertising her services the way doctors did in those days, by placing her name and address under the "Physicians" listings in the 1950 Queens Yellow Pages.[62] But in 1949 fate intervened to prevent her from severing ties with Washington. Dr. Paul Cornely resigned as physician to Howard students, and that summer Dorothy was named acting director of the health service; her salary nearly doubled to six thousand dollars.[63] In Washington she was in charge of a staff of seven doctors, three nurses, a secretary, a clerk, and an attendant. Doctors at the university health service were charged with examining and medically clearing every new student at Howard as well as treating those who took ill. The professional staff was on call 24/7. Office hours at the health service, which was on the second floor of the school's gymnasium, were Monday through Friday from ten in the morning until four in the afternoon and from ten to noon on Saturdays.[64]

The summer the twins graduated from prep school, Dorothy threw an eighteenth birthday bash for them at her posh New York home. As the kids celebrated, the sounds of the bebop that Thurston loved—Charlie Parker, Dizzy Gillespie—played on their 78 RPM records, still in vogue in 1949, poured out of the open windows.[65] Just as the social comings and goings of Dorothy and Claude had been the staple of gossip columns in black papers of the 1920s and 1930s, so too were the frolics of the photogenic Ferebee twins in the 1940s. The party was a media event, with the *New York Age* referring to Dorothy's new home as "their swank Addisleigh Park residence."[66]

It would be the last summer of any true happiness for the Ferebees. Within six months Dolly would be dead, Thurston would spin out of control, Claude would be heartbroken, and it would be Dorothy who, as usual, would take charge and carry on.

15 A Matter for Grave Concern

As 1949 drew to a close, the legendary Mary McLeod Bethune was about to do the unthinkable: retire. For fourteen years Bethune and the National Council of Negro Women were synonymous. The idea that another woman might fill her shoes was sacrilege. Yet a number of them wanted to, including Dorothy; in fact so many of the NCNW's talented members coveted the top spot that they threatened to cause a leadership crisis. "It is obvious that the women are evincing no interest in any office except that of president," wrote Olivia S. Henry, chair of the nominating committee, to Bethune. "This is a matter for grave concern."[1]

As Bethune's physician since 1940, Dorothy knew the icon's health was giving out.[2] Other than Bethune's son, Dorothy was the only person listed as an emergency contact in the little telephone book Bethune carried.[3] For years she had been one of the NCNW president's many devoted followers, who called her "Mrs. Bethune" or "Ma Bethune" and whom she referred to as "my daughters."[4]

Dorothy was a child of privilege. Bethune's parents and most of her sixteen siblings had begun their lives as slaves. Born in South Carolina in 1875, near the end of Reconstruction, Bethune did not learn to read until she was eleven. She graduated from the Moody Bible Institute in Chicago after completing its two-year program in missionary training in 1895.[5] In 1904, with $1.50 in her pocket, she started the Daytona Normal and Industrial Training School for Negro Girls. To pay for teaching supplies she baked sweet potato pies that she peddled for a nickel apiece to workingmen and to tourists passing through Florida.[6] Within two years of opening her school, she had 250 students.[7] In 1929 the school merged with Cookman Institute to become the coeducational Bethune-Cookman College.

The two women shared certain traits: both had strong egos and a patrician bearing, and both loved dressing up. "So much so," in Bethune's case, according to her biographer, Joyce Hanson, "that even her most ardent admirers would later describe her as quite 'vain.'"[8] Their voices were nearly identical, with tight-lipped, upper-class inflections of speech. Dovey Johnson Roundtree, a Washington lawyer who was one of Bethune's many acolytes, once said, "I doubt that anyone who ever heard Dr. Bethune speak could forget her voice—a voice so musical and cultivated that it danced over sentences in the manner of a Shakespearean actor."[9]

Bethune and Dorothy were born into an appallingly racist society and were determined to change it. As racial segregation became legally entrenched at the turn of the twentieth century, "black women increasingly saw the importance of establishing a national organization to systematically address social segregation, economic inequality, and political disfranchisement," wrote Hanson. One of the earliest of these organizations, the National Association of Colored Women (NACW), was formed in 1896. Bethune went to her first NACW meeting at Hampton Institute in Virginia in 1912 to seek support for her school. She was impressed by the women there and worked her way to the top, becoming its president in 1924, a post she held until 1928.[10]

Bethune had one son, Dorothy had her twins, and both women fretted about the limited time they spent with them. In her 1964 biography of Bethune, Rackham Holt (the pen name of Margaret Van Vechten Saunders Holt) wrote, "This phenomenon is fairly common among leaders of causes, who sometimes suffer pangs and misgivings that perhaps their own offspring may have been sacrificed to the larger good by being deprived of intimate, exclusive, parental attention."[11] Holt should have written "intimate, exclusive, *maternal* attention." Powerful women have always faced more criticism than powerful men for putting their career ahead of their children; Dorothy and Bethune were no exceptions.

By the 1930s Bethune was the most visible black woman in America. President Roosevelt placed her in charge of the Division of Negro Affairs in the New Deal's National Youth Administration, where she worked from 1935 until it was disbanded in 1943.[12] She was already sixty when she founded the National Council of Negro Women.[13] Among those sitting at the founding table were Charlotte Hawkins Brown, president of the Palmer

Memorial Institute, a black prep school in North Carolina, and Mary Church Terrell, one of the founders of the NACW. Olyve Jeter from the race relations department of the Federated Council of Churches and Addie Hunton of Alpha Kappa Alpha were there. So were Mabel Keaton Staupers of the National Association of Graduate Nurses; Cecelia Cabiness Saunders, executive secretary of the YWCA of New York City; and Daisy Lampkin, field secretary of the NAACP. Bethune told them, "My appeal to you is to begin to think of the big things done by past leadership who dared to stand for right and let us fight today with Negro womanhood in mind."[14]

The thirty midwives who braved the cold December day to be at the birth of the NCNW voted unanimously to follow Bethune and her dream, but not all of them enthusiastically agreed it was the way to go. (Dorothy wasn't at the meeting.) The most vocal naysayer was Charlotte Hawkins Brown: "I . . . feel that there are too many organizations. There is a need for a Council or Conference but none for an organization." Brown's doubts were echoed by the formidable Terrell: "Theoretically I believe in everything that has been said. But I can't see how this organization can help." Left unspoken was the fear that Bethune's new organization might steal the thunder and the dues-paying members from other black women's groups, particularly the NACW. Despite any misgivings, however, a motion was made and seconded to create the National Council of Negro Women. Terrell wisely nominated Bethune as its first president, and the others agreed.[15] The NCNW incorporated on July 25, 1936, listing the office of Howard University's dean of women, Lucy D. Slowe, as its official address.[16]

Bethune was devoted to her new venture. She rode roughshod over her followers for dues, but two years after she founded the NCNW, there was all of $18.25 in the treasury. In 1937 she held out hope a million women would one day stand under the NCNW umbrella. That year the NCNW received a shot in the arm from Eleanor Roosevelt, the guest of honor at the council's annual dinner at the Harlem YWCA, who turned out to be an excellent draw; 250 women had to be turned away at the door and there were 300 inside. By the early 1940s Bethune claimed to have 800,000 members.[17] When Dorothy was elected president in 1949, the NCNW said it represented 850,000 women through its affiliated member groups.[18] However, if there had been that many dues-paying members Bethune wouldn't have been constantly scrounging around for money.

In 1927, the year before FDR became governor of New York, Bethune was invited to the Roosevelt home on East 65th Street in New York City, where Mrs. Roosevelt hosted a luncheon for thirty-five women leaders. Bethune was there as president of the National Association of Colored Women. She was the only African American invited to the lunch.[19]

As the story goes, when it came time to eat, Bethune caught the sharp eye of the president's mother, Sara Delano, who noticed the southern women casting anxious glances at Bethune, fearful they would be stuck sitting next to her. Sara Delano took Bethune's arm and plopped her down next to Mrs. Roosevelt, to the delight of the servants and the chagrin of the jealous guests.[20] Whether it delighted her daughter-in-law is not certain. In his book about the Roosevelt women, Joseph E. Persico writes, "Upon meeting Mary McLeod Bethune, at the time the nation's most distinguished black educator, Eleanor found herself uncomfortable giving the woman a peck on the cheek."[21]

Eleanor Roosevelt came late to the cause of black equality. "I was more than 15 and in Europe [before] I actually met a Negro," she once wrote.[22] But whatever racial biases she had to overcome to open her heart to Bethune were conquered. Some observers have credited Mrs. Roosevelt as the force behind her husband's appointment of Bethune to the National Youth Administration, a New Deal agency created within the Works Progress Administration to establish educational and training programs for the young and unemployed.[23] Bethune was named director of its Division of Negro Affairs in 1936.[24] In that position she brought together high-level blacks who worked in the Roosevelt administration to form the Federal Council of Negro Affairs. They met informally in her apartment on Friday nights and became so influential in New Deal politics they came to be known as FDR's "Black Cabinet."[25]

Bethune was a regular White House visitor and was among the mourners at the FDR's funeral in the East Room.[26] FDR's cane, a postmortem gift to Bethune from Mrs. Roosevelt, was lovingly preserved in a special corner of Bethune's apartment.[27] Try as she could—and she did—Dorothy could never replicate Bethune's close relationship with the first lady.

The NCNW sponsored a day-long conference on April 4, 1938, on the inclusion of black women in New Deal programs. Bethune insisted the conference be held in a federal building rather than the basement of a local church to underscore the symbolism of being within the halls of power. Mrs. Roosevelt helped Bethune secure space for the conference in the majestic Department of the Interior auditorium in Washington.[28]

Dorothy represented AKA at the conference. It opened with a prayer and a hefty mandate: to draw up a plan of action for increased participation of women in key administration jobs and to get more federal money for programs to help blacks. Bethune told the participants, "I don't think we have been bold enough."[29]

Bethune ran a tight meeting. She appointed a committee to craft a position paper for the first lady in the hope she would put it under FDR's nose. They planned to walk up Pennsylvania Avenue that afternoon in their finery to take tea with Mrs. Roosevelt and place the document in her hand. Time was of the essence. Some of the women wasted that time by praising Bethune and the first lady. But Bethune cut them off: "Mrs. Roosevelt knows how we feel. When you go home you might send a nice little personal letter to her, but this thing is history. . . . We don't want to put any sentiment into this, this is just concrete business."[30]

Dorothy Height once said the secret of Bethune's success was that she "enlisted *anyone* she found worthy to join her. From the beginning she successfully appealed to white benefactors. . . . She believed strongly in interracial cooperation. And she was always task oriented."[31] Dorothy Ferebee was equally awed by Bethune's skill: "She had the secret of getting others to do what she wanted done. She never directed them, but she was able to throw out little ideas and allow others to develop them so that they became eager to do the job on their own."[32]

Dorothy gladly became one of those eager followers. Bethune selected her as one of ten participants at the 1938 conference to draft the final report. What emerged in record time was succinct, well-written, and on point. It cited those agencies that lacked black women in key roles and explained why their absence was harmful to the agency's mission as well as the interests of African Americans. The report recommended that a black woman be placed in authority in the Children's Bureau and that black doctors, administrators, nurses, and nutritionists be hired at the U.S. Public Health Service. It advocated for black women to run Negro chapters of the American Red Cross and to administer programs in the Federal Housing

Administration, and it suggested that a black woman be appointed to the Women's Bureau in the Department of Labor.[33]

Black women's employment was a major issue for the NCNW. At the time, half of all black women worked outside the home, but nine out of ten were domestics or farm laborers. In 1938, 90 percent of all black federal government workers were cleaning floors.[34] It was time to smash the low glass ceiling.

But despite high hopes, six months after the conference, the recommendations in the report languished.[35] In her role as AKA supreme basileus between 1939 and 1941, Dorothy would continue fighting to get a black woman into the Women's Bureau with no luck. In September 1940 she and Jeanetta Welch Brown of the AKA Non-Partisan Council met with Mary Anderson, director of the bureau, to ask why no black women were employed there. The tepid response: two of the last three had left to get married and the other quit.[36]

Unlike AKA, the council did not sponsor racial uplift projects. It was, as Professor Deborah Gray White of Rutgers notes, "dealing with the intangible. It aimed to insert black women into the nation's consciousness so that they would be factored into policy decisions and empowered to participate in decision-making processes."[37]

Bethune had succeeded in bringing together scattered black women's organizations with multiple purposes and giving them a single, overarching goal: to bring them into the mainstream of public life. If nothing else, within three short years after it was founded, the NCNW was a known entity with a voice on matters concerning race and gender, even if it sometimes seemed that nobody was listening. In Jim Crow America, getting on the map was in itself, a stellar achievement.

The press paid attention to the NCNW. Bethune kept a close eye on what was written about her, assigning volunteer minions to carefully clip every mention of her name out of the newspapers. "She looked to the black papers for word from the trenches," wrote Dovey Roundtree, one of those volunteers.[38]

Over the years the FBI too paid attention to the NCNW. The bureau spent considerable time spying on the council, as well as on Bethune and its future presidents, Dorothy Ferebee, Vivian Carter Mason, and Dorothy

Height. What the FBI feared the council and these four women might do, other than draw attention to the terrible treatment of blacks in midcentury America, is not clear. In hindsight the material gathered by J. Edgar Hoover's agents was nothing short of silly. But those were different times.

Bethune's FBI file includes snippets of gossip and innuendo from named and unnamed sources, newspapers clippings, and such trivial tidbits as the fact that she addressed a meeting of the Southern Negro Youth Congress in Richmond in 1937 and spoke at a birthday party for Paul Robeson in New York in 1944. Ridiculously, the FBI even took note of the fact that Bethune's name showed up on a mimeographed list of sponsors of a relief campaign for refugees of the Spanish Civil War along with that of Secretary of the Interior Harold Ickes, Ernest Hemingway, and President Roosevelt's mother.[39] Innocuous as her activities sound, Hoover nonetheless authored a memo in November 1941 to someone whose name has been blacked out: "It is recommended that this individual [Bethune] be considered for custodial detention in the event of a national emergency."[40]

Further, in the 1940s Congressman Dies of the Un-American Activities Committee branded Bethune, revered in the black press as the "First Lady of Colored America," a communist on the House floor, triggering an FBI investigation. Bethune called the label "malicious" and absurd.[41] She was "invited" to come to the FBI, be placed under oath, and answer questions about her loyalty. At the interview she looked the agent in the eye and said, "It startles me just a little to even have anyone surmise . . . from the things I do and stand for that there would be within my thinking any type of belief or action that would bring me under the rays of communistic ideas. . . . It seems I have been so far removed from what my interpretation of a Communist is."[42]

The third NCNW president, Vivian Carter Mason, appeared on the FBI's radar screen following a ten-day trip to Russia with the International Democratic Women's Federation in 1946.[43] Dorothy Ferebee and Dorothy Height, the fourth NCNW president, were under FBI surveillance along with dozens of other civil rights activists during the voting rights campaign in Selma, Alabama, in the autumn of 1963, when they both spoke at a rally at a local Baptist Church.[44]

The NCNW drew its strength from its ability to keep the pressure on government decision makers. Besides lobbying for decent jobs for black women, the council sought equality in education, voting rights, improved maternal and child health, and better treatment for women worldwide. It joined the NAACP to push for federal antilynching legislation, always a losing proposition. The council recognized early the dangerous plight of the European Jews under Hitler and passed a resolution at its 1938 annual meeting condemning their persecution: "As members of an oppressed group in the United States of America, we sympathize with the Jewish minority group in Germany as can no others."[45]

The NCNW supported integration of the armed forces and the inclusion of women in military support roles. In 1941 Congresswoman Edith Nourse Rogers of Massachusetts introduced legislation to create the Women's Army Auxiliary Corps (WAAC). To the extent women could fill administrative roles in the army, men could be freed for combat. Bethune insisted that black women be allowed to join the WAAC officers' candidate school, and the army reluctantly concurred. The War Department appointed her civilian advisor to the WAAC for racial issues.[46]

In 1943 the NCNW hired Jeanetta Welch Brown away from AKA's Non-Partisan Council as its first paid executive director. Working out of Bethune's cramped apartment, she ran telegram and mail campaigns to FDR and federal officials in the name of the NCNW, made speeches, and planned council participation at conferences and in testimony before Congress.[47] The council's stature grew to the point that it was able to lure congressmen, judges, government officials, and, eventually, President Truman to its annual meetings.[48] The NCNW published the *Aframerican Woman's Journal*, its official magazine, and *Telefact*, its monthly newsletter, which brought news of council activities to the membership and the outside world.[49]

Despite all of the positive achievements of the NCNW, the organization could be one big headache for the woman who ran it. There were perpetual problems with money and staff. Bethune wanted a national headquarters commensurate with the NCNW's status, so at the end of 1943 the executive committee authorized a $750 down payment for a $15,500 house at 1318 Vermont Avenue NW. With the help of Eleanor Roosevelt, Bethune secured $10,000 from the Chicago department store magnate Marshall Field toward the cost of the new headquarters.[50]

On the day the executive committee voted to buy the house, the deeply religious Bethune remarked, "God send his blessing on the passage of this motion."[51] Given the precarious state of the NCNW's finances, the council had no business buying a headquarters. The plan was to have it pay for itself by leasing out the top floor. When Bethune stepped out of the committee room for a few moments, the women remaining voted to allow her to live at the headquarters rent free for the rest of her life—something else the NCNW could not afford.[52]

The council house at 1318 Vermont Avenue NW, walking distance from the vibrant African American U Street restaurant and shopping area, was the type of three-story Victorian mansion that Dorothy's ancestors had lived in and Bethune's might have worked in. Built in the 1870s, it was a brick row house with a large bay window dominating the façade and a black wrought-iron fence surrounding it and a small front yard. The first floor had a reception room, a kitchen, and a dining room that could serve as a meeting space. The second floor included office space and a bathroom as well as a small apartment with a bedroom and a dressing room. The small apartment was where Bethune would live. The third floor had four bedrooms, a bathroom, and a kitchenette.[53]

The ribbon-cutting ceremony for the headquarters took place on Sunday, October 15, 1944. Edith Sampson, a Chicago lawyer, presided. It was over-the-top with pomp and circumstance. There were musical excerpts from Dvořák's *New World* symphony and a reading of The Lord's Prayer. Bethune spoke, as did Eleanor Roosevelt. As chair of the Housing Committee, Dorothy had the honor of putting the key in the front door to open the lock, while dignitaries gathered in folding chairs on the lawn uttered their "ooh's" and "ahh's."[54] From the day Dorothy turned that key until a night in January 1966 when a fire caused extensive damage rendering it uninhabitable, 1318 Vermont Avenue NW would be the NCNW's home.[55]

Long before the fire, Bethune and the executive committee realized the house was too small. Bethune tried to work her magic to get the council to buy a bigger, more impressive house,[56] but with money tight at the NCNW, she would make do with what she had. It would not be until 1995, when the council purchased 633 Pennsylvania Avenue NW during the long reign of Dorothy Height, that the NCNW would have a dazzling national headquarters among the government buildings of Washington.[57]

In 1943, the year before the Vermont Avenue council house opened, the NCNW was in such miserable financial shape that Bethune had to beg a grant of six thousand dollars from the liberal Rosenwald Fund to keep it afloat.[58] She took to the speaking circuit, demanding $250 and a first-class travel ticket for each appearance.[59] Three years later, when Dorothy was the NCNW treasurer, the spigot ran dry again. Dorothy was in the unfortunate position of having to tell the executive committee that income from sale of the *Aframerican Woman's Journal* was $692 a year, while the cost of publishing it was $1,943. And there was more bad news: the NCNW took in $6,779 in 1946 and had $23,073 in expenses.[60]

In January 1947 there was $456.61 in the council's bank account and it could not pay the tax bill. The executive director earned $3,600 a year and had to be paid. Members of the inner circle had a heart-to-heart talk about how to convince twenty-five women to dig into their leather handbags and fork over one hundred dollars each to keep the council afloat.[61]

Later that year the NCNW was hit with some bad press when word got out that Bethune was leaving in September for a month-long European trip with Dorothy again at her side as her personal physician and confidante. They planned to attend the International Council of Women's meeting in Paris and from there go to London, Luxembourg, and Sweden. The ICW was founded in 1888 with the goal of establishing a member organization in each self-governing country of the world.[62] In reporting on the proposed trip, the *Chicago Tribune's* columnist Charley Cherokee showed no deference to Ma Bethune. While she traveled the world, he wrote, "her National Council of Negro Women is still flat on its fanny in morale and finances."[63] Recognizing that the trip would be a public relations disaster, Bethune needed a gracious way out, which Dorothy provided. At the postwar conference of the ICW in Philadelphia, which took place shortly before the planned conclave in Europe, Dorothy announced that "due to her physical condition" Bethune would be unable to go. Bethune named Eunice Carter, a New York lawyer and chair of the NCNW executive committee, to go in her place.[64] Most likely Carter paid her own way.

Two years later the financial situation at the NCNW would deteriorate so badly that Edith Sampson, a top contender to succeed Bethune and the lawyer who would handle Dorothy's 1950 divorce, loaned the organization five hundred dollars at Bethune's behest. In a letter to Sampson on February 8, 1949, Bethune got straight to the point: "You are a woman in brown skin, and I can afford to ask you. If you can, send One Thousand Dollars.

Send it at once. We must pull through. We cannot stop here."[65] Sampson immediately sent half that amount. Just as quickly Bethune sent it back, upset because Sampson's check was made out to her rather than to the NCNW. "To secure your faith in the organization, your note will be signed by the Treasurer, Dr. Dorothy Ferebee and myself."[66]

Sampson's note was good for only sixty days, but by mid-May she had not gotten back a dime of her money. "We will try to have payment of the note ready for you by the 15th of June," Bethune wrote to her. "The Council just has no money and I have only $100 in my own check book."[67] This may have been why Bethune did not want her name on Sampson's check.

By 1949 Bethune was done. Although the council had voted in 1941 to make her president for life, she privately told Eleanor Roosevelt and the NCNW executive committee in January that she planned to retire at the end of the year.[68] She offered her failing health as the reason. She would live another six years after her retirement.

Bethune walked on water. "Of course, there will never be another Bethune," wrote a columnist in the *Pittsburgh Courier*.[69] Yet jockeying began immediately among the accomplished women of the council who desperately wanted the grueling, unpaid job. The question was which one, if any, of her "daughters" would Bethune endorse?

Behind the scenes she orchestrated the outcome. She told reporters that the next NCNW president needed a firm educational background, a strong faith, a willingness to sacrifice, an ability to accept constructive criticism, a love of humanity, a broad vision, a warm heart, and a level head.[70] That description fit Dorothy Ferebee, but it fit others as well, like Arenia Mallory and Edith Sampson.[71] Both women were considered stronger candidates than Dorothy in the early days of the contest.[72] Edith Sampson was a beautiful, stylish, and poised attorney who had made her name as the NCNW's delegate to the Town Hall World Tour, a goodwill trip in which representatives of American organizations promoted international understanding in public meetings around the world. As the only black woman participating, Sampson had attracted significant media attention.[73] When the day of the vote approached, the newspapers handicapped the contest. Sampson was considered to have "a legally astute mind and [to be] ingenious enough to surround herself with helpers who may compensate for whatever abilities she may lack." Dorothy, meanwhile, lacked nothing. "Mrs. Ferebee, known for her quiet, sturdy, calm and conscientious thoroughness, has both physical and spiritual nearness to the Council," wrote one journalist.[74]

Four hundred NCNW delegates showed up for the convention, which opened on November 15 and went through the evening of November 18, most of it taking place at the Department of Labor auditorium.[75] It was a private affair with the exception of the International Night celebration and the Bethune testimonial dinner. The days were long and filled with excruciatingly detailed committee chair reports. On November 16 at eight in the evening, Dorothy presented her treasurer's report, in which she announced how "grateful" she was for the trust she was given as treasurer "through difficult and oft times embarrassing moments." The next day the women took a break from committee business and toured the Haitian, Indian, British, Ethiopian, and Mexican embassies.[76] They dressed to the nines for the outing. "The clothes worn by the delegates showed the fruits of a year's careful planning and selection," wrote one journalist. "Practically every fur of the animal kingdom was in evidence, with gorgeous hats to match."[77]

After they returned, they tended to business. A box was placed on the officers' table into which members were instructed to place their ballots. Bethune urged the group to cast aside friendships; the election was not a popularity contest. "Think soberly and wisely," she warned. Nothing less than "our Cause" was at stake.[78]

A sign of the clout wielded by Bethune was the appearance of Harry Truman at International Night, which opened the convention. (Bethune also invited FBI director J. Edgar Hoover, but he declined.)[79] It was the first time the president of the United States had appeared at an NCNW event. It was an evening befitting a queen, and Bethune looked like one in a black velvet gown with a spray of white orchids at her shoulder.[80]

FDR had a reputation for being in sympathy with the suffering of Negroes, but it was Truman who proved more willing to risk political capital to ameliorate that suffering. In his State of the Union message in 1947 he addressed civil rights. A little more than a year later he submitted a civil rights program to Congress, the strongest ever offered by a president up until that time. He called on Congress to enact a federal law to end lynching, poll taxes, and discrimination in interstate travel. He also urged legislators to pass stronger laws to ensure voting rights and fair employment practices.[81]

On International Night Truman lauded Bethune's accomplishments. "She brought to the National Youth Administration a conviction that its program must reach all young people regardless of race, religion or color," the president said. "She has been in the forefront of those who worked for better housing and for larger employment opportunities through improved training and through the extension of fair employment practices."[82]

Before the glow of International Night dimmed, the back-door politicking picked up. Sampson did not have sufficient support within the organization to become president.[83] One anonymous newspaper columnist suggested that Dorothy, not used to playing second fiddle, encouraged a "Stop-Sampson" movement because she was jealous of the dynamic lawyer. "Some Ferebee stage-managers were out to get Sampson's scalp primarily because of the national and international acclaim she enjoys as member of the World Town Hall Seminar."[84] Then there was Arenia Mallory. She was the NCNW southern regional director and had successfully corralled a significant number of new members and hoped they would support her candidacy.[85]

Perhaps because of their physician-patient relationship or because Bethune saw something of her younger self in Dorothy, Bethune anointed her as her successor. Using her gift for gentle manipulation, she convinced Mallory to withdraw and throw her southern support to Dorothy. The irony could not have been lost on Dorothy that her victory depended on the willingness of Mallory to take a dive. Mallory bent to Bethune's wishes and dropped out. But as she withdrew, she made an unfortunate speech calling Dorothy the candidate of "little" women. "By implication, she meant that Sampson was the candidate of the 'select' few. Her speech divided the convention further," wrote Elaine Smith.[86] The resulting debate "became so heated that a motion was made by one delegate to retain Mrs. Bethune in office for another year," reported the *Chicago Defender*. But Bethune, old, tired, and suffering health problems, declined.[87]

For her part, Sampson wanted nothing more to do with it. She sought to get her name off the ballot. But it was too late; the parliamentarian ruled that the names of all candidates would remain. This infuriated the voting body for an obvious reason; it left the impression that the race was open for grabs when everyone knew the fix was in. The anger showed in the numbers. Although four hundred women were eligible to vote, only 141 of them did. Dorothy received ninety-seven votes to Mallory's twenty-five and Sampson's nineteen. A motion to elect Dorothy by acclamation to hide the dissension failed.[88] The *Pittsburgh Courier* reported that "the entire delegation of nearly four hundred women [was] weeping profusely" by the time the brutal election was over.[89]

No matter, within hours Dorothy had fixed her makeup, changed into her black evening gown with an overlay of long-sleeved black lace, and rose to the occasion as mistress of ceremonies for Bethune's farewell party, attended by anywhere from six hundred to eight hundred guests. Dorothy presided over the affair with "her usual poise, grace and dignity."[90]

The new NCNW board of directors showed they were a classy bunch by putting on a united front. Ma Bethune was there to help. Through her body language—she hovered near Dorothy and posed for pictures with her—she made certain the world knew Dorothy's presidency had her blessing. Dorothy's lifelong striving had led to this moment, and it should have been among the happiest of her life, but in photographs taken that evening her face looks tense.

Dorothy wisely kept the focus of the testimonial dinner on Bethune, a loving eulogy to a woman still living. The evening ended with encouraging words from Bethune: "Now I pass the lighted torch to you, with the hope that is flame will burn more brightly."[91] The audience responded with a rousing musical send-off, harmonizing in what had come to be Bethune's theme song, "Let Me Call You Sweetheart."[92]

The next day reality set in. Bethune was off to her retirement home in sunny Florida, and the NCNW was in a huge financial hole. The first order of business when the executive board met on Saturday morning was damage control. The board voted that "a strong statement be sent to the press as to our faith in the new administration; our belief in the principles and purpose of the Council, and our determination to stand by it. The NCNW is not going to disintegrate."[93] There followed a press blitz featuring Dorothy. Everyone was curious about her. "Second President of NCNW at Helm" was the headline in the *Atlanta Daily World*.[94] Other newspapers reported, "Dr. Dorothy Boulding Ferebee ... brings a wealth of experience in several fields to her post as successor to Mrs. Mary McLeod Bethune" and "Dr. Ferebee ably steps into Dr. Bethune's shoes."[95] Dorothy responded with platitudes: "I feel it a signal honor to have been elected to the presidency of such an organization as the National Council of Negro Women."[96]

Not surprisingly readers were hungry for details about Dorothy's personal life. The *New Journal and Guide*, published in her old hometown of Norfolk, reported, "Dr. Ferebee is the former wife of Claude Ferebee, New York City dentist."[97] Although the article was technically wrong, it was sort of true. Dorothy and Claude had not lived together as husband and wife since before the war and were less than a year away from being divorced. Yet Dorothy continued to promote the fiction that her family life was picture-perfect, and she insisted on a correction. The paper accommodated her.[98]

With the war and the Depression long over, the Christmas lights went up and families made plans to gather together. Dorothy had much to be thankful for: she had reached the pinnacle. But her triumph would end in tragedy in less than three months, after which it is unlikely she ever again had a truly happy day.

16 One of the Coldest Winters We Ever Had

In spite of the twins' lousy academic records, one telephone call from their mother most likely could have gotten them into Howard. For whatever reason, Dorothy did not make that call. Dolly applied to several competitive colleges, but they were far beyond her reach given her lackluster academic performance at Northfield. She applied to Vassar, one of the prestigious Seven Sisters schools on par with an Ivy League men's college. She also applied to New York University and her mother's alma mater, Simmons.[1] Nothing survives to prove it, but all three colleges probably rejected her. Although Dolly was a talented singer and professed a desire for a stage career, she so admired her mother that she also aspired to be a physician.[2] However, nothing in her academic background once she left Banneker Junior High showed she would have been capable of handling the rigors of a medical school program.

On September 2, 1949, less than two weeks before classes were to begin, Dolly asked Northfield to forward her transcript to Champlain College in Plattsburg (sometimes spelled Plattsburgh) New York.[3] She was accepted instantly. She and her brother, who was also accepted, packed their winter scarves, hats, and long johns and trundled up to the campus, which hugged the Canadian border. Whether Thurston, near the bottom of his class at Tilton, tried to get into any other schools is unknown. Presumably, as with boarding school, their mother paid for their college educations. Tuition was $240 a year according to the college catalog; although an article in the *New York Herald Tribune* put it at almost twice that.[4]

Originally a junior college and not to be confused with the private school of the same name in Champlain, Vermont, the school opened in the fall of 1946 to meet the emergency need for campus space for GIs returning from the war.[5] In the 1949–50 academic year, when Dolly and Thurston attended, there were 1,710 students; 68 percent were veterans. There were 775 students in the twins' freshman class, about half of them veterans.[6] Because Champlain was a public school relying on federal funds, it could not discriminate on the basis of race.[7]

Getting in was easy. For the 1949–50 academic year 865 students applied to Champlain and all but ten were accepted.[8] The twins probably knew about the school because their friend and stalking horse, Beckley, had enrolled the year before.

Champlain College in New York, which is no longer in existence, was situated on an abandoned army base first used in the War of 1812, in the Adirondack Mountains along the northwestern shore of Lake Champlain.[9] To the east, across the water, lies Vermont. The leafy campus was oval shaped, the heart of which was along the perimeter of a half-mile-long quadrangle.[10] Dolly, Thurston, and the other freshmen reported to college on Wednesday, September 14, 1949.[11] There were 1,682 male students and only 28 females.[12] Dolly was required to live at Hudson Hall, the on-campus dormitory for unmarried women, which was nestled among the faculty row houses.

The school's code of conduct for single women was strict. No living off campus without the dean's approval. No staying out later than 10 p.m. during the week, 12:45 in the morning on Saturday or the night before a holiday. No leaving campus overnight without permission. No men in a coed's room; dates waiting for female students at Hudson Hall were expected to cool their heels in the public reception area.[13] Dorothy's brother had no such restrictions. Thurston immediately settled into a four-man dormitory suite with Beckley and two other students. Given the ratio of males to females on campus, plus the fact that most of the male students were older, it is not surprising the rules for the female students were so strict. One wonders how any parent in that conservative era would have been comfortable allowing a teenage daughter to attend school there.

Classes for the twins began on September 19, an unusually warm late summer day.[14] In what would turn out to be her only semester on campus, Dolly quickly became Miss Popularity. Her beautiful smile, shapely figure, and reputation for kindness made her everyone's sweetheart. She joined the cheerleading squad; each Saturday afternoon in a long blue dirndl skirt, matching sweater, and white blouse—the school colors—she led cheers for the Champlain College Bluejays. "The entire squad made a name for itself in enthusiasm, energy and pep," wrote the editors of the 1950 *du Lac*, the school yearbook. George Jones, a fellow student and left end on the football team in the fall of 1949, remembered Dolly as "a very pretty girl and a very nice person." Among the football players Dorothy cheered on to victory was her brother, who wore number 58 on his blue jersey.[15] At 170 pounds, he played left halfback.[16] Dolly also joined the Women's League, which organized Hudson Hall social and civic activities, including the annual Christmas party and a fund-raising drive to fight polio.[17]

Seemingly benign events that inexorably led to unspeakable tragedy quickly fell into place. First, Cupid's arrow struck. Somewhere on campus Dolly bumped into sophomore Norburt Paul Schreiber, a white Jewish student from the Bronx who was three years older.[18] Then, despite the school's many restrictions on where she could go and when, Dolly probably became pregnant.

Known as Paul and sometimes Buddy, Schreiber was studying at Champlain on the GI Bill, having left City College of New York after a year to enter the military. He had been a foreman in a machine shop before enlisting in the army on June 18, 1946, and was honorably discharged on October 21, 1947, having spent half of his tour in the United States and half in postwar Japan.[19] While in the army, he worked as a noncommissioned officer in administration and was good with an M1 rifle.[20]

Dolly's beau was tall and lean—6'1" and 155 pounds—with thick, dark brown hair that came to a well-defined widow's peak on his forehead. He would keep most of his hair and his lean physique throughout his life, his youthful athletic prowess serving him well in his declining years. He had played triple-A baseball—probably right field—for the New York Yankees' minor league team before entering the army.[21]

It was love at first sight. Dolly and Paul were headed to the altar in June 1950, less than a year after they met. It was a radical, some might say foolhardy idea. In 1950 it was still illegal in twenty-nine states for whites and blacks to marry.[22] But that didn't bother the young lovebirds. Dorothy, with her finely tuned political ear, was well aware how poorly a union between her daughter and a white man would be viewed in 1950s America, but she was far too sensible and open-minded to oppose it. She supposedly met Schreiber in 1949, liked him, and approved of the marriage.[23]

Other than to fall wildly in love, there wasn't much to do at Champlain. Plattsburg was tiny and, as far as social activities went, dead. Margaret Street was the main drag. On one side was the ubiquitous Woolworth's Five and Dime; on the other was the hundred-year-old Union Hotel, where proud parents stayed when attending school events.[24] The Fife and Drum tavern and restaurant, with its red leather seats inside the Witherill Hotel at 25 Margaret Street, was a favorite student hangout.[25] Today Plattsburg's shopping area is charmless, nondescript, and mostly deserted.

Classes during the fall of 1949 continued until November 23, the day before Thanksgiving. It was around this time that Dorothy became one of the most famous women in America as the second president of the National Council of Negro Women. Dolly and Thurston returned to campus the Monday after the holiday and remained until December 17, when everyone scattered for the Christmas recess. The students returned to campus after the holiday to study for exams. Finals began on January 23 and ended on January 28, in time for the students to let loose and return to campus for Winter Weekend,[26] which kicked off on Friday, February 10, with a sleigh ride and a basketball game. On Saturday there was a ski contest, an ice-hockey match, and an ice-sculpting contest. At night there was a semiformal dance featuring Ray McKinley and his Orchestra, still popular in those waning days of swing. McKinley had played with Benny Goodman before the war and, after entering the service, was part of Glenn Miller's American Band of the Allied Expeditionary Forces. He was a logical entertainment choice for the GI-filled campus. Winter Weekend continued on Sunday with church services, a jazz concert, and a movie.[27]

Coeds carried printed dance cards in their evening purses with up to fifteen blank spaces for eager partners.[28] Dolly's dance card surely would have been filled quickly; she might have needed a spare. But she never made it to the semiformal dance or any other Winter Weekend activity. While the Champlain College community was happily preparing for the sleigh ride on Friday, Dolly's body was being buried at Mount Hope Cemetery in Hastings-on-Hudson, New York. She was eighteen years old.

Dorothy survived thirty years after her daughter's death but said next to nothing about the most horrible tragedy ever to befall her. The transcript of the 1979 interview Dorothy gave to Merze Tate for the Black Women Oral History Project, contains only the briefest explanation as to how Dolly died. "It was, 1949 to 1950, one of the coldest winters we have ever had, and Dorothy [Jr.] contracted a dreadful cold and pneumonia. She was ill for about five days before I knew it. In short order, before I could get to her or could bring her to me, she died an untimely death, February 6, 1950. It was on one of the occasions when I was in Washington, dividing my time between that city and New York."[29]

How much of this came directly from Dorothy is unclear. It may have been a recitation of family lore provided either by Thurston, or his wife, Carol, that had been created by Dorothy years before. The statement is in brackets and in the official transcript is a warning: "Material in brackets was added after the interview was recorded."[30] Dorothy did not survive to edit the transcript and it fell to Tate, with the help of Dorothy's son and daughter-in-law to do it.

With all the parties long dead, nobody knows exactly what happened. But among the few surviving friends and family members, the open secret is that the pneumonia story was spun by Dorothy to cover up a botched abortion. There is no smoking gun, but strong circumstantial evidence exists to support the unofficial version. For one thing, the official story doesn't add up: the weather was not unusually cold; Dolly *was* able to get to her mother while still alive; the time span between Dolly's arrival at her mother's and when she died was not as contemporary newspapers reported; and Dolly's death certificate indicated the presence of suspicious health conditions.

The winter of 1949–50 was not one of the coldest; it was one of the warmest.[31] There was a record-breaking high temperature of almost 66 degrees in New York City on January 4.[32] By the middle of the month the mercury hit 42 degrees in what was usually the frigid state capital in Albany.[33] The Champlain College ski team had to cancel three meets that season due to lack of snow.[34] The misleading assertion that the winter was the coldest ever set the stage for the pneumonia story.

Champlain College students had a little more than a week off between the end of exams on January 28 and the beginning of the new semester on

February 6. Those last days of Dolly's life cannot be accounted for. Years later Paul Schreiber told his wife, Nancy, that sometime during the week he put Dolly on a train to Washington. Her fiancé had no idea when he kissed her goodbye at the station that it would be the last time he ever saw her.[35]

Newspaper accounts of Dolly's death vary as to where she was before she was stricken. "Miss Ferebee arrived in Washington from Plattsburgh on Monday morning [February 6, the day she died] and went to NCNW headquarters at 1318 Vermont Ave. NW, where her mother resides," reported the Baltimore *Afro-American*[36] But the *Pittsburgh Courier* had a different story: "She had come here [Washington] from St. Albans, LINY, to visit her mother."[37]

The death of Dorothy Ferebee Jr. received substantial play in the African American newspapers. The source for those articles was never revealed. "Young Miss Ferebee had been a victim of virus pneumonia," reported the *Pittsburgh Courier* without attribution on February 18, 1950.[38] Rushing home to be near her mother, reported the Baltimore *Afro-American*, "she died a few hours later."[39] The *Chicago Defender* wrote, "Funeral services were held here last Friday for Miss Dorothy Boulding Ferebee, Jr. . . . who died suddenly . . . of virus pneumonia."[40]

The very private Paul Schreiber, who died in 2006, kept his own counsel about Dolly. His widow did not even know her last name; she knew only that her husband had been engaged in college to an African American girl named Dorothy who died of pneumonia and had a famous mother.[41] But Nancy is sure about one thing: Dolly had been the love of Paul's young life. Had she been suffering from symptoms of pneumonia, it is unlikely Paul would have allowed her to make a fifteen-hour train trip to Washington alone. Champlain College had a full-service infirmary with a doctor on call 24/7; he could have taken her there.

It is far more likely that Dolly was in perfect health at the end of the exam period and that Paul put her on a train to St. Albans for the winter recess. It would have been a perfect time and place for Dolly to get rid of an unwanted pregnancy on the QT. Any number of illegal abortionists plied their trade in New York City. Her plan might have been to have the procedure, rest at her mother's home in Queens, and return to school in time for Winter Weekend, with none being the wiser.

If Dolly was indeed pregnant in the winter of 1950, Paul was surely the father. Nancy doesn't believe Paul was unaware of Dolly's condition; she thinks he would have tried to help her once she got "in trouble," the phrase for unmarried pregnant girls back then. If she died as the result of an abortion, perhaps one Paul arranged for her, he would have been wracked by his loss as well as by guilt and shame. He might also have feared criminal prosecution for becoming involved, even tangentially. Abortion was illegal in every state in 1950 and had been for at least one hundred years.[42]

Looking back at age eighty-five, George Jones, the Champlain football player who knew and liked Dolly, recalled how hard it was for girls who got in trouble in the 1950s: "There was a lot of pressure on a girl who got pregnant; she took a terrible beating socially. As a result there was a plethora of back-alley sources (for abortions), as far away as Schenectady or Harlem."[43] Because they were performed clandestinely, there is no way to accurately tally the number of abortions in the United States when Dolly may have had hers. The estimates range from 200,000 to 1.2 million per year. In 1950 there were three hundred recorded deaths due to illegal abortions, but the real number was surely higher, with many doctors and families claiming other causes, as Dorothy may have done with her own daughter's death.[44]

A woman seeking an abortion faced a gruesome, often expensive procedure under unsanitary conditions. Women have described going to marginal neighborhoods to visit the dirty apartments of doctors who had lost their license to practice medicine and used unsterilized, pointed objects, leaving them vulnerable to hemorrhaging and infection. Some women submitted to expensive saline injections by abortionists whose medical training consisted of answering phones in a doctor's office. Saline abortions resulted in an expulsion of the fetus; if the uterus failed to empty completely, infection could set in.[45]

Claude Ferebee never stopped blaming Dorothy for their daughter's death; it was the last straw in their broken marriage. He believed Dolly felt pressured to abort because her pregnancy would have mortified her mother in her prominent new role as NCNW president. He even thought Dorothy herself performed the abortion and was the one who botched it. "The children of kings and queens have babies out of wedlock," Claude often said to whoever would listen. "Why did she have to kill my baby?"[46]

There is no proof that Dorothy performed an abortion on her daughter. If she had, there is no reason to believe that with her first-class medical education and years of gynecological training and practice, she would not have done it right. More likely, Dolly went to a back-alley abortionist and sought her mother's help after it was too late. Russ Eberhardt, so close to the Ferebee twins that he was the best man at Thurston's wedding, said sixty years later, "I know that for a fact she died of a botched abortion. It was an interracial affair. I met him after Dolly had died."[47]

Dolly probably took the train to Washington after it became apparent something had gone terribly wrong. Dorothy was supposed to be giving a speech in Boston when her daughter died, but a cold of her own kept her at the NCNW headquarters, where as a perk of being president she had the use of a cozy, two-room apartment on the second floor unless Mary Bethune happened to be in town, in which case Dorothy could use one of the bedrooms on the third floor.[48] When Dolly showed up, Dorothy quickly hustled her upstairs and put her to sleep.

The newspaper accounts describing the last hours of Dolly's life tend toward the melodramatic. "Dr. Ferebee called in Dr. William G. Lofton for consultation, but her daughter collapsed and was dead within three hours," reported the Chicago Defender.[49] In her column in the Pittsburgh Courier Toki Schalk Johnson wrote, "Virus pneumonia . . . the dreaded disease which slips upon an unsuspecting victim . . . claimed this lovely young girl for its own. Within hours, almost, the child was dead."[50] The Baltimore Afro-American, in what purported to be a conversation between the dying Dolly and her mother, dramatized the scene: "'I wanted to be here with you,' Miss Ferebee is said to have told her mother, who noted that her daughter was ill and immediately put her to bed. She died a few hours later."[51]

When read in conjunction with Dolly's death certificate, however, the newspaper stories prove to be pure fiction. Dolly arrived at her mother's apartment at least two days before she died. When Dorothy saw the sorry shape her daughter was in on Saturday, February 4, she called in Dr. Lofton, her friend in the hospital obstetrics department for more than twenty-five years. Dolly did not collapse and die in her mother's arms within hours, as reported; she survived until 3:15 in the afternoon on Monday, February 6. Dr. Lofton signed off on her death certificate.[52] By casting the time of death as shortly after Dolly's arrival in Washington, Dorothy avoided thorny questions about why she did not admit her daughter to Freedmen's Hospital if she suspected she had pneumonia. And none of the press accounts raised the question of why Dorothy chose an obstetrician-gynecologist to treat her daughter. If Dolly had pneumonia-like symptoms, why hadn't she called in a pulmonary expert?

Lofton's son, a gynecologist also named William but known as "Buster," knew Dorothy and the Ferebee twins. The two families were extremely close; Buster's mother, Robbie, was Dorothy's closest friend and was also Dolly's godmother. Now ninety-five, Buster denies any knowledge of an abortion involving Dolly. Yet he did say, cryptically, "Every time Dr. Ferebee got in trouble, she called Daddy."[53]

The arrival on her doorstep of her daughter bleeding uncontrollably due to a botched abortion was indeed trouble. Only a few months earlier Dorothy had won a hard-fought battle to succeed the iconic Mary Bethune. The contest bitterly divided the NCNW and left some of the members with a bad taste in their mouth. Dorothy's new and untested regime might not have survived the scandal of a pregnant unmarried daughter, never mind one who died following an abortion. Dorothy was well aware that the morals of African American women were placed under the microscope. From the earliest days of the club movement the message among these women was to lead by example, and that meant leading an exemplary life. In her book *Too Heavy a Load*, Deborah Gray White writes, "In the club leaders' thinking, moral purity was the key to social and cultural improvement."[54] The behavior of the president of the National Council of Negro Women and her family had to be above reproach, particularly when it came to matters involving sexuality. The power inherent in the NCNW presidency would have evaporated if the race-baiters in Congress knew how the daughter of its new president had died. Already Dorothy had clashed with them, loudly and publicly.

In December 1949, less than a month after assuming her highly visible post, Dorothy went before Alabama senator John Sparkman's housing subcommittee on Capitol Hill to testify about the problems of low-income families. During her appearance she mentioned that passage of President Truman's extensive civil rights program was critical to securing equality for Negroes. Senator Sparkman disagreed. He dismissed the Truman rights package as "legalistic" and one that might "do harm instead of good." Dorothy refused to back down. "I think if we really wanted to do something we would be willing to use 'legalistic methods' along with others," she retorted. The exchange, which became heated, made newspapers nationwide.[55]

Despite being devastated by her daughter's death, Dorothy remained clear-headed. She put the pneumonia story out fast and stuck to it tenaciously. The day after Dolly died she sent a telegram to inform Northfield that Dolly had died of a freak bout of virus-related pneumonia.[56] She adhered to the official version, even with family members, although her grandchildren pegged it as strange once they got older.[57] It struck the students at Champlain College as strange right away. The campus was abuzz about it. The sudden death of a healthy eighteen-year-old girl from pneumonia did not sound plausible, and even without anything more concrete than a hunch, rumors circulated that Dolly had died from an abortion.[58]

Dolly's death certificate listed multiple causes of death. Under "Immediate cause of death," Dr. Lofton wrote, "Virus pneumonia & anemia." Below that, under "Due to," he wrote what appears to be "toxemia" as well as "exhaustion & pulmonary edema." The duration of Dolly's illness was listed as "6 days."[59] Toxemia is a poisoning of the blood which can be caused by an abortion that becomes infected, or septic, due to fetal tissue remaining in the uterus. Sepsis moves fast and can lead to pulmonary edema, which is fluid in the lungs that can occur right before death. Anemia could have been the result of excessive blood loss following a badly performed abortion. Sepsis is not normally associated with viral pneumonia.[60]

Dolly's body was removed to the McGuire Funeral Home at 1820 9th Street NW, where the burials of Washington's African American elite were arranged.[61] From there her casket was shipped to New York City for services at the historic St. Philip's Episcopal Church in Harlem. When filled to capacity, 750 worshippers can fit in the sanctuary. It was New York City's first African American Episcopal parish and *the* house of worship for the African American upper crust.[62]

The funeral took place on February 10 at one in the afternoon. Instead of Dolly's wedding invitations, the Ferebees sadly sent out their daughter's funeral announcements. The small card read: "In profound sorrow we announce the death of Dorothy B. Ferebee, Jr., on Monday the 6th of Feb 1950. Services will be held St. Philips Episcopal Church from Delany's

Funeral Parlor, Feb. 10th at 1 o'clock PM." The mourners were seated shoulder to shoulder. Claude invited NAACP executive secretary Walter White, who preserved the funeral announcement among his personal papers until his own death.[63]

The warmer than normal weather continued on the day of Dolly's funeral, reaching 44 degrees in New York City. Dolly's friends stumbled around in a state of shock. Paul Schreiber went to St. Philip's to say goodbye to the woman he loved; crying his eyes out.[64] When she left the church after the service, Dorothy looked as if she were about to die herself. She was pale and nearly prostrate, supported under one arm by her son and under the other by her equally grief-stricken husband.[65] She later told Russ Eberhardt she would "never, ever" get over the death of her daughter. "Dolly was her pride," he said.[66]

The funeral procession made its way slowly to Mount Hope Cemetery in Hastings-on-Hudson, fifteen miles north of the city, where Dolly was buried beneath a small headstone in a corner of the bucolic burial ground. While Dorothy paid for Dolly's education, it was Claude who paid for Dolly's grave. He purchased a single plot for $100 on the day of her funeral. Two years later he purchased another, larger plot for $240 and had his daughter's body moved there, perhaps contemplating that he would one day be buried next to her, which never happened.[67]

Messages of sympathy poured out after Dolly's passing. The assistant principal of Northfield wrote a sad and touching letter to Dorothy: "She made a real contribution to the life of our school and will continue to make a real contribution in the other world."[68] The editors of the Champlain College *du Lac* devoted a full page in the student yearbook to Dolly, with a beautiful photograph of her in a white blouse wearing a double strand of pearls. Under the dark black heading, "In Memoriam," they wrote in part, "For us, her beauty and grace, her poise and charm, above all, her spirit and vitality, will be a lasting memory."[69]

Mary Bethune telegrammed her condolences to Dorothy and Claude the day before the funeral, filled with references to God, who had sustained the religious Bethune in troubled times. "We must bow in humble submission to God's will. He knows best. Remember He never places upon us more than we can bear. Place your trust in Him and know that He will comfort you."[70] In another letter she sent directly to Dorothy, Bethune wrote, "I want you to be brave and strong, and know that this is a bridge over which you must go. . . . Know that I am always with you."[71]

For her brother and the twins' friends, Dolly's death was devastating.[72] Thurston spun out of control preferring to play poker, practical jokes, and the role of a spoiled Goodtime Charley rather than grow up and become a fully responsible adult.

Paul Schreiber took off for California after Dolly died, having found the state beautiful while stopping there en route to Japan during his army service.[73] But it took him a long time to find true love again. He married and divorced three times; the first was in 1961, the second three years later, and the third in 1972. That marriage lasted a mere two months.[74] Finally, on December 15, 1979, nearly thirty years after Dolly's death, he took a fourth chance on marriage with a May-December romance and got it right. Nancy Simerly was thirty and Paul was fifty-one.[75] They remained together until he died of lung cancer in 2006. He was seventy-eight and had had a long career in corporate accounting and finance before he retired.[76]

Dolly's death did not make much of a dent in Dorothy's professional façade. She spent several unaccounted-for weeks in New York, then she picked herself up by her bootstraps and on March 1, 1950, returned to her duties as NCNW president. In a letter to the executive committee she wrote that day, Dorothy asked them to clear their calendars for a meeting on Saturday, March 11, from eleven to three: "Please make every effort to attend this important meeting as there are matters of importance demanding our immediate attention." In her only concession to the unimaginable tragedy she had just suffered, she added, "I need not tell you how much I have to depend upon each of you now, more than ever before to help me carry forward our great program."[77]

On March 11, one month after lowering her beautiful eighteen-year-old daughter into her dark and lonely grave, Dorothy presided over the monthly meeting of the NCNW executive committee at the same council house where she had been unable to save her daughter's life. Not one word was mentioned at the meeting about what had happened.[78]

17 As Good as I Could

Although both Ferebees were residents of New York by 1950, they could not get divorced there. Until 1967 the only ground for divorce in their home state was adultery, and to prove it meant catching the offending spouse in the act.[1] Given Dorothy's prominence, a messy love triangle would have been sensational front-page news. Claude would never be the household name his wife was in the 1950s, but in New York, out from under her broad shadow, he was able to develop his own solid reputation. In 1948 he was elected president of the North Harlem Dental Society, to which he was reelected for two successive one-year terms.[2] He would be known as the dentist to the black stars; rhythm and blues singer-songwriter Sam Cooke sat in Claude's dental chair.[3]

To end the marriage required creative thinking. The lawyer Dorothy turned to for help was the woman she'd defeated for the NCNW presidency six months earlier, Edith Sampson. Sampson practiced law in Illinois, where divorces could be obtained on the ground of desertion, so Dorothy filed a complaint alleging she had been a resident of Cook County, Illinois, for more than one year prior to seeking a divorce.[4] Claude, representing himself in the action, kept quiet and agreed to end the marriage.[5] Such fraud was frequently committed by couples seeking to end marriages. New York was a particularly harsh jurisdiction for unhappily married couples; it was the last state in the country to enact no-fault divorce and did not do so until 2010.[6] It is hard to be critical of Dorothy or Claude for doing what was necessary to end their misery once and for all.

Although she lied about her residency, Dorothy told the truth about her marriage. She alleged that since July 15, 1942, Claude had willfully "deserted and absented himself from the plaintiff without reasonable cause on the part of the plaintiff for so doing, and has continued . . . to absent himself . . . [despite the fact that] she at all times conducted herself as a true, kind and affectionate wife."[7] The date on which Dorothy alleged that Claude had left her roughly coincided with the time the couple had a showdown over the Madeline Dugger affair. In his legal response Claude took exception to her claim she was "a true, kind and affectionate wife."[8] Dorothy got in her own dig during her inquest in June 1950. When asked in court by Sampson, "While you lived together, how did you treat your husband?" Dorothy replied, "As good as I could." When Sampson asked her, "How did your husband treat you?," Dorothy said, "Indifferent."[9]

In the end Claude was a gentleman. He consented to pay child support for Thurston and to cover Sampson's legal bill.[10] On June 20, 1950, a judge in Cook County granted a default judgment of divorce to Dorothy, meaning Claude did not show up to contest it, and awarded Dorothy custody of Thurston.[11] Just weeks shy of their twentieth wedding anniversary and a little more than four months after their daughter's death, their long and unhappy marriage was finally over.

Afterward, neither breathed a word about it. Three months after the divorce, Dorothy was profiled in the military newspaper, *Stars and Stripes*, for joining something called the Crusade for Freedom. Led by Gen. Lucius D. Clay, the ostensible purpose of the Crusade was to get prominent Americans to tout democracy in the midst of the cold war. (The Crusade was later revealed to have had ties to the Central Intelligence Agency, although whether Dorothy had any inkling of this can never be known. The Agency does not confirm or deny whether a person worked for it.)[12] In the *Stars and Stripes* article, for which Dorothy must have been the source, she was described as living "with her dentist husband in a home at St. Albans, N.Y. [from which she] commutes to her Washington office three days a week, and travels 20,000 miles a year giving out her ideas."[13] The interview was Dorothy's twentieth-century version of her mother's nineteenth-century tall tale about her own disintegrating marriage.

Reporters attempted to ferret out rumors that the couple had split for at least six months before Claude's second marriage in June 1951. Editors at the Baltimore *Afro-American* revealed the lengths to which the Ferebees had gone to sweep it under the rug: "Repeated efforts last March to get both of the Dr. Ferebees to discuss their reported separation always met with rebuffs and even after the marriage announcement, they were hesitant to give a statement for publication." With Claude walking down the aisle, the Ferebees could not keep the lid on it any longer. Dorothy finally told the *Afro-American* they had divorced in Illinois the previous year. The newspaper could not resist making her pay for stonewalling, noting that Dorothy had "emphatically denied oft-repeated reports that divorce papers bordered on the sensational and thus were sealed."[14]

With his parents divorced and his sister dead, Thurston found himself at loose ends. His days at Champlain College were over. Without Dolly there, he wanted no part of life on the campus. He filled the void by marrying Carol Phillips, the young woman he met and fell in love with at Highland Beach.

Carol Sylvia Phillips was born in her grandfather's house on March 21, 1932, to Walter Phillips, a mailman, and his wife, Ruth Todd.[15] She grew up in Washington, not far from the Ferebees. Her paternal grandfather, W. Franklin Phillips, was a longtime physician in Washington.[16] Her family background put her in the same social sphere as the Ferebees. She was a debutante who had her coming-out party in 1949.[17] That same year she graduated from Dunbar High School with the dream of becoming a teacher.[18] She attended Miner Teachers' College, now the University of the District of Columbia, but dropped out after her sophomore year to marry Thurston. Afterward she drew maps for the U.S. Geological Survey for $2,750 a year. She quit at the end of 1952, shortly before she gave birth to Claude Thurston Ferebee III.[19] Like his father, he was nicknamed "Buzzy."

Carol was a lighter-skinned version of Dolly. Like other teenage girls of the 1950s, she wore her wavy brown hair just above her shoulders, pulled back from her face with barrettes, with poufy bangs. She had the same turned-up nose and full, sensuous lips as Dolly. The adjectives used by friends to describe Carol—pretty, sweet, kind, friendly—were the same as those once used about Dolly. "Carol was a good friend and a perfect person," recalled Margo Dean Pinson, her best friend in childhood, who happened to have been delivered by Dr. Dorothy Ferebee. "You could not dislike her; she was so warm. Everyone just gravitated to her. There was no pretense."[20] Carol and her little brother, Vaughn, born two and a half years after she was, were best friends, just as Thurston and Dolly had been.[21] One need not be Freud to figure out that Thurston married a woman as similar to his own sister that he could find.

Carol's family lived for much of her girlhood at 947 S Street NW, the home of her maternal grandparents, Jhonce Calhoun Vaughn Todd, a builder, and Ruth Todd. The S Street Todds came from Kentucky and were supposedly descended from First Lady Mary Todd Lincoln. Family lore had it that one of Mrs. Lincoln's brothers fathered one of Carol's ancestors in the usual way: by taking sexual advantage of a family slave.[22] If true, there were any number of candidates who could have been Carol and Vaughn's ancestor; Mary Todd Lincoln was raised in a well-to-do, slaveholding Kentucky household and had three brothers and four half-brothers.[23]

Jhonce and Ruth's residence was a three-story brick row house with steps leading from the street into a small yard surrounded by a wrought-iron fence. Built in 1885, it had eight bedrooms and four baths, enough for a multigenerational family. Their daughters, Ruth and Alexina, married postal workers. Both remained on S Street with their husbands and children. Grandfather Jhonce got run over by a trolley car, after which "he could walk but he couldn't do much else," Vaughn said. He survived a long time in a debilitated state, until he died in his bed in 1956 at age seventy-nine, following a stroke.[24]

The mailman Ruth Todd married on June 4, 1931, in Washington was Walter Phillips.[25] He was the son of Dr. W. Franklin Phillips and his wife, Carrie, who lived in the largest house on the block at 1023 New Jersey Avenue NW, where the doctor had his medical practice in the basement. Like most doctors of his day he made house calls, but he took a cab to get to them because he did not drive. "He was a good guy," said his grandson Vaughn. "He served the underprivileged community, and when they couldn't pay him, they would barter his medical services for chickens."[26] The Phillipses had three children: Walter and two younger daughters.[27] Dr. Phillips would continue to practice medicine until four months before he died in 1957, when he was seventy-eight.[28]

Vaughn was the heartthrob of his sister's friends. "I had such a crush on Vaughn. He was so handsome," confessed Margo Pinson more than sixty years after the fact.[29] He graduated from Armstrong Technical High

School in the hope of becoming an engineer, then attended the University of Michigan and Howard University but did not graduate from either. He was one of the first African Americans to be hired as an executive at the Hecht Company, a Washington department store, and he also worked in local government before he retired.[30]

Carol and Thurston married on November 1, 1951, a damp and cloudy day.[31] The ceremony took place where her family worshipped, St. Luke's Episcopal Church on 15th Street NW.[32] Dorothy's mother-of-the-groom dress was made of black chiffon, and her own mother wore navy and pink. Carol's mother was in royal blue, and her grandmother, Carrie Phillips, wore aqua. The bride wore a gold ankle-length dress with a sweetheart neckline and short sleeves. Russ Eberhardt was Thurston's best man.[33]

A reception for the newlyweds was hosted by Dr. Phillips and his wife in their New Jersey Avenue home, which was large enough for more than a hundred guests. Dorothy's brothers, Ruffin and Richard, were not at the reception, nor were Dorothy's many Norfolk cousins from her mother's side of the family. With the exception of the groom, none of the guests was a Ferebee. The wedding took place a year into Dorothy's first two-year term as president of the National Council of Negro Women, yet the reception did not include any of Washington's movers and shakers. Some of the male guests had dated the pretty and popular Dolly.[34] Surely her absence cast a pall over the celebration.

There had been another Ferebee wedding in 1951. On June 10 fifty-year-old Claude quietly tied the knot in his parents' living room in Norfolk.[35] His second wife was not Mrs. Dugger, his "Concerto" who inspired so much Sturm und Drang during World War II. Nor was the bride the chic, sophisticated Bobbie Branche of the NAACP in New York City he had dated. Instead Claude married a chubby, thirty-six-year-old New York divorcée, Hazel Irene Jones Hardy.[36]

Hazel couldn't hold a candle to Dorothy Celeste Boulding Ferebee. Her father, Norman Jones, was a janitor, and her mother, Maude Lee, was a housewife. Hazel was born in 1913 or 1914 and lived in Selma, Alabama.[37] At the time she and Claude married, she was a dietician at a New York hospital.[38] ("That's what my grandfather needed, a woman who could cook," laughed granddaughter Dorothy Ruth Ferebee.)[39] Hazel later worked as the office manager and bookkeeper in Claude's dental office in Harlem.[40]

The second Mrs. Ferebee had none of Dorothy's style, fame, panache, or power, which may have been exactly why Claude married her.

News of the marriage dropped like a bomb on the Ferebees' social world. "The East Coast society set buzzed this week over the sudden announcement" of the Ferebee-Hardy nuptials, reported the *New York Amsterdam News*. The much younger Hazel had flitted around the periphery of that society set because of the clout of her first husband, James B. Hardy, who was a behind-the-scenes political player in Harlem.[41]

Hazel may have crossed paths with Claude earlier in life. She earned a bachelor of science degree at Howard University in 1939,[42] where, during her freshman year, which would have been in the spring of 1936, she was one of the "ladies in waiting" to the queen of Howard's annual May Festival. An estimated two thousand students, faculty, staff, and random gawkers strolled past Frederick Douglass Hall on the Howard campus on a Tuesday afternoon to catch a glimpse of the queen and her court posing for pictures outside.[43] Claude Ferebee, still teaching about crowns and bridges that year, might have been there, perhaps bewitched by the young coed.[44] It would not have mattered, though; back then Hazel had eyes for another.

By 1937 Hazel was slipping up to New York during her Easter recess from classes to be with her future husband.[45] James Hardy was a politically connected Harlem businessman and a successful fund-raiser for African American office-seekers.[46] After they married, Hazel and James lived in a prewar building at 312 Manhattan Avenue, at the corner of West 113th Street near Morningside Park, once a classy central Harlem address.[47] They had no children.

After her marriage, Hazel's name surfaced in the press, not for starting a settlement house, testifying before Congress, providing medical care to the poor in the Mississippi, or leading one of the nation's most powerful group of women, but for her social activities and reasons that would have horrified Dorothy, namely, her public fights with her husband. Mr. and Mrs. Hardy reportedly got into a "fistic encounter" during the 1939 Christmas holiday. They were at it again in June 1940 in front of a bar on 116th Street, following a fraternity banquet. Hazel finally had enough and moved out.[48]

Claude could have crossed paths with Hazel at Harlem social events. She organized balls and enjoyed socializing at the upscale Theresa, Harlem's hottest hotel.[49] When she married Claude she was living at 555 Edgecombe

Avenue, a Beaux Arts apartment building at the corner of 160th Street that is now a National Historic Landmark.[50] The bluff on which the apartment house sits was dubbed "Sugar Hill" because life there was said to be so sweet.[51]

The couple sneaked away to Norfolk, took out a marriage license on July 9, and got married the next day in a small ceremony officiated by the Reverend James R. Johnson Jr. of St. John's AME Church, where Claude's family had worshipped for years.[52] Once again the house on Chapel Street was decked out for a celebration. The living room stairway was lined with fragrant white peonies, snapdragons, potted plants, and slender candles. Just as Dorothy had done for her a decade earlier, Claude's sister Maxine Ferebee Burrell served as the new Mrs. Ferebee's matron of honor. For her second stroll down the aisle on what was a very hot day, Hazel wore a powder-blue crepe dress and carried a bouquet of white orchids. Little sister Connie's husband, William Laurence Jones, was his brother-in-law's best man.[53] Immediately after the wedding the newlyweds returned to New York to attend a Dental Society dinner at the Hotel Theresa and then left for a long honeymoon at an undisclosed location.[54]

Despite the considerable age difference and Claude's history as a ladies' man, his marriage to Hazel would last forty-five years, until his death in 1996. The glue that held the couple together might have been an understanding that Claude would be the top dog. They were also bound by a mutual and relentless criticism of any and all things having to do with Dorothy Boulding Ferebee.

"The Major held on to his anger toward Gam (the family nickname for Grandmother Dorothy) the whole time he was married to Hazel," said Lisa Ferebee, the widow of Claude Thurston Ferebee III (Buzzy). "It came out while we visited them and the conversation about her came up, and for some reason, it always did. . . . The feeling was that it was 'normal' in his and Hazel's marriage for Gam to be talked about, negatively always."[55] Claude rarely visited Washington after he and Dorothy divorced. "Washington's not big enough for the two of us," he told his grandson Todd.[56]

Long after Dorothy was dead, Claude still couldn't let it go. In 1986 Buzzy videotaped an oral history with Claude, who looked straight into the camera and said, "I took a whole lot of stuff to the army—golf clubs, archery targets, tennis rackets—because when I left Washington, DC, I never had it in mind to go back. Period." After he spoke his face took on a faraway, unhappy expression, and then he ordered Buzzy to turn off the camera: "Okay, let's take a break."[57]

Dorothy did not fail to get in a few shots of her own, although Thurston told the *Washington Post* for a profile of his mother, "She has never said a derogatory word about my father," thus proving he was as adept at dissembling as she was.[58] He left out the part about Dorothy's propensity for claiming his father was dead even though he was very much alive, or about her grousing to her grandchildren about how little Claude did for them.

Claude's bitterness was likely rooted in an ego fractured from having been married to an icon and unresolved anger over the death of his daughter. Hazel's zest for going after Dorothy and egging on Claude to join her was probably due to jealousy. Dorothy's feelings were more complicated; she blamed their breakup on professional envy, but she knew that was only partially true. He was a cheater, and he blamed her for their daughter's death; no marriage could withstand that. Dorothy could never set the record straight because the truth cut to the core of the image she projected to the world. To admit her husband blamed her for her daughter's death would have required her to come clean about the facts surrounding it. Even years later, as a leader in the pro-choice movement, when the story of her daughter's death would have been so poignant, she could not do it. Sadly she missed the chance to give her daughter's brief life and tragic death some greater purpose.

It poured in Washington on the night Claude married Hazel. But if the weather matched Dorothy's mood over her husband's wedding, she did not show it. Instead on that night, she did what she loved doing best: she stood at the podium in the Crystal Ballroom of the historic Hotel Willard wearing an evening gown and presiding over an NCNW dinner for two hundred guests. The event was an awards night, celebrating select women who had contributed to the betterment of society.[59] In her keynote speech Dorothy said, "In honoring these women, the National Council of Negro Women has honored itself, through its recognition of their exceptional services in the fields of race relations, art, government, statesmanship, theatre, human relations, social welfare and international affairs."[60] She was describing a woman exactly like herself and exactly the kind of woman Claude no longer wanted.

18   You Were Grand as Ever

Weeks after Dolly's funeral, Dorothy was on the move and kept on moving for the next thirty years. Among the duties of the NCNW president was to wave the flag at regional meetings and speak before civic and church groups. Dorothy was game for all this. She traveled to Greensboro, North Carolina, a month after Dolly was buried and three months before her divorce to speak at Bennett College, where, ironically, the theme of the program was "Keys to Successful Family Living."[1] She attended the North Atlantic regional meeting of AKA in April.[2] In May 1950 she and her two rivals for the NCNW presidency, Edith Sampson and Arenia Mallory, were the featured speakers at a regional meeting in Dallas.[3] The trio "rocked the sessions for three days" with "dynamic speeches" demonstrating "femininity, spirit and leadership."[4] Dorothy offered a different kind of leadership than Bethune, ushering in an era where how the NCNW president looked was as important as what she said. "The national president of the NCNW spoke constructively, charmingly and in her prettiest voice before several hundred eager patrons," wrote Toki Schalk Johnson in the *Pittsburgh Courier* after Dorothy's November 1950 visit there. "Dr. Ferebee chose to speak in a black taffeta and velvet frock . . . taffeta cocktail dress topped with a velvet (with taffeta trim) jacket . . . and a head hugging hat misted with veiling."[5]

Although Dorothy traveled extensively, the one place she seemed unable to go was back to her apartment at the NCNW headquarters where Dolly died. After Dorothy was elected president, she had quarters at 1318 Vermont Avenue whenever she had business in Washington, as had Bethune. But before the end of 1950 she moved to a pleasant row house at 47 V Street NW, just a few blocks from where she and Claude and the twins had lived as a family in the 1930s.[6]

Dorothy never did return to live at the council house, remaining on V Street until she finally sold her New York home in the late 1950s and returned to the capital permanently at which time she bought her own small place in a northeast Washington neighborhood that rapidly went downhill.[7] (She would be mugged outside that home at 2960 13th Street NE in the 1970s. She was dazed and angry after the incident but not hurt, the mugger having received a taste of Dorothy's medicine—she tussled with him—before he ran off.)[8]

Those around Dorothy knew she was grieving over her daughter. A week after Dolly's death, NCNW executive director Jeanetta Welch Brown wrote to the executive committee, "Of course you know of the great tragedy that has just befallen our very capable and enthusiastic President. She needs you and your help now as never before."[9] Perhaps it was concern for their president's well-being that inspired the council to send her on a nice long trip the following year. At its November 15, 1950, meeting, the executive board chose Dorothy to represent the NCNW at the International Council of Women's Triennial Conference meeting in Greece in March 1951, with a cryptic entry as to how to pay for it: "By common consent it was agreed that expenses involved be referred to the Budget Committee."[10] At the same meeting the council voted to give Bethune $9,375 "in appreciation of the services she has rendered NCNW" during the fourteen years she served in her unpaid position as president.[11] That was real money—worth about $89,000 today.

Nothing had changed insofar as the NCNW's dismal finances were concerned, and the wisdom of making such a generous payment to Bethune and sending Dorothy abroad is questionable. In February 1950 Jeanetta Brown reported that there was $89.91 in the NCNW's bank account and the council was unable to pay its utility bills, insurance, office expenses, or salaries. Shamelessly Brown sent letters to each executive committee member, begging for money and underlining for emphasis, "send to the national office immediately, $25.00, 50.00 or $100.00."[12]

The Greek trip might have been good for Dorothy's psyche and her image as a citizen of the world but her extended absence from Washington undermined her position as the NCNW's leader. It fostered the idea that Bethune was still running the show. It also provided fodder for editorial writers and regional officers who suspected the NCNW was pouring money down the drain. An unsigned column in the *Chicago Defender* read, "And if that's grumbling you hear in the background over how the NCNW's president Dorothy Ferebee can be galivanting in Greece with the council on the financial rocks, we'd join in the refrain."[13]

Even before Dorothy's trip, there were signs that she was not enjoying the respect Bethune had. She was subject to criticism that would never have been thrust at the First Lady of Black America. In 1942, the Voice of America began to bring U.S. government-sponsored news programming to war-torn countries or places where censorship was prevalent.[14] The NCNW's Intercultural Committee was upset at the lack of top-level African American personnel at the VOA, and in July 1950 a story broke in the *Chicago Defender*, obviously leaked by a disgruntled council member, revealing that the Intercultural Committee sought to confront the VOA about it. Dorothy vetoed the idea. "Whatsamatter, gals, couldn't be that you fear not being invited to attend more international conferences or serve on more special committees?" the unsigned *Defender* column chided. "The time for window dressing is over and we've got to bear down where it's needed and when it's needed, else face the consequences."[15]

In the fall of 1950 Jeanetta Welch Brown, a powerhouse of efficiency and energy, dealt a blow to the council by resigning, although she stayed on through the summer of 1951. At a meeting of the board of directors in November 1950—a full year after Dorothy took the helm—Arenia Mallory suggested that Bethune get the last word on the selection of Brown's replacement, which had to have hit Dorothy like a slap in the face.[16]

Mallory apparently had not made peace with Bethune's order to step aside in the 1949 election. She sent Dorothy a letter praising her performance at her first NCNW annual meeting as president in November 1950: "You were grand as ever." But in the same letter she pouted because Dorothy had neglected to send her a congratulatory letter for the silver anniversary of the Saints' Industrial School: "Guess you forgot, know how busy you are." In a final poke she reminded Dorothy that Bethune had remembered and that the matriarch still spoke for the council: "Mrs. Bethune sent long lovely wire for herself and NCNW, so we received that."[17] Shortly before the 1951 annual convention, Mallory griped about not yet having an assignment for the convention and about being "overlooked" once again: "Each year I have to remind you. Why? Others feel as I do, only they are not frank enough to tell you, they tell others. I let it remain between us."[18]

Commiserating with Dorothy not long after she was elected, Ida Jackson, who had had her fill of Mallory years earlier, wrote wryly from California, "I have heard little of the activity of the Council here more than the petty striving of old self styled leaders who do little but retard the progress of those who might do a job. My best wishes for your success."[19]

Amazingly Dorothy kept turning the other cheek. "Every one of my executive committee has been wonderful to me, though I know the world expected a different story," she wrote to Mallory that fall. "I am grateful to them, for it has demonstrated a one-ness to keep the banner flying from the house top as a great tribute to Mrs. Bethune."[20]

After Dorothy's first year at the helm, the press questioned whether the NCNW could survive. "A choice morsel in the capital is about the meager 230-odd delegates including locals who attended the 15th annual conference of the National Council of Negro Women [the first of Dorothy's presidency] and the $16,000 they are in the red," reported a Cleveland, Ohio, newspaper, the *Call & Post*. Making matters worse, the author of the unsigned piece suggested that Dorothy was not up to the task of running the organization: "Then could it be that the recently elected president does not carry the dynamic punch and personality of Ma Bethune." Although she was never a quitter, all of this took its toll on Dorothy, who vacillated about whether she wanted to run for a second two-year term at the end of 1951.[21]

Dorothy must have felt the walls closing in on her. Nobody was serenading *her* with "Let Me Call You Sweetheart" as the council had for Bethune. While Claude and Hazel were planning their double-ring ceremony, Dorothy packed her bags for ten days in Greece for the ICW conference, after which she would spend two months in Germany on a goodwill tour.[22] She set sail aboard the *Queen Elizabeth* from New York Harbor to Athens on March 20, 1951.[23]

At the time of her trip Dorothy was the acting director of the Howard University Health Service.[24] President Mordecai Johnson, always supportive of her extracurricular work, generously gave her a leave of absence, something her busy travel schedule would require him to do routinely over the next seventeen years until she retired.[25]

As she was preparing to leave, there was still no money to pay for the trip. Ruth Scott, then the NCNW's northeast regional director, asked one hundred of Dorothy's closest friends to chip in at least one dollar.[26] She raised

$650.[27] Before departing for Greece, Dorothy was given an elaborate send-off by the NCNW. "You are cordially invited to wish BON VOYAGE to Dr. Dorothy Boulding Ferebee. . . . We hope you will come and bring your friends," at four dollars each, the invitation read.[28] Some five hundred guests joined Dorothy at the Hotel Governor Clinton in Midtown Manhattan on Sunday, March 11.[29] The event yielded between four hundred and five hundred dollars. Mary Bethune auctioned off the orchid she wore to the party for fifteen dollars.[30] Eventually well-wishers raised $1,500 for Dorothy's trip.[31]

Among those invited to the going-away party were Bethune; Dorothy Height; Rachel Robinson, who was Dorothy's St. Albans neighbor and the wife of Brooklyn Dodger Jackie Robinson; Juanita Hall, who was playing "Bloody Mary" on Broadway in *South Pacific*; and the wives of Ralph Bunche and former New York governor Herbert Lehman. Dorothy attended the party with her ever-present mother. Both sat at the head table with Bethune. Dorothy wore a dark suit and what looked like a man-eating corsage; it covered the entire front of her jacket from her breast to the top of her shoulder.[32]

The transatlantic crossing aboard the luxury liner took a week. Dorothy arrived in Paris on March 27, where she boarded an Air France prop-plane for a grueling seven-and-a-half-hour nonstop flight to Athens. To today's traveler, lucky to get a cup of coffee and a package of stale crackers on an airliner, Dorothy's description of the meal served on board—several kinds of meat, mushrooms, vegetables, cheeses, rolls, pastries, wines, liquors, and champagne—seems incredible.[33] The delegation was greeted by Queen Frederika once they settled in Athens. The queen opened the ICW conference.[34]

The ICW was founded to foster peaceful settlement of international disputes. Looking back, the positions taken by the ICW mirrored those proffered a generation later when debate over the Equal Rights Amendment was raging in the United States in the 1970s. In 1951 the women sought to end gender discrimination on all levels; they wanted equal access to education for men and women, legal and contractual rights for married women, freedom from forced marriages and elimination of child marriages, equal pay for equal work for women, and gender fairness in pension distributions.[35]

From Greece it was off to Germany to join a group of women leaders invited by the High Commission of Germany with the cooperation of the

U.S. State Department and the Department of Labor to observe postwar conditions.[36] Certainly part of the mission was to foster positive U.S. government propaganda, whether or not Dorothy recognized she was being used for that purpose. She had a high old time, proud that she was chosen as the group's spokeswoman. In a letter to Jeanetta Brown from Munich, Dorothy offered "just a tiny glimpse" of her "wonderful experiences":

> I personally have had a most satisfying trip. For two days after our arrival, I had the privilege of making my first impression when the High Commissioner Mr. John J. McCloy, asked me to make a radio broadcasting with his wife, Mrs. McCloy. It was all very flattering, though I knew deep down, it was more or less a test case for me, to see how I was thinking, and how I handled myself before the Mic. Luck was with Me! The questions the interviewer put to me were fortunately ones I could manage, with the very good result of my being made the spokesman for the group of 11 American women![37]

Meanwhile back in Washington, the NCNW was imploding. "Dear Dear Doctor: How happy we are you are having such a good time. We have been having a h of a time here, but things are looking up now," Brown wrote sardonically. First the executive committee called an emergency meeting because the House Un-American Activities Committee reported the names of persons who signed a peace petition and casted suspicion on their loyalty to the country. The release by HUAC chairman Representative John S. Wood of Georgia; "Report on the Communist 'Peace' Offensive: A Campaign to Disarm and Defeat the United States" was the catalyst for the NCNW to throw itself into a tizzy. From today's perspective the report is nonsense. It was filled with the usual allegations that communists had either inspired or infiltrated left-wing peace groups populated by the usual suspects— artists and writers—and anyone who attended the meetings or signed a petition calling for disarmament was not a good American.[38] "The president of the Brooklyn chapter was named therein several times," wrote Brown.[39] At the emergency meeting it was determined that all activities of the Brooklyn Council be suspended pending an investigation—showing how frightened the women were of being affixed with the label of disloyalty.[40]

The executive committee voted to publish a warning in the April issue of *Telefact* that local chapters should stay away from "the many spurious peace crusades and statements being issued by the forces that would 'preach peace but practice aggression.' "[41] NCNW members whose names appeared in the HUAC report were asked to "prove" the allegations were false. Besides Brooklyn Council president Ada Jackson, the name of none other than the national vice president Vivian Carter Mason, one of Dorothy's rivals in 1949, also appeared in the HUAC report. Mason and Jackson were directed to respond within fifteen days.[42] Mason complied, but the Brooklyn president did not. "And now the fireworks begin with Brooklyn, they have protested," Brown told Dorothy.[43]

Other headaches awaited Dorothy when she returned. The board was forced to take out another loan to pay the bills. The head of the NCNW Intercultural Committee took it upon herself to organize a Caribbean Tour on Pan American Airlines and bill it as the "National Council of Negro Women Caribbean Tour," with plans to visit various heads of state and no plans to clear it with Dorothy. But the executive committee "clipped her wings" and canceled the trip, Brown wrote. Finally one of the regional directors refused to hold a meeting as required under the NCNW by-laws. Brown left Dorothy with a few handwritten parting words: "*Have a good time* forget everything & *live for once*."[44]

Dorothy's long-awaited homecoming was dramatic. She breezed into council headquarters in Washington on June 9 directly from the airport after a three-month absence, smack in the middle of an executive committee meeting. She put down her bags, caught her breath, and picked up her gavel. The women were only too happy to have her back so they could dump the entire Brooklyn Council HUAC mess in her lap. Dorothy promised to act quickly, after first consulting with the council's legal committee.[45]

Ironically Dorothy's trip to Germany sucked her into the vortex of the Red Scare. Two years after she returned she was summoned to an executive session of Senator Joseph McCarthy's Subcommittee on Investigations. McCarthy, his chief counsel, the ruthless Roy Cohn, Senator Stuart Symington of Missouri, and Senator Henry Jackson of Washington wanted to know who had sponsored her trip and what purpose it had served. They tried to bait her into naming names of friends or fellow professors who were communists, but she did not bite. On June 8, 1953, after swearing to tell the truth, she told McCarthy's panel she had been invited by the International Division of the Department of Labor's Women's Bureau to "meet with women's groups and lecture, talk with their townspeople in and around Germany."[46] The session never became heated; Dorothy said little and revealed nothing.

> *Senator Symington*: You have never been a member of the Communist party?
> *Dr. Ferebee*: No, I have not. . . .
> *Senator Symington*: Do you have any friends who are Communists?
> *Dr. Ferebee*: None that I know of.
> *Senator Symington*: Do you have any relatives who are Communists?
> *Dr. Ferebee*: No, I have not. . . .
> *Senator Symington*: Do you know any Communist party members in the faculty at Howard University?
> *Dr. Ferebee*: No, I don't. I don't know of any personally.[47]

Dorothy was thanked for her testimony, praised by Senator Jackson as a "very fine witness," and Senator McCarthy promised her testimony would remain secret unless she chose to reveal it.[48] Throughout the ordeal Dorothy maintained her dignity and self-respect. Not surprisingly, outside of telling family members, she never spoke of being called before Senator McCarthy.[49]

Although Dorothy was a good citizen and did an appropriate amount of flag waving as NCNW president, she was not blind and not willing to sit by when her race and gender were being unfairly treated—even by a president she largely admired. In a letter to President Truman after her return from Germany, she was honest about the fact that the American Dream did not exist for her people. She described of her visits to black soldiers while in Germany: "I need not tell you that the presence of the segregated military units belies the democratic principles we extolled, and reeks damage that cannot be repaired by hundreds of good-will emissaries."[50] She asked if she might call on the president to discuss it further but got a polite brush-off from his secretary, Matthew J. Connelly: "All that you say has been most carefully noted and I am indeed sorry that it is not possible to arrange the interview with the President that you request."[51]

As NCNW president Dorothy was the face of the organization and responsible for its stewardship. Within weeks of her election, she put forth a program to make the council more relevant and effective. She created nine departments—labor and industry, human relations, social welfare, publicity, citizenship education, international relations, youth conservation, junior councils, and history—and organized the council's activities around them. Within those departments the council would work across racial lines, lobby for civil rights legislation, educate members on how to be more involved in public life while improving their family lives, participate in government conferences, and maintain an archive of the achievements of black women.[52]

During the four years Dorothy led the NCNW, the group continued to participate in White House conferences on issues involving women and children.[53] She made appearances at NCNW regional meetings around the country, and she testified on Capitol Hill, her medical background often putting her and the NCNW at the forefront of health issues. In the fall of 1951 she testified before the Senate Rules Committee to urge that it end "the undemocratic process of filibuster," which was used to kill civil rights legislation.[54] Dorothy was blunt in her criticism of the practice, telling the committee that during her recent sojourn to Germany, those she met "repeatedly questioned America's hypocrisy in championing democracy around the world, while using at home, every device at hand to thwart the extension of civil rights to its citizens. . . . I can say with great honesty and emphasis that they saw very little difference between our brand of racism and that of the Hitler regime."[55]

In the spring of 1952 Dorothy appeared before Congress at least twice, once before the Senate Subcommittee on Health to testify for government-funded health care for the families of low-paid enlisted men in the military. Shortly thereafter she testified before the Senate Committee on Banking and Currency in favor of extending the emergency price controls established by the government during the Korean War.[56]

Dorothy wrote a regular newspaper column as NCNW president and made speeches on every possible topic of importance to the civil rights struggle.[57] The council often shot off telegrams to President Truman. In December 1951 Dorothy complained in one telegram that no black doctor had been appointed to a national commission to promote public health: "If this is true, there has been a serious oversight and the National Council of Negro Women representing 850,000 throughout the country urge you to make such an appointment."[58]

Unfortunately Dorothy's attention was drawn away the council's substantive policy work because she had to keep it afloat. Not more than a month after her daughter died, she berated the executive committee for adjourning its March 1950 meeting "without specific action on any of the crucial and immediate problems of the Council."[59] With her nerves understandably frayed, she wrote a blunt letter to her executive committee:

> There is no positive direction left for me as to how to meet the next pay roll period; how the staff would be paid from then on; how the accrued indebtedness could be reduced, or how the current loan of $1,200 could be liquidated.
>
> As an endorser of the latest loan, I feel that I have indicated my interest and willingness to give concrete proof of my faith in this organization, but I must make it absolutely clear that I shall not again assume financial responsibility for the organization, especially when the responsible officers seem unable to evolve some financial plans to assure its future.[60]

After that dressing-down, the council leaders devised a number of fundraising schemes, some wackier than others. Someone came up with the idea of a "mid-century register of women," in which council members would pay one dollar each for the privilege of putting their names in a time capsule that would be opened in 2000.[61] The council offered to produce a concert for First Daughter Margaret Truman, who had a middling singing career while her father was in the White House, with part of the proceeds going to the NCNW, but Miss Truman politely declined.[62] There was a ten-dollar-a-ticket fashion show at the Waldorf-Astoria in New York (eighty-eight in today's dollars) and in 1952 a boat ride on the Potomac to celebrate the seventy-seventh birthday of Mrs. Bethune—minus the presence of the birthday girl.[63]

In February 1951 the NCNW hosted a tea in honor of Jane Barkley, the new thirty-eight-year-old bride of seventy-one-year-old vice president Alben Barkley, at the Shoreham Hotel in Washington.[64] It was an interracial event at a time Washington was still strictly segregated. Dorothy corralled five hundred guests in the Main Ballroom, where white and black women poured and shared tea with one another. The wife of Supreme Court Justice Tom Clark poured tea next to the dean of women at Howard

University. The council made four hundred dollars on the event (about nine thousand in today's dollars).[65]

The council hosted two concerts in 1951 featuring major talent: Hazel Scott, the beautiful concert pianist who in 1945 married New York congressman Adam Clayton Powell, and Josephine Baker, the sensuous stage performer whose dance in a banana skirt in the 1920s made her the most famous woman on earth. The Hazel Scott concert on May 14 at Carnegie Hall took place while Dorothy was in Greece.[66] Scott was the star at Café Society, an integrated nightclub in New York. Patrons included Paul Robeson, Langston Hughes, Leonard Bernstein, Nelson Rockefeller, and Eleanor Roosevelt. Scott cut albums, appeared on Broadway, made movies in Hollywood, and in 1950 was the first black woman to host her own television show, *The Hazel Scott Show*, on which she played the piano while wearing sparkly diamonds and glittery gowns.[67]

But Scott also tangled with HUAC. After her name appeared in the right-wing pamphlet *Red Channels*, which published names of those it considered "Red" or "Pink," Scott volunteered to go before HUAC to "clear" her name. Within a week after she testified on Capitol Hill, her television show was canceled.[68]

Dorothy was back from Europe in time to host the Josephine Baker concert. Baker got her big career break in the chorus of the 1923 black revue, *Shuffle Along*, and in 1925 went to Paris, where she performed her infamous dance wearing a skirt made of sixteen bananas and not much else. She became the highest paid performer in Europe and a heroine of the French Resistance in World War II, smuggling messages to anti-Nazi fighters in her sheet music and her underwear. In the 1950s she returned more frequently to the United States to participate in civil rights' activities.[69]

When Baker arrived in Washington on July 2, 1951 for the NCNW concert she was treated as if she were visiting royalty. "A motorcade of 50 cars escorted the exotic toast of Paris to the Council house where she met the press and was served refreshments," read one news account.[70] The concert was Jeanetta Brown's swan song with the council; she dreamed up the idea and got the green light from the executive committee, and she and Vivian Mason made it happen in record time. Brown had proposed to the executive committee on June 9 that it invite the diva to perform in Washington just three weeks later. Volunteers were recruited, the giant National Guard Armory was reserved, and Brown found a printing company to run off tickets ranging in price from $1.80 to $6.[71] Baker did not donate her services to the beleaguered council; she demanded four thousand dollars up front to perform (thirty-five thousand dollars today), and the council paid her.[72] Hazel Scott, in contrast, performed for the NCNW without charge.[73]

Brown and Mason handled every aspect of the concert with Dorothy's full support. They worked from nine in the morning until midnight of the evening Josephine Baker walked onstage. They helped secure a local backup band, rented a Steinway piano to accompany her, negotiated with the stage hands union for lighting, and commandeered local businesses as ticket-selling agents. They convinced the manager of the Dunbar Hotel at 15th and U Streets, in the heart of the African American business district, to donate space for a temporary ticket office. They sold a souvenir program and advertising space. They worked with Baker's public relations man to negotiate reduced rates for newspaper ads and free public service air time on the radio and to distribute one thousand placards and fifty thousand flyers announcing the concert.[74]

Dorothy held Presidential Box H for Harry Truman and offered an unlimited number of tickets for him and his guests, which he declined.[75] As if Baker herself had just been elected president of the United States, the council arranged for a fifty- to one hundred–car motorcade up Pennsylvania Avenue in her honor. Dorothy wrote to the major of the Metropolitan Police Department seeking permission for a procession of cars to lead Baker from Union Station up Pennsylvania Avenue to 15th Street NW and then north to U Street NW and through the streets of Washington to the NCNW headquarters on Vermont Avenue NW.[76]

Baker's plane was scheduled to arrive at National Airport at 2:20 on the day of the concert. A hostess committee hustled out to the runway to form a "guard of honor" to lead her from the ramp of the plane to a reception room, where she was welcomed by Dorothy, presented a key to the city by District of Columbia commissioner F. Joseph Donahue, greeted by a representative of the French Embassy, and given an armful of roses. Following a brief news conference, Dorothy and Baker climbed into the backseat of a convertible with several airport dignitaries and headed downtown.[77]

During the two-and-a-half-hour concert that began at 8:30 that evening, Baker changed into selections from the forty-three French designer gowns she brought along for the show.[78] Dorothy stuck to one elegant black dress with a natural waist and a bodice of short-sleeved lace. She wore fingerless black lace gloves and peep-toed black sandals with an ankle strap. She pulled her hair back and tied it with a white flower at the nape of her neck. She looked exquisite. She walked to the stage to present Baker with the NCNW Scroll of Honor "for her fearless and forthright stand against discrimination and segregation in America."[79]

The Baker concert was a huge success, and it filled the NCNW's bank account. There were six thousand in the audience, and crowds had to be turned away at the door.[80] Thanks to Josephine Baker, at the September 1951 executive committee meeting the NCNW members dined on boiled ham and potato salad, coffee, and grapes and sat down to happily count their money rather than nervously wring their hands over where their next dollar was coming from. After all the bills were paid, the Josephine Baker concert account had more than $2,800 in it.[81] But neither the euphoria nor the money lasted long; by the spring of 1952, the NCNW had exactly $152.02 in the bank, forcing it to lay off a typist and another staff member.[82]

For all the carping against President Ferebee, she ran unopposed for a second term.[83] (Dorothy won with ninety-seven votes, indicating that a small group of the inner circle essentially ran the organization.)[84]

For the remainder of 1951 Dorothy occupied herself by becoming a traveling NCNW saleswoman, offering her services as a lecturer on the black college campus circuit for a fee. In the summer letters went out to dozens of schools, mostly in the South.[85] While it was admirable of her to offer to traipse all over the country for the good of the NCNW, it was exhausting, time-consuming, and not a particularly effective way to get the council permanently out of the red.

At the end of 1952 Dorothy returned to Germany for a month at the invitation of the Bonn government.[86] But by the end of her second two-year term, she was done. She was fifty-five years old in the fall of 1953, which was not "the new forty" back then. She did not smoke cigarettes and did not drink more than nipping an occasional teaspoon or two of Jamaica Rum when she made one of her favorite recipes, New England Suet

Pudding and Hard Sauce, one of a number included in an NCNW fund-raising cookbook. But despite her healthy living and boundless energy she looked and probably felt her age.[87] And she may have suffered a more serious, undisclosed health problem. In February 1952, the NCNW's Arabella Denniston wrote to Bethune: "Dr. Ferebee is back and looking almost like herself again. She is still taking treatments in New York, however."[88]

While she had been running the NCNW, she was also directing the Howard University Health Service, teaching in the obstetrics department of the hospital, treating patients, and delivering babies. She did not have speech writers, publicity agents, or a personal assistant. She put on the reading glasses that she had been wearing since 1929 and spent her weekends writing speeches in longhand on yellow legal pads while she sat aboard pokey trains and noisy prop planes for hours, crisscrossing the country.[89]

The well-known *Pittsburgh Courier* reporter Hazel Garland aptly described what was at stake for the woman who would replace Dorothy at the end of 1953 at the helm of the council: "Although there are a number of other officers of the NCNW, it functions largely as a 'one-woman' organization. That is why the presidency is so important. And interest at this time is tantamount to that of electing a president of the United States."[90]

The new president would have her work cut out for her. The council house was a mess, and the Vermont Avenue, NW, neighborhood in which it was located was deteriorating. The executive director hired to replace Jeanetta Brown quit within two years.[91] The incoming Eisenhower administration was not likely to be closely aligned with the interests of the NCNW.

The final NCNW annual convention of Dorothy's presidency took place in November 1953. In one of her last official acts, she presided over a packed house at what had become a regular event, International Night at the Department of Labor auditorium. Nelson Rockefeller, then the undersecretary of the Department of Health, Education and Welfare, was the main speaker.[92] The conference was a success and afterward select members of the council were invited to the White House by First Lady Mamie Eisenhower.[93]

Dorothy was impressed with the young Dorothy Height of New York and wanted to see her elected as her successor. As those in power often do, during her last year in office she began grooming Height to take over.[94] Bethune wanted Vivian Carter Mason to be president in 1953. In an unheard-of situation, Dorothy and Bethune ended up arguing over it, so vigorously that the exchange of words saw the light of day in at least one newspaper. "Political maneuverings leading up to the election of a new president for the National Council of Negro Women narrowed down to a word battle between outgoing president Dorothy Ferebee of Washington DC, and the organization's president-emeritus Mary McLeod Bethune," wrote a columnist for the *Pittsburgh Courier*.[95]

Proving that Dorothy never enjoyed Bethune's status or influence, the members elected Bethune's candidate.[96] Immediately after the election, Dorothy headed to New York to check into the Edward S. Harkness Eye Institute, part of Columbia University Hospital, to treat a minor medical problem—probably cataracts—that she had ignored while she was busy running the council.[97]

19 A Bad Bitter Pill

The civil rights movement heated up as Dorothy's visibility was winding down. Vivian Mason was at the helm of the NCNW in 1954 when the U.S. Supreme Court handed down its landmark decision in *Brown v. Board of Education*, one of many death knells for legalized segregation. And it was during Mason's tenure that Rosa Parks's arrest ignited the Montgomery bus boycott and launched the career of the charismatic young minister Dr. Martin Luther King Jr. As characterized by the Pulitzer Prize–winning author Diane McWhorter in her Pulitzer Prize–winning book *Carry Me Home*, "the modern civil rights movement had been born. . . . The struggle had moved out of the hands of the talented tenth and into the streets."[1]

Ironically, with no children at home Dorothy became more focused on family life. She adored Buzzy's children and was a doting grandmother. "Gam" was all their infant tongues could do with the word "grandma." She *loved* the nickname. Gam was their baby-sitter, role model, and beach pal at her home on the Jersey Shore.

Four years after his sister's death, Thurston was still reeling. He entered the air force reserve in June 1954 as a clerk. Four months later he enlisted in the regular air force and was sent to Sampson Air Force Base in central New York. He remained in the air force until 1960, when he was honorably discharged as an airman, first class. During his years in the service he also was stationed at Mac Dill Air Force Base in Tampa and at the Air Force Command in Denver.[2]

For part of the time her son was away, Dorothy's daughter-in-law, Carol, and their firstborn son, Buzzy, lived with her in St. Albans. Dorothy was in heaven. "She is very fond of the baby and devotes a good deal of time to his interest," Ruth Scott wrote in a gossipy note to Bethune in the mid-1950s. "She even has him speaking French."[3]

Dorothy remained a relentless joiner. While still running the NCNW, she was named to the national board of the YWCA,[4] where could emphasize her devotion to her Christian faith. She was, after all, a church lady at heart. She called membership in the YWCA an opportunity to "make a spiritual impact upon the forces of racial and religious discrimination."[5] The national leadership of the YWCA took a progressive view on integration; it adopted a no-discrimination policy in 1960, which put its board at odds with branches in the South that were segregated.[6] Dorothy's board responsibilities brought her to New York City periodically for meetings throughout the 1950s and early 1960s and provided a platform for talks around the country, long after most of her NCNW public appearances were behind her.[7]

With few women in power on the national scene and even fewer when it came to women of color, Dorothy's name surfaced when a politician needed what she could offer. John F. Kennedy's presidential election in 1960 opened doors for Dorothy at the White House. Among his "New Frontier" initiatives was the Food for Peace program, led by the future South Dakota senator and presidential candidate George McGovern. The program was intended to promote international goodwill by selling or donating surplus food and commodities to underdeveloped countries.[8] JFK appointed Dorothy in May 1961 to the Food for Peace Council, a ninety-five-member blue-ribbon panel of advisors and public speakers who could tout the program to special interest groups. Along with business leaders, journalists, academics, lawyers, and state agriculture officials, the panel included a few glamorous figures like Hollywood stars Yul Brenner and Danny Kaye, singer Marian Anderson, and Pulitzer Prize–winning author James A. Michener.[9]

Dorothy was also among those JFK called on to lend a hand with his landmark civil rights bill. Despite victories in the federal courts, the civil rights movement was stalled in legislatures and town halls and at lunch counters all over the South. Realizing the federal government could no longer sit still, Kennedy appeared on national television on June 11, 1963, and told the listening world, "We are confronted primarily with a moral issue. It is as old as the Scriptures and is as clear as the American Constitution."

With that, he introduced the most sweeping civil rights bill since Reconstruction.

For the rest of the summer JFK summoned community leaders to drum up support. Dorothy joined some 350 black and white women of note who were invited to the White House for an off-the-record session on the bill.[10] Before the meeting began in the East Room, presidential advisor Charles A. Horsky slipped JFK a note with the names of four women he could call on who were "primed to speak." Dorothy was on the list; Horsky identified her as one of two "Negroes."[11]

The president received a standing ovation from the women, who were dressed in their best summer suits, matching hats, and wrist-length white gloves. The White House pulled out all the stops; Attorney General Robert Kennedy, Vice President Lyndon Johnson, and Secretary of State Dean Rusk all showed up. Afterward, on what was a gorgeous summer afternoon, the president thrilled his guests by giving them a personal tour of the Rose Garden.[12]

Just as Bethune stepped up to the plate when Dorothy needed her and her health permitted, Dorothy too made herself available for her successors. When Vivian Mason practically forced her way into a meeting with FBI director J. Edgar Hoover in 1956 to discuss increasing violence against African Americans in the South, Dorothy was at her side. Mason, Dorothy, and a contingent from the executive committee of the NCNW had met with Attorney General Herbert Brownell in mid-December 1955 and then walked over to the FBI director's office to see him too. Hoover stalled as long as he could but eventually agreed to see them. The meeting they had several months later is a shameful chapter in the story of the FBI's tepid responses to continued lawlessness against blacks during the civil rights era.[13]

After fourteen-year-old Emmett Till of Chicago was murdered by white men in August 1955 for supposedly making an indecent remark to one of their wives, a picture of his battered face in an open coffin ignited worldwide outrage. The FBI never investigated, determining that no violation of federal law was involved. That same month Lamar Smith, a sixty-three-year-old African American, was shot and killed on the courthouse lawn in Brookhaven, Mississippi, after urging blacks to cast absentee ballots in the upcoming election for governor. The FBI did not investigate that one either, preferring to leave the matter to local officials.[14]

The FBI's attitude toward the NCNW representatives was equally appalling. First, the director tried to push the delegation off to an underling. When Mason insisted they meet with the director, Hoover's response was, "Just what do we know [about] the Council?"[15]

Not surprisingly the meeting that went on for an hour and a half on February 28, 1956, went nowhere. Hoover made no promises to investigate civil rights abuses and before the meeting ended launched into a patronizing discourse in which he blamed racial unrest on "extremists" on both sides of the civil rights issue, as opposed to racists in southern governments or horrifying lynchings, and he called for "calm deliberation and understanding."[16]

Two years after Bethune died in 1955, Dorothy Height finally became president of the NCNW, defeating the perennial candidate Arenia Mallory.[17] Like Mason, she too called on Dorothy for help. Dorothy went to Capitol Hill in the winter of 1958 with NCNW executive director Elsie Austin to convince Congress to exempt the NCNW building from real estate taxes.[18] President Eisenhower signed the bill on behalf of the council and one of the pens he used was later presented to Dorothy on behalf of the NCNW.[19]

In the mid-1960s the council's constitution and by-laws were changed to eliminate term limits for the NCNW president.[20] Consequently Height remained in office for years. In 1963 she asked Dorothy to join her in Selma to help in the fight for voting rights. Certainly this demonstrated she respected Dorothy and wanted to work with her. Yet as Dorothy aged, she is said to have resented Height, although it is not clear what exactly soured the relationship. The Ferebee grandchildren continued to harbor ill feelings toward Height years after both women were dead. Basically Dorothy and her family thought she never received the credit she deserved for her groundbreaking work as a race leader. To an extent they were right. Dorothy and Vivian Carter Mason, the Norfolk social work administrator who followed her as NCNW president, were sandwiched between a pair of icons.[21] Bethune founded the council, made it into a political force, and ran it for fourteen years. Mother Bethune's symbolic importance is embodied in a larger-than-life bronze statue of her that hovers over Lincoln Park, just blocks from the Capitol building in Washington.

During the entire four years of her uncompensated presidency, Dorothy was digging into her handbag to help the council stay afloat, while she also ran the Howard student health service and treated patients in her medical offices in New York and Washington. Height was associated with the NCNW for more than seventy years.[22] At some point the presidency became salaried and she was well-paid.[23]

Height achieved what had been unattainable by Bethune, Ferebee, and Mason: tax-exempt status for the NCNW. By getting the NCNW designated as a 501(c)(3) charitable organization in 1966, Height put the council on solid financial ground,[24] freeing it from paying federal income taxes and making it eligible for large foundation grants. Donors could deduct contributions to the NCNW from their own income taxes. Never again would the president of the council be forced to beg its members for gifts of money, ask bank officers for loans that could not be repaid, and make speeches in obscure locales for a pittance. If Height had done nothing else during the years she was president, obtaining nonprofit status for the council would have been sufficient to place her on a pedestal.

The Ferebee grandchildren resented the fact Height became, in essence, "president for life," ignoring the fact she did so with consent of the NCNW's voting members. The official council website in 2014 contained photographs of only two of its first four presidents: Bethune and Height. The NCNW's current national headquarters, a majestic structure at 633 Pennsylvania Avenue NW, strategically situated between the Capitol Building and the White House, is named the Dorothy I. Height Building.

Susan Goodwillie Stedman, Height's executive assistant at the council in the early 1960s, said, "Over time, Dorothy Height just became a presence." NCNW by-laws or not, by the mid-1960s "there was no one else who could have possibly succeeded her. She was the matriarch of the black community in this country."[25] Ferebee and Height were significant figures in mid-twentieth-century America, yet Height's outsized reputation leaves the impression that she alone was in the trenches. When she died in 2010 she was "widely credited" according to her New York Times obituary with being the "first person" in the movement to recognize the dual problems of racial and gender equality as "a seamless whole," allowing her to merge "concerns that had been largely historically separate."[26] Actually both Bethune and Ferebee considered those issues to be intertwined long before Height came along. The historian Joyce A. Hanson wrote, "Bethune distinguished herself from other race leaders by steadfastly incorporating the struggle for gender equality within her efforts for black equality."[27] Dorothy had also been saying the same thing for years; it was the theme of her speech the night she and Height shared a podium in 1963 at the First Baptist Church in Selma at the voting rights rally.

Height was on the platform when President Obama was inaugurated in 2009, just as Dorothy had been when FDR was sworn in for a fourth term in 1945.[28] When Dorothy died, Patricia Roberts Harris, a lawyer with a string of firsts in her own career—first African American woman to hold a cabinet post (Carter administration), to serve as an ambassador (Luxembourg), and to run a law school (Howard)—gave the eulogy at Howard's Rankin Memorial Chapel to a standing-room-only crowd.[29] When Height died, President Obama gave a thirteen-minute eulogy at her funeral at the National Cathedral in Washington.[30] Prior to her death, Height had visited the Obama White House twenty-one times, including once during a blizzard while in a wheelchair for a meeting of black leaders about unemployment.[31] Dorothy Ferebee rubbed elbows with multiple presidents and first ladies—Franklin and Eleanor Roosevelt, Harry and Bess Truman, Ike and Mamie Eisenhower, JFK and Jackie, LBJ and Lady Bird, as well as First Lady Patricia Nixon. But she could not boast of being invited to the White House nearly two dozen times by the same president. Ironically there seemed to be little competition when they were both alive and working for equality. When the chips were down, Height did not hesitate to turn to Dorothy for help, and Dorothy did not hesitate to give it.

In October 1963 Susan Goodwillie Stedman, then Susan Goodwillie, was working at her desk at the NCNW headquarters and received a telephone call from Prathia Hall, an organizer with the Student Non-Violent Coordinating Committee (SNCC). "I took that call. The urgency in her voice was palpable and I knew it was important," she remembered.[32] SNCC activists had gone into Selma, Alabama, to organize a voter registration drive. After four young African American girls were killed by a bomb in the basement of the 16th Street Baptist Church in Birmingham on Sunday morning, September 15, 1963, SNCC beefed up its voter registration campaign in Selma in the hope of defeating Governor George Wallace.[33]

The younger and edgier of the civil rights organizations, SNCC sometimes butted heads with the established Southern Christian Leadership Conference, run by Martin Luther King, whose godlike status was such that SNCC's inner circle irreverently called him "de Lawd."[34] SNCC had enlisted local high school and college students for the Selma voter drive, and they were getting arrested by the dozens. There was talk the youngsters were being mistreated in the local jails. Prathia Hall begged Dorothy Height to come down and see for herself. "They really were trying to build more of a climate of support around these young people and also to bring to public attention the way they were being treated," Height later said.[35]

A month before the church bombing, 250,000 people descended on Washington for the March on Washington for Jobs and Freedom, best remembered today for King's "I Have a Dream" speech. Height was on the platform in front of the Lincoln Memorial when King spoke. As president of the NCNW, it would have been fitting for her to have addressed the crowd, but the event's coordinator, Bayard Rustin, wouldn't hear of it. Although Height tempered her remarks for her memoir, *Open Wide the Freedom Gates*, she was steamed about it. "She fought very, very hard to have a woman up there," recalled Stedman years later.[36]

The marginalization of women at that march indirectly led to SNCC's invitation to the NCNW to come to Selma. The day after the march, Height and Pauline "Polly" Spiegel Cowan, the heiress to the Spiegel mail-order catalogue fortune and a liberal social activist, organized a biracial women's meeting in Washington to discuss housing, education, and employment. Prathia Hall attended and told the women about SNCC's campaign. Height offered her help.[37]

Hall reached out two months later, after three hundred black children— some as young as eight—were arrested in Selma for encouraging their parents, relatives, and neighbors to vote. Height put together an interracial team to go to Selma. She chose two white women, Polly Cowan and Shirley Smith, the executive director of the National Women's Committee for Civil Rights, to join her and Dorothy.[38]

Dorothy was about to turn sixty-five. Having paid her dues to the civil rights movement years before, she could have easily taken a pass when Height called, and spent a pleasant autumn weekend at her home on the Jersey shore instead. In her memoir Height said she chose those three women because "we already had been working closely together on civil rights issues. We knew and respected each other."[39] Certainly Dorothy's medical degree and work with the student population at Howard figured into the invitation. Her reputation for fearlessness was surely another factor. Her contemporaries had known of her daring work in Mississippi in the 1930s.

In Selma SNCC had been organizing a voter registration drive for the better part of a year. The executive secretary James Forman led the drive; he was a man described years later in his *New York Times* obituary as having had a "fiercely revolutionary vision."[40] He was also known as "the SNCC hothead."[41] Prathia Hall, the daughter of a Baptist minister and a graduate of Temple University in Philadelphia, was one of SNCC's first women field organizers.[42]

In 1963 half of Selma's 28,600 inhabitants were black, but they accounted for less than 1 percent of the city's registered voters.[43] After a slow start, SNCC attracted a few Selma high school students who became intrigued, then captivated, and then energized by what was happening in their city. They went door-to-door to ask adults if they were registered voters. Frightened residents slammed the doors in their faces.[44] By April 1963 something just short of a miracle happened: one hundred black adults went downtown and stood on line all day to register to vote, albeit with little or no success.[45] They risked a lot to be there; their employers checked the line implying that they would be fired if found on it. Law enforcement officers took pictures of those waiting on the registration line, leading to fears of violent reprisals.[46]

Fanning the flames of violence was Sheriff James Gardner Clark Jr. of Dallas County, who could have come right out of central casting. Jim Clark was a doughy-face, double-chinned bulldog of a white man who was 6'2" tall, weighing 220 pounds. He wore an electric cattle prod at his waist and a pin on his lapel with one word printed on it: "Never."[47]

With a deputized posse of armed, good-ol' white boys and with help from Col. Albert J. Lingo of the Alabama Department of Public Safety, Clark bullied blacks into submission and arrested child demonstrators en masse.[48] The posse members carried their own hunting rifles and shotguns. The editor of the local *Selma Times-Journal* reportedly said, "Damn lucky they haven't killed anyone yet."[49]

By the early fall of 1963, the situation was out of control. The FBI had undercover agents running around Selma taking pictures of SNCC organizers and teletyping reports to Director Hoover back in Washington.[50] Colonel Lingo's state police—the eyes and ears of Governor Wallace—infiltrated rallies and meetings in plainclothes, but half of Selma knew who they were.[51] Celebrities descended on the city to lend support; there were rumors that Martin Luther King was en route.[52]

SNCC's James Forman called on five hundred to one thousand blacks to register to vote on what he was calling "Freedom Monday," October 7.[53] Height and Ferebee boarded a plane for Montgomery, Alabama. They were to be picked up at the Montgomery airport by Amelia Boynton, a local civil rights activist, who would drive them forty-two miles to Selma and straight to the First Baptist Church to meet with youngsters released from jail. They were under time pressure; their plane wasn't scheduled to land until 3:20 in the afternoon, and they were supposed to meet with the children at 4:00. The other women, Cowan and Smith, planned to rent a car at the airport and drive to their motel on the white side of Selma. Their plan was to meet quietly with those white women in the city who were at least somewhat open-minded toward the voter registration drive.[54]

While on the plane they encountered James Forman, who was on his way to the First Baptist Church to lead a rally, and the black activist and comedian Dick Gregory.[55] Gregory's wife, who was three months pregnant, was among those who had been arrested in Selma the week before, and she was still sitting in jail.[56] At the airport something went wrong. Either Mrs. Boynton never showed or, if she did, she picked up Forman and Gregory, leaving no room in her car for Height and Dorothy.[57] Height's interracial team was forced to travel together in one rental car, dangerous at any time in Alabama in the 1960s but more so given the heightened tension brought on by the standoff between SNCC and Sheriff Clark.

Polly Cowan credited Dorothy for staving off disaster. "Dr. Ferebee said there was only one thing to do. If we had to ride in an integrated car, Shirley and I had to ride in the front; Dorothy Height and Dorothy Ferebee had to ride in the back; and if we were stopped, they would act as our cooks," Cowan wrote in an unpublished memoir. "Even then," she added, "we were in danger."[58] (In her memoir Height claimed the idea was hatched by both Dorothy *and* her: "The two of us in the backseat said we'd claim to be the hired help if the police stopped us, and we all laughed.") Height wrote that for the two days they were in Selma "two suspicious-looking cars . . . followed us wherever we went."[59] That was true; FBI files show that the bureau was monitoring the comings and goings of the four women during the entire time they were in Selma. What would have shocked and saddened them was that among those feeding the FBI information was an unnamed "Negro source."[60]

Cowan and Smith dropped off Ferebee and Height at the First Baptist Church, but instead of going to their motel, they decided it would be more interesting to stick around and listen. The participation of the white women in the events that unfolded at the all-black First Baptist Church created a problem: it pushed away those few liberal and moderate white women they had been hoping to enlist in the voting rights struggle. Once the out-of-town white women became visibly aligned with the black activists, local white women were too fearful of reprisals from their racist neighbors to embrace their cause.[61]

At the First Baptist Church that afternoon, sixty-five teenagers released from jail waited to tell their stories to Height and Dorothy. Their experiences were indeed as rumored: they were crammed into cells with no blankets, no drinking water, and no private bathroom facilities; their food—scant enough as it was—was mixed with sawdust to make it stretch; instead of sugar for their coffee, their sadistic jailors gave them salt. The girls were constantly under threat of sexual assault and, because of it, too afraid to go to sleep.[62]

Despite the teenagers' experiences, a sense of excitement filled the sanctuary. Signs hung from the rafters: "FREEDOM TO VOTE. REGISTER MONDAY." Each person who entered the church that night got a slip of paper: "Freedom Day, October 7, 1963—9 a.m. Register to VOTE NOW, Dallas County Court House."[63] Although it was early autumn, it was warm all over Alabama on October 4, with temperatures in the mid-70s.[64] By 7:30, 750 people, half of them children, made their way through the doors of the church. Scattered here and there in the pews were FBI agents, Alabama state troopers, and Selma city police officers in plainclothes.[65] Also present was Alan Ribback, who would later change his name to "Moses Moon." In spite of a limp from childhood polio, he lugged heavy, awkward, reel-to-reel tape recorders along with boxes of blank tapes, microphones, plugs, extension cords, and wires. Moon had run a Chicago folk music club, the Gate of Horn, until he was arrested on obscenity charges in 1962 along with the comedians Lenny Bruce and George Carlin. After he was convicted, his club was shut down and he took to the road with his microphone to bear witness to the historic civil rights struggle. One hundred fifteen reels of his recordings of interviews, songs, meetings, and demonstrations during the civil rights era in the South survive. He recorded the October 4, 1963 rally at the First Baptist Church in its entirety.[66]

The meeting opened with Freedom Songs. Years of singing in the church choir trained the voices in the audience to carry a beautiful tune. Everyone knew the words. James Forman, the master of ceremonies, apologized to the crowd for the long songfest. "We had to sing to purge our souls. When we sing a long time, we try to get it out of our guts. Segregation is a bad, bitter pill. You have to do something to get rid of it."[67]

Forman invited the NCNW women to take seats on the platform in the front of the church and asked them to speak. Height had been denied that opportunity in Washington by Bayard Ruskin six weeks earlier, but Forman recognized the importance of having the support of the NCNW behind the SNCC voting rights effort. Height said, "On behalf of the National Council of Negro Women . . . there is very little that any of us can bring to you. We can only take from you the sense of dedication to the whole cause of freedom and assure you that your sisters and brothers across this land are with you."[68]

After speaking, Height graciously asked Ferebee to take a bow, telling the audience that "it was to her that Mary McLeod Bethune passed on her mantel." Forman interrupted: "While we certainly don't want to prevail upon her, yet, if she feels moved, we would like her to come up and say something." He added, erroneously, "Because you see girls, this is very important, this lady is head of a medical school." Neither woman bothered to correct him, but his mistake made for a good teaching point to the young crowd. "And it is important that we as young Negroes understand that we don't have to be pickin' no cotton fields all the time and scrubbing Jim Clark's floor, that we can do something else."[69]

As Forman continued to talk, Dorothy Ferebee made her way to the microphone. "I think she's coming up so we should give her a big hand," he said, oblivious to the fact that wild horses could not have kept her away from that microphone once she saw that huge, energized audience at her feet. She acknowledged, as had President Kennedy in his inaugural address, that the torch had been passed to a new generation, and she encouraged them to run with it. Her feminist message presaged the emergence of the woman's movement by at least five years and demonstrated that even as she approached retirement, new ideas continually dominated her thinking.

> I bring you greetings from the students of Howard University and from the young women of the National Council of Negro Women. They have been captivated and inspired by your diligence and your vigilance and your wonderful dedication to the job that you're doing for freedom. . . . You know, there was a time when women were not expected to participate in any work of the community, in any work of society or anything that contributed to human betterment. But we know quite differently now, that the young women are standing shoulder-to-shoulder with the men. And we know that the whole range of potential abilities that belong to men, also belong to the women.
>
> . . . . I think that all of the young people of this country are an inspiration and a prod to we older people. Keep on prodding us. Keep on being the beacon of light and being the beacon of hope that you are. I thank you and I commend you for your magnificent spirit for your magnificent work and for your courage.[70]

The audience cheered. When Dick Gregory followed her onto the stage several minutes later, he paid homage to Ferebee and Height. Making reference to the undercover police in the audience, Gregory remarked, "I'm glad they was in here tonight to witness two Negro women . . . and you don't even have to put them together, any one of them probably have more education and more intelligence than this whole police department put together."[71]

The rally lasted four hours. As it drew to a close sometime after eleven, the audience grew increasingly nervous. Forman told them, "There's a big posse outside. . . . We have to be very careful on our way home."[72] In her autobiography Height described the scene: "As we got to the door we saw that the building was surrounded by a sea of state troopers wearing yellow helmets with Confederate flags painted on them. Each trooper carried what seemed to be standard equipment: club, pistol, carbine, riot gun, submachine gun, tear gas bomb, and electric cattle prod. It was an armed camp." Height recalled that she, Dorothy, Cowan, and Smith were warned by a white photographer from an out-of-state newspaper to leave fast. "Instinctively we four women knew we should not acknowledge one another as we walked out," wrote Height. "Dorothy Ferebee and I moved in one direction and Shirley Smith and Polly Cowan in another as we headed for our accommodations on opposite sides of town."[73]

Ferebee and Height spent the night at Mrs. Boynton's and got out of town fast the next day.[74] Before nine in the morning the local police arrived with summonses for the two women, accusing them of contributing to the delinquency of minors, but the two were already gone.[75] Height put it succinctly: "I never returned to Selma."[76]

The voting rights campaign would drag on for two more years, until President Johnson signed the Voting Rights Act into effect. The impact of the act was immediate and profound; by the end of 1965 a quarter of a million new black voters were registered.[77]

But all of that was later. Within six weeks of the NCNW team's visit to Selma, the entire course of history would change. President Kennedy would be shot in Dallas and the decade would be engulfed in violence.

20 A Citizen Concerned with International Affairs

All the world became Dorothy's stage. She toured Africa in July 1960 on a grant from the Women's Africa Committee of the DC-based African-American Institute, which sponsored educational opportunities in America for African exchange students. She was vice chair of the committee Institute, whose members and advisors included Dorothy Height, the playwright Lorraine Hansberry, Barnard College's president Millicent McIntosh, and Esther Peterson, director of the Women's Bureau of the U.S. Department of Labor.[1]

Dorothy's observations about Africa were filtered through her belief in the strength of women. "The education level varies," she told a reporter for the *New York Herald Tribune*, "from very educated to illiterate to bush women. But even among the illiterates in the market place you would be amazed at how they could transact business. Women are the traders of Africa. They handle the money."[2] A year later she transacted business of her own, hosting a "Doll Tea" at the Ghanaian ambassador's home in Washington, where the price of admission was a brown-colored doll: baby dolls, walking dolls, dolls in native costume. After the party the dolls were packed up and mailed as Christmas gifts to children in Africa.[3]

As she had fifteen years earlier when she went to San Francisco to attend the birth of the United Nations, Dorothy kept journals of her trips abroad. They provide a bird's-eye view of the African struggle for independence from colonial powers and a rare window into her private thoughts.[4] Even while traipsing around in some of the poorest, remotest places on earth, Dorothy was fashion conscious. On a subsequent visit to Africa in 1964, she wore peach to visit the Korle Bu Hospital in Accra and put on a white suit to attend a buffet dinner later that evening. She got back into the white suit three days later to visit the Winneba Nurses Training School and slipped into a dark-green sleeveless dress the next day to go shopping.[5]

While in Africa in 1960 Dorothy participated in a woman's conference sponsored by the Ghana Organization of Women at the University College of Accra. Great changes were occurring all over the continent. Ghana became Africa's first independent state in 1957. In June 1960 the Belgian Congo became the Democratic Republic of the Congo, with Patrice Lumumba as its first elected prime minister. This was a "tense moment in the Congo emergency," Dorothy wrote in her journal. "In Accra [Ghana's capital], day & night, hundreds of thundering USAF and Soviet planes airlifted food, supplies and UN troops to [the] Congo."[6] Dorothy met Lumumba in July and got his autograph as he came through Ghana en route to the United Nations to seek help maintaining stability in his new country. In her journal she wrote that she "heard him speak in French—[he] is tall, thin, young & calm."[7] Within six months of their meeting, Lumumba was assassinated by political enemies with the support of the U.S. Central Intelligence Agency.

In an article she later wrote for the Simmons College alumni magazine, "Africa: The Continent of the Hour," Dorothy described the Ghana conference as a congenial gathering that focused on the importance of educational and business opportunities for women there through lectures and discussions. The only wrinkle, she wrote, was a proposed resolution condemning the policies of racial segregation in the United States and South Africa. While the U.S. delegation was not about to cheer for the sorry state of race relations in the United States, it bitterly resented having its country lumped in the same category as South Africa. "The dilemma was successfully met by offering two distinct resolutions, one deploring the apartheid policy of South Africa and another urging the people of the United States to hasten their progress toward their national goal of freedom and equality for all its citizens," Dorothy wrote.[8]

In her private diary she was less sanguine. She said the conference was marred by "great confusion, stress and tensions." The political upheaval in the region was reflected in the politics of the conference. She complained of the U.S. delegation's selection of the left-leaning Shirley Graham Du Bois

(W. E. B. Du Bois's wife) as chair. "In 1st meeting 16 of them against only me there to stem tide of threat of capture of conf. by Pro-Soviet block [sic]," Dorothy wrote. She managed to get herself elected to a steering committee and took credit for changing the tenor of the delegation, although she gave no specifics. Perhaps it was her influence that led to the two resolutions she mentioned in her Simmons article.[9]

Following the tumultuous conference, Dorothy visited African hospitals and schools. She traveled to what was then Southern Rhodesia which she described as "quiet on surface, but . . . a real seething pot underneath. The Africans are determined to achieve their rights and freedom and even small children when planes fly overhead, cry out 'Freedom Now.'"[10]

Her journal is filled with descriptions of mishaps associated with travel in the Third World. She suffered a thirty-hour delay in Kano, Nigeria, because of a diversion of aircraft for emergency airlifts and engine problems. She arrived in South Africa without a visa, and customs agents confiscated her passport until she left. It was winter in the Southern Hemisphere in August and the temperature in South Africa was 38 degrees. "Had to put on three dresses to feel warm," she wrote. In her spare time during the trip, she took a stab at learning Swahili. Her notebook contains actual and phonetic spellings for phrases she tried to master: "Hello," "Goodbye," "I am sorry," "Remove your shoes before entering," "Do not take photograph."[11]

Once back home Dorothy tried to convince Congress to focus on Africa's development. In the spring of 1962 she testified before the Senate Foreign Relations Committee in support of the Foreign Assistance Act. She said Africans needed schools, teachers, and hospitals. Their struggles, she told the committee, were similar to those faced by American blacks: "They are seeking self-determination, they are seeking dignity and equality and justice for themselves and all their people."[12]

Dorothy's travel schedule throughout the early 1960s would have been punishing for anyone, let alone a woman near retirement age. In 1963 she made at least a half-dozen trips around the country to speak on behalf of either the Girl Scouts or the YWCA, organizations she became closely involved with as she got older.[13] Bitten even harder by the travel bug, Dorothy took a one-year leave of absence from Howard University in the spring of 1964 to work for $15,640 ($117,000 today) as a consultant to the

U.S. Department of State, to report on the health conditions of U.S. government personnel assigned to work in the Third World. In her job application, she said she hoped to travel "frequently."[14] It was the opportunity of a lifetime, the Mississippi Health Project all over again. Only this time, on the world stage. The *Washington Post* reported that Dorothy was handpicked by Secretary of State Dean Rusk.[15]

From a personal standpoint, it was a good time to go. Her beloved mother had died in Dorothy's home in December 1959 of an inflammation of the heart wall and hardening of the arteries.[16] Thurston was discharged from the air force in 1960 and focused on getting his career on track and taking care of his growing family, which now included four children. Dorothy loved them dearly and they loved her, but she and Carol Ferebee did not see eye-to-eye. Some of this was due to normal tensions between mother-in-law and daughter-in-law. Todd Ferebee recalled, "She always used to say, 'Your Mother and Father don't need to spend money on a housekeeper/maid when they have four strapping children.' I can only imagine what she said to my Mother."[17]

Within a month of her appointment, Dorothy was off for South America, Africa, and, initially, Southeast Asia. Some thirty-six well-wishers from the Howard University Faculty Women's Club, of which she was president, squeezed into her tiny house in northeast Washington for a bon voyage party.[18] A week later Thurston, Carol, the grandchildren, and a few friends saw her off at the airport as she started her 73,000-mile journey. Her first stop was La Paz, Bolivia (delayed by engine trouble and an emergency landing in Panama), whose location at thirteen thousand feet above sea level created headaches—literally—for State Department employees stationed there.[19] Dorothy visited twenty countries in a little over three months and evaluated hospitals and clinics in sixteen of them. On average she stayed about five days in each country. The schedule was grueling for a sixty-five-year-old.[20]

Her imminent arrival in a country was given a big buildup by Washington. Dr. Harold Beeson, the assistant medical director of the State Department's Overseas Programs, wrote, "Dr. Ferebee is a forceful talker, has a charming and friendly manner, and a missionary zeal to carry her messages to our people."[21] Once she stepped on foreign soil, she gave at least two lectures to State Department personnel and their families and met informally with government workers and, most important, with their wives, to have frank discussions about their anxieties and fears about living in settings so different from home.[22]

The embassies arranged for her to tour local hospitals and health care facilities, which gave Dorothy an idea of the level of medical treatment available for American employees. In some postings conditions were abysmal. "The medical facilities in Recife in Northern Brazil were unbelievably inferior," she reported, "under staffed, under equipped and unsanitary in every aspect." She observed health care facilities and sanitary conditions in Senegal, Liberia, Togo, Uganda, Kenya, and Tanzania and pronounced most of them inadequate.[23]

In three months she visited and issued reports on fifty-five hospitals and clinics. But something went awry in the middle of Dorothy's year-long assignment. She cited "professional commitments to Howard University [that] precluded leave of absence for more than five months." As a result of her truncated leave, she scratched Southeast Asia from her itinerary.[24] It is intriguing that in August 1964, when Dorothy would have been touring Southeast Asia, the long-simmering Vietnam conflict exploded. The North Vietnamese were accused of attacking two U.S. destroyers in the infamous Gulf of Tonkin incident, allowing President Johnson to mount a full-scale, undeclared war. Perhaps it was official Washington and not Howard that put the kibosh on Dorothy's continued consulting arrangement. The State Department may have determined that it was too politically charged for a doctor working for the U.S. government to be wandering around Southeast Asia inspecting hospital facilities.

Dorothy kept traveling until her health gave out. In 1961, as a national officer in the Girl Scouts of America, she attended a conference in Uganda.[25] In June 1975, although feeling shortness of breath from the congestive heart failure that would eventually kill her, she went to the International Women's Year Conference in Mexico City as chair of the DC delegation. While there she broke her ankle; at first refusing to go to the hospital, she acquiesced and was given crutches. Rather than lean on them, however, she waved them over her head to celebrate getting out of the hospital.[26]

Among Dorothy's personal effects when she died were her travel journals; some were little leather books that after thirty years had dried out, and others were cheap steno pads. Although she recorded the political temperature of the places she visited as well as the local history and culture, she often focused on the mundane. She kept track of the money she spent abroad, sometimes down to the penny. She made lists of French wines according to price. She practiced words and phrases in the languages of the countries she visited. She made lists of the names of the people back home to whom she sent postcards. On a 1969 trip to Russia and Finland she sent seventy-five cards; among the recipients were Ruth Scott, Dr. Lofton, her AKA sisters, and her grandsons, Buddy (Todd) and Carl (nicknamed "Bucky"). In 1970, on a trip to London and Lisbon, she sent sixty-three cards to friends and relatives, including her son and his children, her brother Ruffin, and Ida Jackson. In Germany in 1952 she sent cards or letters to 221 people.[27]

There is something profoundly sad about these journals and all the postcard writing. Dorothy seemed utterly alone as she wrote; a woman traveling the world in a single seat, observing from the outside looking in, passing through other people's homes and lives on the way to the next conference, the next speaking engagement, the next meeting, the next country, the next diary entry, the next few lines on a postcard. One cannot imagine anyone who had truly close friends, deep family connections, a happy marriage, or a loving relationship living this way.

Dorothy's overseas adventures did give her something she very much enjoyed besides her souvenir collection of small metal dogs and bells: entrée to the highest rung of the ladder of power.[28] She sat in one of nine seats at President Johnson's table on October 24, 1967, at a White House state luncheon in honor of the president of the Federal Republic of Cameroon.[29] After enjoying Wouri River shrimp, veal, potatoes, crème roulade, and cabernet sauvignon, Dorothy had her picture taken with LBJ, which he later autographed and sent to her.[30]

Dorothy was in the corner of LBJ's eye throughout his presidency. He appointed her one of five U.S. delegates to the twentieth assembly of the World Health Organization in Geneva in the spring of 1967.[31] She was on the short list for a seat on the DC Council, which was a presidential appointment before Washington had an elected local government.[32] In the spring of 1968 Lady Bird Johnson invited her to a White House luncheon with other recognized health and social welfare leaders to discuss improving child health.[33] On Dorothy's résumé in the White House files, which she presumably provided, she described herself as a widow with one son.[34]

Although she was not appointed to the DC Council, Dorothy moved back to the nation's capital. There was nothing keeping her in New York. She sold the outsized house in St. Albans, Queens, in November 1957 to a woman who assumed her $17,000 mortgage and paid her another $4,500.[35] A year earlier, after eight years of holding down the fort as the acting director of the Howard University Health Service, she was finally promoted. She remained at Howard until she reached the age of mandatory retirement, which came in 1968. Forever slicing years off her age, she fibbed in her oral history, claiming she did not retire from Howard until 1972.[36]

After she finished her work for the state department and returned from her leave of absence —already sixty-six years old—she continued as the $13,680-a-year medical director of the Howard student health service. Besides initiating all programs for preventive medicine and offering hands-on health care to 7,500 students at the university, Dorothy supervised thirteen professional and clerical employees, ran three infirmaries for in-patient and out-patient care for sick students, supervised the campus pharmacy, and worked with the administration to promote sound student health.[37] She was also an assistant professor of preventive medicine.[38]

Student health services were introduced on college campuses early in the twentieth century. When higher education was restricted to the children of the upper classes, they were presumed to have access to top-quality health care back home. Not so when college students were the children of immigrants, the working classes, or African Americans. Howard University, in a segregated town where most white doctors were unwilling to treat black patients, took seriously its obligation to protect student health. Directing the health service was a good opportunity for Dorothy, as it had been for many women in medicine in the twentieth century. Perhaps because it required working with young people, the position of student health director at colleges and universities was often reserved for female physicians, according to Heather Munro Prescott, who wrote a book about campus health services. Notwithstanding, Dorothy always asserted that her elevation to the post, for which she credited her supervisor, Dr. Paul Cornely, and Mordecai Johnson, engendered jealousy among the male doctors on the Howard faculty.[39]

Contemplating her return to Washington, Dorothy bought a modest home for fourteen thousand dollars at 2960 13th Street NE.[40] She opened a medical office in the basement, where she kept limited hours, from six to eight each evening.[41] Over the years she would periodically take out mortgages against the property, the last one for almost forty-four thousand dollars at a whopping 11.5 percent interest rate the year before she died.[42] Mostly likely these loans were to help her son.

The Washington to which Dorothy returned looked very different from the one she first called home about forty years before. By 1968 African Americans made up 67 percent of the population, the highest percentage in any major American city. Racial tensions were high. Middle- and upper-class whites were fleeing to the suburbs of Montgomery County, Maryland, and Fairfax and Arlington counties in Virginia. The DC public schools had become 92 percent black.[43] Not only were whites leaving Washington, but the Talented Tenth were taking off too.

Dorothy's son began his exodus from Washington not long after his mother moved back home. He and his family moved from a brick duplex in a working-class African American neighborhood at 775 Oglethorpe Street NE, where they lived until 1964, to 7208 Blair Road in the Takoma Park section of the city, near the Maryland border. The shingled Ferebee house on Blair Road was detached, set back from the street, and framed with lush foliage. He moved again and from 1972 until he died in 1981 Thurston and his family lived in the affluent suburb of Chevy Chase, Maryland, at 3215 Brooklawn Terrace. The house was a sprawling brick split-level, not far from Rock Creek Park, with a big lawn in the front and a concrete bomb shelter in the back. The kids had fun in that; Bucky painted the inside with black florescent paint and cartoon characters and called it "the bong shelter." The neighborhood was mostly white and Jewish; the Ferebee grandchildren jokingly called the winding, tree-lined street on which they lived "Bar Mitzvah Boulevard."[44]

By the late 1960s downtown Washington was a tinderbox waiting to ignite. The spark came from Memphis on April 4, 1968, where the Rev. Martin Luther King Jr. was shot and killed on the balcony of the Lorraine Motel. All hell broke loose in at least 120 American cities, including the nation's capital. The areas hit hardest in Washington included once-vibrant black sections of town that had been deteriorating for years: 14th and U Streets NW, the H Street NE business district, 7th Street NW near Howard, and Anacostia.

The day King was shot was warm and sunny, but by nightfall it had turned cool and rainy in Washington. It was the Thursday before Palm Sunday, the middle of Cherry Blossom Season.[45] Once word got out that King was dead, a crowd gathered at the People's Drug Store on the corner of 14th and U Streets, and within two hours rioting, looting, and arson had begun.[46]

The Ferebee grandchildren, living on Blair Road, slipped out of their house and ran to the yard of a small synagogue nearby, which gave them a clear view of the smoke from fires raging on Georgia Avenue downtown. Like most DC parents, the Ferebees kept their children home from school the next day.[47]

By the 1960s the civil rights movement of which Dorothy had so long been a part was no longer run by the Talented Tenth, who shared a homogeneous goal of integration and equality. Dorothy and her crowd were considered stuffy and old-fashioned by most of the New Guard. *Black power* had become the operative phrase. And Dorothy was suddenly a target.

Muhammad Speaks was a newspaper published by the Nation of Islam to raise money for the religious movement that until 1964 included Malcolm X.[48] On November 8, 1963, the paper published an article about what was purported to be "the great debate" over the question "Should Negroes welcome moral support from Chinese foes of 'our white folks'?" According to the newspaper, Chairman Mao Zedong of the People's Republic of China had made a statement acknowledging that blacks were oppressed in the United States and expressing solidarity with their struggle. The newspaper reported that Chairman Mao's effort at outreach was "rebuffed" by the NAACP's executive secretary Roy Wilkins and the director of the Congress of Racial Equality, James Farmer. It is unclear whether any part of the story was true, but at least one part was false: the response to Wilkins in the newspaper purportedly written by the "medical specialist and well-known civic leader," Dr. Dorothy Ferebee.

Under her byline, alongside a picture of a woman who may or may not have been her, and with the title, "Open Letter to Wilkins," a feisty "Dorothy" excoriated Wilkins for rejecting support from Chairman Mao: "As a 'leader' in the movement of a people struggling to get out from under the yoke of oppression, how dare you reject an expression of support and solidarity from China?" The article was filled with venom. The author referred to Wilkins as one of the white man's "lackeys" who had "mastered the art of being [one of the] 'good Negroes.'"[49]

Although the language in the open letter *sounded* like Dorothy when she had a head of steam, she never wrote a word of it. Humiliated and furious, she sued the paper and its editor for libel in federal court, seeking a half-million dollars in damages.[50] The lawsuit turned out to be a time-consuming nightmare. First, the defendants avoided service.[51] Finally, after nearly two years of their stonewalling, the judge had enough and entered a default judgment in Dorothy's favor.[52] The case went to trial on the issue of damages. A jury was selected, Dorothy Height and Ruth Scott were asked to testify as to how the article hurt Ferebee's reputation, and in January 1967 the jury returned a verdict in her favor for ten thousand dollars.[53] It is unlikely she ever collected a dime.

Dorothy's forty-one-year connection to Howard ended with her mandatory retirement at age seventy. A ceremony was held for her and the other retirees on June 4, 1968.[54] The next night Senator Robert F. Kennedy was shot in Los Angeles after winning the California Democratic presidential primary. It was turning out to be one of the most violent years in history.

After retiring, Dorothy commuted to Boston to serve as an adjunct lecturer in preventive medicine at her alma mater, Tufts.[55] In 1971 she was given the prestigious Edward C. Hitchcock Award, named for the physician who established the first college health service, at Amherst College in 1861. The award honors those members of the American College Health Association who have made outstanding contributions to protecting the health of college students.[56]

Even before her retirement Dorothy started racking up awards. She was presented with the first Distinguished Achievement Award from Simmons College in 1959.[57] Although it was supposed to be top-secret, Dorothy had been tipped off by an old college chum to ensure she'd be there to accept.[58] "I'll probably explode from sheer joy and pride before the day," she wrote to the alumnae president when told about it, "but I promise to do my very best to contain myself."[59] When she arrived in Boston in June to accept the award, she came dressed to the nines in a polka-dot silk summer dress with matching jacket, a double strand of pearls around her neck, her signature corsage, and a small black hat with a veil. She was visibly touched and smiling from ear to ear when her fellow alums gave her a standing ovation. She told her former classmates, too, that she was a widow.[60]

Simmons continued to recognize Dorothy even after her death. It dedicated a student lounge in one of the dormitories in her name in 1986.[61] And, in a gesture that would have given her no end of pleasure, with the Class of 1992 Simmons awarded six minority students four-year scholarships in her name. To get one, a student had to demonstrate leadership potential, community involvement, and academic achievement.[62] Tufts honored her as well, putting her on the cover of its alumni bulletin in the spring of 1968 and recalling the prophetic write-up her peers gave her in the 1924 Tufts yearbook: "Dot, we're sure that Tufts will some day be as proud of your accomplishments as your friends are today."[63]

Wearing a pretty flowered dress with her hair swept up in an elegant French twist, Dorothy was the guest of honor at a testimonial dinner in November 1965 at the Sheraton Park Hotel in Washington. It was a very public valentine to a woman who had lived a very public life. While she and her guests sat in the Grand Ballroom eating broiled breast of Virginia capon, green beans, potatoes, and a toasted snowball with chocolate sauce, Esther Peterson, the special assistant to President Johnson for consumer affairs, gave the speech honoring her for her many years of service to her profession and the community.[64] When it came time to give her an award, her nine-year-old grandson, Todd, was among the presenters. He had a little speech prepared—with the help of the honoree, who made him practice, practice, and practice—and was so small he had to stand on a wooden milk crate to reach the microphone as he recited it.[65]

As a precursor to the event, the *Washington Post* published a feature about Dorothy titled "Hard Work Can Topple the Barriers," perhaps without realizing the irony; after forty years of activism, Dorothy had finally toppled the barrier into the white press.[66] The awards continued for the rest of her life. Just four months before she died the DC City Council passed a resolution honoring her for her many contributions to society.[67]

Vogue magazine did a spread in its May 1969 issue featuring five super-achieving African American women, including Dorothy. The article honored them as women who "have the ropes of power in their hands." Sharing the billing were Coretta Scott King, New York congresswoman Shirley Chisholm, Dr. Mildred Mitchell-Bateman, a psychiatrist who was head of the West Virginia Department of Mental Health, and Elma Lewis, director of the National Center of Afro-American Artists in Boston. In typical woman's magazine hyperbole, Dorothy was described as a woman who "charms birds off trees" and as "strong, buxom, shrewd, voluble, with the kind firmness of an archetypal mother."[68]

Accompanying the brief articles on each of the women were photographs taken by the renowned Irving Penn. Dorothy traveled to Penn's studio on West 40th Street in Manhattan to sit for the portrait.[69] The picture is artistic perfection; softly lit, it brilliantly shows the inner Dorothy, a handsome woman of substance. She is serious, but with a slightly upturned mouth in a small, closed-lip smile. Her eyes look wise and kind. It is a masterpiece, but the Ferebees weren't crazy about it. "My family didn't warm up to the photograph. They thought it too dour, too bloated, too un-like me," Dorothy wrote to the associate editor after she saw the issue. "I scotched all the critics with the suggestion that the photographer probably did the best he could with what he had to work with." She graciously thanked the editor for including her in the "illustrious group of women."[70] And on she went. There was still work to do before she could rest.

21 Woman Power

In the decade before she died, Dorothy turned what energy she had left—considerable, as it turned out—to women's issues. Women's Liberation, or "Women's Lib," as the movement was initially called, emerged as *the* movement of the 1970s. Dorothy was ahead of the game. She had maneuvered in a man's world her entire life and had been an advocate for equal treatment for women since her youth.

In the early days of feminism, as befuddled male public officials grappled with what women wanted, they formed study commissions to figure it out. The DC Commission on the Status of Women was created in 1967.[1] Mayor Walter Washington appointed Dorothy to an unpaid term on the commission in February 1968.[2] Within the year she was chairing it.[3] Once at the helm, Dorothy championed abortion rights. Between 1967 and the Supreme Court's 1973 decision in *Roe v. Wade* striking down all antiabortion laws, one-third of the states had begun liberalizing their laws. Although a proposal had been pending in DC to permit abortion if necessary for the mother's "health," Dorothy thought whether to have an abortion was a decision to be made by the pregnant woman herself.[4]

In November 1969, in a letter to the editor, she congratulated the *Washington Post* on behalf of the commission for supporting liberalized abortion. She predicted that once women were able to obtain safe, legal abortions "the number of women admitted for treatment after tragic home or 'back-alley' attempted abortions" would decline. But she avoided any mention of the abortion tragedy that had shrouded her own family for almost twenty years.[5]

Dorothy chaired the Commission on the Status of Women until 1974.[6] Besides advocating for abortion on demand, the commission called for more DC policewomen and supported the doomed Equal Rights Amendment.[7] She fought for better treatment of women in jail and called for more drug-treatment programs and halfway house spaces for women convicted of petty crimes or being held on bail pending trial.[8]

Women's organizations substituted for an extended family for Dorothy in the 1970s as the members of her small family of origin passed on. After Florence Boulding's death in 1959, it fell to Richard to clean out what personal effects she still had in Norfolk. He sold his mother's piano and household furniture for fifteen cents on the dollar, apologizing to his sister for the paltry sum. "I did the best I could," he wrote her. He complained in the same letter about having a hard time "with these 'white-people,'" who had hauled him into court twice over some unexplained dispute. Apparently without a stable place to live after his mother's death, he told Dorothy he would be residing with friends on a temporary basis and provided only a post office box where he could be reached.[9] Dorothy did not offer him her mother's old room in her three-bedroom house in Washington.

Richard died in 1980 in Norfolk of heart failure, seven months before Dorothy succumbed to the same disease. Continuing with her tradition of putting only the family's best foot forward, she told city authorities filling out her brother's death certificate that he was a retired postal worker, although he had not worked as a mailman in nearly forty years.[10]

Ruffin Boulding had died four years earlier, on May 31, 1976, from an acute bowel obstruction caused by a strangulated hernia.[11] After his early success in Oklahoma, Ruffin moved to Charlotte, North Carolina, his wife Julia's home state. She died of heart failure in 1970.[12] Charlotte was not the friendliest place for an African American lawyer; at the end of World War II there were but a handful of black lawyers in the rigidly segregated city, who were unwelcome in the local bar association. Ruffin hung in, his booming voice and the peck-peck-peck of the typewriter emanating from his one-man law office. He also had a real estate business on the side.[13]

Ruffin had a direct and not altogether pleasant way of dealing with people. His letters to his siblings are bossy and lack warmth. He wrote to Richard in late 1963, asking questions about their recently deceased uncle: "Who's handling Leslie's [R. G. L. Paige's oldest son] estate matter? Since all his children are grown, Leslie's house should be sold to one of the children or to someone else and their sale money divided and distributed.

Answer. Yours, Ruffin."[14] The year before their mother died, Ruffin sold timber from the family land in Crewe, Virginia, and wrote to Dorothy with instructions to deposit the money in her bank account. "In doing so, this money should be earmarked for future Crewe taxes, needed repairs for the Norfolk home, and Mama's medicine, etc," he wrote, as if his sister would dream of shirking her fiscal responsibilities or her duties to their mother.[15]

A neighbor found the body of eighty-year-old Ruffin inside his modest brick bungalow in Charlotte a few hours—or days—after he died. Seventy-eight and ailing, Dorothy traveled 330 miles south to make the funeral arrangements. On the morning Ruffin was buried, she and a cousin of Ruffin's late wife were the only mourners at the grave.[16]

Like her brother, parents, and grandparents, Dorothy appreciated the importance of owning property. After the war she bought land in Morris Beach, near Egg Harbor Township on the South Jersey Shore. She amassed four lots, intending to leave one to each of her four grandchildren. Morris Beach was New Jersey's answer to Maryland's Highland Beach, an enclave of African American professionals who banded together after being shut out of other summer resorts. Its namesake was Jennie Morris, a Philadelphia undertaker who bought 154 acres from white landowners in 1939 for fifteen thousand dollars and then subdivided it for vacation homes for upper-class blacks from Philadelphia, Baltimore, and Washington.[17] Dorothy bought her first parcel in 1946 for two thousand dollars, a second in 1963, and two more in 1977.[18]

Surprisingly Dorothy, who had always been on the move, enjoyed staying put in Morris Beach. Peter Shelton, whose family had property there since the 1950s, had fond memories of the Ferebees: "Dorothy was a proper lady who never flaunted her education. I remember Dorothy as dignified, grandmotherly looking, and casually dressed. She loved to soak her feet in the salt water bay while her grandchildren were usually outside playing, crabbing and fishing." He recalled her regaling her summer neighbors with tales of her exotic travels. While listening, her audience contended with the mosquitoes and green-headed biting flies that were common at the Jersey Shore.[19]

By the summer of 2008, nearly thirty years after Dorothy's death, her white asbestos-shingled cottage was a wreck. There were gaping holes in the roof, the front picture window was broken, and the screen door leading into the thousand-square-foot house was falling from its hinges. The only inhabitants were feral cats. In 2012 the cottage still needed extensive repairs, and the two surviving Ferebee grandchildren could not afford to do it. With her heirs unable to pay the taxes, the county put the properties up for sale.[20]

A fixture at the Morris Beach house with Dorothy was Ruth Scott, a woman the Ferebee grandchildren called "Cousin Ruth." Some friends and family members suspect Dorothy and Scott were lovers, but others adamantly disagree. Dorothy was a pack rat who saved drafts of speeches, programs from obscure conferences, and a tiara made of pipe-cleaners that she wore at a dinner commemorating the fiftieth anniversary of Alpha Kappa Alpha. She saved a form letter asking her to join the American Foreign Service Association, yet she kept few personal letters.[21] Either she never got any—which is highly unlikely—or, recognizing her significance to twentieth-century history, she may have suspected that her papers would one day be open to the public. A woman as careful of her image as Dorothy would have been scrupulous about destroying anything that threatened to tarnish it, as an intimate relationship with a woman certainly would have in her day.

Scott was large and masculine in appearance and never married. Dorothy was feminine and in her youth was the object of serious attention from male admirers. But after her divorce there was never any hint of a romance between Dorothy and another man. That being said, there is no evidence that would prove the existence of a romance between Dorothy and Scott.

Ruth Adelaide Scott was the same age as Dorothy.[22] She graduated from the University of Pennsylvania, left Philadelphia to attend graduate school at Columbia University in New York, and returned to a forty-year career teaching in the Philadelphia public schools. Like Dorothy, she was immersed in the activities of AKA and the NCNW, where she served as a regional director for many years.[23]

Scott and Dorothy probably met in 1935 at an Alpha Kappa Alpha meeting in Philadelphia.[24] Dorothy convinced Scott to join the Mississippi Health Project, and while there Scott grew to admire her to the point of hero worship. In writing about the 1940 health project, Ruth described ripping her hair out over the 100-degree heat, flying insects, and screaming kids about to be vaccinated. Then she looked at Dorothy, "who was swamped with children. . . . I observed that radiant, sympathetic, and patient countenance which is always inspiring and indicative of her rare personality. I suddenly felt ashamed and returned to my work with renewed determination to endure at any cost." Scott outlived Dorothy by five years, dying in Philadelphia in 1985.[25]

The last decade of Dorothy's life was impacted by her slowly failing health and the rapidly changing times. She did her best to keep up, throwing herself into her work on the national board of the Girl Scouts. Although the Girls Scouts would seem to be one of the least controversial organizations on earth, Dorothy managed to stir the pot in 1970 by dreaming up the idea of an all-black Girl Scout conference.[26] It did not go over well with some local chapters that found it unnecessarily divisive.

The Girl Scouts have been around since 1912.[27] Yet despite the group's policy to include all girls in scouting, it has historically been a mostly white organization. Even today, 65 percent of the nation's 2.2 million Girl Scouts are white.[28] Dorothy became involved with the Girl Scouts as a regional advisor in 1955, was elected to the national board of directors in 1957, and between 1969 and 1972 served a term as one of four national vice presidents.[29] In the fall of 1969 she chaired the national task group on race relations and dreamed up the idea of a minority conference to discuss making scouting more relevant to African American girls.[30]

Regional councils chose representatives from selected cities to attend the conference in Atlanta, and forwarded their names to Dorothy. Those selected had to be black.[31] Dorothy led the conference on March 13 and 14, 1970, in which 150 black senior Girl Scouts, volunteer adults, and scouting professionals participated. The Girl Scout hierarchy recognized the conference would be controversial.[32] News reporters were only given access to Dorothy's opening and closing remarks. "I had hoped that it would not have been necessary for me to even mention that this meeting is not a separatist movement," she said. "But there is a kind of paranoia in this country, a thinking that every time black members of an institution want to get together, it is automatically a separatist movement."[33]

In 1973 after many years as an active board member of the YWCA, she was made an honorary member, meaning she could still come to board meetings but it would have to be on her dime. That didn't stop her.[34] After her work on the DC Commission on the Status of Women was completed,

Mayor Washington gave her another unpaid appointment, as a member of the DC Commission on Human Rights. She remained on the commission until the year before she died.[35]

What never changed was the thrill Dorothy got when she stepped onto a podium. In the summer of 1974 she was an honored guest among the eighteen thousand spectators at the Mary McLeod Bethune Memorial dedication in Lincoln Park, not far from the Capitol.[36] Three days of nonstop festivities surrounded the unveiling of a ten-foot statue of the NCNW founder.[37] It had taken the council thirteen years to raise the $400,000 needed to fund it and three years to build it. The dedication ceremony took place on July 10, a broiling hot day that would have been Bethune's ninety-ninth birthday. There was a parade to the Capitol from Lincoln Park for those able to make it without suffering heat stroke. There were embassy parties and a "Salute to Women" banquet at the Sheraton Park Hotel the night after the unveiling. Dorothy stood before the microphone at the Sheraton addressing two thousand banquet guests, mostly women.[38] At seventy-six she was no longer coloring her hair, which had become infiltrated by gray. In describing Bethune for the friendly audience, she could have been talking about herself: "She believed that when women were bound together they would be a powerful force in the world."[39]

Two days later Dorothy and other VIPs from the NCNW were invited to the White House by the first lady for a very exclusive afternoon tea. Within the month President Nixon would resign in the wake of the Watergate scandal, but Patricia Nixon nonetheless summoned the grace to ask some of the Bethune celebrants to join her for refreshing tall glasses of iced tea garnished with sprigs of fresh mint.[40] Ferebee, Mrs. Nixon, and Height posed for pictures together.

Even as Dorothy was winding down in public life, one grandchild or another was still chauffeuring her to the few house calls she continued to make, mainly to the older patients she had treated for years. She was particularly diligent about collecting her fee for her services, telling her granddaughter Dolly, "I've got to go get my check before it turns into a ham on someone's table."[41]

Before Dorothy died she had one final cause to take on, and her toughest challenge: Thurston. Once criticized for not being sufficiently involved with her children, she put herself in charge of her adult son's life. She was not amused when he dropped out of college. She might have resented Carol, thinking that he sacrificed his education to get married. Dorothy wanted him in medical school. His father wanted him in dental school in New York.

Thurston and Carol did not have it easy. Carol gave birth to five children in less than a decade; Claude Thurston III ("Buzzy"), in February 1953, followed by Michael Charles, who died of crib death when he was only three months old. In 1955 Carol had Carl Phillips ("Bucky"), followed the next year by Todd Boulding ("Buddy"). Their last child and only girl, Dorothy Ruth ("Dolly"), was born in 1959.[42] Overwhelmed by so many children with her husband away in the air force, Carol ceded control of them—particularly Buzzy—to Dorothy. He spent so many of his early years with his grandmother that even though he was the oldest of the five children Carol bore, he never recalled seeing her pregnant.[43]

Once Thurston was discharged from the air force, the tug-of-war over his future began in earnest between his parents. "Dr. Dr. Ferebee (Claude) and Mrs. Dr. Ferebee had a big struggle with him over whether he would be a doctor or a dentist, and he played it," remembered John Beckley.[44] Dorothy refused to acknowledge such a test of wills ever took place, because to do so would mean she lost. When asked during her oral history, "Did his father influence him in this choice of profession?," she answered with a curt "I think not."[45]

Thurston was a Mama's boy. He stopped by Dorothy's house five times a week. His wife was forever competing with his mother for his attention. A mere thirteen months after Dorothy's death, Thurston's rapidly metastasizing pancreatic cancer killed him. "When he died, my mother cried, 'She took him with her,'" said Todd Ferebee.[46]

Just as Dorothy once chided Mary Bethune for overindulging in cakes and pies, she breathed fire at her son for his own love of sweets, fast food, and his wife's tasty cooking, which he enjoyed to excess after a lifetime of avoiding his mother's awful meals. His waistline thickened until his good friend, Sam Singleton, nicknamed him "Buddha," and he became borderline diabetic.

Once Thurston returned to college, Dorothy micromanaged his education. "She did everything she could to get him through Howard except to go to class for him," remarked Timmy Johnson.[47] After he was accepted to a postgraduate course in oral surgery in 1967 at New York University that cost $1,800, Dorothy went straight to the top and contacted Congressman Melvin R. Laird, with whom she had been a delegate to the World Health Organization in Geneva, to help her obtain a scholarship for her son from the National Institutes of Health.[48]

Thurston graduated from Howard University's dental school in 1966, no small feat given his less than stellar academic record at Tilton. Because of Dorothy's affiliation with the school, he paid no tuition.[49] But he still had six mouths to feed. Irresponsible as his friends thought he was, he held down a job as a night guard at the magnificent National Building Museum, also known as the Pension Building, while making his way through school.[50] Each evening he strapped on a gun, put on his uniform, and headed to work for his all-night shift. He came home a little before seven, grabbed a few hours of sleep, and went to class. After school he took a cat nap in the late afternoon before returning to work.[51]

Carol helped support the family while Thurston was in school by taking a series of low-level government jobs. From September 1962 through the summer of 1968 she engraved maps for the U.S. Geological Survey, never earning more than $3.74 an hour. In the 1970s she was able to obtain more substantial positions. She drafted aeronautical charts for the National Oceanic and Atmospheric Administration, earning close to nineteen thousand dollars by the end of the decade (about sixty-one thousand in today's dollars).[52] After Thurston graduated from Howard, he moved to New York to complete a dental internship at Harlem Hospital, returning to his family on weekends. Carol was left to play the role of a single working mother with four children during the week.[53]

While doing postgraduate work at Harlem Hospital, Thurston was not living the life his father had a generation earlier. There were no debutante balls or dinners at supper clubs. Harlem had become dangerous, and Thurston's nights were not filled with jazz and swing but with gunshots and police sirens. His days were an education in how to fix teeth knocked out in street fights or neglected due to dire poverty.

In 1967 Thurston was licensed to practice dentistry in New York and returned home to open his own practice with a partner in southwest Washington.[54] He fixed the teeth of his wife, his children, and his mother.[55]

Unable to make ends meet solely through private practice, he took a part-time job in 1970 as the associate dental officer with the DC Department of Corrections' Lorton Correctional Complex at a salary of nearly $14,200. He eventually worked full time at Lorton; at his death in 1981 he was the chief dental officer, earning $50,112 (about $129,000 today).[56]

Everyone who ever knew Thurston described him as a happy-go-lucky bon vivant. Some blamed the early death of his sister for his refusal to act like a grown-up, but Thurston was like that before she died. He was an indifferent student and a good athlete with prodigious appetites for food, fun, and the women who attracted his roving eye. He and the rest of the "Filthy Five" "loved life and they lived it as they loved it," said Todd Ferebee.[57]

The Five had been through a lot together. Thurston and Timmy had known each other since they were toddlers. Timmy had a crush on Dolly and, it so happens, on Carol Phillips before she married Thurston. Sam Singleton's first encounter with Thurston was when Sam stole a toy from him as a child. Sammy's mortified mother dragged him to 1809 2nd Street NW to apologize to Dorothy and her son, and the boys struck up a friendship. Sam started working at Howard as Mordecai Johnson's driver and worked his way up to station commander of the Howard University security force.[58] Thurston met Russ Eberhardt in St. Albans.

The Filthy Five all more or less ended up at Howard. Johnson attended Morehouse College in Atlanta, dropped out, and earned a degree in electrical engineering from Howard. He worked for the Defense Department and NASA.[59] Beckley graduated from pharmacy school there. Eberhardt went to Howard, joined the air force, and worked in computers at Grumman Aircraft. He later became a homicide detective in New York and was a jazz pianist on the side, playing in bars and nightclubs on Long Island, where he lived.[60]

The Five were loyal friends and closer than brothers. Eberhardt and Beckley cleaned out Dolly's room at Champlain after she died. They partied together, attended each others' weddings, became godfathers to each other's children, and were pallbearers at one another's funerals, Thurston's being the first. The only time some of them hung back was when it came to taking seats around Thurston's dining room table for his infamous Friday night poker games. Players sat amid clouds of smoke and knocked back cocktails mixed by Thurston's daughter, Dolly. They played for big money; on some nights, thousands of dollars would be piled in the center of the table. The men—and at least one woman—in the game were some of Washington's biggest movers and shakers.[61] Washington's mayor Marion Barry, with a walkie-talkie on the table in case of emergency, Congressman Bill Clay of Missouri, Ernie Jarvis, the first husband of DC Councilwoman Charlene Drew Jarvis, and the director of the Jarvis Funeral Home, all found seats at Thurston's poker games. When Ernie Jarvis couldn't make it, Charlene played his hand. Bill Fitzgerald, president of the black-owned Independence Bank of Washington, played.[62]

John Beckley took a seat at the poker table from time to time, but only if Marion Barry wasn't there. Johnson mostly stayed away. "Thurston was always acting immaturely most of his life," explained Johnson. "I had a security clearance to protect and I took that seriously."[63] Thurston's adult son Buzzy avoided the game because he was a police officer. Charlene Jarvis stopped playing poker with Thurston and the boys once she was elected to the District Council in 1979.[64]

Charlene Jarvis came by the house at other times because she was a close friend of Carol's, whose circle of loyal friends also included Margo Pinson. In the small world of Washington's black elite, Charlene's father was famous at Howard for his work in blood plasma; Margo was the daughter of Buddy Dean, the dentist to whom Claude Sr. left his Washington practice when he moved to New York after the war, and Dorothy delivered Margo. Carol's group called themselves "the Chatterboxes" and met once a month at one another's homes to share dinner, friendship, and gossip.[65]

Thurston was determined to replicate for his children the same experiences his parents gave him and his sister, except it cost far more to do so in the 1970s. He sent his sons to Tilton. Buzzy, who attended from September 1969 through June 1972, was the only one to graduate.[66] Bucky and Buddy attended Tilton from September 1971 until Buzzy left in 1972, at which time tuition was over three thousand dollars a year.[67] Once Thurston bought the house in Chevy Chase, he sat his two younger boys down and told them the facts of life: as tuition was then approaching $3,600 a year, he said they could return to Tilton, but if they did, the cost of college would be on them. The two younger boys stayed home, graduating from Bethesda–Chevy Chase High School, along with their sister, Dolly. It is ironic that none of the Ferebee grandchildren graduated from college.[68] It was one more thing that did not sit well with Dorothy and provided an excuse for her to continue to meddle in her son and daughter-in-law's parenting methods.

22 I Should Not Be Here but I Had to Come

In the end, "Go-to-Meeting Ferebee" could not help herself. The summer before she died, old and frail with a failing heart, Dorothy traveled to Atlanta to attend an AKA Boule. Struggling to get out of a taxi, she told the supreme basileus, "I should not be here but I had to come."[1]

Dorothy may have been driven by a lifetime of determination to overcome her chronic illness to participate in the sorority event she loved, or she may have been motivated to travel more than six hundred miles from home by the loneliness and boredom of old age. But she was going to die as she lived: dressed in a tailored suit with matching earbobs while standing behind a podium.

A week before she died of congestive heart failure on September 14, 1980, at Georgetown University Hospital in Washington, Dorothy donned a white summer suit with contrasting window-pane checks, support hose, and white pumps to attend a community celebration for her pride and joy, Southeast House, which she had founded fifty years earlier. Looking old among the five hundred neighborhood children who came to enjoy fresh fruit snacks and free pony rides, Dorothy was given a plaque commemorating her creation of the historic settlement. She proudly held it up in front of her audience. She was held up herself by Washington's congressional delegate Walter E. Fauntroy, who stood on one side of her, and by her handsome, twenty-something grandson, Buddy, who stood on the other.[2] Fauntroy sang a George Benson song, "The Greatest," and dedicated it to Dorothy, while the children in the audience, who may have had no clue who she was, cheered and shouted, "We love you, we love you."[3]

After her death AKA Supreme Basileus Barbara Phillips wrote a fitting tribute to Dorothy in the *Ivy Leaf*: "We honor her memory and pledge ourselves to remember her deeds and seek to emulate her best efforts: her work to bring about good physical health, her emotional stamina . . . her social involvements provided through gregariousness and emphatic expressions and contact with people, her logic and intellectual capacity and farsightedness . . . and her spirituality in her relationships with her God and with her fellowmen."[4]

Dorothy outlived her two brothers and her own daughter. She represented a Negro aristocracy long gone from her adopted city of Washington by 1980. The neighborhood near Howard University where she had first lived fifty years earlier was a boarded-up ghetto. The Lincoln Colonnade, where the young, stylish Dorothy and her handsome Claude danced with the smart set at What Good Are We parties in the 1930s, was crumbling. The U Street corridor where she once bought stylish hats and snappy suits burned to the ground in the 1968 riots and had yet to be rebuilt. Drive-by shootings were rampant in the city that had come to be called the "murder capital of the world."[5] Gentrification would be a generation away.

The city was dying, but there was life in Dorothy until the end. She loved a good time as much as the Filthy Five, zipping around the streets of Washington, pedal to the metal of her Oldsmobile, "Granite Foot Gam." She kicked in money to help her youngest grandson, Buddy, buy his first car, a pearl-white Triumph TR-6. "She used to love to ride around in it with the top down," he recalled. She still whipped up her favorite dessert now and again: bread pudding from the recipe printed in the NCNW cookbook, one tablespoon of Myers's rum for the mixing bowl, one for Dorothy. Not used to spirits, she would giddily tie one on before it came out of the oven.[6] If a woman's group needed a speaker, Dorothy still hoisted herself into the saddle.

Dorothy's failing health drove her crazy. "For anybody who traveled around as fast as I did for 40 years to be on a cane and slow down and have somebody help me out of a chair, is pretty difficult," she said after slowly shuffling to the podium a year before her death.[7] Some of what she did in old age seemed sad, as though she were watching the parade passing by. In 1974, when Walter Washington became the first elected mayor of the nation's capital in more than one hundred years, Dorothy attended his inaugural ball. Although he had appointed her to two district commissions, she didn't go as one of the mayor's inner circle but instead stood on line in a flowered gown, paid her fifteen-dollar general admission, and sat at a small table at the back of the cavernous hall. "We've never had an inaugural ball before and I wanted to see how it moved," she told a reporter for the *Washington Evening Star-News*.[8]

Having dedicated her life to knocking down barriers, Dorothy reflected near the end of her life on which one was heavier: the one society erected against her race or the one against her gender. She determined that sexism was tougher. At a speech before a panel sponsored by the National Endowment for the Humanities and the NCNW in 1979, she said sexism was harmful because "many women have lost faith in themselves, they don't really believe that they are as good as they are."[9]

As difficult as slowing down was for Dorothy, there was a silver lining. She had time for her grandchildren that she had not had for her twins. Her house on 13th Street NE had a revolving door for them; at times they lived there, at times they merely visited, but they always felt welcome. There was a special place in her heart for her firstborn grandson, Claude Thurston Ferebee III. The boy's birth in 1953, so soon after Dolly's death, cemented their bond. He inherited his father's nickname, Buzzy. And he named her "Gam."[10]

After graduating from Tilton, Buzzy went no further in his education than Montgomery County Community College. His father and grandfather worked on him to consider dental school, but it fell on deaf ears. In 1975, when Buzzy was twenty-two, he joined the Montgomery County Police Department. Being a policeman may not have been as prestigious or as lucrative as being a dentist, but his parents and Gam were proud of his career choice.[11]

In his tan uniform with his .38 revolver at his side, Claude Thurston Ferebee III looked handsome and pleased with himself the day he graduated from the police academy. His career choice was a good professional fit. He was a people person and had the aura of authority. His younger siblings sought his counsel, and his baby sister, Dolly, relied on his protection from the rough and tumble of a family of boys. Throughout her life Dolly would name him her favorite sibling.[12]

Buzzy became a policeman when there were far fewer African American cops in uniform than there are today. As he entered middle age, he was a menacing presence at 6′3″ tall and 275 pounds. But he was a gentle giant, a practical joker who was well-liked by his brother officers and who served as a role model for the few black ones on the force. "He took me under his wing and was like a second father to me," said Sgt. Brent Kearney, an African American who was trained as a motor patrolman by Buzzy Ferebee.[13]

When Buzzy was twenty-four he moonlighted as a chaperone for the DC Youth Orchestra. He also served as the orchestra's semiofficial photographer. His watchful eye fell on a pretty blond cellist barely out of childhood. Only fifteen, Lisa Marie Kleinman had already devoted six years of her young life to her instrument. By the time she graduated from high school, she was a Youth Orchestra faculty member teaching cello classes and private lessons and performing professionally. She won a music scholarship to the University of Maryland but lasted in college only a few months. On November 11, 1980, soon after she turned eighteen, she and Buzzy married at a chapel on the Howard University campus. Two months earlier Lisa had played the cello at Dorothy's funeral at the nearby Rankin Chapel, also on the campus.[14]

Youngest grandson Buddy's relationship with Dorothy was also special. When he was sick with some childhood ailment, nothing comforted him more than "seeing her smile and hearing her once she would come into my room with her ever-present medical bag to check me out." He lived with his grandmother while he attended Howard.[15] The price to pay for her good company was to suffer at her dinner table. "I heard stories of her re-frying fried chicken she'd bought and pancakes stiff enough to use as Frisbees," recalled Lisa Ferebee. "And things like mixing four boxes of different cereals to 'stretch it.'" But Gam was wise to herself. The first time she met Lisa she pulled her aside and said, "I don't know if you heard, but they say I can't cook." Lisa usually went to Gam's bearing her own home-baked banana bread, which Dorothy loved. Gam's home-decorating skills were not much better. There were dusty, plastic floral arrangements on the toilet tanks in her bathrooms and on her bookshelves.[16]

Lisa and Gam took to one another instantly. Dorothy appreciated Lisa's talent and dedication to her craft, and Lisa admired the old warrior. When

Lisa wanted to buy a $14,000 cello and was $1,500 short, Dorothy made up the difference. How it happened, Lisa never knew because she did not ask her for it. Buzzy apparently told Dorothy outside Lisa's presence and then came home with the money, which he said Gam insisted he take. Lisa said, "She just loved women accomplishing anything. . . . I felt like she wanted to support this gift I had."[17]

Dorothy may have seen a combination of her own lineage and a little of her young Claude when she looked at Buddy. A charmer and raconteur, in adulthood he was at 6', tall like his older brothers, but at 185 pounds not so hefty. He bears an eerie resemblance to Dorothy's grandfather, the young R. G. L. Paige. Dorothy started Buddy on his career path; when he was twelve she gave him a book about the architect Frank Lloyd Wright.[18]

Buddy attended the Howard University School of Architecture and Planning between 1974 and 1979 but never earned a degree. He had wanted to take a year off after graduating from Bethesda–Chevy Chase High School in 1974, but Dorothy would not hear of it. Just as her great-aunt Emma had swooped in and whisked her to Boston for a good education before World War I, Dorothy pounced on Buddy to get him into college. When September came around and Buddy was still not in school, she marched him over to the administration building at Howard, pushing past the secretary into the office of Dr. Carl Edwin Anderson, vice president for student affairs. She was on a first-name basis with him, and within twenty minutes her grandson was signed up for twelve credit hours, whether he wanted to be or not.[19]

While they lived together, Buddy drove her to the few house calls she was still making to patients in the late 1970s, and he prepared warm water and Epsom salt baths in the tub so she could sooth her aching feet. Like his father, Buddy married early, cutting short his education to marry in 1979.[20] Gam was sorely disappointed.[21]

When Buddy was unavailable to squire Gam to house calls, baby sister Dolly served as a backup. In her teenage years Dolly was as beautiful as her aunt. In middle age she resembled Gam: light-skinned, high cheek bones, medium height, and a sturdy build. She attended Montgomery County College briefly and then opted for a computer technical school. She became an IT technician for the Washington DC Housing Authority. Dolly harbored a huge secret from the family when she was young, although

Buzzy figured it out fairly early: she was a lesbian.[22] Dorothy died without her granddaughter ever revealing to her the truth.

Memories clash among family members about the days leading up to Dorothy's death. Buddy said the family knew Gam was dying; she was under hospice care on oxygen and hooked up to machines that were monitoring her vital signs.[23] Lisa Ferebee recalls it differently: that Gam checked herself into Georgetown University Hospital a few days before she died and at the hospital was her old self, running the show and greeting the doctors from her gurney. "We thought she'd be home the next day after some tests," recalled Lisa.[24]

Dorothy died at 6:40 on the evening of September 14, 1980. The cause was blood clots caused by chronic congestive heart failure brought on by a decade of hardening of the arteries. Her death certificate indicated that she was born not in 1898, as she sometimes claimed, but in 1896, which, if true, would have made her eighty-three.[25]

The day Dorothy died was unusually sticky for September, even in swampy Washington. Temperatures reached 94 degrees by late afternoon, and the humidity was 100 percent.[26] There were scattered thunderstorms, and Buddy swears that when he learned Gam died—through a phone call from his father—the skies opened up with thunder, lightning, and a massive downpour.[27] At the time of Dorothy's death the world was fixated on what had occupied it for the previous ten months: the fate of fifty-two Americans held hostage in Iran.[28]

Four days after she died, Dorothy's body was dressed in a pink suit—one of the colors of AKA—and was laid out in an open casket at the Rankin Chapel at Howard University for a four-hour wake. Nearly 150 of her AKA sisters turned out, most of them from a new generation, to pay tribute to their role model. Each soror walked past the coffin and placed a twig of ivy—the sorority plant—on it. Throughout the chapel the sorors grasped hands, sang the AKA anthem, and cried over the loss of their former leader.[29]

To her sorority admirers, Dorothy looked lovely in her casket, "as if she was asleep—getting a well deserved rest," one wrote.[30] But Buddy, who would turn twenty-four the next day, was appalled. In his eyes Gam was a gaunt shadow of her former self. He complained to his father about the open coffin: "My father just told me that there was nothing he, me or anybody could do because the AKA's were running lead on this part of the service and that they [were] only trying to do honor to their fallen soror and former leader."[31]

The scene was different the next morning, when Dorothy's family and friends and the African American aristocracy came to her funeral. The five-hundred-seat Rankin chapel was packed. The eulogy was given by Patricia Roberts Harris, former dean of the Howard Law School, who was the secretary of the Department of Health and Human Services under President Carter.[32]

Dorothy Height, the NCNW president, also spoke, as did Barbara Phillips, the supreme basileus of Alpha Kappa Alpha. Four of the Filthy Five—minus Dorothy's son—carried her casket. A couple of Thurston's Friday night poker pals were honorary pallbearers: Mayor Marion Barry and Congressman William Clay. Former mayor Walter Washington was also one. City Councilwoman Charlene Drew Jarvis, Dr. Montague Cobb, and Dorothy's one-time boss at the Howard Health Service, Dr. Paul Cornely, came to pay their respects.[33] Lisa Kleinman—she was not yet a Ferebee—performed the first movement of Eduardo Lalo's Concerto in D Minor on the cello Gam helped her purchase. The piece was "very moving and fitting for Gam because it was a very intense, serious and statement making piece: Gam herself in a nutshell," Lisa said.[34]

At the conclusion of the hour-and-a-half-long service, Dorothy's body was returned to the McGuire Funeral Home for cremation. The mourners made their way through Washington to Thurston's home on Brooklawn Terrace in Chevy Chase, Maryland, for an all-day reception. AKA sorors assisted with a picnic spread of chicken, turkey, potato salad, and greens. Liquor flowed until 10 o'clock at night.[35] Thurston needed it. His sister's name was invoked during the funeral service, which brought the chapel to tears. At the reception Thurston broke down occasionally as guests recalled his mother.[36] He thought it right that he call his father and let him know of Dorothy's passing. What was said in that phone conversation went with them to their graves.[37]

It fell to the grandchildren to clean out Dorothy's house. They sorted through piles of unread medical journals, yellowing pages of handwritten notes for speeches, photographs, newspaper clippings, scrapbooks, old record albums of classical symphonies, metal dog and bell collections,

AKA memorabilia, clothing, and other personal effects collected during her more than eighty years. They found hundred-dollar bills stuck in books here and there and greeting cards from presidents of the United States and other well-known political figures.[38] Lisa and Buzzy took Gam's mahogany rocker with maple inlay—sturdy enough for big Buzzy. They also took Dorothy's old upright piano. Buddy and his wife took Gam's dining room hutch. Thurston and Carol kept her papers.[39]

Like her own father, Dorothy died without having written a will. This suggests, as did her faulty memory when interviewed for the Black Women Oral History Project in December 1979, that she may have been on the brink of dementia before she died. Or maybe she just wasn't ready to go and thought she could control that too. It turned out to be a costly mistake for her family. It took nearly four years to straighten out her postmortem financial affairs, leaving the burden on Claude III's broad shoulders, who took over as administrator after his father became terminally ill.[40]

Dorothy was well off at the time of her death, at least she seemed to be on paper. She owned her home at 2960 13th Street NW, which had a forty-four-thousand-dollar mortgage, and the bungalow and land in Morris Beach outright. She had four properties in North Carolina that had been left to her by Ruffin, including the house in which he and Julia had lived at 2218 Celia Street in Charlotte. Her real estate holdings alone were estimated to be worth about $130,550. She had another forty-four thousand dollars in cash and household furnishings, including her Oldsmobile Cutlass, valued at five hundred dollars. Even factoring in the cost of her funeral, she left only about $1,500 in debts.[41]

Her son, however, had saddled her with nearly ninety-four thousand dollars in debt that ended up making her estate next to worthless to his wife and children after he died. He was a better dentist than he was a businessman. It seems that on June 16, 1978, Thurston entered into a lease agreement for equipment to outfit a new dental office. Five months later, on November 22, 1978, Dorothy agreed to act as a guarantor. In accordance with the lease agreement, two deliveries were made to Thurston, one on March 5, 1979, and the other on March 29. But he got into a dispute with the supplier and on October 1, 1980, within two weeks of his mother's death, he defaulted. The bank holding the lease went after Dorothy's estate, seeking what Thurston owed plus interest and attorney's fees.[42]

By the fall of 1980 Thurston was gravely ill himself with pancreatic cancer diagnosed shortly after Gam's death. Within months he went from being a large man to a skeletal one, all of 120 pounds. He endured harsh chemotherapy.[43] At the time of his death, although he was still technically employed at Lorton, he had used all his sick days and more. He might have been kept on at the government job as a humanitarian gesture so his family could keep his health insurance and not be bankrupted by his illness.[44]

Thurston was only fifty when he died at the Washington Hospital Center on October 21, 1981. Once again, as they had for Dorothy's funeral, the Ferebees and their friends congregated at the Rankin Chapel.[45] This time Claude and his wife, Hazel, attended. One can only imagine the heartbreak he must have felt at having lived to bury both his children. The Filthy Five were down to four, and they carried Thurston's coffin to the waiting hearse.[46] His body was cremated, and in honor of his service to his country in the air force, his remains were placed in a mausoleum at Arlington National Cemetery.

In old age Dorothy moved to the side of the world stage, each receding step making her unhappier. Yet even after she died she never completely disappeared. In 1990, at the suggestion of DC School Board member R. Calvin Lockridge, the Washington Highland Elementary School at 8th and Yuma Streets SE was renamed the Ferebee-Hope Elementary School in honor of Dorothy and her first director at Southeast House, Marion Conover Hope.[47] Unfortunately the school left something to be desired over the years. In 1995 it was discovered that the water fountains were contaminated with lead, leaving the children without drinkable water. That same year it was considered so troubled the DC Schools superintendent wanted to turn its operation over to private managers.[48] Then a judge determined it was unfit to open because of local fire-code violations.[49] In 2009 the Ferebee-Hope School was visited by First Lady Michelle Obama, who read to its third graders.[50] But it was closed at the conclusion of the 2013 school year.[51]

Today even a casual search of "Dorothy Boulding Ferebee" on the internet yields several thousand results. The organizations with which she was involved in her lifetime continue to post references to her and her many achievements. The home she shared with her former husband and the twins at 1809 Second Street NW in Washington DC is now a tourist attraction and instructions on how to get there may be found on the city's "cultural tourism" website.[52]

Dorothy's four beautiful grandchildren did not have the lives their grandmother might have hoped for. Buzzy, an experienced motorcycle patrol officer, enjoyed recreational riding on the weekends. On August 27, 2000, while riding his motorcycle off-duty with friends in West Virginia, an unexpected rain shower left the highway damp. He skidded on wet leaves, lost control of his bike, and struck an oncoming vehicle. He was killed instantly, leaving his wife of nineteen years and their two teenage sons. Buzzy was forty-seven years old.[53] "His death wrecked that unit of the family," lamented their cousin Laurence Jones.[54] His funeral was attended by scores of brother officers.[55] After her husband was cremated and his ashes scattered in rural Pennsylvania, where he used to go hunting, Lisa and her sons moved to Bowie, Maryland. Several years later she met a new man. The two of them live in North Carolina, where she continues to perform professionally. She is now a grandmother.[56]

Middle son Bucky was troubled. It is likely he suffered from undiagnosed attention deficit disorder and today would be medicated and under a doctor's care. But in the 1950s and 1960s teachers in elementary school probably just wondered why he had ants in his pants and couldn't sit still.[57] Little brother Buddy caught up to Bucky academically and was promoted ahead of him in school.[58] Bucky grew to be a large man—about 6'2" and 245 pounds. He went to St. Mary's University in Nova Scotia, Canada, where he played football, but he never graduated. He returned home when he learned his father was ill.[59] Although Bucky was considered a talented cartoonist and worked intermittently as a housepainter, he had a substance abuse problem on top of his other difficulties and was unable to hold a steady job. He lived at home with his parents and never married. Just two years after his oldest brother was killed in the accident, Bucky died of leukemia. He, too, was forty-seven at the time of his death.

The marriage for which Buddy left Howard University did not last. He had one son with his first wife, divorced, remarried, had a second son, and divorced again. His first wife died of a brain tumor. The economic collapse of 2008 was rough on him. After he lost his job at an architectural firm in Philadelphia it took several years to pull himself back up. For a time he worked as a salesman at Sears outside Philadelphia. Recently he moved back to Washington, and as the economy improved, so did his job choices. He is currently working in architecture.[60]

Dolly came out of the closet after Gam's death. Society changed radically since the tragic death of her aunt, so that when *this* Dolly became the single mother of a son in 1988, nobody blinked an eye. Her son served in the army and was sent to Afghanistan, leaving Dolly with many nights of nail-biting. He came home safely and followed in the footsteps of his late Uncle Buzzy, becoming a police officer in suburban Maryland. Dolly is the doting grandmother to her son's little girl.[61]

Claude Ferebee, the husband Dorothy claimed over and over again was dead, outlived her by sixteen years. He died on July 23, 1996, in Selma at age ninety-five. At his death the man who strayed so far when he was with Dorothy had been married to Hazel for forty-five years.[62] In 1993 he and Hazel abruptly sold their home in White Plains and headed to Hazel's hometown without giving notice to his grandchildren.[63] Buzzy, in particular, was hurt. He and Lisa had grown close to Claude because Lisa was studying the cello with a teacher in New York and while there would stay at Claude's home a few times a year.[64]

It was surprising that Claude and Hazel chose to leave New York. Hazel was overjoyed that Cab Calloway lived down the street from them in White Plains. "She was quite hooked on image," said Lisa.[65] The grandchildren became so estranged from Claude after he and Hazel left New York that Hazel never let them know he died. After Buzzy found out somehow, he called Hazel; the conversation was not pleasant. "She was nasty to him, saying she didn't want 'any of you' coming to try to take his stuff," Lisa said.[66]

Why Hazel resented Claude's offspring so much, other than perhaps the fact that they shared Dorothy's DNA, is not clear. But she may have had her own problems. She was thirteen years younger than Claude, who had just turned ninety-two when they left New York. It may well be that the sharp, disciplined, and exacting Claude she married was gone. When they sold their house, Claude turned over power of attorney to Hazel in a document with a shaky signature that bore little resemblance to the artist's penmanship visible in the letters to his "Concerto," Madeline. He may have become quite feeble; perhaps they returned to Selma so her family could help her take care of him. Hazel outlived Claude by more than a decade, dying in 2007 when she was ninety-three years old.[67]

Claude's parents had died years earlier, his father in 1956 and his mother in 1961.[68] Claude's two sisters outlived him, but not by much. Baby sister Constance died the year after Claude in a Norfolk hospital of a ruptured abdominal aorta. She was eighty-five. She had retired years earlier from her job as an English teacher at Booker T. Washington High School.[69] A year later her older sister, Maxine Burrell, died at age ninety-five.[70]

Death, which seemed ever present in the Ferebee household after Gam passed away, struck again in 1988, when Carol Ferebee died of abdominal cancer. She had been ill for some time, and her stomach had been swelling before she was finally diagnosed. She died just months later.[71] She was fifty-six. Carol was cremated and her ashes placed in an urn next to her husband's at Arlington. After Thurston died, it had fallen to her to be the caretaker of the mounds of memorabilia Dorothy left behind. Given that her formidable mother-in-law had been so bossy and often difficult, a lesser woman might have dumped Dorothy's papers at the curb. But living up to her reputation for being kind and thoughtful, Carol donated them to Howard University, recognizing what Dorothy always knew: that one day researchers would want to read them.

Epilogue
Going Home

Nobody still alive can remember for sure, but Buzzy probably chose a warm autumn day and went alone to the Paige cemetery in Norfolk to scatter his grandmother's ashes on his great-grandmother's grave. He stored Gam's ashes, which weighed about four pounds, in a container on the back of his "baby," a Yamaha XS Special, and took off on the three-and-a-half-hour trip from Maryland.[1] Whether he ever found the cemetery, let alone his great-grandmother's grave once he got there, is anyone's guess. The burial ground developed by his wealthy great-great-grandfather, R. G. L. Paige, in the nineteenth century had become a patch of overgrown weeds and vandalized headstones long before his grandmother died. This ignominious spot would be the last stop for the world-traveling Gam.

Even in the twenty-first century cremation is not the choice of most African Americans; when Dorothy died in 1980, it was even less popular. It seems strange that a woman so honored in life, and so proud of all the honors she earned, would have chosen to be scattered without any headstone marking her final resting place or any monument to the many contributions she made to society. But four days after her death, obviously in accordance with her last wishes, Washington authorities cleared her body for cremation.[2]

Probably the last time Dorothy visited the Paige cemetery was when her mother was buried there more than twenty years earlier. She may not have been aware how badly it had fared since. Articles in the Norfolk paper lamented the eyesore the cemetery, also known as Mt. Olive, had become. "Berkley's Mt. Olive Cemetery is a resting place for the dead, a link with the community's history, and an occasional haven for muggers, robbers and even a man convicted of murder," reported the Norfolk *New Journal and Guide* in 1962. The newspaper blamed the weedy, overgrown appearance of the grounds for providing cover for criminals.[3]

The last descendants of R. G. L. Paige to worry about the condition of the cemetery were Dorothy's uncles: Joseph Paige, a pharmacist, who died in 1962, and Leslie Paige, a lawyer, who died in 1963.[4] After they were gone the grounds were untended except by members of civic organizations who occasionally pitched in to clean up. Leslie's death left ownership of the burial ground in doubt and city officials at a loss as to what to do with it. Every few years newspaper articles would appear touting another beautification effort, but for the most part it remained a neglected rubbish dump.[5]

Today, with a greater appreciation for the contributions of African Americans to society and a heightened sensitivity about the need to keep burial grounds sacred, the Paige cemetery is cared for by city landscapers. The twelve-foot obelisk that Lillie Paige built to her beloved R.G.L. looms large over the peaceful graveyard. But no stone marks the spot where his daughter, Dorothy's mother, Florence Paige Boulding, was buried. Therefore there is no way of knowing where Buzzy may have scattered Dorothy's ashes.

In the end, more than accolades, headlines, stone monuments, or other earthly glory, what mattered to Dorothy was to be back in the protective circle of her Norfolk family and in the ethereal arms of her loving mother. After the thousands of miles she had traveled in her lifetime, making speeches, tending to the poor and the sick, fighting for the rights of her race and gender, and managing the lives of her children and grandchildren, she needed peace and quiet. If there is a hereafter, one can imagine Dorothy has finally found eternal happiness in it—as a child with the wealthy, cultured, family that so lovingly encouraged her dreams and gave her the promise of hope as she fixed the wings of wounded birds.

Far from the Paige cemetery is the grave of another daughter. No arms encircle her. More than 350 miles north in the very small, very wealthy, very white village of Hastings-on-Hudson, in New York's Westchester County, is the grave of a different Dorothy Ferebee, the twin daughter born to Dorothy and Claude in the hot summer of 1931. Dolly's grave lies forgotten in the pastoral Mount Hope Cemetery, a lovely oasis nestled since 1886 near the Harlem and Saw Mill Rivers, overlooking the Palisades.[6] A small headstone marks that resting place. The stone is covered with so much lichen and mold sixty years after it was erected that the name on it is all but obscured. Dolly's grave is described by cemetery officials as "neglected." It has been visited so rarely that since the autumn of 2012 my inquiries about it have prompted several bills for its upkeep, the latest one on March 17, 2014, for $116 for grass care, reseeding, and ground leveling.[7]

When Dolly was buried there, thirty years before her famous mother died, the cause of her death had so threatened to disgrace the family that an elaborate ruse was concocted to cover it up. But, as so often happens with the passage of time, what once seemed important no longer matters. It is not clear whether Dorothy ever visited the grave during her lifetime.

Once, Dolly's father might have considered sharing the bucolic spot for eternity with his precious daughter. But Claude's marriage a little more than a year after Dolly's death to Hazel, a woman for whom his children and grandchildren held little charm, doomed that possibility, as did Claude's own longevity and possible descent into dementia. When he died in 1996, he was buried in Selma, Alabama, next to an empty spot that awaited Hazel when her time finally came in 2007.

At first glance, Dolly's headstone is nearly impossible to read. Some gentle rubbing helps. Missing from that headstone are tender words of love, longing, and despair often carved into the grave markers of children who predecease their parents, ruining the natural order of things. Phrases like "Our beloved daughter"; "We miss you every day"; "Until we meet again in heaven." Instead the small stone reads, "Ferebee Dorothy, 1931–1950." Also missing from the headstone is the suffix "Jr." given to the deceased at birth, which back in the day had also meant so much to her famous mother.

As Dorothy's other child, Thurston, lay dying at the Washington Hospital Center less than a year after she passed, his troubled middle son, Bucky, was visiting with his cousin, Laurence Jones. While the two of them were helping to turn over Thurston's wasted body as he lay in bed, Bucky poignantly remarked, "I wish there was a reset button."[8] Were such an option available, would Dorothy have availed herself of it and started anew, making different choices and setting new priorities? We will never know. What we do know is that by making the choices she did make, by following her often lonely and difficult path, she shut certain doors to her personal happiness. We also know that those same choices opened the doors to the future for African Americans and women that had been closed to Dorothy in the past. And in the end, that is her monument and the one she would have wanted.

NOTES

The author's personal interviews were conducted between 2008 and 2014 by various means.

INTRODUCTION

1. Tom Ward, "Medical Missionaries of the Delta: Dr. Dorothy Ferebee and the Mississippi Health Project, 1935–1941," *Journal of Mississippi History* 63.3 (2001): 203.
2. J. D. Ratcliff, "Cotton Field Volunteer Clinic," *Reader's Digest* (September 1940): 102.
3. Ratcliff, "Cotton Field Volunteer Clinic," 100.
4. Mary King, *Freedom Song: A Personal Story of the 1960's Civil Rights Movement* (New York: William Morrow, 1987), 218.
5. "Dr. Dorothy B. Ferebee, Charms Birds off Trees," *Vogue*, May 1969, 173.
6. J. Y. Smith, "Dorothy Ferebee Dies: Fought for Rights of Women, Blacks," *Washington Post*, September 16, 1980.
7. Editorial: "Dorothy Boulding Ferebee," *Washington Post*, September 18, 1980.
8. "Bury Daughter of NCNW Prexy: Dr. Ferebee's Daughter Dies in Washington," *Chicago Defender*, February 18, 1950.
9. "AFRO Columnist to Speak at Bennett," (Baltimore) *Afro-American*, March 25, 1950.
10. Deborah Gray White, *Too Heavy a Load: Black Women in Defense of Themselves, 1894–1994* (New York: Norton, 1999), 87, 88.
11. Eulogy delivered by Barrington Parker Jr. for Robert L. Carter, Cathedral of St. John the Divine, New York, March 1, 2012, courtesy of Judge Parker.
12. "Dorothy Boulding Ferebee."

PROLOGUE

1. Julius Eric Thompson, *Lynchings in Mississippi: A History, 1865–1965* (Jefferson NC: McFarland, 2007), 92.
2. J. D. Ratcliff, "Cotton Field Clinic," *Survey Graphic* 29 (September 1940): 465.
3. Ratcliff, "Cotton Field Clinic," 465–67.

4. Susan L. Smith, *Sick and Tired of Being Sick and Tired: Black Women's Health Activism in America, 1890–1950* (Philadelphia: University of Pennsylvania Press, 1995), 158.

5. Bernard A. Weisberger, ed., *The WPA Guide to America: The Best of 1930s America as Seen by the Federal Writers' Project. Selections from the American Guide Series, 1935–1941* (New York: Pantheon Books, 1985), 180.

6. Marjorie Holloman Parker, notes on the Mississippi Health Project, Moorland-Spingarn Research Center, Howard University, Dorothy Boulding Ferebee Papers, Box 183-17, Folder 3.

7. Thompson, *Lynchings in Mississippi*, 98; "20 Lynchings in 1935, Says Tuskegee Inst.," *Chicago Defender*, January 4, 1936; "Lynching in America: Statistics, Information, Images," http://law2.umkc.edu/faculty/projects/ftrials/shipp/lynchstats.html, accessed August 7, 2014.

8. Walter White, *Rope and Faggot: A Biography of Judge Lynch* (Notre Dame IN: University of Notre Dame Press, 2001), 232.

9. Thompson, *Lynchings in Mississippi*, 91; Ratcliff, "Cotton Field Clinic," 466.

10. Hon. John Carter, New York State Supreme Court, son of the late U.S. District Judge Robert L. Carter, interview with the author.

11. Minutes of the Eighteenth Annual Boule of Alpha Kappa Alpha Sorority, December 27–30, 1935, Richmond VA, 51, AKA Archives, MSRC-HU.

12. Ratcliff, "Cotton Field Clinic," 465–66.

13. Ratcliff, "Cotton Field Clinic," 466.

14. Dr. Rosier Davis Dedwylder II interview with the author.

15. Elsie Ann Ervin, "Doctor Ded," unpublished manuscript, Delta State Teachers College, 1951, 9, used with permission of James Ervin and obtained courtesy of Dr. Rosier Davis Dedwylder II.

16. Dedwylder interview with the author.

17. Black Women Oral History Project, Dorothy Ferebee interview with Merze Tate, December 28 and 31, 1979, OH 31, Schlesinger Library on the History of Women in America, Radcliffe Institute, Harvard University, Cambridge MA, 26, 28 (hereafter, Ferebee Oral History). (Tate later wrote, and placed in parentheses on page 1 of the transcript, that the interview took place on December 30, 1979.)

18. Dorothy Boulding Ferebee letter to Ida Louise Jackson, June 30, 1935, MSRC-HU, Ferebee Papers, Box 183-5, Folder 18.

1. PUSH, PLUCK, PROMINENCE, AND MERIT

1. J. Y. Smith, "Dr. Dorothy Ferebee Dies; Fought for Rights of Women, Blacks," *Washington Post*, September 16, 1980.

2. Barbara A. Kridel, "Dreams Do Come True," *Simmons Review* 31.3 (1949): 21.

3. Ellen S. More, *Restoring the Balance: Women Physicians and the Profession of Medicine 1850–1995* (Cambridge MA: Harvard University Press, 1995), 4–5.

4. W. E. B. Du Bois, "The Talented Tenth," September 1903, http://www.teachin gamericanhistory.org/library/index.asp?document=174, accessed September 18, 2008.

5. George Freeman Bragg Jr., Letter to Monroe N. Work, *Journal of Negro History* 5 (April 1920): 242; Bragg, "Stories about Some Noted Virginians: Hon. Richard G. L. Paige," (Norfolk) *New Journal and Guide*, n.d.

6. "The Virginia Outrage," *New York Herald*, January 21, 1880.

7. Ferebee Oral History, 2.

8. 1850 U.S. Census (Thomas S. Page), www.ancestry.com, accessed December 20, 2014; 1850 U.S. Census Slave Schedules (Thomas S. Page), www.ancestry.com, accessed December 20, 2014.

9. Paige's date of birth is carved into his grave marker, a twelve-foot obelisk at the Paige Cemetery in Norfolk, visited by the author on May 14, 2012; R. G. L. Paige obituary, *Norfolk Landmark*, September 23, 1904. The obituary says Paige died the day before, but his headstone lists his date of death as September 21, 1904, which is probably correct.

10. William Still, *The Underground Railroad: A Record of Facts, Authentic Narratives, Letters & Etc. . . .* (Chicago: Johnson, 1970), 169, 336–45, 591; *Quinquennial Catalog, Harvard Law School, 1817–1889* (Cambridge MA: 1890), 7.

11. "Obituary: The Hon. George S. Hillard," *Boston Daily Globe*, January 22, 1879; "New England Leaders of the Bench and Bar . . . George Stillman Hillard, a Lawyer Famous as a Brilliant Writer and as an Orator," *Boston Daily Globe*, March 15, 1917; "Longfellow and the Fugitive Slave Act," Longfellow National Historic Site, National Park Service, http://www.nps.gov/long/historyculture /henry-wadsworth-longfellow-abolitionist.htm, accessed May 19, 2010.

12. *Quinquennial Catalog, Harvard Law School*, 100; "Judge George Ruffin: Outline of the Life of the First Colored Man Ever Elevated to the Bench in the North . . . ," *Boston Advertiser*, November 20, 1883; "Josephine St. Pierre Ruffin," Biographies, http://www.pbs.org/blackpress/news_bios/newbios/nwsppr/Biogrphs/josephruff /joseph.html, accessed June 14, 2008.

13. "Judge George Ruffin," *Boston Advertiser*, November 20, 1883.

14. Luther Porter Jackson, *Negro Office-Holders in Virginia 1865–1895* (Norfolk: Guide Quality Press, 1945), 32–33; *Official Register of the United States Containing a List of Officers and Employees . . . on the First of July, 1883 . . .* , vol. 2 (Washington DC: Government Printing Office, 1884), 733.

15. Ruffin Family Bible, Amistad Research Center, Tulane University, New Orleans LA, Heslip-Ruffin Family Papers, Box 2.

16. Norfolk County, Virginia, Deed Book 90: 626–28; 1880 U.S. Census (Richard G. L. Paige).

17. Vicki Lewis, "Grace Episcopal to Celebrate 100th Anniversary with Services," *Virginian-Pilot/Ledger-Star*, November 2–3, 1983.

18. "Mrs. Boulding, Ex-Teacher, Daughter of Legislator," (Washington DC) *Evening Star*, December 3, 1959.

19. "Society: Devoted to All the Activities of Women; The Bible Union Sisters," (Norfolk) *New Journal and Guide*, February 19, 1921.

20. 1900 U.S. Census (Dorthy C. Bolden [sic]), www.ancestry.com, accessed December 20, 2014.

21. Application of Dorothy B. Ferebee, Federal Programs Branch, Division on Exchange of Persons, U.S. Department of State, January 30, 1951.

22. Ferebee/Boulding, Marriage License Application, Chester Co. (PA) Archives and Records, Lic. No. 30290, Dkt. 22, p. 302, http://dsf.chesco.org/archiveindex/marriage/1931/searchresults.asp, accessed September 8, 2010.

23. Letter to the author from S. Simmons, office services specialist, Virginia Department of Health, January 25, 2012.

24. Ferebee Oral History, 2.

25. U.S. World War I Draft Registration Cards, 1917–18 (Ruffin Paige Boulding); U.S. World War I Draft Registration Cards, 1917–18 (Benjamin Richard Boulding), both available on www.ancestry.com and accessed December 20, 2014.

26. *Bison*, Howard University yearbook, 1925, Howard University Archives.

27. Certificate of Death, Lillie A. Paige, No. 17439, Commonwealth of Virginia, Department of Health, Division of Vital Records; Will of Lillie A. Paige, June 17, 2011, Norfolk County Will Book 13: 290.

28. References to Richard Boulding's employment show up in the Norfolk city directories over the years as well as in his draft registration cards: World War I Draft Registration Cards, 1917–18 (Benjamin Richard Boulding); World War II Draft Registration Cards (Benjamin Richard Boulding), www.ancestry.com, accessed May 14, 2012.

29. Ferebee Oral History, 2.

30. "B. R. Boulding Jr., Post Office Veteran," *Virginian Pilot*, February 22, 1980.

31. Benjamin Richard Boulding, Personnel File, U.S. Post Office, National Archives and Records Administration, National Civilian Personnel Records Center, St. Louis MO, Freedom of Information Act request by the author.

32. "Mrs. Boulding, Ex-Teacher"; 1919 Norfolk and Portsmouth City Directory, 266; 1924 Norfolk and Portsmouth City Directory, 277; 1927 Norfolk and Portsmouth City Directory, 233; 1928 Norfolk City Directory, 193; 1930 Norfolk City Directory, 191; 1931 Norfolk City Directory, 191.

33. Ferebee Oral History, 37.

34. *Hampton Graduates, 1871–1899*, May 1899, 132, states that Boulding was born in Burkeville. An untitled article about him in the *Colored American Magazine*, November 1903, says he was born in Crewe. Both publications courtesy of Hampton University Archives.

35. *Colored American Magazine*, November 1903, n.p.; 1900 U.S. Census (Brujac* K. Boulding–Benjamin R. Boulding), www.ancestry.com, accessed May 22, 2012. (The "Brujac* K" entry is apparently a reference to the way the name appears in the original records due to the poor penmanship of the census taker.)

36. 1900 U.S. Census (Brujak* K. Boulding–Benjamin R. Boulding).

37. Partition Deed, Flossie P. Boulding and others, heirs of B. R. Boulding, Nottoway County Circuit Court, Deed Book 65: 254.

38. *Hampton Graduates, 1871–1899*, 132, 165.

39. *Official Register of the United States Containing a List of Officers and Employees . . . on the First of July 1893*, vol. 2 (Washington DC: Government Printing Office, 1894), 428; *Twenty-Two Years' Work of the Hampton Normal and Agricultural Institute: Records of Negro and Indian Graduates and Ex-Students* (Hampton VA: Normal School Press, 1893), 267, courtesy of Hampton University Archives.

40. Susan B. Carter et al., eds., *Historical Statistics of the United States: Earliest Times to the Present, Part B: Work and Welfare*, millennial ed., vol. 2 (New York: Cambridge University Press, 2006), 2–265.

41. *Colored American Magazine*, November 1903; *Official Register of the United States*, 428.

42. Benjamin R. Boulding Jr. and Florence C. Paige, Certificate of Marriage, Virginia Department of Health, Division of Vital Records.

43. Norfolk County, Virginia, Deed Book 184: 218–19; Sharon Rea Gamble and Truitt M. Bonney, *Norfolk County Virginia Marriage Licenses 1850–1899 (non-white)*, vol. 3 (Suffolk VA: Privately published, 2008), 25, courtesy of Sargeant Memorial Room, Norfolk Public Library.

44. Untitled article, *Norfolk Landmark*, September 29, 1903, courtesy of Hampton University Archives.

45. "To Appeal for Colored Children; 4,000 Negro Children Crowded Out, It Is Claimed, Ask for a High School; Citizens Educational Association Ask That Princess Anne Avenue Building Be Used as Colored School," *Norfolk Landmark*, June 30, 1908.

46. "Mr. Benjamin R. Boulding, Norfolk, Virginia," *Alexander's Magazine*, September 1906, 51; "Benjamin R. Boulding, 31 Avenue A, Norfolk, VA," *Southern Workman*, October 1905, both publications courtesy of Hampton University Archives; Samuel R. Spencer Jr., *Booker T. Washington and the Negro's Place in American Life* (Boston: Little, Brown, 1955), 123.

47. Untitled publication, courtesy of Hampton University Archives, April 1901.

48. U.S. Mail Railway Post Office, "The Railway Mail Service," Railway Mail Service Library Publication, 1995, 4.

49. "Nine Killed in Wreck; Fast Mail Jumped from Trestle Near Danville. Postal Clerks Killed . . . ," *Norfolk Landmark*, September 29, 1903; "Saved Tons of Mail,

Postal Property Rescued by a Norfolk Clerk. Aided Wounded Also. B. R. Boulding, of This City, Was One of the First on the Scene of the Wreck of the Southern New York–New Orleans Fast Mail Train—Assisted in Rescuing Fellow Mail Clerks from the Debris," *Norfolk Landmark*, September 29, 1903.

50. "Saved Tons of Mail."

51. "Hero of the Wrecked Fast Mail Train No. 97," *Richmond Planet*, October 3, 1903.

52. "Statistics of Population—Table 24—Native and Foreign Born and White and Colored Population," Census Reports 1, *Twelfth Census of the United States: Population*, 1900, part 1, vol. 1, 682.

53. John Hope Franklin, *From Slavery to Freedom: A History of Negro Americans*, 4th ed. (New York: Knopf, 1974), 253; Jane Dailey, *Before Jim Crow: The Politics of Race in Post Emancipation Virginia* (Chapel Hill: University of North Carolina Press, 2000), 14, 201n132.

54. Norfolk County, Virginia, Deed Book 233: 197–98.

55. Ferebee Oral History, 3.

56. Dorothy Ruth Ferebee interview with the author.

57. "Mrs. Boulding, Ex-Teacher."

58. Franklin, *From Slavery to Freedom*, 115, 176.

59. Ferebee Oral History, 3–4.

60. Norfolk County, Virginia, Deed Book 335: 146–47.

61. Norfolk County, Virginia, Deed Book 155-B: 586; William Inge, archivist, Sargeant Memorial Room, Norfolk Public Library, email to author, October 19, 2011.

62. Norfolk, Virginia, Deed Book 335: 146–47.

63. "Salary Record, B. R. Boulding, Jr.," NARA, National Civilian Personnel Records. Both Dorothy's father and her brother were often referred to in official documents or publications with the suffix "Jr." The notation on the salary record indicating the employee had died reads "7-9-10," and obviously refers to Dorothy's father.

64. "The New Public School for Colored Children," *Norfolk Virginian*, December 16, 1886.

65. Ferebee Oral History, 4.

66. "Flag Raising and Patron's Day," program, Cumberland Street School, May 24, 1911, courtesy of Dorothy Ruth Ferebee.

67. Ferebee Oral History, 4.

2. AMONG THE FAVORED FEW

1. Transcript, Girls' High, City of Boston Archives.

2. Transcript, Girls' High; Deed Book, Suffolk County, Massachusetts, Book 2967: 257; Book 2969: 524–25.

3. 1910 Census of the United States (Emma Ruffin), www.ancestry.com, accessed December 20, 2014.

4. *City of Boston List of Residents 20 Years of Age and Over as of April 1, 1923* (Ward 13, Pct. 1): 2; 1910 U.S. Census; 1920 U.S. Census (Emma Ruffin), www.ancestry .com, accessed December 20, 2014.

5. Transcript, Girls' High.

6. Kenneth L. Mark, *Delayed by Fire: Being the Early History of Simmons College* (Concord NH: Rumford Press, 1945), 7.

7. *A Brief History of Simmons College: The Early Years, 1899–1919*, Simmons College Archives, www2.simmons.edu/library/archives/exhibits/438.php, accessed March 28, 2015.

8. Bryon Farwell, *Over There: The United States in the Great War 1917–1918* (New York: Norton, 1999), 35–36.

9. Farwell, *Over There*, 51; World War I Draft Registration Cards, 1917–18 (Ruffin Paige Boulding).

10. Ferebee Oral History, 2; State of Virginia, War History Commission, Military Service Record for Ruffin Paige Boulding, Library of Virginia, http://image.lva .virginia.gov/wwl/pages/045/0027.html, accessed December 11, 2014.

11. Farwell, *Over There*, 53, 132.

12. Farwell, *Over There*, 130.

13. Farwell, *Over There*, 132.

14. Dorothy C. Boulding, "Lynching as an Expression of Americanism," Simmons College, 1920, MSRC-HU, Ferebee Papers, Box 183-14, Folder 23.

15. "Lynchings: By Year and Race," Archives, Tuskegee Institute, http://law2.umkc .edu/faculty/projects/ftrials/shipp/lynchingyear.html, accessed May 2, 2012.

16. "Colored Girl at Simmons Writes on Lynching," unnamed newspaper, n.d., Ferebee Simmons scrapbook, courtesy of Lisa Ferebee.

17. Boulding, "Lynching."

18. "Dorothy Celeste Boulding," *1920 Microcosm*, 51.

19. Graduation figures for the class of 1920 and information about commencement, courtesy of Simmons College.

20. U.S. Department of Agriculture, Weather Bureau, "Daily Local Record, Boston, Massachusetts Weather Station," June 14, 1920.

21. Invitation to Dorothy Celeste Boulding graduation reception, Dorothy Ferebee scrapbook, courtesy of Lisa Ferebee.

22. Dorothy Celeste Boulding, application for admission to Tufts College Medical School, August 22, 1920.

23. Dr. Frank E. Haskins letter to Dorothy C. Boulding, September 13, 1920, Dorothy Ferebee scrapbook, courtesy of Lisa Ferebee.

24. "Tufts College Medical and Dental Schools," *Boston Medical and Surgical Journal* 184 (February 24, 1921): xv.

25. Boulding application for admission to Tufts College Medical School.

26. Henry H. Banks, *A Century of Excellence: The History of Tufts University School of Medicine, 1893–1993* (Boston: Tufts University Press, 1993), 7.

27. Minutes of the meeting of the faculty of Tufts College Medical School, May 28, 1924, courtesy of Hirsch Health Sciences Library, Tufts University.

28. *1921–22 Tufts College Medical School Bulletin*, 50–51, Hirsch Health Sciences Library, Tufts University.

29. Minutes of the meeting of the faculty of the Tufts College Medical School; "Washington Society," *Chicago Defender*, January 3, 1925.

30. Dorothy Celeste Boulding, "History of '24," in *1924 Caduceus*, 50, Tufts University, digital collection and archives, Medford MA.

31. U.S. Department of Agriculture, Weather Bureau, "Daily Local Record, Boston, Massachusetts Weather Station," Wednesday, April 2, 1924.

32. *1924 Caduceus*, 57, 184, n.p. (photograph of the Senior Class Banquet, April 2, 1924).

33. "James Ernest Martin, Jr.," *1921 DenTufts* 56; "Figurative Dope," *Tufts Weekly* 24, September 29, 1920, 3.

34. "Dorothy Celeste Boulding," *1924 Caduceus*, 64.

35. Paul G. Richter letter to Dartmouth College Alumni Records Office, December 29, 1973, "James Ernest Martin, Jr.," Alumni Files, courtesy of Dartmouth College Library.

36. Dorothy Ferebee scrapbook, courtesy of Lisa Ferebee; U.S. Department of Agriculture, Weather Bureau, "Daily Local Record, Boston, Massachusetts Weather Station," April 13, 1921.

37. Priscilla White, secretary of Zeta Phi fraternity, Epsilon Chapter, Tufts College Medical School, letter to Miss Boulding, February 13, 1922; Calendar, Epsilon Chapter, Zeta Phi Fraternity, 1923–24, all from Dorothy Ferebee scrapbook, courtesy of Lisa Ferebee.

38. "Epsilon Chapter of Zeta Phi," *1923 Caduceus*, 131.

39. Ferebee Oral History, 31; Joellen Elbashir, curator, manuscript division, MSRC-HU, home of the Ferebee papers, email to the author, February 15, 2012.

40. Toki Schalk, "Toki Types: About People Here and There: Stopping By," *Pittsburgh Courier*, August 7, 1943; "History," Bluefield State College," http://www.bluefield state.edu/about/history, accessed April 15, 2012; The information regarding when Martin married comes from his answers to a pair of questionnaires he filled out for the Dartmouth College Alumni Records office. In the first, submitted in 1965, he said he married in 1924, in the second, submitted in 1971, he said he married in 1925. "James Ernest Martin, Jr."

41. E. Franklin Frazier, *Black Bourgeoisie* (New York: Free Press Paperbacks, 1997), 177.

42. "Miss Boulding Wins Zeta Phi," unnamed newspaper clipping, n.d., Ferebee scrapbook, courtesy of Lisa Ferebee.

43. "Feurtado's Column," unnamed newspaper, July 12, 1924, Ferebee scrapbook.

44. Frazier, *Black Bourgeoisie*, 174.

45. "Feurtado's Column."

46. Editorial: "Dorothy Boulding Ferebee," *Washington Post*, September 18, 1980.

47. "Hospital Appointments," *1924 Caduceus*, 127–30.

48. Ellen S. More, *Restoring the Balance: Women Physicians and the Profession of Medicine, 1850–1995* (Cambridge MA: Harvard University Press, 1999), 107n45, citing *Journal of the American Medical Association* 82 (1924): 992–94.

49. "Medical Interne," unnamed newspaper clipping, n.d., Ferebee scrapbook, courtesy of Lisa Ferebee.

50. Ferebee Oral History, 6.

3. AS IF I HAD THROWN A BOMB INTO THE ROOM

1. Ferebee Oral History, 38; Jacqueline Trescott, "Making a Practice of Persistence: Dorothy Ferebee, the Elegant Doctor with a Social Conscience," *Washington Post*, May 5, 1978.

2. *1925 Bison*, Howard University, 92.

3. Buck Colbert Franklin, *My Life and an Era: The Autobiography of Buck Colbert Franklin*, edited by John Hope Franklin, and John Whittington Franklin (Baton Rouge: Louisiana State University Press, 1997), xv, 1, 147, 203.

4. Linda D. Wilson, "Wewoka," *Encyclopedia of Oklahoma History and Culture*, Oklahoma Historical Society, http://www.digital.library.okstate.edu/encyclopedia/entries/W/we023.html, accessed July 2, 2012; "Wewoka, Oklahoma," http://www.city-data.com/city/wewoka-oklahoma.html, accessed December 18, 2014.

5. Franklin, *My Life and an Era*, 203.

6. "Ruffin Boulding to Share in $25,000 in Attorneys' Fees," (Norfolk) *New Journal and Guide*, December 11, 1926; "Indian Files a Suit to Regain Valuable Land: Papers Prepared and Entered by Law Offices of Ruffin P. Boulding, Former Norfolk Lawyer," (Norfolk) *New Journal and Guide*, September 18, 1926.

7. Franklin, *My Life and an Era*, 208.

8. *Mirror: Annual Yearbook of the Teachers College of Howard University*, vol. 1, 1915, 118.

9. "Taught in Norfolk: Mrs. Julia W. Boulding Passes in Charlotte," (Norfolk) *New Journal and Guide*, March 28, 1970.

10. Marriage License No. 000023, Boulding, Ruffin P./Wyche, Julia I., issued August 10, 1927, Mecklenburg County, North Carolina (Boulding, Ruffin) meckrod.manatron.com/marriage/searchresults.aspx, accessed December 18, 2014.

11. 1930 U.S. Census (Charles F. Goodloe), www.ancestry.com, accessed December 20, 2014.

12. W. Montague Cobb, "A Short History of Freedmen's Hospital," *Journal of the National Medical Association* 54.3 (1962): 277, 279; Annual catalogue of Howard University, 1929–30, 52.

13. Cobb, "Short History of Freedmen's Hospital," 272.

14. W. A. Warfield, "Annual Report to the Secretary of the Interior," August 8, 1921, in *Report of the Freedmen's Hospital to the Secretary of the Interior for the Fiscal Year Ended June 30, 1921* (Washington DC: Government Printing Office, 1921), 7.

15. W. A. Warfield, "Annual Report to the Secretary of the Interior," August 21, 1925, in *Report of the Freedmen's Hospital to the Secretary of the Interior for the Fiscal Year Ended June 30, 1925* (Washington DC: Government Printing Office, 1925), 7.

16. Randall Bond Truett, ed., *Washington, DC: A Guide to the Nation's Capital, "Howard University,"* rev. ed. (New York: Hastings House, 1968), 54–55.

17. Constance McLaughlin Green, *The Secret City: A History of Race Relations in the Nation's Capital* (Princeton NJ: Princeton University Press, 1967), 89–96.

18. David Levering Lewis, *District of Columbia: A Bicentennial History* (New York: Norton, 1976), 74.

19. Green, *Secret City*, 204.

20. Green, *Secret City*, 207.

21. Harry S. Jaffe and Tom Sherwood, *Dream City: Race, Power, and the Decline of Washington, DC* (New York: Simon & Schuster, 1994), 28–29.

22. Charlene Drew Jarvis interview with the author.

23. Dr. William Lofton Jr. interview with the author.

24. Louis R. Lautier, "Under the Capitol Dome; Washington Society," *Chicago Defender*, April 30, 1927; "What Good Are We? Dance Eclipses Former Events: Elite from Various Sections of Country Are in Attendance," *Pittsburgh Courier*, May 30, 1931; "Turkey Day Calendar in Washington Brimming with Festive Holiday Glory; Annual Howard-Lincoln Football Game Will Be Center of Much Gayety," *Pittsburgh Courier*, November 24, 1934; Lynette Gittoes, "What's What in Washington," *New York Amsterdam News*, February 10, 1945.

25. Ferebee Oral History, 6.

26. Minutes of the Washington DC Board of Medical Supervisors, July 31, 1925, Washington DC Department of Health, FOIA request by the author; DC Department of Health FOIA Officer Phillip L. Husband email to author, April 11, 2012; Office of the Board of Medical Supervisors of the District of Columbia letter to Dr. Dorothy Boulding, August 1, 1925, courtesy of Dorothy Ruth Ferebee; DC Commission on Licensure Healing Arts Practice Act letter to Dr. Dorothy Boulding Ferebee, April 5, 1934, courtesy of Dorothy Ruth Ferebee.

27. "Norfolk Young Woman Winning Recognition," (Norfolk) *New Journal and Guide*, October 31, 1925.

28. Dean Harden, citation letter to Dorothy upon her retirement, June 4, 1968, Howard University Archives.

29. "Quarter-Century of Strong African-American Progress in Medical School Education May Be Coming to an Abrupt Halt," *Journal of Blacks in Higher Education* 18 (Winter 1997–98): 14.

30. Richard McKinney, *Mordecai: The Man and His Message. The Story of Mordecai Wyatt Johnson* (Washington DC: Howard University Press, 1997), 60, 79; Annual Catalogue of Howard University, 1929–30, 51, Howard University Archives.

31. Dorothy B. Ferebee, MD, "A Statement of Appreciation," Funeral Services for Dr. Mordecai Wyatt Johnson, 1890–1976, September 14, 1976, Andrew Rankin Memorial Chapel, Howard University, courtesy of Rankin Memorial Chapel.

32. William Howard Johnson interview with the author; John Beckley interview with the author; Harry G. Robinson III and Hazel Ruth Edwards, *The Long Walk: The Placemaking Legacy of Howard University* (Washington DC: Howard University Press, 1996), 218.

33. Program for "Sex Education for the Adolescent," February 25, 1928, and letter to Dorothy Boulding from Sarah C. Fernandis, n.d., courtesy of Dorothy Ruth Ferebee.

34. "Home Place for Sex Education League Hears: Dr. Dorothy Boulding Tells Women Parent Is Best Sex Teacher . . . ," (Baltimore) *Afro-American*, March 3, 1928.

35. Jean H. Baker, *Margaret Sanger: A Life of Passion* (New York: Hill and Wang, 2011), 116, 124.

36. Carole R. McCann, *Birth Control Politics in the United States, 1916–1945* (Ithaca NY: Cornell University Press, 1994), 73, 75.

37. Baker, *Margaret Sanger*, 5.

38. McCann, *Birth Control Politics*, 114.

39. "Home Place for Sex Education League Hears."

40. Program, "Conference on Social Hygiene and Juvenile Delinquency," Federation of Parent-Teacher Associations, Garnett-Patterson Junior High School, May 3, 1929, courtesy of Dorothy Ruth Ferebee.

41. Program, Washington Council of Social Workers, 1929–30, courtesy of Dorothy Ruth Ferebee.

42. Minutes of the Executive Committee of the Board of Trustees of Howard University, June 5, 1930, 8, and Minutes of the Executive Committee of the Board of Trustees of Howard University, September 25, 1930, 5, Howard University Archives.

43. Minutes of the Board of Trustees of Howard University, February 5, 1929, Howard University Archives.

44. "Students Taught Health," *Hilltop* 6 (October 16, 1930), Howard University Archives.

45. Vernon C. Thompson, "SE Neighborhood House to Stay Open," *Washington Post*, March 29, 1979.

46. Ferebee Oral History, 6.

47. Jacqueline Trescott, "Making a Practice of Persistence: Dorothy Ferebee, the Elegant Doctor with a Social Conscience," *Washington Post*, May 5, 1978.

48. Ferebee Oral History, 7.

49. Ferebee Oral History, 7.

50. Ferebee Oral History, 7–8.

51. Ferebee Oral History, 8; Washington Welfare Association, Application, DC Community Chest, December 9, 1929, MSRC-HU, Ferebee Papers, Box 183-24, Folder 10.

52. Ferebee Oral History, 8–9.

53. Ferebee Oral History, 9.

54. Minutes of the Meeting of the Board of Directors of Friendship House, March 19, 1929, Friendship House Association Records, MS 2142, Special Collections, Gelman Library, George Washington University, Box 15, Folder 2.

55. Draft letter from Lydia Burklin, April 16, 1929, Friendship House Association Records, George Washington University, Box 4, Folder 10.

56. Ferebee Oral History, 8.

57. Chairman of Budget Committee of the Community Chest letter to Dorothy Boulding, February 28, 1930, MSRC-HU, Ferebee Papers, Box 183-3, Folder 13.

58. Cordelia A. Winn, YMCA letter to Dr. Dorothy C. Boulding, June 18, 1929; Helen L. Thomas, YMCA letter to Dr. Dorothy C. Boulding, July 1, 1929.

59. Sara Pelham Speaks, "DC Society: Lofton Party," (Baltimore) *Afro-American*, June 15, 1929.

60. "Gets H.U. Post," (Norfolk) *New Journal and Guide*, September 7, 1929.

4. THE COUNT

1. Jonathan Gill, *Harlem: The Four Hundred Year History from Dutch Village to Capital of Black America* (New York: Grove Press, 2011), 184.

2. Lillian R. Gaines, "History of College Class of '23," 1923 *Wilberforcean*, 26.

3. Wilberforce University, "History," http://www.wilberforce.edu/welcome/history.html, accessed February 16, 2009.

4. 1923 *Wilberforcean*, 154.

5. Claude Thurston Ferebee videotaped oral history interview with Claude Thurston Ferebee III, January 20, 1986, courtesy of Lisa Ferebee.

6. 1923 *Wilberforcean*, 19.

7. 1923 *Wilberforcean*, 26.

8. 1923 *Wilberforcean*, 18, 62, 77, 97, 101; 1923–24 *Wilberforce University Catalog*, 134.

9. "Greater Norfolk, Personal Brevities, Society-Fraternities: City Personals," (Norfolk) *New Journal and Guide*, June 30, 1923.

10. 1920 Census of the United States, *Population*, vol. 3 (Washington DC: Government Printing Office, 1922), 1069.

11. Claude Thurston Ferebee videotaped oral history interview.

12. Claude Thurston Ferebee, SS-5, Application for Social Security card, NARA, from the Social Security Administration, Office of Earnings Operations, Baltimore MD, FOIA request by the author.

13. U.S. Social Security Death Index, 1935–2014, (Maxine F. [Ferebee] Burrell), (Constance [Ferebee] Jones), www.ancestry.com, accessed August 7, 2012.

14. World War I Draft Registration Cards, 1917–18 (Charles S. Ferebee); Nannie J. Ferebee Certificate of Death, No. 1225, Virginia Department of Health, Division of Vital Records, filed June 22, 1961.

15. Marriage Register Book 3: 57, Marriage License No. 229, Circuit Court Clerk, City of Norfolk VA.

16. Charles S. Ferebee Federal Service Records, Post Office Department; Norfolk VA, Postmaster R. W. Shultice letter to Charles S. Ferebee, March 1, 1940, NARA, National Civilian Personnel Records Center, St. Louis MO, FOIA request by the author.

17. "Charles Ferebee, Mail Carrier 30 Years, Dies," (Norfolk) *Journal and Guide*, April 28, 1956; Lisa Ferebee email to the author, September 3, 2012.

18. Lisa Ferebee email to the author, September 3, 2012.

19. James McGill, "Junior Mendelssohn Clef Club Celebrates Fourth Anniversary," (Norfolk) *New Journal and Guide*, December 9, 1916.

20. Capt. Claude Thurston Ferebee letter to Madeline K. Dugger, April 1, 1942, National Park Service, Mary McLeod Bethune Council House NHS, National Archives for Black Women's History, Madeline Kountze Dugger Kelley Papers, Series 2, Subseries 5, Box 3, Folder 9 (hereafter, NPS, NABWH, Dugger Papers).

21. 1860 U.S. Census (John Jordan), www.ancestry.com accessed December 3, 2011; 1870 U.S. Census (Hannah Jordan), www.ancestry.com accessed December 3, 2011; 1880 U.S. Census (Hannah Jordan), www.ancestry.com, accessed December 3, 2011; Claude Thurston Ferebee videotaped oral history interview.

22. Cathy Aldridge, "Moles Bow with Party, Dinner Dance, Lunch," *New York Amsterdam News*, March 11, 1967.

23. Laurence Jones interview with the author.

24. Norfolk County, Virginia, Deed Book 274: 290, 1908 Norfolk and Portsmouth City Directory.

25. Norfolk County, Virginia, Deed Book 268-A: 503.

26. Laurence Jones interview with the author.

27. Norfolk County, Virginia, Deed Book 1119: 412.

28. Claude Thurston Ferebee videotaped oral history interview.

29. Constance Curtis and Chollie Herndon, "Dentists Must Unite Medicine with Fine Art; Talents Needed for Success," *New York Amsterdam News*, May 21, 1949; Todd Boulding Ferebee interview with the author.

30. *Columbia University Bulletin of Information: School of Dentistry and Oral Surgery, Announcement 1924–1925*, 16, Archives and Special Collections, Columbia University A. C. Long Health Sciences Library.

31. Dr. Robert L. Harris, national historian, Alpha Phi Alpha, interview with the author.

32. Bessye J. Bearden, "Tid-Bits of New York Society," *Chicago Defender*, January 12, 1929.

33. 1930 U.S. Census, (Kathleen Vogelsang), www.ancestry.com, accessed October 23, 2012; Gerry, "Society," *New York Amsterdam News*, April 16, 1930; "New York: The Social Whirl," (Baltimore) *Afro-American*, January 24, 1931; "Club Chats," *New York Amsterdam News*, June 7, 1933.

34. Certified Academic Record of Claude Thurston Ferebee, courtesy of the Office of the Registrar, Medical Center Campus, Columbia University.

35. 1924–25 *Columbia Dental School Bulletin*, 18.

36. Claude Thurston Ferebee Academic Record.

37. Claude Thurston Ferebee Academic Record; "Photograph—Class of 1929," *Columbia Dentor*, n.p.

38. Connie F. Mitchell, New York State Education Department, letter to author, December 31, 2012; New York State Office of the Professions, Verification Searches (Claude T. Ferebee, Sr.), http://www.nysed.gov/coms/op001/opsc2a?profcd=50&plicno=010130&namechk=FER, accessed December 21, 2014.

39. Gill, *Harlem*, 227, 281, 320, 324.

40. "Changes in Dental Faculty Stir Howard: Seek Reason for Doctor's Resignation; Staff Members Split into Two Camps," *Chicago Defender*, September 28, 1929; Claude Thurston Ferebee videotaped oral history interview.

5. PETUNIA TICKLEBRITCHES

1. Rayford W. Logan, *Howard University: The First Hundred Years, 1867–1967* (New York: New York University Press, 1969), 312. The student yearbook, the 1930 *Bison* (Howard University Archives), put the number of dental students that year at seventeen.

2. Annual Catalogue of Howard University, 1929–30, 335.

3. Annual Catalogue of Howard University, 1931–32, 390–91.

4. Dr. William Lofton Jr. interview with the author on standard delivery fees in the 1930s among black doctors and their patients in Washington DC; minutes of the June 5, 1930 meeting of the Executive Committee of the Howard University Board of Trustees, 8, Howard University Archives.

5. Minutes of the meeting of the June 5, 1930 Executive Committee of the Howard University Board of Trustees, 8; Dr. William Lofton Jr. interview with the author.

6. Ferebee Oral History, 12–13.

7. Minutes of the September 25, 1930 meeting of the Executive Committee of the Howard University Board of Trustees, 5; Minutes of the June 5, 1930 meeting of the Executive Committee, 8; Annual Catalogue of Howard University, 1929–30, 433, all from the Howard University Archives.

8. Heather Munro Prescott, *Student Bodies: The Influence of Student Health Services in American Society and Medicine* (Ann Arbor: University of Michigan Press, 2007), 74–78.

9. Ferebee Oral History, 12–13.

10. Dorothy Ruth Ferebee interview with the author.

11. Ferebee Oral History, 13.

12. Campbell C. Johnson letter to Marion Conover, January 14, 1930, MSRC-HU, Ferebee Papers, Box 183-6, Folder 1.

13. Claude Thurston Ferebee and Dorothy Boulding Ferebee, Marriage License Application No. 30290, Commonwealth of Pennsylvania, County of Chester.

14. Certificate of Birth No. 348505, Claude Thurston Ferebee II; Certificate of Birth No. 348506, Dorothy Boulding Ferebee Jr., Government of the District of Columbia, Department of Health.

15. "Dr. Boulding to Resume Duties," *Hilltop* 6.4 (October 30, 1930).

16. "Median Age at First Marriage, 1890–2010," U.S. Bureau of the Census, www.infoplease.com, accessed November 18, 2012.

17. Dorothy Ruth Ferebee interview with the author.

18. Ferebee honeymoon album, courtesy of Lisa Ferebee; Jerry, "New York: The Social Whirl," (Baltimore) *Afro-American*, July 12, 1930. Although the by-line reads "Jerry," it should probably read "Gerry," as it was the occasional pen name of journalist Geralyn Dismond.

19. Jerry, "New York."

20. "Doctor and Dentist Just Married," (Norfolk) *New Journal and Guide*, July 12, 1930.

21. New York City 1940 Online Telephone Directory, http://directme.nypl.org/directory/manhattan, accessed December 21, 2014.

22. "Dr. Thomas H. Walters, a Retired Dentist, Dies," *New York Times*, March 20, 1980.

23. Untitled column, (Baltimore) *Afro-American*, August 2, 1930.

24. Jerry, "New York; Personals," (Baltimore) *Afro-American*, September 6, 1930.

25. W. E. B. Du Bois letter to Dorothy Boulding Ferebee, August 19, 1930, MSRC-HU, Ferebee Papers, Box 183-4, Folder 5.

26. *Boyd's 1931 Directory of the District of Columbia*, 278, 606.

27. "Nearly 50 Race Doctors at White House Confab: One-Third of Those Invited Attend," *Pittsburgh Courier*, February 28, 1931.

28. J. L. Jenkins, "Maryland State: Baltimore," *Chicago Defender*, April 4, 1931.

29. Capitola, "Washington," (Norfolk) *New Journal and Guide*, May 23, 1931.

30. Stanley Lebergott, "Actual Estimates of Unemployment in the United States, 1900–1954," in *Measurement and Behavior of Unemployment* (Cambridge MA: National Bureau of Economic Research, 1957), 215, http://www.nber.org/chapters/c2644, accessed January 19, 2015.

31. Ferebee Oral History, 15.

32. "Weather," *Washington Post*, August 2, 1931.

33. "14 Are Overcome by Extreme Heat: Second Highest Mark for Year Reached; Five Treated from Cell Block," *Washington Post*, August 4, 1931.

34. "Heat to Continue: Cooler by Night; Official Temperature Rises to 97, but Tube at Kiosk Was 102," *Washington Post*, August 9, 1931.

35. Claude Thurston Ferebee II and Dorothy Boulding Ferebee Jr., birth certificates.

36. Ferebee Oral History, 14.

37. "The Notebook of the Guide's Society Editor," (Norfolk) *New Journal and Guide*, August 22, 1931; "Washington, DC," *Chicago Defender*, August 15, 1931; Gerry, "The New York Social Whirl," (Baltimore) *Afro-American*, September 5, 1931.

38. "Personals," (Norfolk) *New Journal and Guide*, August 15, 1931.

6. EVERYTHING WAS PRECISE

1. 1933 *Boyd's Directory of the District of Columbia*, 238, 567.

2. Ferebee Oral History, 13.

3. John Beckley interview with the author.

4. Ferebee Oral History, 13, 14.

5. Ferebee Oral History, 15.

6. 1933 *Boyd's Directory of the District of Columbia*, 238, 567.

7. "Husband, Wife Killed in Early Morn Crash: Injuries Fatal to Mr. and Mrs. E. C. Crocker; 2 Recover," (Norfolk) *New Journal and Guide*, February 24, 1934.

8. "Lawyer's Bond in Larceny Case Fixed at $1,500: Case Goes to Grand Jury without Police Court Hearing," (Norfolk) *New Journal and Guide*, October 6, 1934.

9. "Renew Efforts for Pardon in Paige Case: Motion for Suspended Sentence Denied by Judge Goode," (Norfolk) *New Journal and Guide*, October 24, 1936.

10. John Beckley interview with the author.

11. Ferebee Oral History, 15.

12. Ferebee Oral History, 15.

13. Ferebee Oral History, 13, 18.

14. "H.U. Cuts Faculty," (Baltimore) *Afro-American*, May 16, 1936.

15. Claude Thurston Ferebee videotaped oral history interview.

16. "March 20, 1933," www.nps.gov/hofr/upload/march%2020%20and%2022.pdf, accessed November 26, 2012; "The New Deal: 1933," http://www.rooseveltinstitute .org/policy-and-ideasroosevelt-historyfdr/new-deal, accessed November 26, 2012.

17. Minutes of the April 11, 1933 meeting of the Howard University Board of Trustees, 12–13, Howard University Archives.

18. Special Correspondent, "Howard U. Ax Said to Have Hit Bartsch, Scurlock, Cromwell, Jackson; The Ousting of Dr. Ferebee May Mean That Howard Will Go Back to the Old System of Having Co-eds Examined by a Male Physician . . . ," (Baltimore) *Afro-American*, April 22, 1933.

19. Minutes of the April 28, 1933 Special Meeting of the Howard University Board of Trustees, 5, Howard University Archives.

20. "Howard U. Ax Said to Have Hit."

21. "Howard Co-Eds Want Woman Doctor Kept: Physician among Those Slated to Go under Axe," (Norfolk) *New Journal and Guide*, May 13, 1933.

22. "Howard Law Alumni Oppose Dismissal of Dr. Ferebee: Urge Faculty Representation," (Norfolk) *New Journal and Guide*, June 17, 1933.

23. Annual Catalogue, Howard University, 1933–34, 76, Howard University Archives.

24. Minutes of the April 13, 1934 meeting of the Executive Committee of the Howard University Board of Trustees, Howard University Archives.

25. Claude Thurston Ferebee videotaped oral history interview.

26. "Many Out-of-Town Visitors Attend What-Good-Are-We Dance," (Baltimore) *Afro-American*, June 3, 1933.

27. "Many Out-of-Town Visitors."

28. Claude Thurston Ferebee Military Records, NARA, National Military Personnel Records Center, St. Louis MO, FOIA request by the author.

29. V. A. Silverman, General Heating Co., letter to Dr. Boulding, October 13, 1931, MSRC-HU, Ferebee Papers, Box 183-4, Folder 10.

30. Marion Grace Conover, "Annual Report of the South East House," June 22, 1932, MSRC-HU, Ferebee Papers, Box 183-24, Folder 10.

31. Richard Pearson, "Dorothy Howard Dies: Founded Nursery School," *Washington Post*, September 1, 1988; John Beckley interview with author.

32. Pearson, "Dorothy Howard Dies."

33. Ferebee Oral History, 16.

34. Aurelia Roberts Brooks email to author, December 6, 2012.

35. Aurelia Roberts Brooks email to author; Lynn C. French email to author, August 3, 2013.

36. Aurelia Roberts Brooks email to author; William Bushong, *Historic Resource Study: Rock Creek Park, District of Columbia*, August 1990, 1, 37, www.nps.gov/rocr, accessed December 7, 2012; Lynn C. French email to author.

37. Aurelia Roberts Brooks email to author.

38. Susan L. Smith, *Sick and Tired of Being Sick and Tired: Black Women's Health Activism in America, 1890–1950* (Philadelphia: University of Pennsylvania Press, 1995), 151–52; Marjorie H. Parker, *Alpha Kappa Alpha through the Years 1908–1988* (Chicago: Mobium Press, 1990), 184.

39. Ida Louise Jackson, "Service Project: 'Summer School for Teachers'—Saints Industrial School, Lexington, Mississippi," *Ivy Leaf* 12.3 (1934): 9.

40. "Ida Louise Jackson: 8th Supreme Basileus 1934–36," *Ivy Leaf* (Spring 1980): 10; Jesuit University in Silicon Valley, Markkula Center for Applied Ethics, "Ida Jackson," http://www.scu.edu/ethics/architects-of-peace/Ida-Jackson/homepage .html, accessed June 27, 2008.

41. Ida Louise Jackson, "Overcoming Barriers in Education," BANC MSS 91/148c, an oral history, conducted in 1984 and 1985 by Gabrielle Morris, Regional Oral History Office, Bancroft Library, University of California, Berkeley, 1990, 2–3 (hereafter Jackson Oral History).

42. "Our Past National Basilei: Ida L. Jackson," *Ivy Leaf* (June 1940): 5.

43. Parker, *Alpha Kappa Alpha*, 57; Jackson Oral History, 13, 18.

44. Anjulet Tucker, "'Get the Learnin' but Don't Lose the Burnin': The Socio-Cultural and Religious Politics of Education in a Black Pentecostal College," PhD dissertation, Emory University, 2009, 13, 43, 66–67.

45. Charles C. Bolton, *The Hardest Deal of All: The Battle over School Integration in Mississippi, 1870–1980* (Jackson: University Press of Mississippi, 2007), 31.

46. Smith, *Sick and Tired*, 152.

47. Jackson Oral History, 28, 42.

48. Jackson, "Service Project," 10.

49. Minutes of the Seventeenth Annual Boule of Alpha Kappa Alpha Sorority, December 26–29, 1934, New York City, 72, MSRC-HU, Alpha Kappa Alpha Archives.

7. WE WENT, WE SAW, WE WERE STUNNED

1. Ida L. Jackson, "My Reflections on Alpha Kappa Alpha's Summer School for Rural Teachers and the Mississippi Health Project," *Ivy Leaf* 52.1 (1976): 12.

2. Marjorie H. Parker, *Alpha Kappa Alpha through the Years 1908–1988* (Chicago: Mobium Press, 1990), 185–86.

3. Jackson, "My Reflections," 12; Irving Stone, ed., "Ida L. Jackson," in *There Was a Light: Autobiography of a University. Berkeley: 1868–1968* (Garden City NY: Doubleday, 1970), 261.

4. Ida Jackson letter to Ferebee, January 21, 1935, MSRC-HU, Ferebee Papers, Box 183-5, Folder 18.

5. Susan L. Smith, *Sick and Tired of Being Sick and Tired: Black Women's Health Activism in America, 1890–1950* (Philadelphia: University of Pennsylvania Press, 1995), 150.

6. Alpha Kappa Alpha Sorority, Inc., "Centennial Celebration: 1908–2008," http://www.aka1908.com/centennial, accessed December 21, 2012.

7. Introduction to Alpha Kappa Alpha Incorporated Boule Minutes 1918–2008, AKA Archives, MSRC-HU.

8. Joellen ElBashir, curator, manuscript division, MSRC-HU, email to author, February 15, 2012.

9. Minutes of the Seventeenth Annual Boule of Alpha Kappa Alpha, 72, 115, 117, AKA Archives, MSRC-HU.

10. Sabrina Tavernise, "Disparities in Life Spans Narrow, but Remain: Four Years Separate Whites and Blacks," *New York Times*, July 18, 2013.

11. Felix Underwood, *Twenty-Ninth Biennial Report of the State Board of Health of the State of Mississippi, July 1, 1933 to June 30, 1935*, Jackson MS, 1935, 19–20.

12. Underwood, *Twenty-Ninth Biennial Report*, 136.

13. Youth of the Rural Organizing and Cultural Center (Holmes County, Mississippi), *Minds Stayed on Freedom: The Civil Rights Struggle in the Rural South—An Oral History* (Boulder CO: Westview Press, 1991), 5, 7.

14. Felix Underwood, *Twenty-Eighth Biennial Report of the State Board of Health of the State of Mississippi—July 1, 1931 to June 30, 1933*, Jackson MS, 1933, 10, 53, 137–38.

15. Ferebee letter to unnamed AKA recipients, n.d., MSRC-HU, Ferebee Papers, Box 183-17, Folder 4.

16. Ida L. Jackson letter to Ferebee, June 17 (the context indicates it was written in 1935), MSRC-HU, Ferebee Papers, Box 183-5, Folder 18.

17. Dovie Marie Simmons and Olivia L. Martin, *Down Behind the Sun: The Story of Arenia Conelia Mallory* (Memphis TN: Riverside Press, 1983), 1–2. Mallory's middle name is sometimes written as "Cornelia."

18. Simmons and Martin, *Down Behind the Sun*, 6–7; "Eddie Mallory Dead at 54: Ex-Husband of Ethel Waters," *New York Amsterdam News*, March 25, 1961.

19. Simmons and Martin, *Down Behind the Sun*, 3–4.

20. E. M. Lashley, "Glimpses into the Life of a Great Mississippian and a Majestic American Educator, 1926–1976," unpublished manuscript, 1977, n.p., OCLC No. 221384064, University of California, Davis.

21. Lashley, "Glimpses into the Life," n.p.

22. "In Brand New Work; Wed to Accountant," *New York Amsterdam News*, September 30, 1939; "Toki Types," *Pittsburgh Courier*, August 5, 1972; "Visitor Robbed of $2,000 in Gems: Bandleader's Kin Here for the Holidays. Jewelry Stolen from Car Parked at 107th St., Near Broadway," *New York Amsterdam News*, December 24, 1949.

23. Mary E. Williams, "The Newer Techniques of Health Education for Children," *Ivy Leaf* 14.4 (1936), 11. See photo accompanying article.

24. "Soror Mary Williams," *Ivy Leaf* 16.3 (1938): 7–8.

25. John M. Barry, *Rising Tide: The Great Mississippi Flood of 1927 and How It Changed America* (New York: Touchstone, 1998), 322–23, 382, 388–89 (Colored Advisory Commission group photo).
26. "Soror Mary Williams," 7–8; Williams, "Newer Technique," 11.
27. Mary E. Williams letter to Ida L. Jackson, February 6, 1935, MSRC-HU, Ferebee Papers, Box 183-5, Folder 18.
28. Mary E. Williams letter to Miss Jackson, n.d., MSRC-HU, Ferebee Papers, Box 183-7, Folder 17.
29. Ida L. Jackson letter to Mary E. Williams, February 20, 1935, MSRC-HU, Ferebee Papers, Box 183-5, Folder 18.
30. Mary E. Williams letter to Ferebee, March 7, 1935, MSRC-HU, Ferebee Papers, Box 183-7, Folder 17.
31. Mary E. Williams letter to Ferebee, March 12, 1935, MSRC-HU, Ferebee Papers, Box 183-7, Folder 17.
32. Mary Williams letter to "Dot" (Dorothy), March 18, 1935, MSRC-HU, Ferebee Papers, Box 183-7, Folder 17.
33. Dr. Roscoe C. Brown, National Negro Health Movement, letter to Ferebee, February 27, 1935, MSRC-HU, Ferebee Papers, 183-3, Folder 3.
34. Ferebee letter to Dr. C. J. Vaughn, March 31, 1935, MSRC-HU, Ferebee Papers, Box 183-7, Folder 10.
35. Dr. C. J. Vaughn letter to Ferebee, April 4, 1935, MSRC-HU, Ferebee Papers, Box 183-7, Folder 10.
36. Thompson, *Lynchings in Mississippi*, 1, 83, 91.
37. *Minds Stayed on Freedom*, 6.
38. See Jackson, "My Reflections," 11; "Actual Budget," Mississippi Health Project 1935, MSRC-HU, Ferebee Papers, Box 183-17, Folder 4.
39. Ferebee letter to "Ida, Ida, Ida," June 5 (the context makes it clear it was written in 1935), MSRC-HU, Ferebee Papers, Box 183-5, Folder 18.
40. Letter from Ethel H. Lyle to Dorothy, May 13, 1935, MSRC-HU, Ferebee Papers, Box 183-2, Folder 13.
41. Ida L. Jackson letter to Ferebee, June 17 (the context makes it clear it was written in 1935), MSRC-HU, Ferebee Papers, Box 183-5, Folder 18.
42. Ferebee letter to Soror Lyle, June 19, 1935, MSRC-HU, Ferebee Papers, Box 183-2, Folder 13.
43. Ferebee letter to U.S. Secretary of Labor, June 5, 1935; Ferebee letter to U.S. Surgeon General Hugh S. Cumming, June 8, 1935, both in MSRC-HU, Ferebee Papers, Box 183.
44. Mary E. Williams letter to "Dot," June 15, 1935; Mary E. Williams letter to "Dot," June 20, 1935, both in MSRC-HU, Ferebee Papers, Box 183-7, Folder 17.
45. Mary E. Williams letter to "Dot," April 15, 1935, MSRC-HU, Ferebee Papers, Box 183-7, Folder 17.

46. Ferebee letter to Dr. Frederick D. Patterson, June 13, 1935, MSRC-HU, Ferebee Papers, Box 183-6, Folder 24.

47. F. D. Patterson letter to Ferebee, June 28, 1935, MSRC-HU, Ferebee Papers, Box 183-6, Folder 24.

48. Telegram from A. Mallory to "Dr. B Farebee [sic]," June 27, 1935, MSRC-HU, Ferebee Papers, Box 183-6, Folder 7.

49. Ida L. Jackson letter to Ferebee, June 17.

50. "A.K.A.'s Directing Health Work Day Down Mississippi," *Pittsburgh Courier*, May 18, 1935.

51. "Eighty-One Sorors Attend Fifth Annual Conference," *Chicago Defender*, June 8, 1935.

52. "What Good Are We Dance Colorful and Gay: About Six Hundred at Most Exclusive Hop of the Season," *Chicago Defender*, June 1, 1935.

53. Ida L. Jackson letter to Ferebee, June 30, 1935, MSRC-HU, Ferebee Papers, Box 183-5, Folder 18.

54. Ferebee Oral History, 25–26.

55. Dorothy B. Ferebee, MD, "The Alpha Kappa Alpha Mississippi Health Project," *Ivy Leaf* 52.1 (1976): 14.

56. "Alpha Kappa Alpha Sorority: Sponsored a Health Project in Lexington, Miss.," *Negro Star (Wichita KS)*, October 25, 1935.

57. Dr. H. Jack Geiger email to the author, February 13, 2013.

58. Dr. Count D. Gibson Jr. memo to Dr. H. Jack Geiger, May 12, 1967, Delta Health Center Records, No. 4163, Southern Historical Collection, Wilson Library, University of North Carolina at Chapel Hill.

59. Ferebee letter to "Ida, Ida, Ida."

60. Ferebee letter to Miss Cain, June 27, 1935, MSRC-HU, Ferebee Papers, Box 183-3, Folder 10.

61. Mary Williams letter to "Dot," June 15, 1935.

62. Williams letter to "Dot," July 1, 1935, MSRC-HU, Ferebee Papers, Box 183-7, Folder 17.

63. Ferebee letter to "Soror Anne," May 25, 1976, MSRC-HU, Ferebee Papers, Box 183-2, Folder 14.

64. Ferebee letter to Ida L. Jackson, June 30, 1935, MSRC-HU, Ferebee Papers, Box 183-5, Folder 18.

65. Ferebee letter to Ida L. Jackson, June 30, 1935.

66. "Mississippi Health Project" (Alpha Kappa Alpha, 1935), Ferebee scrapbook, Mississippi Health Project, Howard University, Box 183-30.

67. Ida L. Jackson, "A Message from Our Supreme Basileus: The Health Project—In Appreciation," *Ivy Leaf* 13.3 (1935): 3.

68. "The Weather," *Washington Post*, July 6, 1935.

69. Ferebee letter to Miss Cain.

70. Ferebee letter to Ida Jackson, June 30, 1935.

71. "91 Are Killed in U.S. on 4th: 35 Hurt Here. Auto Crashes Claim 27 Lives and 16 Are Drowned . . . ," *Washington Post*, July 5, 1935.

72. "Mercury at 87.2, Hottest of Year: Three Prostrations Reported in the City as Torrid Wave Sweeps the Country . . . ," *New York Times*, July 6, 1935; Ferebee letter to Zenobia Gilpin, June 27, 1935, MSRC-HU, Ferebee Papers, Box 183.

73. Ferebee draft, AKA Mississippi Health Project Report, 1935, MSRC-HU, Ferebee Papers, Box 183-17, Folder 4.

74. Ferebee letter to Arenia Mallory, June 30, 1935, MSRC-HU, Ferebee Papers, Box 183-6, Folder 7.

75. Ferebee notes re Mississippi Health Project, 1935, MSRC-HU, Ferebee Papers, Box 183-17, Folder 3.

8. STUPID, VACANT, AND VOID OF HOPE

1. J. D. Ratcliff, "Cotton Field Volunteer Clinic" *Survey Graphic*, September 1940.

2. Susan L. Smith, *Sick and Tired of Being Sick and Tired: Black Women's Health Activism in America, 1890–1950* (Philadelphia: University of Pennsylvania Press, 1955), 155; Ferebee letter to Ida Jackson, June 30, 1935.

3. Anne Read Purnell Heath interview with Heath Hardage Lee (conducted for the author).

4. Dorothy B. Ferebee, "The Alpha Kappa Alpha Mississippi Health Project," *Ivy Leaf* 52.2 (1976): 14–15.

5. Ferebee Oral History, 28.

6. Ida Jackson, "My Reflections on Alpha Kappa Alpha's Summer School for Rural Teachers and the Mississippi Health Project," *Ivy Leaf* 52.2 (1976): 13; Ratcliff, "Cotton Field Clinic"; "Sorors Shocked by Discovery of Wretched Condition of Cotton's Slaves in Mississippi: Employ 'Trigger Men' to Keep Tenants Tied to Land," *New York Amsterdam News*, December 7, 1935.

7. Ferebee Oral History, 28.

8. Ferebee scrapbook, MSRC-HU, Ferebee Papers, Box 183-30.

9. Photographs from Ferebee's Mississippi Health Project scrapbook, MSRC-HU, Ferebee Papers, Box 183-30.

10. Charles C. Bolton, "Farmers without Land: The Plight of White Tenant Farmers and Sharecroppers," *Mississippi History Now*, http://www.mshistory.k12.ms.us/index.php?id=228, March 2004, accessed December 28, 2014.

11. John M. Barry, *Rising Tide: The Great Mississippi Flood of 1927 and How It Changed America* (New York: Touchstone, 1998), 116, 326.

12. Thompson, *Lynchings in Mississippi*, 29, 94.

13. Tom Ward, "Medical Missionaries of the Delta: Dr. Dorothy Ferebee and the Mississippi Health Project, 1935–1941," *Journal of Mississippi History* 63.3 (2001): 195.

14. Alpha Kappa Alpha, "Mississippi Health Project Report, July 1935," MSRC-HU, Ferebee Papers, Box 183-17, Folder 4.

15. Ferebee Oral History, 28.

16. Ida L. Jackson, "A Message from Our Supreme Basileus: The Health Project—In Appreciation," *Ivy Leaf* 13.3 (1935): 3.

17. Ferebee, "Alpha Kappa Alpha Mississippi Health Project," 15.

18. Ward, "Medical Missionaries of the Delta," 194, 196.

19. "Buzzard's Feather around Neck Helps Baby's Teeth Grow, Is One of Delta's Many Superstitions," *Pittsburgh Courier*, December 14, 1935.

20. "Sorors Shocked."

21. Ella Payne Moran, *A Project Conducted in Mississippi: Alpha Kappa Alpha Sorority Health Project, Mississippi 1935–1942*, Howard University, Education 290, August 1942, 4, MSRC-HU, Ferebee Papers, Box 183-17, Folder 6.

22. B. L. Patterson letter to Dorothy, July 9, 1935, MSRC-HU, Ferebee Papers, Box 183-6, Folder 22.

23. Ferebee letter to "Bessie," July 14, 1935, MSRC-HU, Ferebee Papers, Box 183-6, Folder 22.

24. Jackson, "Message from Our Supreme Basileus," 3.

25. Marion Carter letter to Ferebee, August 17, 1935, MSRC-HU, Ferebee Papers, Box 183-3, Folder 10.

26. Parker, *Alpha Kappa Alpha*, 187.

27. Minutes of the Eighteenth Annual Boule of Alpha Kappa Alpha Sorority, December 27–30, 1935, Richmond VA, 54–55, AKA Archives, MSRC-HU.

28. Smith, *Sick and Tired*, 166–67.

29. "Alpha Kappa Alpha Sorority: Sponsored a Health Project in Lexington, Miss." (Wichita KS) *Negro Star*, October 25, 1935; "Sorors Shocked."

30. Ferebee letter to Ida Jackson, October 24 (from the context of the letter it was written in 1935), MSRC-HU, Ferebee Papers, Box 183-5, Folder 18; "Alpha Kappa Alpha Sorority"; "Sorors Shocked."

31. Ferebee letter to Ida Jackson, October 24.

32. Ida Louise Jackson letter to Ferebee, October 22 (from the context of the letter, it was written in 1935), MSRC-HU, Ferebee Papers, Box 183-5, Folder 18.

33. Dr. Dorothy Boulding Ferebee letter to Mrs. Franklin D. Roosevelt, December 2, 1935, Franklin D. Roosevelt Presidential Library and Museum, Hyde Park NY, "Appointments," Box 1186, Series 170.

34. Malvina T. Scheider letter to Dr. Dorothy Boulding Ferebee, December 9, 1935, Franklin D. Roosevelt Presidential Library and Museum, "Appointments," Box 1186, Series 170.

35. "The First Lady and Some Guests at the White House," *New York Times*, May 2, 1935; see also "May Basket for Mrs. FDR," *Gettysburg Times*, May 7, 1935; "Daughter of Norfolkians at White House," (Norfolk) *New Journal and Guide*, May 11, 1935.

36. Jackson, "Message from Our Supreme Basileus."

37. Marion Carter letter to Dorothy, December 18, 1935, MSRC-HU, Ferebee Papers, Box 183-3, Folder 10.

38. Jackson, "Message from Our Supreme Basileus."

39. Marion Carter letter to Dorothy, December 18, 1935.

40. Minutes of the Organizational Meeting of the National Council of Negro Women, December 5, 1935, National Park Service, Mary McLeod Bethune Council House NHS, National Museum of Black Women's History, Records of the National Council of Negro Women (hereafter NPS, NABWH, Records of the NCNW), Series 2, Box 1, Folder 1.

41. Minutes of the Eighteenth Annual Boule, cover.

42. "Capital Has 'White' Christmas as Snow Still Covers Streets," *Washington Post*, December 25, 1935.

43. "The Weather," *Washington Post*, December 27, 1935.

44. Irma Clarke, "A Delegate Reviews the Boule," *Ivy Leaf* 14.1 (1936): 23.

45. Minutes of the Eighteenth Annual Boule, 102, 106–7, 121–22.

46. "7-Inch Snow Blankets District as Storm Sweeps over South: Five Die in Oklahoma; Damage in Atlanta Is $2,000,000; Virginia, Maryland and Carolinas Hit . . . ," *Washington Post*, December 30, 1935.

47. Ida L. Jackson, "The Conference with Mrs. Roosevelt," *Ivy Leaf* 14.2 (936):4.

48. Jackson Oral History, 69; "The Weather," *Washington Post*, January 1, 1936.

49. "Capital Greets Dawn of 1936 in Gay and Noisy Celebrations. . . ." *Washington Post*, January 1, 1936; Daily Calendar of First Lady Eleanor Roosevelt, December 31, 1935, Franklin D. Roosevelt Presidential Library and Museum.

50. Daily Calendar of First Lady Eleanor Roosevelt, December 31, 1935.

51. "The White House Museum: Red Room," http://www.whitehousemuseum.org /floorl/red-room.htm, accessed January 27, 2013; Jackson, "Conference with Mrs. Roosevelt," 4.

52. Daily Calendar of First Lady Eleanor Roosevelt, December 31, 1935; Jackson, "Conference with Mrs. Roosevelt," 4; "White House!," *Pittsburgh Courier*, February 1, 1936.

53. "Mrs. Roosevelt Interested in Health of Negroes in South: Conference at White House Is Encouraging; AKA Representatives Discuss Health Project, Jim Crow," (Norfolk) *New Journal and Guide*, February 1, 1936.

54. Jackson, "Conference with Mrs. Roosevelt," 4.

55. "Mrs. Roosevelt Interested in Health of Negroes."

56. Ellen S. More, *Restoring the Balance: Women Physicians and the Profession of Medicine, 1850–1995* (Cambridge MA: Harvard University Press, 1999), 168.

57. Ferebee letter to Ida Louise Jackson, October 24.
58. Ferebee letter to Ida Louise Jackson, October 24.

9. AS THE MOONLIGHT TURNED BARN ROOFS TO SILVER

1. (Norfolk) *New Journal and Guide*, January 11, 1936.
2. Ferebee 1936 Mississippi Health Project Scrapbook.
3. "Dr. Dorothy Boulding Ferebee," *Ivy Leaf* 14.1 (1936): 23.
4. Dr. M. O. Bousfield letter to Ferebee, March 9, 1936, MSRC-HU, Ferebee Papers, Box 183-3, Folder 9.
5. Senator Harrison letter to Dr. Thomas Parran Jr., U.S. Public Health Service, June 19, 1936, MSRC-HU, Ferebee Papers, Box 183-8, Folder 18.
6. Marjorie H. Parker, *Alpha Kappa Alpha through the Years 1908–1988* (Chicago: Mobium Press, 1990), 61, 188.
7. Ferebee letter to "My darling Marita," February 17, 1936, MSRC-HU, Ferebee Papers, Box 183-8, Folder 2.
8. Florence O. Alexander letter to Ferebee, January 26, 1936; MSRC-HU, Ferebee Papers, Box 183-2, Folder 12.
9. Wirt A. Williams, ed., *History of Bolivar County, Mississippi* (Jackson: Mississippi Delta Chapter, Daughters of the American Revolution, 1948), 1, 5, 9.
10. *Twenty-Ninth Biennial Report of the State Board of Health of Mississippi, July 1, 1933 to June 30, 1935*, 105, 98–106.
11. Ferebee letter to Dr. Felix J. Underwood, March 31, 1936; Dr. H. C. Ricks letter to Ferebee, April 11, 1936, both in MSRC-HU, Ferebee Papers, Box 183-6, Folder 28.
12. Dr. Count Gibson memo to Dr. H. Jack Geiger, "Report of Interview with Dr. Dorothy Ferebee, May 8, 1967," May 12, 1967, Delta Health Center Records, No. 4613, Southern Historical Collection, Wilson Library, University of North Carolina, Chapel Hill; Susan L. Smith, *Sick and Tired of Being Sick and Tired: Black Women's Health Activism in America, 1890–1950* (Philadelphia: University of Pennsylvania Press, 1995), 156.
13. Dr. R. D. Dedwylder letter to Ferebee, April 14, 1936, MSRC-HU, Ferebee Papers, Box 183-3, Folder 15.
14. Dr. Count Gibson memo to Dr. H. Jack Geiger; "New Yorker Helps A.K.A. Health Work," *New York Amsterdam News*, October 2, 1937.
15. See, e.g., Ola L. DeNeal letter to Ferebee, February 11, 1936, MSRC-HU, Ferebee Papers, Box 183-3, Folder 15.
16. Ferebee letter to Dr. R. D. Dedwylder, April 20, 1936, MSRC-HU, Ferebee Papers, Box 183-3, Folder 15.
17. Minutes of the Nineteenth Annual Boule of Alpha Kappa Alpha Sorority, December 27–30, 1936, Lexington KY, 13, AKA Archives, MSRC-HU.
18. Dennis Hevesi, "Barrington D. Parker, 77, Is Dead: Trial Judge for Reagan's Attacker," *New York Times*, June 5, 1993.

19. Marjorie Holloman, "I Remember Mississippi," n.d., unpublished essay, MSRC-HU, Ferebee Papers, Box 183-17, Folder 5; James P. Dawson, "Crowd of 30,000 Sees Louis Stop Sharkey in Fight at the Yankee Stadium . . . Louis Knocks Out Sharkey in Third . . . ." *New York Times*, August 19, 1936.
20. Holloman, "I Remember Mississippi"; "Forecast of Weather over the Nation and Abroad," *New York Times*, August 21, 1936.
21. Holloman, "I Remember Mississippi."
22. Bessie E. Cobbs, "Health on Wheels in Mississippi: The Mississippi Rural Health Project of the Alpha Kappa Alpha Sorority," *American Journal of Nursing* 41.5 (1941): 552.
23. Ferebee letter to Eugene Booze, August 8, 1936, MSRC-HU, Ferebee Papers, Box 183-3, Folder 8.
24. Williams, *History of Bolivar County*, 265–67.
25. "Negro City to Celebrate: Mound Bayou, Founded by Ex-Slaves, to Mark 50th Year," *New York Times*, July 8, 1937.
26. "Mound Bayou Mourns Slave Who Founded Negro City: Isaiah T. Montgomery Grew Up in Household of Brother of Jefferson Davis—His Community Is Managed Entirely by Colored People," *New York Times*, April 27, 1924.
27. Webb Waldron, "Drippings from Other Pens: All Black a Unique Negro Community," *Chicago Defender*, February 18, 1939 (reprinted from *Southern Workmen*).
28. "Negro City to Celebrate."
29. "Born a Slave, Heads Town, Mississippi Negro Tells How He Rose to $200,000 Wealth," *New York Times*, August 24, 1912.
30. "Mound Bayou Mourns Slave."
31. "Mound Bayou Astir over Brutal Killing; Citizens Denounce Booze for Leading Officers to Kill Wife's Sister," *Chicago Defender*, October 14, 1939; "Free Two in Poison Case; Murder Plot Evidence Is Thrown Out; Mr. and Mrs. Booze Win in Court," *Chicago Defender*, August 20, 1927.
32. M. Estelle Montgomery letter to W. E. B. Du Bois, June 5, 1927, Special Collections and University Archives, University of Massachusetts, Amherst Libraries, MS 312, http://oubliette.library.umass.edu/view/full/mums312-b039-i493, accessed March 20, 2013; "Montgomery Poison Case Dismissed for Lack of Evidence; Daughter of Mound Bayou Founder Still Insists Story Is True—Blames Doctor," *New York Amsterdam News*, August 23, 1927.
33. "Free Two in Poison Case."
34. "Mound Bayou Astir over Brutal Killing."
35. "Police Kill Sister of Mrs. Booze: Victim Was Daughter of I. Montgomery," *Atlanta Daily World*, October 9, 1939.
36. "Mound Bayou Astir over Brutal Killing."

37. "E. P. Booze, GOP Leader Is Slain in Mississippi," *New York Amsterdam News,* November 11, 1939.

38. Eugene P. Booze letter to Ferebee, July 21, 1936, MSRC-HU, Ferebee Papers, Box 183-3, Folder 8.

39. Eugene P. Booze letter to Ferebee, August 12, 1936, MSRC-HU, Ferebee Papers, Box 183-3, Folder 8.

40. Elsie Ann Ervin, "Dr. Ded (Dr. Rosier Davis Dedwylder 1883–1948)," second-place prize-winning essay, Delta State Teachers College, 1951, 1, 9, 12–13, courtesy Dr. Rosier Davis Dedwylder II.

41. Dr. Rosier Davis Dedwylder II interview with the author. Although Dr. Dedwylder II is Dr. Ded's grandson, Dr. Ded's son was not a Junior; his name was Rozier (spelled with a "z") Tyrone Davis.

42. Dr. Rosier Davis Dedwylder II interview with the author.

43. Tom Ward, "Medical Missionaries of the Delta: Dr. Dorothy Ferebee and the Mississippi Health Project, 1935–1941," *Journal of Mississippi History* 63.3 (2001): 198.

44. Dr. Rosier D. Dedwylder II email to author, January 12, 2009; "Tennessee Walking Horse," http://www.ansi.okstate.edu/breeds/horses/tennesseewalking, accessed February 1, 2013.

45. Ervin, "Dr. Ded," 2–3.

46. Dr. Rosier D. Dedwylder II interview with the author.

47. Sharon D. Wright Austin, *The Transformation of Plantation Politics: Black Politics, Concentrated Property and Social Capital in the Mississippi Delta* (Albany: State University of New York Press, 2006), 26.

48. Dr. Rosier Davis Dedwylder II interview with the author.

49. "Negro Sorority to Conduct Free Health Clinic," *Cleveland Enterprise*, August 5, 1936.

50. "2nd Year at Clinic: Sorority Gives Free Service to 3,500," *New York Amsterdam News*, September 19, 1936.

51. "The Mississippi Health Project," *Ivy Leaf* 14.3 (1936): 5.

52. "Forecast of Weather over the Nation and Abroad"; "The Weather over the Nation and Abroad," *New York Times*, August 23, 1936.

53. Holloman handwritten, untitled memoir, beginning with "Perhaps someone might be interested . . . ," Ferebee Papers, MSRC-HU, Box 183-17, Folder 3.

54. Alpha Kappa Alpha Sorority Clinic Schedule, August 21–September 1, 1936, MSRC-HU, Ferebee Papers, Box 183-17, Folder 4; Holloman, "I Remember Mississippi."

55. "A.K.A.'s Health Clinic Boom to Mississippi," *Pittsburgh Courier*, October 3, 1936.

56. AKA Sorority Clinic Schedule.

57. "The Mississippi Health Project," *Ivy Leaf* 14.3 (1936): 5.

58. Alpha Kappa Alpha, "The 1936 Mississippi Health Project in Bolivar County," MSRC-HU, Ferebee Papers, Box 183-17 Folder 4.

59. AKA Sorority Clinic Schedule.

60. The Mississippi Health Survey of the Alpha Kappa Alpha Sorority, Schedule B (for Women), MSRC-HU, Ferebee Papers, Box 183-17, Folder 3; Holloman, "I Remember Mississippi."

61. Holloman, "Perhaps someone might be interested."

62. Holloman, "I Remember Mississippi."

63. Alpha Kappa Alpha, "1936 Mississippi Health Project in Bolivar County."

64. Zhenghai Dong, "From Postbellum Plantation to Modern Agribusiness: A History of the Delta and Pine Land Company," PhD dissertation, Purdue University (May 1993), 106, 108, 159.

65. Eugene Booze, "AKA's Close Miss. Clinic; 3,500 Treated, 'Time,' Photographer Makes Movies of Staff at Work . . . ." (Norfolk) *New Journal and Guide*, September 19, 1936; Dong, "From Postbellum Plantation to Modern Agribusiness," 155–56.

66. Alpha Kappa Alpha, "1936 Mississippi Health Project in Bolivar County."

67. Fred C. Smith, "The Delta Cooperative Farm and the Death of a Vision," *Journal of Mississippi History* 71.3 (2009): 237.

68. Alpha Kappa Alpha, "1936 Mississippi Health Project in Bolivar County."

69. Ida Jackson, "A Message from Our Supreme Basileus: The Delta Co-Operative Farm," *Ivy Leaf* 14.3 (1936): 3.

70. Ferebee, "Tentative Financial Statement [1936 Health Project]," courtesy Dorothy Ruth Ferebee.

71. R. D. Dedwylder letter to Ferebee, September 3, 1936, MSRC-HU, Ferebee Papers, Box 183-3, Folder 15.

72. Holloman, "I Remember Mississippi."

10. TELL CLAUDE FEREBEE TO KEEP HIS SHIRT ON

1. "Dr. Dorothy Ferebee Not a Candidate for A.K.A. Presidency," *Capital Plaindealer*, January 3, 1937.

2. Marjorie H. Parker, *Alpha Kappa Alpha through the Years 1908–1988* (Chicago: Mobium Press, 1990), 189, 191.

3. Helen Finley, "A Regional Director Describes the 1936 Boule," *Ivy Leaf* 15.1 (1937): 7.

4. "Friendship House Plans Celebration: Pageants and Play to Mark Silver Anniversary of Southeast Center; Building Is Historic," *Washington Post*, September 15, 1929; New Home Campaign Southeast House, Washington DC, October 1937, publicity pamphlet, Franklin D. Roosevelt Presidential Library and Museum, Hyde Park NY, "personal correspondence," Series 100, Box 647.

5. "Friendship House Dedication Today," *Washington Post*, November 28, 1937; Lydia Burklin, "History of Friendship House, 1950," 5, Friendship House

Association Records, Special Collections Research Center, Gelman Library, George Washington University, Box 3, Folder 11.

6. Ferebee letter to Mrs. Franklin D. Roosevelt, October 23, 1937, Franklin D. Roosevelt Presidential Library and Museum, "personal correspondence," Series 100, Box 647.

7. Ferebee letter to Mrs. M. T. Scheider, October 23, 1937, Franklin D. Roosevelt Presidential Library and Museum, "personal correspondence," Series 100, Box 647.

8. Eleanor Roosevelt note to M. T. Scheider, October 25, 1937, Franklin D. Roosevelt Presidential Library and Museum, "personal correspondence," Series 100, Box 647.

9. Harold E. Snyder, *Clarence Pickett—A Memoir*, edited by Walter Kohoc, n.p., 1966; and excerpted as "Clarence E. Pickett, 1884–1965," http://www.picketten dowment.quaker.org/about.php, accessed January 4, 2015.

10. Richard Hurst Hill letter to Clarence Pickett, November 20, 1937, Franklin D. Roosevelt Presidential Library and Museum, "personal correspondence," Series 100, Box 647.

11. Eleanor Roosevelt draft letter to Dorothy Ferebee, December 7, 1937, Franklin D. Roosevelt Presidential Library and Museum, "personal correspondence," Series 100, Box 647.

12. Ferebee and Mae C. Hawes letter to Mrs. Franklin Delano Roosevelt, February 28, 1939, Franklin D. Roosevelt Presidential Library and Museum, "Requests for Donations," Series 150.2.

13. Note to author from Virginia Lewick, n.d., Franklin D. Roosevelt Presidential Library and Museum, "File (when written on a piece of correspondence) means there was no response."

14. "New Officers Are Elected by DC Chest . . . ," *Washington Post*, February 5, 1938.

15. Harry B. Anderson, "Meet Your Neighbor," (Baltimore) *Afro-American*, February 26, 1938.

16. "AKA Sorority Forms Congressional Lobby: Setup as Aftermath of DC Meeting," (Norfolk) *New Journal and Guide*, April 2, 1938.

17. Bettye Collier-Thomas, *N.C.N.W., 1935–1980* (Washington DC: National Council of Negro Women, 1981), 3.

18. Elaine Smith, "Historic Resources Study: Mary McLeod Bethune and the National Council of Negro Women, Pursuing a True and Unfettered Democracy," NPS, Mary McLeod Bethune Council House, September 2003, 47–55.

19. "Ferebee Weds Hazel Hardy," *New York Amsterdam News*, June 16, 1951.

20. "Norfolkian Heads DC Dentists," (Norfolk) *New Journal and Guide*, December 10, 1938.

21. "Wilberforce Club Meets," (Baltimore) *Afro-American*, June 10, 1939.

22. "300 View Paintings by Jones," (Baltimore) *Afro-American*, February 27, 1927.

23. Truman K. Gibson Jr. Office Memorandum, "Conference with Brig. Gen. Leigh Fairbank, re: Utilization of Negro Dentists," January 27, 1941, Library of Congress, Manuscript Division, African Americans in the Military, Part 2: Subject Files of Judge William Hastie, Reel 1:0756.

24. "Variety of Events Liven Social Life in Dee Cee," *Pittsburgh Courier*, October 26, 1940; T.E.B., "Chatter and Chimes," *New York Star and Amsterdam News*, October 19, 1940.

25. Dorothy Boulding-Ferebee, "Our 1937 Mississippi Health Project," *Ivy Leaf* 15.3 (1937): 8.

26. Parker, *Alpha Kappa Alpha*, 189; "Twenty-Second Boule in Boston, December 27–30, Soror Mary C. Wright, General Boule Chairman," *Ivy Leaf* 17.4 (1939): 5.

27. Ferebee, Mississippi Health Project Scrapbook, MSRC-HU, Ferebee Papers, Box 183-30.

28. Parker, *Alpha Kappa Alpha*, 190. Parker refers to Dr. Wright as Dr. Mary C. Thompson of Boston. In that there was only one dentist with the health project, Dr. Mary C. Wright, also of Boston, and Marjorie Holloman Parker did not write her book until 1990, it would seem Dr. Wright either married or remarried in the interim.

29. Ferebee financial statement, National Health Project, August 1937, courtesy of Dorothy Ruth Ferebee.

30. Ferebee telegram to Ida Louise Jackson, August 28, 1937, BANC MSS 2006/166, Ida Louise Jackson Papers, 1917–2003, Bancroft Library, University of California, Berkeley, Box 1, Folder 8.

31. "Post Graduate Work Sought by Many," (Norfolk) *New Journal and Guide*, July 9, 1938; "Personal Mention," (Norfolk) *New Journal and Guide*, September 16, 1939.

32. "Volunteer Sorors Hold Health Clinics in South," *Chicago Defender*, October 2, 1937.

33. Ferebee, "Our 1937 Mississippi Health Project."

34. Jerry W. Dallas, "The Delta and Providence Farms: A Mississippi Experiment in Cooperative Farming and Racial Cooperation, 1936–1956," *Mississippi Quarterly* 4.3 (1987): 285, 287–88; Fred C. Smith, *Trouble in Goshen: Plain Folk, Roosevelt, Jesus, and Marx in the Great Depression South* (Jackson: University Press of Mississippi, 2014), 114–16, 119, 120–21.

35. Smith, *Trouble in Goshen*, 122–23.

36. Smith, *Trouble in Goshen*, 7, 122–23; Dallas, "Delta and Providence Farms," 289.

37. Smith, *Trouble in Goshen*, 125.

38. Smith, *Trouble in Goshen*, 125, 128.

39. Smith, *Trouble in Goshen*, 8.

40. 1937 Guest Register, Delta Cooperative Farm, Allen Eugene Cox Papers, MSS.45, Special Collections Department, Mississippi State University Libraries.

41. 1938 and 1939 Guest Registers, Delta Cooperative Farm, Allen Eugene Cox Papers.

42. Minutes of the Twenty-Third Annual Boule of the Alpha Kappa Alpha Sorority, December 27–31, 1940, Kansas City MO, 40, AKA Archives, MSRC-HU.

43. Minutes, Alpha Kappa Alpha National Health Conference, April 1–2, 1942, Chicago IL, BANC MSS 2006/166, Ida Louise Jackson Papers, 1917–2003, Bancroft Library, University of California, Berkeley, Box 1, Folder 1.

44. Smith, *Trouble in Goshen*, 126, 131–32.

45. Smith, *Trouble in Goshen*, 129, 132, 136.

46. Parker, *Alpha Kappa Alpha*, 192.

47. Letter from R. D. Dedwylder to H. C. Ricks, April 7, 1938, Ferebee Papers, MSRC-HU, Box 183-3, Folder 15; Poster advertising the 1938 Mississippi Health Project, Ferebee scrapbook, Ferebee Papers, Box 183-30.

48. Eugene P. Booze letter to Ferebee, May 23, 1938; Benjamin A. Green letter to Ferebee, May 23, 1938, both in MSRC-HU, Ferebee Papers, Box 183-3, Folder 6.

49. Melva L. Price, "We Observe," in 1938 Mississippi Health Project, Fourth Annual Report, December 1938, MSRC-HU, Ferebee Papers, Box 183-17, Folder 5.

50. Health Project, Expenses of Portia Nickens's Car, Schomburg Center for Research in Black Culture, New York Public Library, Melva L. Price Papers, MG 596.

51. 1938 Mississippi Health Project, Fourth Annual Report.

52. Parker, *Alpha Kappa Alpha*, 190.

53. Louis Lauter, "Only 250 of 32, 522 CMTC Enrollees Were Colored; Youths Are Eligible for Commissions," (Norfolk) *New Journal and Guide*, July 23, 1938.

54. Ferebee letter to Melva Price, Thursday, August [n.d.], MSRC-HU, Ferebee Papers, Box 183.

55. Ferebee letter to Melva Price.

56. 1938 Mississippi Health Project Report, Fourth Annual Report.

57. Marjorie Holloman, "Concerning the Health Project," *Ivy Leaf* 16.4 (1938): 49.

58. Irma F. Clarke letter to Soror [Melva] Price, December 2, 1938, SCRBC-NYPL, Melva L. Price Papers, MG 596.

59. "Weather Reports from over the Nation and Abroad," *New York Times*, December 29, 1938.

60. "Heads A.K.A. Project," *Chicago Defender*, December 31, 1938.

61. Hazel L. Reed, "The Twenty-First Annual Boule: 21st Annual Boule Held in Detroit, Dec. 27–30, 1938," *Ivy Leaf* 17.1 (1939): 4; "The Weather," *New York Herald Tribune*, December 30, 1938; "New Cold Wave Due after Let-up Today: Snow Forecast for Tonight or Tomorrow—Mercury at 19.4° Here as Nation Suffers," *New York Times*, December 29, 1938.

62. Allan Keiler, *Marian Anderson: A Singer's Journey* (New York: Lisa Drew/Scribner, 2000), 185–86.

63. John Lovell Jr. letter to Col. West A. Hamilton, February 19, 1939, Records of the Marian Anderson Citizens Committee, MSRC-HU, Box 1 Folder 13.

64. Marian Anderson, *My Lord, What a Morning* (New York: Viking Press, 1956), 189.

65. Keiler, *Marian Anderson*, 209, 210; "Lincoln Memorial," http://www.nps.gov /nr/travel/wash/dc71.htm, accessed May 13, 2013.

66. Todd Boulding Ferebee email to the author, May 21, 2013.

67. "Three Negroes on American Food for Peace Council," *Jet Magazine*, May 25, 1961, 5.

68. Ella Payne Moran, "A Project Conducted in Mississippi: Alpha Kappa Alpha Sorority Health Project, Mississippi 1935–1942," 4, MSRC-HU, Ferebee Papers, Box 183-14, Box 6.

69. "Eugene P. Booze Shot: Negro G.O.P. Leader," *Cleveland Enterprise*, November 8, 1939.

70. Ferebee, "Demonstrational Dietotherapy Project," MSRC-HU, Ferebee Papers, Box 183-17.

71. Susan L. Smith, *Sick and Tired of Being Sick and Tired: Black Women's Health Activism in America, 1890–1950* (Philadelphia: University of Pennsylvania Press, 1995), 163.

72. "A.K.A.'s Thwarted in Attempt to Extend Program Which Will Prevent Malnutrition: State Officials Give No Reason for Delay," *Pittsburgh Courier*, August 12, 1939.

73. Ferebee Oral History, 29.

74. Leighla Whipper Lewis, "Capital Caviare," (Baltimore) *Afro-American*, January 21, 1939.

75. "Denounce Dies Committee as Race Baiter: Say Group Not Interested in Questioning the Ku Klux Klan," *Chicago Defender*, November 4, 1939.

76. Introduction to American League for Peace and Democracy Collected Records, 1933–39, Swarthmore College Peace Collection, CDG-A, http://www.swarthmore .edu/Library/peace/cdga.a-l/alpd.htm, accessed December 28, 2014.

77. "Dies, Martin Jr. (1900–1972)," *Biographical Directory of the United States Congress, 1774–Present*, http://www.bioguide.congress.gov/biodisplay.pl?index=d000338, accessed December 28, 2014.

78. David Brinkley, *Washington Goes to War* (New York: Knopf, 1988), 17.

79. Statement of Senator Hoffman, 85 *Cong. Rec.* 1043 (1939); "Denounce Dies Committee as Race Baiters."

80. "Denounce Dies Committee as Race Baiters."

81. M. A. Jones memorandum to Mr. Nichols, February 17, 1956, referring to prior investigation of Ferebee under File No. 101-2335-11, Federal Bureau of Investigation, FOIA request by the author.

82. Grayce Kellogg, "The Social Side of the Medical Convention Radiant with Lovely Events for the Women: Milady Kept Busy While Medics Go 'So Scientific,'" *Pittsburgh Courier*, August 26, 1939.

83. Minutes of the Twenty-Second Annual Boule of the Alpha Kappa Alpha Sorority, December 27–30, 1939, Boston MA, 54, AKA Archives, MSRC-HU.

84. Parker, *Alpha Kappa Alpha*, 65.

85. Minutes of the Twenty-Second Annual Boule, 62.

86. "A.K.A.'s Give $1,000 for Legislative Lobby: $2,000 for Health Project . . . ," (Norfolk) *New Journal and Guide*, January 13, 1940.

87. "'James Crow', Honor Guest at FDR Inauguration: Jim Crow Party Is Arranged for Negroes," (Cleveland) *Call and Post*, January 25, 1941.

88. Claude Thurston Ferebee letter to Attorney William Hastie, Special Assistant Secretary of War, January 24, 1941, LOC-MS Division, African Americans in the Military, Part 2: Subject Files of Judge William Hastie, Reel 1:0758.

89. Claude T. Ferebee Military Records; U.S. Army Brig. Gen. R. H. Mills memorandum to William H. Hastie, July 18, 1942, LOC-MS Division, African Americans in the Military; Subject Files of Judge William Hastie, Reel 1:0600.

90. Claude T. Ferebee Military Records.

11. MADELINE, MY CONCERTO

1. T.E.B., "Chatter and Chimes," *New York Star & Amsterdam News*, January 11, 1941.

2. Minutes of the Twenty-Third Annual Boule, 40, AKA Archives, MSRC-HU.

3. "National President AKA Sorority Makes Plea for Masses in Broadcast: Dr. Ferebee Appeals to College Women to 'Do Something'—Not Talk!," *Philadelphia Tribune*, February 29, 1940; Minutes of the Twenty-Third Annual AKA Boule, 29.

4. Judge Anna Johnston Diggs interview with the author.

5. Henry Perlstadt, "The Development of the Hill-Burton Legislation: Interests, Issues and Compromises," *Journal of Health and Social Policy* 6.3 (1995): 80, 82; "National Hospital Bill Reported Out of Committee," *Public Health Reports* 55.19 (1940): 847–48.

6. "The Weather," *Washington Post*, March 20, 1940.

7. "Spoke for Hospital Act," *Atlanta Daily World*, March 26, 1940.

8. "Statement of Dr. Dorothy Boulding Ferebee, Washington DC," Sen. Subc. of the Comm. on Education and Labor on S. 3230, 76th Cong., 3d Sess., March 18 and 19, 1940, 90.

9. "Dr. Ferebee on Health Week Program," *Philadelphia Tribune*, April 11, 1940.

10. "National Negro Health Week," *Journal of the National Medical Association* 26.1 (1934): 33.

11. Sandra Crouse Quinn and Stephen B. Thomas, "The National Negro Health Week, 1915 to 1951: A Descriptive Account," *Minority Health Today* 2.3 (2001): 48.

12. M. A. Jones memorandum to Mr. Nichols, February 17, 1956, Ferebee FBI File No. 101-2335-11.

13. "Negro Congress Convenes Friday: National Issues Face Third Negro Congress," *Chicago Defender*, April 27, 1940.

14. "Dr. Ferebee Visits 20 Cities in Year: Has Many Interests," (Norfolk) *New Journal and Guide*, May 10, 1941.

15. "Dr. Ferebee Will Speak in Richmond: AKA Sorority Sponsors Sunday Meeting," (Norfolk) *New Journal and Guide*, May 4, 1940.

16. Roy Wilkins letter to Dr. Dorothy Boulding Ferebee, May 13, 1940, LOC-MS Division, Records of the NAACP, Group II, Box A-19, Folder 7.

17. "Norfolk AKA's Elect Officers: Give Shower for Bride-to-Be," (Norfolk) *New Journal and Guide*, June 7, 1941.

18. David Gelernter, *1939: The Lost World of the Fair* (New York: Free Press, 1995), 356.

19. American Labor Party Petition, New York World's Fair Negro Week Records, MG 42, Schomburg Center for Research in Black Culture (hereafter SCRBC), New York Public Library, Box 1, Folder 5.

20. Dorothy Ferebee, "The Alpha Kappa Alpha Mississippi Health Project," 5, draft of article for *Ivy Leaf* (1976), MSRC-HU, Ferebee Papers, Box 183.

21. Katherine Gardner letter to Ida Louise Jackson, June 23, 1937, Ida Louise Jackson Papers, BANC MSS 2006/166, Correspondence, 1936–42, Carton 1:8, Bancroft Library, University of California, Berkeley.

22. Ella Payne Moran, "A Project Conducted in Mississippi: Alpha Kappa Alpha Sorority Health Project, Mississippi 1935–1942," 5, unpublished manuscript, 1942, MSRC-HU, Ferebee Papers, Box 183-17, Folder 6; Everett L. Perry, "National Council of Churches," in *Encyclopedia of Religion and Society*, edited by William H. Swatos Jr., http://www.hirr.hartsem.edu/ency/ncc.htm, accessed June 28, 2013; Minutes of the Twenty-Fourth Annual Boule of Alpha Kappa Alpha Sorority, December 27–30, 1941, Philadelphia, 60, AKA Archives, MSRC-HU.

23. Moran, "A Project Conducted in Mississippi,"6–7; Minutes of the Twenty-Fourth Annual Boule, 7, 10, 11, 60.

24. Minutes of the Twenty-Fourth Annual Boule, 14–15, 60.

25. Kay Davis, "Portrait of America: *Survey Graphic* in the Thirties," Spring 2001, http://xroads.virginia.edu/~ma01/davis/survey/intro/introduction3.html, accessed September 29, 2011.

26. J. D. Ratcliff, "Cotton Field Clinic," *Survey Graphic* 29 (September 1940): 467.

27. "NAACP, Women's Group, Holds Meet in Charleston," *Chicago Defender*, October 12, 1940; "Two Women Doctors to Be Honored . . . ," (Norfolk) *New Journal and Guide*, October 19, 1940.

28. Raymond Pace Alexander, "A Short Summary of the Life of Dr. Alexander," pamphlet for the Doctor Virginia M. Alexander Scholarship Foundation (March 1, 1961), 2–3, 5, 8–10, courtesy of Howard University Archives.

29. "Two Women Doctors to Be Honored."

30. Elizabeth Galbreath, "Typovision," *Chicago Defender*, November 2, 1940.

31. Galbreath, "Typovision."

32. Minutes of the Twenty-Third Annual Boule, 51.

33. Rebecca Stiles Taylor, "Activities of Women's National Organizations: National Negro Advisory," *Chicago Defender*, January 10, 1942.
34. "Birth Control Called Cure for Harlem Crime: Federation Convention Gets Appeal for Public Clinics to Benefit Negro Women," *New York Herald Tribune*, January 30, 1942.
35. "Doctor Will Urge Planning of Families: Dr. Ferebee to Speak for Parenthood League at Palmer House," *Chicago Defender*, April 25, 1942.
36. Rebecca Stiles Taylor, "Women Take Army Stand at DC Confab," *Chicago Defender*, November 2, 1940.
37. Taylor, "Women Take Army Stand."
38. Robert Franklin Jefferson, "Making the Men of the 93rd: African American Servicemen in the Years of the Great Depression and the Second World War, 1935–1947," PhD dissertation, University of Michigan, 1995, 203, citing Henry Stimson Papers (Diary of 27 September, 1940, Henry Stimson), Yale University.
39. William Hastie memorandum to the Surgeon General, "Negro Participation in Army Medical Program," December 16, 1940, LOC-MS Division, African Americans in the Military, Part 2: Subject Files of Judge William Hastie, Reel 16:0580–82.
40. U.S. War Department, "Examination for Candidates for Commissions in the Army Medical Corps," press release, October 14, 1940, LOC-MS Division, African Americans in the Military, Part 2: Subject Files of Judge William Hastie, Reel 16:0575.
41. Claude Ferebee letter to members of the National Dental Association, December 20, 1940, LOC-MS Division, African Americans in the Military, Part 2: Subject Files of Judge William Hastie, Reel 16:0441.
42. Truman K. Gibson Office Memorandum, "Conference with Brig. Gen. Leigh Fairbank, re: Utilization of Negro Dentists," January 27, 1941, LOC-MS Division, African Americans in the Military, Part 2: Subject Files of Judge William Hastie, Reel 1:0756.
43. Todd Boulding Ferebee interview with the author.
44. Claude T. Ferebee Military Records.
45. Claude T. Ferebee Military Records; "News about 366th at Fort Devens," (Norfolk) *New Journal and Guide*, June 21, 1941.
46. Ferebee letter to Dr. R. D. Dedwylder, June 18, 1941, MSRC-HU, Ferebee. Box 183-3, Folder 15.
47. Claude T. Ferebee Military Records.
48. Ferebee letter to Dr. R. D. Dedwylder, June 18, 1941.
49. "AKA Basileus Congratulated," *Chicago Defender*, July 26, 1941.
50. Jackson letter to Dr. L. B. Austin, November 27, 1941, Ida Louise Jackson Papers, Correspondence, 1936–42, Carton 1:8, Bancroft Library, University of California, Berkeley.

51. Ida Louise Jackson letter to Irma Clark, February 2, 1942, Ferebee Papers, MSRC-HU, Box 183-5, Folder 18.

52. Ethel Lyle letter to Ida Louise Jackson, June 10, 1942, Ferebee Papers, MSRC-HU, Box 183-5, Folder 18.

53. Edna L. Griffin letter to Ida Louise Jackson, August 10, 1942, Ferebee Papers, MSRC-HU, Box 183-5, Folder 18.

54. Minutes of the Twenty-Fourth Annual Boule, 51, 55–56.

55. "Dr. Ferebee Visits 20 Cities in Year."

56. History of Fort Devens, http://www.fortdevensmuseum.org/history.php, accessed July 2, 2013; "Welcome to Fort Devens," http://www.military.com/base-guide /fort-devens, accessed July 2, 2013.

57. Headquarters 366th Infantry Office of the Special Service Officer, Fort Devens, "Special Service Report," April 5, 1943, LOC-MS Division, African Americans in the Military, Part 2: Subject Files of Judge William Hastie, Reel 8:0196–99.

58. Madeline Kountze Dugger Personal History Statement, U.S. War Department, October 13, 1941, NARA, National Civilian Personnel Records Center, St. Louis MO, FOIA request by the author.

59. Meghan K. Winchell, *Good Girls, Good Food, Good Fun: The Story of USO Hostesses during World War II* (Chapel Hill: University of North Carolina Press, 2008), 1.

60. "Mother of Six Gets LLB Degree at Portia Law: Mrs. Madeline K. Dugger of Jerome Street Is Wife of Maj. Edward Dugger of 372 Infantry," *Medford Mercury*, July 1, 1932, courtesy of Karen Green, Special Collections Librarian, New England Law School.

61. Dugger Personal History Statement, U.S. War Department, October 13, 1941.

62. Claude Ferebee letters to Madeline Dugger, July 26 and August 2, 1942, National Park Service, Mary McLeod Bethune Council House NHS, National Archives for Black Women's History, Madeline Kountze Dugger Garnett Kelley Papers, Series 2, Subseries 5, Box 3, Folder 9 (hereafter Dugger Papers, NPS, NABWH).

63. Claude Ferebee letter to Madeline Dugger, August 7, 1942, Dugger Papers, NPS, NABWH, Series 1, Subseries 1, Folder 5.

64. Dr. Ione D. Vargus interview with the author.

65. Dr. Ione D. Vargus interview with the author.

66. Claude Ferebee letter to Madeline Dugger, August 2, 1942, Dugger Papers.

67. Madeline Dugger letters to Nannie Ferebee, June 6, 1942, and April 19, 1944, Dugger Papers, NPS, NABWH, Series 2, Subseries 5, Box 3, Folder 9.

68. Claude Ferebee letter to Madeline Dugger, April 1, 1942, Dugger Papers, NPS, NABWH, Series 2, Subseries 5, Box 3, Folder 9.

69. Claude Ferebee letters to Madeline Dugger, August 2, 1942, and August 7, 1942, Dugger Papers.

70. Claude Ferebee letter to Madeline Dugger, July 26, 1942, Dugger Papers.

71. Claude Ferebee letter to Madeline Dugger, July 26, 1942, Dugger Papers.

72. Madeline Dugger letter to Col. West Hamilton, March 12, 1942, Dugger Papers, NPS, NABWH, Series 2, Subseries 5, Box 3, Folder 9.

12. THE SKIPPER

1. "Norfolkian, Captain in Army, Here," (Norfolk) *New Journal and Guide*, July 4, 1942.

2. "Brig. Gen. Benjamin O. Davis Sr.," military.com, http://www.military.com /content/morecontent?file=ML_bendavis_bkp, accessed December 28, 2014.

3. "Community Chest Trustees Elected," (Baltimore) *Afro-American*, April 6, 1929.

4. Madeline Dugger letter to Colonel Hamilton, March 12, 1932, Dugger Papers, NPS-NABWH, Series 2, Subseries 5, Box 3, Folder 9.

5. Claude Ferebee letter to Madeline Dugger, August 7, 1942.

6. Madeline Dugger letter to Colonel Hamilton, March 12, 1932.

7. Madeline Dugger Veteran Preference Claim, October 8, 1946, Madeline K. Dugger Personnel Records, FOIA request by the author, NARA, National Civilian Personnel Records Center.

8. H. V. Stirling, hospital director of finance, letter to Madeline Dugger, April 11, 1939, Dugger Papers, NPS, NABWH, Series 2, Subseries 5, Box 3.

9. Boston Post Office Employees Credit Union letter to Madeline Dugger, March 22, 1939; W. W. Howes, first assistant postmaster, letter to Madeline Dugger, April 28, 1939, both in Dugger Papers, NPS, NABWH, Series 2, Subseries 5, Box 3.

10. G. A. Willhauck, collection agent, letter to Madeline Dugger, September 5, 1940, Dugger Papers, NPS, NABWH, Series 2, Subseries 5, Box 3.

11. Irwin T. Dorch, president Boston NAACP, letter to Madeline Dugger, March 22, 1938, Dugger Papers, NPS, NABWH, Series 2, Subseries 5, Box 3.

12. Robert F. Bradford letter to Madeline Dugger, July 6, 1938; Mary M. Lake letter to Madeline Dugger, September 26, 1938, both in Dugger Papers, NPS, NABWH, Series 2, Subseries 5, Box 3.

13. Massachusetts Senator Harris S. Richardson letter to Madeline Dugger, March 11, 1939; Gladys R. Holmes, Massachusetts State Union of Women's Clubs, letter to Madeline Dugger, December 18, 1939, both in Dugger Papers, NPS, NABWH, Series 2, Subseries 5, Box 3; Madeline Dugger letter to Eleanor Roosevelt, July 9, 1940, Dugger Papers, NPS, NABWH, Series 2, Subseries 5, Box 3, Folder 7.

14. Madeline Dugger letter to President Roosevelt, April 14, 1939, Dugger Papers, NPS, NABWH, Series 2, Subseries 5, Box 3, Folder 4.

15. Madeline Dugger letter to Eleanor Roosevelt, July 9, 1940.

16. Ralph Magee letter to Mrs. Edward Dugger, July 11, 1940, Dugger Papers, NPS, NABWH, Series 2, Subseries 5, Box 3.

17. Madeline Dugger Application for Position as Hostess, U.S. Army, Madeline Dugger Personnel File, NARA, Nation Civilian Personnel Records.

18. War Department Notification of Personnel Action to Madeline Dugger, January 11, 1946, Madeline Dugger Personnel File, NARA, National Civilian Personnel Records.

19. Request for Personnel Action, Madeline D. Kelley, Personnel File, NARA, National Civilian Personnel Records.

20. Claude Ferebee letter to Madeline Dugger, April 1, 1942.

21. Dr. Ione Dugger Vargus interview with author.

22. Claude Ferebee letter to Madeline Dugger, August 2, 1942.

23. Madeline Dugger letter to Nannie Ferebee, June 6, 1942, Dugger Papers, NPS, NABWH, Series 2, Subseries 5, Box 3, Folder 9.

24. Madeline Dugger letter to Nannie Ferebee, June 6, 1942.

25. Claude Ferebee letter to Madeline Dugger, July 26, 1942.

26. Claude Ferebee letter to Madeline Dugger, August 7, 1942.

27. New York Domestic Relations Law §235(5).

28. Claude Ferebee letter to Madeline Dugger, November 22, 1943, Dugger Papers, NPS, NABWH, Series 2, Subseries 5, Box 3, Folder 10.

29. Capt. Lloyd L. Crabtree, Internal Memorandum to Commanding General, Boston Port of Embarkation Army Base, Boston, "Mrs. Madeline Dugger, Hostess, Service Club #4, Camp Myles Standish, Mass.," January 12, 1945, Madeline Dugger Personnel File, NARA, National Civilian Personnel Records.

30. Claude Ferebee letter to Madeline Dugger, July 26, 1942.

31. Claude Ferebee letter to Madeline Dugger, August 2, 1942.

32. Claude Ferebee letter to Madeline Dugger, August 2, 1942.

33. "Norfolkian, Captain in Army, Here"; "Dental Corps Officer Visits Home," (Norfolk) New Journal and Guide, July 11, 1942.

34. Claude Ferebee letter to Madeline Dugger, September 22, 1942, Dugger Papers, NPS, NABWH, Series 2, Subseries 5, Box 3, Folder 9.

35. Ferebee Oral History, 19.

36. Claude Ferebee letter to Madeline Dugger, April 19, 1944, Dugger Papers, NPS, NABWH, Series 2, Subseries 5, Box 4, Folder 1.

37. Claude Ferebee letter to Madeline Dugger, September 22, 1942.

38. Claude Ferebee letter to Madeline Dugger, September 22, 1942.

39. Claude Ferebee letter to Madeline Dugger, August 7, 1942.

40. Claude Ferebee letter to Madeline Dugger, September 22, 1942.

41. Claude Ferebee letter to Madeline Dugger, November 22, 1943.

42. Claude Ferebee letter to Madeline Dugger, November 22, 1943.

43. Truman K. Gibson Jr. with Steve Huntley, Knocking Down Barriers: My Fight for Black America (Evanston IL: Northwestern University Press, 2005), 153.

44. Gibson, Knocking Down Barriers, 155.

45. Claude Ferebee letter to Madeline Dugger, July 26, 1942.

46. Gibson, *Knocking Down Barriers*, 132–33.

47. "93rd Infantry Division (Colored) Combat Narrative," 168, U.S. Army Heritage and Education Center, Carlisle PA.

48. Claude Ferebee letter to Walter White, May 1, 1945; Claude Ferebee letter to Walter White, September 16, 1945, both letters from the LOC-MS Division, Records of the NAACP U.S. Army 93rd Division 1943–46, Group II, Box A648, Folder 6; Claude T. Ferebee Military Records.

49. Claude Ferebee letter to Walter White, September 27, 1945, LOC-MS Division, Records of the NAACP, Group II, Box A648, Folder 6.

50. Claude Ferebee letter to Walter White, August 19, 1945, LOC-MS Division, Records of the NAACP, Group II, Box A648, Folder 6.

51. "Meet Captain Ferebee," (Baltimore) *Afro-American*, August 19, 1944.

52. "93rd Infantry Division (Colored) Combat Narrative," 168.

53. Walter White, *A Man Called White* (New York: Viking Press, 1948), 286; "Bougainville Island," Encyclopedia Britannica, http://www.britannica.com/echecked/topic/75436/bougainville-island, accessed December 28, 2014.

54. Walter White, untitled draft article, *New York Post*, February 12, 1945, LOC-MS Division, Records of the NAACP, Group II, Box A648, Folder 6.

55. Robert F. Jefferson, "Making the Men of the 93rd: African American Servicemen in the Years of the Great Depression and the Second World War, 1935–1947," PhD diss., University of Michigan, 1995, 354.

56. Officers of the 93rd Infantry Division letter to Walter White, LOC-MS Division Records of the NAACP, Group II, Box A648, Folder 6.

57. Walter White letter to Maj. Gen. Harry H. Johnson, August 7, 1945, LOC-MS Division Records of the NAACP, Group II, Box A648, Folder 6.

58. Thomas Dyja, *Walter White: The Dilemma of Black Identity in America* (Chicago: Ivan R. Dee, 2008), 45.

59. Claude Ferebee letter to Walter White, August 19, 1945, LOC-MS Division Records of the NAACP, Group II, Box A648, Folder 6.

60. White, *Man Called White*, 277, 288.

61. Walter White letter to "Skipper" (Claude Ferebee), June 26, 1945; Claude Ferebee letter to Walter White, August 19, 1945, both letters from LOC-MS Division Records of the NAACP, Group II, Box A648, Folder 6.

62. Walter White letter to "Skipper" (Claude Ferebee), June 26, 1945; Claude Ferebee letter to Walter White, August 19, 1945.

63. Claude Ferebee letter to Walter White, May 1, 1945, LOC-MS Division Records of the NAACP, Group II, Box A648, Folder 6.

64. Claude Ferebee letter to Walter White, August 19, 1945.

65. Claude Ferebee letter to Walter White, August 19, 1945.

66. "Gets Bronze Star," (Norfolk) *New Journal and Guide*, October 13, 1945.

67. Claude Ferebee letter to Walter White, September 27, 1945, LOC-MS Division Records of the NAACP, Group II, Box A648, Folder 6.

68. Claude T. Ferebee Military Records; Claude Ferebee letter to Madeline Dugger, November 22, 1943.

69. "Dr. Ferebee Opens Dental Offices in New York," (Norfolk) *Journal and Guide*, December 7, 1946.

13. SOME STUFF

1. David Brinkley, *Washington Goes to War* (New York: Knopf, 1988), 81, 107–9.

2. Doris Kearns Goodwin, *No Ordinary Time, Franklin and Eleanor Roosevelt: The Home Front in World War II* (New York: Simon & Schuster, 1994), 263–64, 275; Harry McAlpin, "50 Negro Leaders at FDR Inaugural," *Chicago Defender*, January 27, 1945; "Inaugural History—1945—The 40th Inauguration," http://www.cbsnews.com/htdocs/politics/inauguration/history.pdf, accessed August 26, 2013.

3. Brinkley, *Washington Goes to War*, 265; "Swearing-in Ceremony for President Franklin D. Roosevelt," 40th Inaugural Ceremonies, January 20, 1945, http://www.inaugural.senate.gov/swearing-in/event/franklin-d-roosevelt-1945, accessed August 26, 2013.

4. Elaine H. Smith, "Historic Resource Study: Mary McLeod Bethune and the National Council of Negro Women, Pursuing a True and Unfettered Democracy," Report for the Mary McLeod Bethune Council House National Historic Site, September 2003, 221.

5. Ferebee letter to Ida Louise Jackson, November 5, 1941, "The twins and my mother send you much love," Ferebee Papers, MSRC-HU, Box 183-5, Folder 18.

6. Brinkley, *Washington Goes to War*, 127, 253.

7. Goodwin, *No Ordinary Time*, 357.

8. Ferebee letter to Ida Louise Jackson, "Thurs. noon," otherwise n.d., Ferebee Papers, MSRC-HU, Box 183-5, Folder 18.

9. Minutes of the National Health Committee of Alpha Kappa Alpha, April 1–2, 1942, Chicago, 2–4, 4–8; Ida Louise Jackson Papers, 1917–2003, BANC 2006/166, Bancroft Library, University of California, Berkeley, Carton 1:1, AKA Sorority, 1932–64.

10. Marjorie H. Parker, *Alpha Kappa Alpha through the Years 1908–1988* (Chicago: Mobium Press, 1990), 192.

11. Ida Louise Jackson letter to "My Dear Sorors," April 25, 1943, Ferebee Papers, MSRC-HU, Box 183-5, Folder 18.

12. Minutes of the Twenty-Fifth Annual Boule, Alpha Kappa Alpha Sorority, February 18–20, 1944, Chicago IL, 37, AKA Archives, MSRC-HU.

13. Minutes of the Twenty-Sixth Annual Boule, Alpha Kappa Alpha Sorority, August 8–13, 1946, Los Angeles CA, 32, AKA Archives, MSRC-HU.

14. Dr. Dorothy Boulding Ferebee, "AKA Mississippi Health Project Aids 15,000 Poverty Stricken," untitled newspaper, Cleveland OH, October 21, 1941.

15. Parker, *Alpha Kappa Alpha*, 194.

16. Undine Davis Young, "Highlights of Social Activities in Norfolk," (Norfolk) *New Journal and Guide*, January 2, 1943.

17. "Visits Family," (Norfolk) *New Journal and Guide*, June 26, 1943.

18. Carole R. McCann, *Birth Control Politics in the United States, 1916–1945* (Ithaca NY: Cornell University Press, 1994), 166n104.

19. "Dr. Ferebee Urges Planned Parenthood," *New York Amsterdam News*, May 2, 1942.

20. Dorothy Boulding Ferebee, MD, "Project Reports," speech to the annual meeting of the Birth Control Federation of America, New York, January 29, 1942, Margaret Sanger Papers, Sophia Smith Collection, Smith College, Northampton MA, Box 22, Folder 2.

21. Charlie Cherokee, "National Grapevine," *Chicago Defender*, February 14, 1942.

22. McCann, *Birth Control Politics*, 23–24, 113.

23. McCann, *Birth Control Politics*, 170–71.

24. McCann, *Birth Control Politics*, 165n101.

25. Florence Rose letter to Margaret Sanger, January 24, 1942, Margaret Sanger Papers, Box 22, Folder 2.

26. Dorothy Ferebee Application for Federal Employment as a consultant to the U.S. Department of State (date illegible, but file contents indicate late 1963), Federal Bureau of Investigation, Files of Dorothy Boulding Ferebee, Nos. 62-HQ-88217 and 140-HQ-28823; Dr. William Lofton Jr. interview with the author.

27. "Woman's Journal Gets New Writers," *Atlanta Daily World*, May 14, 1943.

28. Toki Schalk, "Liberty Ship *Harriet Tubman* Is Launched with Impressive Ceremonies in Portland," *Pittsburgh Courier*, June 10, 1944.

29. "Liberty Ships Built by the United States Maritime Commission in WWII," http://www.usmm.org/libertyships/html, accessed September 25, 2013.

30. Schalk, "Liberty Ship *Harriet Tubman* Is Launched;" "They Sponsored USS Harriet Tubman," *Chicago Defender*, June 17, 1944.

31. Dorothy Boulding Ferebee, "Remarks on the Christening of the *Harriet Tubman* Ship: Our Challenge," June 3, 1944, Portland ME, courtesy of Franklin D. Roosevelt Presidential Library and Museum, Hyde Park NY, "News Items," Box 979, Series 130.

32. Ferebee letter to Eleanor Roosevelt, June 9, 1944, Franklin D. Roosevelt Presidential Library and Museum, Box 979, Series 130.

33. "Secretary to Mrs. Roosevelt" letter to Ferebee, June 13, 1944, Franklin D. Roosevelt Presidential Library and Museum, Box 979, Series 130.

34. Townsend Hoopes and Douglas Brinkley, *FDR and the Creation of the UN* (New Haven: Yale University Press, 1997), 133, 179, 181.

35. David McCullough, *Truman* (New York: Simon & Schuster, 1992), 347–48.

36. Annie Laurie Adams letter to Jeanetta Welch Brown, March 30, 1945, NPS, NABWH, Records of the NCNW, Series 5, Box 1, Folder 5.

37. Dorothy Ferebee, NCNW Recorded Interview, NPS, NABWH, Records of the NCNW, Series 15, Subseries 6, Folder 73, Side 1, July 11, 1976. Dorothy participated in an oral history for the National Council of Negro Women when it launched its National Archives for Black Women's History. To distinguish this interview from the Merze Tate one for the Schlesinger library, this will be referred to as the "Ferebee NCNW Recorded Interview."

38. W. E. B. Du Bois, "The Winds of Time: Recognition at Frisco," *Chicago Defender*, April 28, 1945; "United Nations Parley: Mrs. Bethune Added to Frisco Advisors," *Chicago Defender*, April 28, 1945; Walter White, *A Man Called White* (New York: Viking, 1948), 295.

39. Ferebee NCNW Recorded Interview.

40. Ferebee letter to Dr. James Lowell Hall, October 15, 1948, NPS, NABWH, Records of the NCNW, Series 5, Box 15, Folder 9.

41. "An Address by Mrs. Mary McLeod Bethune at Bethel AME Church," *San Francisco News*, n.d., LOC-MS Division, Mary McLeod Bethune Papers: Bethune Foundation Collection, Part 1: Writings, Diaries, Scrapbooks, Biographical Materials, and Files on the National Youth Administration and Women's Organizations, 1918–55, Reel 9:0161, Bethune UN Scrapbook. Like Dorothy, Bethune maintained a 182-page scrapbook of her experiences while attending the United Nations founding conference in San Francisco in the spring of 1945. It contains newspaper clippings (often without listing the name or date of publication). The entire scrapbook is on Reel 9, Frames 0001–182.

42. P. L. Prattis, "Conference Confetti!," *Pittsburgh Courier*, May 5, 1945.

43. "Mrs. Bethune Reveals Hope for Unity and Brotherhood," n.p., n.d., LOC-MS Division, Mary McLeod Bethune Papers: Bethune Foundation Collection: Part 1: Reel 9:0018.

44. Dorothy Ferebee, "Notes and Impressions En Route to San Francisco—Calif for the United Nations Conference on International Organization, April 19 to May 10," NPS, NABWH, Records of the NCNW, Series 5, Box 34, Folder 495: 1.

45. Ferebee, "Notes and Impressions," 1–2, 4.

46. Mary McLeod Bethune to "My dear Children," April 22, n.y., NPS, NABWH, Records of the NCNW, Series 5, Box 4, Folder 74.

47. Ferebee, "Notes and Impressions," 10.

48. "Mrs. Bethune, Walter White Feuding: Unofficial Observers Plead for Equality," *Pittsburgh Courier*, May 5, 1945.

49. "Mrs. Bethune, Walter White Feuding."

50. Prattis, "Conference Confetti!," LOC-MS Division, Mary McLeod Bethune Papers: The Bethune Foundation Collection: Part 1: Reel 9:0155.

51. Ferebee, "Notes and Impressions," 10–12.

52. Rand Richards, *Historic Walks in San Francisco: 18 Trails through the City's Past* (San Francisco: Heritage House, 2008), 196.

53. Charles McClain, "California Carpetbagger: The Career of Henry Dibble," QLR 28.885 (2009), http://scholarship.law.berkeley.edu/facpubs/660, accessed September 1, 2013; Cary Reich, *The Life of Nelson Rockefeller: Worlds to Conquer, 1908–1958* (New York: Doubleday, 1996), 321, 329.

54. Ferebee, "Notes and Impressions," 13, 74, 75–76, 107.

55. Ferebee, "Notes and Impressions," 14.

56. Ferebee, "Notes and Impressions," 15–17.

57. Reich, *Life of Nelson Rockefeller*, 321, 323, 328, 332–34.

58. Thurston Clarke, *JFK's Last Hundred Days: The Transformation of a Man and the Emergence of a Great President* (New York: Penguin Press, 2013), 217.

59. Ferebee, "Notes and Impressions," 25.

60. Ferebee, "Notes and Impressions," 132.

61. Ferebee, "Notes and Impressions," 73, 74, 122–28.

62. Ferebee Oral History, 19.

63. Constance Curtis and Chollie Herndon, "Dentists Must Unite Medicine with Fine Art," *New York Amsterdam News*, May 21, 1949.

64. Walter White letter to Maj. Gen. Harry H. Johnson, August 7, 1945, LOC, NAACP Collection, Group II, Box A648, Folder 6.

65. Claude T. Ferebee Military Records, NARA, Army Service Forces, Ninth Service Command Headquarters Separation Center, Camp Beale CA, February 19, 1946.

66. Gill, "Harlem," 334.

67. Curtis and Henderson, "Dentists Must Unite Medicine with Fine Art."

68. Thelma Berlack-Boozer, "Celebrities See Don Budge Trim McDaniel . . . ," *New York Amsterdam News*, August 3, 1940; "Socialites Go to Chinatown: Many Enjoy Meal at Port Arthur in Aid of 'Y,'" *New York Amsterdam News*, May 25, 1940.

69. Mildred Bond Roxborough interview with the author.

70. Queens County, New York, Deed Book 5545: 501.

71. Tom Topousis, "Cream of the 'Bop': Queens Nabe Rich in Jazz History to Be Landmarked," *New York Post*, February 10, 2010.

72. Theresa C. Noonan, Addisleigh Park Historic District Designation Report, Landmarks Preservation Commission, February 1, 2011, 103.

73. John Russell Eberhardt III interview with the author.

74. "Ferebee Weds Hazel Hardy," *New York Amsterdam News*, June 16, 1951.

14. EVERY BONE IN THE BODY

1. Jack and Jill of America, Homepage, http://www.jackandjillinc.org/test-page, accessed October 5, 2013; Lawrence Otis Graham, *Our Kind of People: Inside America's Black Upper Class* (New York: HarperCollins, 1999), 22.

2. Mabel Alston, "Overheard in the Capital: Tots 'Adopt' Chinese Babes, Socialites in War Work, Gifts to Soldiers Suggested," (Baltimore) *Afro-American*, November 7, 1942; Todd Boulding Ferebee interview with the author.

3. William H. Johnson interview with the author.

4. William H. Johnson interview with the author.

5. Cultural Tourism DC: St Mary's Episcopal Church, African American Heritage Trail, http://www.culturaltourismdc.org/portal/st.-mary-s-episcopal-church -african-american-heritage-trail#.VKtD3SVF-So, accessed January 5, 2015.

6. Aurelia Roberts Brooks interview with the author.

7. John Beckley interview with the author.

8. Rayford W. Logan, *Howard University: The First Hundred Years, 1867–1967* (New York: New York University Press, 1969), 251.

9. John Beckley interview with the author.

10. John Beckley interview with the author.

11. "Lucretia Mott," Woman's Rights National Historical Park, New York, http://www.nps.gov/wori/historyculture/lucretia-mott.htm, accessed September 29, 2013.

12. "Benjamin Banneker Biography," http://www.biography.com/people/benjamin -banneker-9198038, accessed September 29, 2013.

13. Dorothy Ferebee Jr. Transcript, Banneker Junior High School, courtesy of Northfield Mount Hermon School (hereafter NMH); Claude Thurston Ferebee II Transcript, Tilton School (includes Banneker grades for his freshman year, 1944–45), courtesy of Tilton School.

14. Claude Thurston Ferebee II Transcript.

15. Town of Highland Beach, Maryland, "History of Highland Beach," http://www.highlandbeachmd.org, accessed January 5, 2015.

16. John Beckley and Aurelia Roberts Brooks interviews with the author.

17. "Dr. Charles Drew," http://www.cdrewu.edu/about.cdu/drcharlesrdrew, accessed January 5, 2015.

18. Charlene Drew Jarvis interview with the author.

19. Aurelia Roberts Brooks interview with the author.

20. John Beckley interview with the author.

21. Ferebee Oral History, 17.

22. Ferebee letter to Headmaster of Northfield Academy, May 23, 1945, and Director of Admissions Northfield School for Girls letter to Ferebee, May 29, 1945, both courtesy of NMH.

23. "Hartford ACE Sponsors Lecture by Psychologist," *Hartford Courant*, January 2, 1938; "Social Agencies Directors to Hear Dr. I. M. Altaraz," *Hartford Courant*, April 29, 1937.

24. "More School Rest Periods Held Needed: Rigidity of Programs Prevents Progress, Says Dr. I. M. Altaraz at Clinic Reception," *Hartford Courant*, May 2, 1937.

25. Ferebee Oral History, 17.

26. Claude Thurston Ferebee II Altarez [sic] School Transcript, courtesy of Tilton School; Dorothy B. Ferebee Transcript showing Altaraz School incomplete grades for Latin II and Algebra II, courtesy of NMH.

27. Dorothy Ferebee Jr. letter to Director of Northfield Seminary, December 31, 1945, courtesy of NMH.

28. Sally Atwood Hamilton, ed., *Lift Thine Eyes: The Landscape, the Buildings, the Heritage of Northfield Mount Hermon School* (Mount Hermon MA: Northfield Mount Hermon, 2010), ix.

29. "NMH's History," http://www.nmhschool.org/about-nmh-history, accessed January 5, 2015; Peter Weis, archivist NMH, interview with the author.

30. "D. L. Moody, NMH Founder," http://www.nmhschool.org/about-nmh-dl-moody, accessed October 3, 2013.

31. Margaret Gale, Northfield League, memo for Miss Tower, February 7, 1946, and Rev. E. A. Christian letter of reference for Miss Dorothy B. Ferebee to Northfield, February 12, 1946, both courtesy of NMH.

32. Secretary to the Director of Admissions letter to Ferebee, March 26, 1946, courtesy of NMH.

33. Margaret L. Mensel, assistant director of admissions, memo to unknown recipient re: Dorothy Ferebee Jr. admissions interview, April 3, 1946, courtesy of NMH.

34. Unnamed Principal letter to Dorothy Ferebee Jr., May 1, 1946, courtesy of NMH; Peter Weis interview with the author.

35. Dorothy Boulding Ferebee Jr., Application for Admission to Northfield Seminary, January 25, 1946, courtesy of NMH.

36. "Enrollment by Year," courtesy of NMH; Mira B. Wilson, "Colored Students Are an Asset," *Independent School Bulletin* 3 (February 1949): 13.

37. Wilson, "Colored Students Are an Asset," 13.

38. Judge Anna Johnston Diggs Taylor interview with the author.

39. Dorothy Ferebee Jr. Transcript, NMH.

40. Assistant principal letter to Dorothy Ferebee Jr., August 29, 1947, courtesy of NMH.

41. Aurelia Roberts Brooks interview.

42. Dorothy Ferebee Jr. letter to Jeannette G. Daboll, September 4, 1947, courtesy of NMH.

43. "Dorothy Boulding Ferebee," *Highlights*, June 1949, 19.

44. Judge Taylor interview with the author.

45. Uncle Dave Lewis, "Jacob Gade," http://www.allmusic.com/composition/jalousie-jealousy-tango-for-orchestra-mc0002360335, accessed October 14, 2013; Peter Weis email to author, October 19, 2011; Ferebee letter to Marietta Tower, assistant principal Northfield School, April 3, 1949, courtesy of NMH.

46. Letter to Jerome Burtt, Champlain College, November 27, 1950, courtesy of NMH. (The author is probably Mira B. Wilson, Northfield School principal.)

47. John Beckley interview with the author.

48. "Tilton School—About Us," http://www.tiltonschool.org, accessed February 12, 2009.

49. Meg Rand, assistant librarian, Tilton School, email to author, October 24, 2013.

50. John Beckley interview with the author.

51. Claude Thurston Ferebee II Transcript, Tilton School.

52. John Beckley interview with the author.

53. John Beckley interview with the author.

54. "Claude Thurston Ferebee II," *Tower* 1949.

55. Louis Lautier, "Capital Spotlight: Kappas to L.A.," *Baltimore Afro-American*, July 19, 1947.

56. Louis Lautier, "Capital Spotlight," *Baltimore Afro-American*, May 21, 1949.

57. Toki Schalk Johnson, "Inaugural Ball Gala Scene of Breathtaking Beauty . . . ," *Pittsburgh Courier*, January 29, 1949.

58. "Weather: Official Forecast," *Boston Globe*, June 6, 1949.

59. Claude Thurston Ferebee II Transcript, Tilton School.

60. Dorothy Ferebee Jr. Transcript, NMH.

61. John Beckley interview with the author.

62. Dorothy B. Ferebee, New York Medical License No. 048961, http://www.nysed .gov/coms/op001/opsc2a?profcd=60&phcno=048961&nameck=fer, accessed September 29, 2013; *Queens, New York City Alphabetical Telephone Directory, Yellow Pages*, April 1950, 590.

63. Logan, *Howard University*, 428; Ferebee Application for Federal Employment as consultant to the U.S. State Department, Ferebee FBI file.

64. "Information Manual of the University Health Service," Howard University, 1950–51.

65. Gary Marmorstein, *The Label: The Story of Columbia Records* (New York: Thunder's Mouth Press, 2007), 165–70.

66. David Johnson, "Teen Age," *New York Age*, August 20, 1949.

15. A MATTER FOR GRAVE CONCERN

1. Olivia S. Henry memorandum to Mrs. Mary McLeod Bethune, November 7, 1949, NPS, NABWH, Records of the NCNW, Series 2, Folder 45.

2. Ferebee Recorded NCNW interview, July 11, 1976, NPS, NABWH, Records of the NCNW, Series 15, Subseries 6, Folder 73, Side 1.

3. Mary McLeod Bethune Personal 1949 Telephone Directory, LOC-MS Division, Mary McLeod Bethune Papers: Bethune Foundation Collection, Part 1, Reel 5:0604.

4. Such endearments show up throughout surviving letters between Bethune and the younger women who worked with her, many of which are on microfilm at the Library of Congress, Manuscript Reading Room, Mary McLeod Bethune Papers, Part 2: Correspondence Files 1914–55; see e.g., Ruth Scott letter to "Dearest Ma," (Bethune), July 9, 1953, Reel 10:0365; Mary McLeod Bethune letter to Ruth Scott, November 15, 1954, referring to her followers as "my daughters," Reel 10:0394–95; Ferebee, "Notes and Impressions (diary of the 1945 U.N. San Francisco conference)," 1–2; see also NPS invitation to Bethune celebration, Saturday, July 10, 2010, "Mary McLeod Bethune Celebration: Remembering Her Eldest Daughter, Dorothy Irene Height, 1912–2010," sent to the author.

5. Rackham Holt, *Mary McLeod Bethune: A Biography* (Garden City NY: Doubleday, 1964), 2, 20; Joyce A. Hanson, *Mary McLeod Bethune and Black Women's Political Activism* (Columbia: University of Missouri Press, 2003), 43–45; Richard Wormser, "Jim Crow Stories: Mary McLeod Bethune (1875–1955)," http://www.pbs.org/wnet /jimcrow/stories_people_beth.html, accessed December 9, 2013.

6. Dorothy Ferebee, "The Mary McLeod Bethune Legacy," undated speech to commemorate Mary McLeod Bethune Memorial Week (which was in July 1974), Ferebee Papers, MSRC-HU, Box 183-9, Folder 27; Blanche Wiesen Cook, *Eleanor Roosevelt*, vol. 2: *1933–1938* (New York: Viking, 1999), 160.

7. Wiesen Cook, *Eleanor Roosevelt*, 60.

8. Hanson, *Mary McLeod Bethune*, 41.

9. Katie McCabe and Dovey Johnson Roundtree, *Justice Older than the Law: The Life of Dovey Johnson Roundtree* (Jackson: University Press of Mississippi, 2009), 45, 123.

10. Hanson, *Mary McLeod Bethune*, 99, 104–5.

11. Holt, *Mary McLeod Bethune*, 125.

12. Next New Deal: The Blog of the Roosevelt Institute, "National Youth Administration," August 30, 2011, http://www.nextnewdeal.net/national-youth-administration, accessed February 24, 2014.

13. Mary McLeod Bethune, "Stepping Aside . . . at Seventy-Four," *WomenUnited*, October 1949, 14–15.

14. Minutes of the organizational meeting of the National Council of Negro Women, New York City, December 5, 1935, 3, NPS, NABWH, Records of the NCNW, Series 2, Box 1, Folder 1.

15. Minutes of the organizational meeting of the National Council of Negro Women, 4.

16. NCNW Certificate of Incorporation, July 25, 1936, NPS, NABWH, Records of the NCNW, Series 1, Box 1, Folder 1.

17. Elaine H. Smith, "Historic Resource Study: Mary McLeod Bethune and the National Council of Negro Women, Pursuing a True and Unfettered Democracy," Report for the Mary McLeod Bethune Council House National Historic Site, September 2003, 43, 45, 163; "'Our Problem a Decent Living for Everybody,' Mrs.

Roosevelt Tells 300 Cheering Women at New York Dinner, 250 Unable to Get in . . . ," (Baltimore) *Afro-American*, December 25, 1937.

18. "Dr. Ferebee Is Winner of Mrs. Bethune's Post: Edith Sampson, Third in Hot Ballot Fight," *Chicago Defender*, November 26, 1949.

19. Wiesen Cook, *Eleanor Roosevelt*, 159.

20. Holt, *Mary McLeod Bethune*, 178.

21. Joseph E. Persico, *Franklin and Lucy: President Roosevelt, Mrs. Rutherford, and the Other Remarkable Women in His Life* (New York: Random House, 2008), 134.

22. James R. Kearney, *Anna Eleanor Roosevelt: The Evolution of a Reformer* (Boston: Houghton Mifflin, 1968), 60.

23. Kearney, *Anna Eleanor Roosevelt*, 71. "National Youth Administration," *Encyclopedia of Oklahoma History and Culture*, Oklahoma Historical Society, http://www.digital.library.okstate.edu/encyclopedia/entries/n/na014.html, accessed January 3, 2015.

24. Wiesen Cook, *Eleanor Roosevelt*, 160; "Eleanor Roosevelt Papers Project: Teaching Eleanor Roosevelt Glossary, Mary McLeod Bethune (1875–1955)," http://www.gwu.edu/~erpapers/teachinger/glossary/bethune-mary.cfm, accessed November 24, 2013.

25. Wiesen Cook, *Eleanor Roosevelt*, 160.

26. Smith, "Historic Resource Study," 123.

27. Bethune, "Stepping Aside," 15.

28. Minutes of the NCNW Conference on the Participation of Negro Women and Children in Federal Programs, 12, NPS, NABWH, Records of the NCNW, Series 4, Box 1, Folder 5.

29. Minutes of the NCNW Conference on the Participation of Negro Women and Children in Federal Programs, 10–12.

30. Minutes of the NCNW Conference on the Participation of Negro Women and Children in Federal Programs, 34–35.

31. Dorothy Height, *Open Wide the Freedom Gates* (New York: Public Affairs, 2003), 84.

32. Ferebee Oral History, 31.

33. Minutes of the NCNW Conference on the Participation of Negro Women and Children in Federal Programs, 51, 89, 90–92.

34. Smith, "Historic Resource Study," 30, 46.

35. Smith, "Historic Resource Study," 53.

36. "Seek to Place Negro Workers: Women's Bureau Queried in DC," *New York Amsterdam News*, September 20, 1941.

37. Deborah Gray White, *Too Heavy a Load: Black Women in Defense of Themselves, 1894–1994* (New York: Norton, 1999), 155.

38. McCabe and Roundtree, *Justice Older than the Law*, 45–46.

39. Mary McLeod Bethune FBI File No. 101-HQ-1823, Parts 1 and 2, FOIA request by author. Over the years the bureau kept multiple files on Bethune, numbering close to one thousand pages.

40. Mary McLeod Bethune FBI File No. 101-HQ-1823, Part 1, Memorandum from John Edgar Hoover to undisclosed person, November 12, 1941.

41. "Mrs. Bethune Calls Dies' Accusations 'Malicious, Absurd,'" *Pittsburgh Courier*, October 3, 1942.

42. Transcript of FBI interview with Mary McLeod Bethune, April 14, 1942 included in Bethune FBI File No. 101-HQ-1823, Part 1.

43. Report of unnamed Norfolk Special Agent in Charge on Vivian Carter Mason, May 8, 1956, Vivian Carter Mason FBI File No. 157-HQ-141903, FOIA request by the author.

44. Teletype from Special Agent in Charge, Mobile AL, to Director, FBI, "Racial Situation, State of Alabama, Selma," October 5, 1963, FBI File No. 157-HQ-6-61, Sec. 5, FOIA request by the author.

45. Smith, "Historic Resources Study," 142–43, 144.

46. McCabe and Roundtree, *Justice Older than the Law*, 49–51, 53.

47. Smith, "Historic Resources Study," 133–35.

48. Smith, "Historic Resources Study," 139; "Dawson to Present President to NCNW," *Atlanta Daily World*, November 6, 1949.

49. Smith, "Historic Resources Study," 165.

50. Smith, "Historic Resources Study," 215–16; Meeting of the NCNW Executive Committee, December 18, 1943, NPS, NABWH, Records of the NCNW, Series 3, Box 1, Folder 25.

51. NCNW Executive Committee Meeting, December 18, 1943.

52. NCNW Executive Committee Meeting, December 18, 1943.

53. Smith, "Historic Resources Study," 216–18.

54. Smith, "Historic Resources Study," 218–19.

55. "Determining the Facts; Reading 4: The National Council of Negro Women: Beyond Bethune," http://www.nps.gov/nr/twhp/wwwlps/lessons/135bethune/135facts4 .htm, accessed December 1, 2013.

56. Hanson, *Mary McLeod Bethune*, 108; White, *Too Heavy a Load*, 156.

57. "History of 633 PA Avenue," National Council of Negro Women, Inc., http:// www.ncnw.org/about/633history.htm, accessed December 8, 2013.

58. Smith, "Historic Resources Study," 170.

59. Mary McLeod Bethune letter to W. Kent Alson, September 20, 1945, NPS, NABWH, Records of the NCNW, Series 5, Box 1, Folder 5.

60. Board of Directors Meeting, October 5, 1946, NPS, NABWH, Records of the NCNW, Series 3, Box 1, Folder 2.

61. Board of Directors Meeting, January 25, 1947, NPS, NABWH, Records of the NCNW Series 3, Box 1, Folder 3.

62. "Historical Note: International Council of Women Records, 1888–1959," MS 352, Sophia Smith Collection, Smith College, North Hampton MA.

63. Charley Cherokee, "National Grapevine: The People Passing By," *Chicago Defender*, August 9, 1947.

64. Eve Lynn, "International Council of Women Holds Conclave in Philadelphia," *Pittsburgh Courier*, September 27, 1947; "Eunice H. Carter among Delegates to Paris Talks," *Chicago Defender*, September 13, 1947.

65. Mary McLeod Bethune letter to Edith Sampson, February 8, 1949, Edith Sampson Papers, MC 397, Schlesinger Library on the History of Women in America, Radcliffe Institute, Harvard University, Box 9, Folder 188.

66. Mary McLeod Bethune letter to Edith Sampson, February 18, 1949, Edith Sampson Papers, Box 9, Folder 188.

67. Mary McLeod Bethune letter to Edith Sampson, May 16, 1949, Edith Sampson Papers, Box 9, Folder 188.

68. Smith, "Historic Resource Study," 272; NCNW Executive Committee Meeting, January 23, 1949, NPS, NABWH, Records of the NCNW Series 3, Box 1, Folder 27; "Dr. Ferebee Is Winner of Mrs. Bethune's Post."

69. Toki Schalk Johnson, "Toki Types: If Bethune Retires . . . Then What? . . . ," *Pittsburgh Courier*, September 24, 1949.

70. Revella Clay, "Mrs. Bethune Lists Qualifications for New President of Council: Favorites Headed by Name of Chicago Attorney Edith Sampson," *Pittsburgh Courier*, November 12, 1949.

71. "Edith Sampson, Arenia Mallory Vie in Race for Mrs. Bethune's Job . . . ," *Chicago Defender*, November 19, 1949.

72. "Crystal Gazing," *Chicago Defender*, November 5, 1949; Clay, "Mrs. Bethune Lists Qualifications for New President of Council"; "Edith Sampson, Arenia Mallory Vie in Race."

73. Helen Laville and Scott Lucas, "The American Way: Edith Sampson, the NAACP, and African American Identity in the Cold War," *Diplomatic History* 20.4 (1996): 568–71.

74. Clay, "Mrs. Bethune Lists Qualifications."

75. "National Council of Negro Women's Convention Attracts 400 Delegates: Meeting to Be Marked by Retirement from Presidency of Mrs. Mary McLeod Bethune," *Washington Afro-American*, November 19, 1949.

76. Cleonia M. Donan, handwritten notes of the November 15–19, 1949, annual meeting of the NCNW, NPS, NABWH, Records of the NCNW, Series 2, Folder 46, 18, 21.

77. "NCNW Hits Washington with Spirit," (Norfolk) *New Journal and Guide*, November 26, 1949.

78. Donan, handwritten notes, 16.

79. President Harry S. Truman, "Address at the Annual Meeting of the National Council of Negro Women, Inc.," November 15, 1949, Papers of the Presidents, Harry S. Truman (1945–53), Harry S. Truman Library and Museum, Independence MO, https://www.trumanlibrary.org/publicpapers/index.php?pid=1337, accessed September 13, 2013; undated entry by unknown author in Mary McLeod Bethune FBI File No. 101-HQ-1823, Section 2.
80. Smith, "Historic Resources Study," 272–74.
81. David McCullough, *Truman* (New York: Simon & Schuster, 1992), 531–32, 586–87.
82. President Truman address at the annual meeting of the NCNW, November 15, 1949.
83. Smith, "Historic Resource Study," 278–79.
84. "Plain Talk," *Chicago Defender*, November 26, 1949.
85. Smith, "Historic Resource Study," 279.
86. Smith, "Historic Resource Study," 280.
87. "Dr. Ferebee Is Winner of Mrs. Bethune's Post."
88. Smith, "Historic Resource Study," 280.
89. "Women Shed Tears as Bethune Retires: Dorothy Ferebee Voted President in Hot Election," *Pittsburgh Courier*, November 26, 1949.
90. Smith, "Historic Resource Study," 280–281; "Leaders Pay Tribute to Mrs. Mary Bethune," *Chicago Defender*, November 26, 1949.
91. Smith, "Historic Resource Study," 282.
92. "Program, Mary McLeod Bethune Testimonial Dinner," November 18, 1949, NPS, NABWH, Records of the NCNW, Series 2, Folder 48.
93. Minutes of the Executive Committee Board, November 19, 1949, 2, NPS, NABWH, Records of the NCNW Series 3, Folder 27.
94. "Second President of NCNW at Helm," *Atlanta Daily World*, November 27, 1949.
95. Lois Taylor, "Meet the President," (Baltimore) *Afro-American*, December 3, 1949; "Dr. Ferebee Ably Steps into Dr. Bethune's Shoes," (Norfolk) *New Journal and Guide*, November 26, 1949.
96. "'It's a Signal Honor,' Declares Dr. Ferebee as She Takes Over NCNW," *Chicago Defender*, December 3, 1949.
97. "Dr. Ferebee Ably Steps into Dr. Bethune's Shoes."
98. "Corrections Noted in Nov. 26 Paper," (Norfolk) *New Journal and Guide*, December 3, 1949.

16. ONE OF THE COLDEST WINTERS WE EVER HAD

1. Dorothy Boulding Ferebee Jr., academic record, courtesy of NMH.
2. Letter from Dorothy Ferebee Jr. to Miss Daboll, NMH, June 14, 1946, NMH.
3. Dorothy Boulding Ferebee Jr. academic record.

4. "Associated Colleges of Upper New York—Champlain College—Middletown Collegiate Center, Catalog Number 1949–1950," 28, Bobst Library, NYU Archives, ACUNY Records, MC 82, Box 3, Folder 14; "Champlain Now Accepts Women in 'Experiment in Co-education': 29 Are in Residence Now and 200 More Will Be Accepted in January," *New York Herald Tribune*, November 3, 1946.

5. Ali Simpson and Debra Kimok, "Guide to the Champlain College Collection 86.6," Special Collections, Benjamin F. Feinberg Library, Plattsburgh State University College, September 2008, revised by Debra Kimok, May 2012, 1.

6. Minutes of the Board of Trustees of Associated Colleges of Upper New York, May 26, 1950, 14–15, Bobst Library, NYU Archives, ACUNY Records, MC 82, Box 1, Folder 14.

7. Kimok, "Guide to the Champlain College Collection," 1.

8. Minutes of the Board of Trustees of Associated Colleges of Upper New York, 4.

9. Tom O'Hara, "1,007 Students at New College at Plattsburg . . . ," *New York Herald Tribune*, September 22, 1946.

10. "Across the Campuses of the Associated Colleges of Upper New York," school brochure, Bobst Library, NYU Archives, ACUNY Records, MC 82, Box 3, Folder 11; "Associated Colleges of Upper New York—Champlain College—Middletown Collegiate Center, Catalog Number 1949–1950," 16.

11. "Associated Colleges of Upper New York: Champlain College Catalog 1949–50," 6, Champlain College Collection, 86.6, Feinberg Library, SUNY-Plattsburgh, Box 2.

12. Minutes of the Board of Trustees of Associated Colleges of Upper New York, 15.

13. Mrs. H. Osgood and Dr. E. E. Masters, "Rules for Single Women Students Not Living at Home, Champlain College," October 15, 1946, Champlain College Collection, 86.6, Feinberg Library, SUNY-Plattsburgh, Box 1 (School Information), Folder 1.

14. "Champlain College Catalog 1949–50," 6; "Weather," *New York Times*, September 20, 1949.

15. "Cheerleaders," 1950 *du Lac* (Champlain College Yearbook), n.p.; George Jones interview with the author.

16. Football Program, "Champlain-Ithaca," November 12, 1949, courtesy of George Jones.

17. "Women's League, 1950 *du Lac*, n.p.

18. "Obituary: N. Paul Schreiber," *Fresno* (CA) *Bee*, November 8, 2006; Nancy Schreiber email to the author, June 25, 2013.

19. Nancy Schreiber email, June 25, 2013; "Norburt P. Schreiber: Enlisted Record and Report of Separation," Norburt P. Schreiber Military Records, NARA, National Military Personnel Records Center, St. Louis MO, FOIA request by the author.

20. Schreiber Enlisted Record and Report of Separation.

21. "Obituary: N. Paul Schreiber"; Nancy Schreiber email, November 1, 2013.

22. *Perez v. Lippold*, 32 Cal. 2d 711 (1948).

23. Nancy Schreiber email, November 1, 2013.

24. "Union Hotel Expands, Modernizes Facilities: Continuing Renovation Scheduled," *Plattsburgh Press-Republican*, August 14, 1956.

25. George Jones interview with the author.

26. "Champlain College Catalog 1949–50," 6.

27. "Legends of Big Band Swing: Ray McKinley," http://www.swingmusic.net/mckinley_Ray.html, accessed January 6, 2015; Invitation, 1950 Winter Weekend, Champlain College Collection 86.6, Feinberg Library, Plattsburgh State University College, Box 1, Folder 5.

28. Invitation, 1950 Winter Weekend.

29. Ferebee Oral History, 17–18.

30. Ferebee Oral History, 1.

31. "Bear Mountain Basks in a Ski-less Spring Sun," *New York Times*, January 3, 1950.

32. "Spring Visits East Coast, City Gets Record 65.6: Then Sets 3d Record at 62 after Midnight . . . ," *New York Herald Tribune*, January 5, 1950.

33. "The Weather," *Washington Post*, January 14, 1950.

34. "Ski Team," 1950 *du Lac*, n.p.

35. Nancy Schreiber email, June 25, 2013.

36. "Death Claims One of Ferebee Twins," (Baltimore) *Afro-American*, February 18, 1950.

37. "Prexy of NCNW Buries Daughter," *Pittsburgh Courier*, February 18, 1950.

38. "Prexy of NCNW Buries Daughter."

39. "Death Claims One of Ferebee Twins."

40. "Bury Daughter of NCNW Prexy: Dr. Ferebee's Daughter Dies in Washington," *Chicago Defender*, February 18, 1950.

41. Nancy Schreiber email, June 25, 2013.

42. Nancy Schreiber email, November 3, 2013; Linda Greenhouse and Reva B. Siegel, *Before Roe v. Wade: Voices That Shaped the Abortion Debate before the Supreme Court's Ruling* (New York: Kaplan, 2010), 3.

43. George Jones interview with the author.

44. Rachel Benson Gold, "Lessons from before Roe: Will Past Be Prologue?," *Guttmacher Report on Public Policy* 6.1 (2003): 2, http://www.guttmacher.org/pubs/tgr/06/1/gr060108.html, accessed November 7, 2013.

45. Ellen Messer and Kathryn E. May, *Back Rooms: Voices from the Illegal Abortion Era* (New York: St. Martin's Press, 1988), 5–9, 26–27, 125–29.

46. Todd Boulding Ferebee interview with the author.

47. J. Russell Eberhardt III interview with the author.

48. "Death Claims One of Ferebee Twins"; Elaine H. Smith, "Historic Resource Study: Mary McLeod Bethune and the National Council of Negro Women, Pursuing a True and Unfettered Democracy," Report for the Mary McLeod Bethune Council House National Historic Site, September 2003, 217, 233.

49. "Bury Daughter of NCNW Prexy."
50. Toki Schalk Johnson, "Toki Types: Tragedy Strikes," *Pittsburgh Courier,* February 11, 1950.
51. "Death Claims One of Ferebee Twins."
52. Dorothy Boulding Ferebee (Jr.), Certificate of Death, No. 495531, District of Columbia Health Department, Bureau of Vital Statistics.
53. William Lofton interview with author.
54. Deborah Gray White, *Too Heavy a Load: Black Women in Defense of Themselves, 1894–1994* (New York: Norton), 70.
55. "Leaders Debate Negroes' Rights," (Washington DC) *Times Herald,* December 21, 1949; "Civil Rights' Effect Debated in Hearing," *Washington Post,* December 21, 1949; "Civil Rights Dispute Flares at Hearing," *Abilene* (TX) *Reporter-News,* December 21, 1949; "Ferebee Fights with Dixiecrat," *New York Amsterdam News,* December 24, 1949.
56. Unsigned note in Dorothy Ferebee Jr. school file, February 7, 1950, courtesy of NMH.
57. Todd Boulding Ferebee interview with the author.
58. George Jones interview with the author.
59. Dorothy Boulding Ferebee (Jr.) Certificate of Death.
60. Laurie R. Goldstein MD, OBGYN, email to the author, November 13, 2013.
61. Dorothy Boulding Ferebee (Jr.) Certificate of Death.
62. "St. Philip's Episcopal Church," http://www.nycago.org/organs/nyc/html/StPhilip Epis.html, accessed April 19, 2013.
63. Dorothy Boulding Ferebee Jr. Death Announcement, Beinecke Rare Book and Manuscript Library, Yale University, Walter Francis White and Poppy Cannon White Papers, JWJ MSS 38, Series 1, Box 2, Folder 60.
64. "Bury Daughter of NCNW Prexy"; Aurelia Roberts Brooks interview with the author; "Weather: Summary," *New York Herald Tribune,* February 11, 1950.
65. "Bury Daughter of NCNW Prexy."
66. John Russell Eberhardt III interview with the author.
67. Single Grave Certificate No. 12137, Mount Hope Cemetery Association, Claude Ferebee, February 10, 1950; Deed No. 7347, Mount Hope Cemetery Association Deed Register, Dr. Claude T. Ferebee, August 18, 1952, courtesy of Mount Hope Cemetery Association.
68. Unnamed assistant principal, NMH, letter to Ferebee, February 14, 1950, courtesy of NMH.
69. "In Memoriam: Miss Dorothy B. Ferebee, 1931–1950," 1950 *du Lac,* n.p.
70. Mary McLeod Bethune telegram to Ferebee and Claude Ferebee, February 9, 1950, NPS, NABWH, Records of the NCNW, Series 6, Box 1, Folder 1.
71. Mary McLeod Bethune letter to Ferebee, March 9, 1950, NPS, NABWH, Records of the NCNW, Series 6 Box 1, Folder 2.

72. Aurelia Roberts Brooks interview with the author.

73. Nancy Schreiber email, June 28, 2013.

74. All the Paul Schreiber marriages are found in the California Marriage Index, 1960–85, www.ancestry.com, accessed June 18, 2013; divorce between Schreiber and his third wife from, California Divorce Index, 1966–84, www.ancestry.com, accessed June 18, 2013.

75. California Marriage Index, 1960–85, www.ancestry.com, accessed June 18, 2013.

76. "Obituary: N. Paul Schreiber."

77. Ferebee letter to officers of the NCNW, March 1, 1950, NPS, NABWH, Records of the NCNW, Series 6, Box 1, Folder 1.

78. Executive Committee Meeting of the NCNW, March 11, 1950, NPS, NABWH, Records of the NCNW, Series 3, Box 1, Folder 28.

17. AS GOOD AS I COULD

1. William E. Nelson, *Legalist Reformation: Law, Politics, and Ideology in New York, 1920–1980* (Chapel Hill: University of North Carolina Press, 2001), 233.

2. *Constitution and By-Laws: North Harlem Dental Society*, New York City, October 1952, 14, courtesy of James Weldon Johnson Memorial Collection of Negro Arts & Letters, Yale University Library.

3. Todd Boulding Ferebee interview with the author.

4. *Dorothy B. Ferebee v. Claude T. Ferebee*, Complaint for Divorce, No. 6605, May 25, 1950, City Court of Calumet City, Cook County IL.

5. *Dorothy B. Ferebee v. Claude T. Ferebee*, No. 6605, Claude T. Ferebee, Appearance *Pro Se*, May 31, 1950, City Court of Calumet City, Cook County IL.

6. Carlyn Kolker and Patricia Hurtado, "Divorce Easier as New York Law Ends Need to Lie," *Bloomberg News*, August 16, 2010, http://www.bloomberg.com/news/2010-08-16/breaking-up-not-so-hard-to-do-as-new-york-s-divorce-law-ends-need-to-lie.html, accessed December 15, 2013.

7. *Dorothy B. Ferebee v. Claude T. Ferebee*, Complaint for Divorce.

8. Claude T. Ferebee, Answer to the Complaint for Divorce, *Dorothy B. Ferebee v. Claude T. Ferebee*, No. 6605, City Court of Calumet City, Cook County IL.

9. *Dorothy B. Ferebee v. Claude T. Ferebee*, No. 6605, Bill for Divorce, Certificate of Evidence, Transcript of the Inquest of Dorothy B. Ferebee, June 6, 1950, City Court of the City of Calumet, Cook County IL.

10. *Dorothy B. Ferebee v. Claude T. Ferebee*, No. 6605, Signed "Agreement," City Court of the City of Calumet, Cook County IL.

11. *Dorothy B. Ferebee v. Claude T. Ferebee*, No. 6605, Decree for Divorce, June 20, 1950, City Court of the City of Calumet, Cook County IL.

12. Kenneth A. Osgood, "Hearts and Minds: The Unconventional Cold War," *Journal of Cold War Studies* 4.2 (2002): 93; Mark Landler, "Diplomatic Memo: As U.S.

Looks to Nuclear Deal, Book Faults Handling of Iranian Defector," *New York Times*, May 19, 2014.

13. Phyllis Battelle, "Those United States," *Stars and Stripes*, September 17, 1950.

14. "End 20-Year Marriage: Wedding Bares Ferebee Split: Social Circles Buzz over Well-Kept Secret," Baltimore *Afro-American*, June 30, 1951.

15. Carol Sylvia Phillips, Certificate of Birth No. 347779, Health Department, District of Columbia.

16. "Dr. Phillips, Physician for Half Century," *Washington Post*, September 12, 1957.

17. Revella Clay, "Roving with Revella," unnamed newspaper clipping, n.d., courtesy of Dorothy Ruth Ferebee.

18. "Carol Sylvia Phillips," 1949 *Liber Anni*, Dunbar High School, Washington DC, 47, courtesy of Charles Sumner School Museum and Archives, Washington DC.

19. Carol Sylvia Phillips Ferebee, Application for Federal Employment, May 26, 1951, and November 15, 1951; Carol P. Ferebee, Notification of Personnel Action, December 13, 1951; Carol P. Ferebee, Notification of Personnel Action, December 31, 1952, NARA, National Civilian Personnel Records, St. Louis MO, FOIA request by the author.

20. Margo Dean Pinson interview with the author.

21. Vaughn Phillips interview with the author.

22. Vaughn Phillips interview with the author.

23. "First Lady Biography: Mary Lincoln," http://www.firstladies.org/biographies/firstladies.aspx?biography=17, accessed December 18, 2013.

24. Vaughn Phillips' interview with the author; John C. Vaughn Todd, Certificate of Death No. 56-3542, District of Columbia, Department of Health.

25. "Walter F. Phillips, District of Columbia Marriages, 1811–1950," District of Columbia Marriages 1811–1950, index and images, Family Search, https://familysearch.org/ark:/61903/1:1:VNTH-9-Ql, accessed January 6, 2015, citing District of Columbia Records Office, Washington DC, FHL microfilm 2,399,058.

26. Vaughn Phillips interview with the author.

27. 1920 U.S. Census, "Carrie E. Phillips," www.ancestry.com, accessed January 15, 2014.

28. "Dr. Phillips, Physician for Half Century."

29. Margo Dean Pinson interview with the author.

30. Vaughn Phillips interview with the author.

31. Claude Thurston Ferebee Jr. [*sic*] and Carol Sylvia Phillips, Marriage License No. 361028, District of Columbia Archives; "The Weather in the Nation," *New York Times*, November 2, 1951.

32. Claude Thurston Ferebee Jr. [*sic*] and Carol Sylvia Phillips, Marriage License.

33. "Newlywed Thurston Ferebees Honorees at Wedding Reception," Baltimore *Afro-American*, December 22, 1951.

34. "Newlywed Thurston Ferebees Honorees at Wedding Reception."

35. "Ferebee-Hardy Vows Spoken on June 10th," (Norfolk) *New Journal and Guide*, June 30, 1951.

36. "End 20-Year Marriage."

37. 1930 U.S. Census (Hazel Jones), www.ancestry.com, accessed June 9, 2012; 1920 U.S. Census (Hazel Jones), www.ancestry.com, accessed June 9, 2012.

38. Arnold de Mille, "Along Celebrity Row," *Chicago Defender*, June 23, 1951.

39. Dorothy Ruth Ferebee interview with the author.

40. Sondra Kathryn Wilson, *Meet Me at the Theresa: The Story of Harlem's Most Famous Hotel* (New York: Atria Books, 2004), 239.

41. "Ferebee Weds Hazel Hardy," *New York Amsterdam News*, June 16, 1951.

42. "Hazel Irene Jones," *Howard University Alumni Directory, 1867–2005* (Chesapeake VA: Harris Connect, 2005), 156, 265.

43. "May Festival Lends Festive Air to Campus," 13 *Hilltop*, June 5, 1936.

44. Howard University Annual Catalogue, 1935–36, 409–11.

45. Archie Seale, "Around Harlem with Archie Seale: This Town of Ours," *New York Amsterdam News*, April 3, 1937.

46. Julius J. Adams, "Reveals Details of Harlem Leaders $6000 Job Dinner: Hunt Guest Who Talked to Sampson; Diners Agreed Clubs Needed Money; Sought Same from Candidates," *New York Amsterdam News*, January 31, 1948.

47. T.E.B., "Chatter and Chimes: Questions on Juicy Topics," *New York Amsterdam News*, June 15, 1940; "312 Manhattan Avenue," http://www.emporis.com/building/312-manhattan-avenue-new-york-city-ny-usa, accessed January 9, 2014.

48. T.E.B., "Chatter and Chimes."

49. "The Social Swirl," *New York Amsterdam News*, September 20, 1947; Wilson, *Meet Me at the Theresa*, 158.

50. "Ephemeral New York: The Most Elite Apartment Building in Harlem," http://www.ephemeralnewyork.wordpress.com/2013/05/15/the-most-elite-apartment-building-in-harlem/, accessed January 12, 2014; Claude Thurston Ferebee–Hazel Jones Hardy, Certificate of Marriage, No. 14503, June 10, 1951, Commonwealth of Virginia Department of Health, Division of Vital Records.

51. "A Walk about Harlem's Historic Sugar Hill," http://www.sugarhillmap.com/about.asp, accessed January 12, 2014.

52. Claude Thurston Ferebee–Hazel Jones Hardy, Certificate of Marriage.

53. "Ferebee-Hardy Vows Spoken on June 10th."

54. de Mille, "Along Celebrity Row."

55. Lisa Ferebee email to the author, July 14, 2011.

56. Todd Boulding Ferebee interview with the author.

57. Claude Thurston Ferebee videotaped interview with Claude Thurston Ferebee III, January 20, 1986, courtesy of Lisa Ferebee.

58. Jacqueline Trescott, "Making a Practice of Persistence: Dorothy Ferebee, the Elegant Doctor with a Social Conscience," *Washington Post*, May 5, 1978.

59. Invitation to NCNW Outstanding Women of the Year Event, June 10, 1951, NPS, NABWH, Records of the NCNW, Series 7, Box 7, Folder 14.

60. "A Memorable Evening," *Telefact*, May–June 1951, 1, NPS, NABWH, Records of the NCNW, Series 13, Box 2, Folder 37.

18. YOU WERE GRAND AS EVER

1. "AFRO Columnist to Speak at Bennett," (Baltimore) *Afro-American*, March 25, 1950.

2. "Alpha Kappa Alpha Sorority Holds 19th North Atlantic Regional Conference in New York City: 194 Delegates at 19th AKA's North Atlantic Regional Meet," (Baltimore) *Afro-American*, April 29, 1950.

3. Tomi Ayers, "West Coast Roundup: About People and Places," *Chicago Defender*, May 13, 1950.

4. Jessie Mae Brown, "Your Social Chronicler," *Los Angeles Sentinel*, June 1, 1950.

5. Toki Schalk Johnson, "Toki Types: Dorothy Ferebee Scores . . . ," *Pittsburgh Courier*, November 18, 1950.

6. White Pages Directory, Washington DC, November 1951, "Ferebee, Dorothy Boulding, MD," 340.

7. White Pages Directory, Washington DC, September 1958, "Ferebee, Dorothy Boulding, MD," 368.

8. Lisa Ferebee email to the author, January 25, 2014.

9. Jeanetta Welch Brown letter to Vivian Carter Mason, February 15, 1950, NPS, NABWH, Records of the NCNW, Series 6, Box 1, Folder 1.

10. Action Taken at Executive Board Meeting NCNW, November 15, 1950, 3, NPS, NABWH, Records of the NCNW, Series 3, Folder 5.

11. Minutes of Executive Board Meeting, NCNW, November 15, 1950, 1, NPS, NABWH, Records of the NCNW, Series 3, Folder 5.

12. Jeanetta Welch Brown letter to Vivian Carter Mason, February 15, 1950.

13. "Random Notes," *Chicago Defender*, May 5, 1951.

14. "Inside VOA: Our People, Programs & Events," http://www.insidevoa.com/info/about_us/1673.html, accessed April 5, 2014.

15. "The Time Is Right Now," *Chicago Defender*, July 29, 1950.

16. Minutes of Board of Directors Meeting, National Council of Negro Women, November 19, 1950, 2, NPS, NABWH, Records of the NCNW, Series 3, Folder 5.

17. Arenia Mallory letter to Ferebee, December 20, 1950, NPS, NABWH, Records of the NCNW, Series 6, Box 1, Folder 6.

18. Arenia Mallory letter to Ferebee, October 12, 1951, NPS, NABWH, Records of the NCNW, Series 6, Folder 11.

19. Ida Louise Jackson letter to Ferebee, March 12, 1951, MSRC-HU, Ferebee Papers, Box 183-5, Folder 18.

20. Ferebee letter to Arenia Mallory, October 12, 1950, NPS, NABWH, Records of the NCNW, Series 6, Box 1, Folder 6.

21. "Is the Nat'l Council of Negro Women Folding?," (Cleveland OH) *Call and Post*, December 2, 1950; unsigned letter (probably Arabella Denniston) to Bethune, September 27, 1951.

22. Aileen S. Miles, "Hand of Friendship," in *Information Bulletin of the Office of the U.S. High Commissioner for Germany*, July 1951, 1–8; "President of Council of Women Sails for Greece," *Atlanta Daily World*, March 23, 1951.

23. Baggage ticket, Dr. Dorothy B. Ferebee, Cunard White Star, March 20, 1951, courtesy of Dorothy Ruth Ferebee.

24. Theodore M. Brown and Elizabeth Fee, "Paul B. Cornely (1906–2002): Civil Rights Leader and Public Health Pioneer," *American Journal of Public Health*, Supp. 1, 101 (December 2011): 164.

25. Ferebee Oral History, 24–25.

26. Ruth Scott letter to Mary McLeod Bethune, February 13, 1951, LOC-MS Division, Mary McLeod Bethune Papers, Part 2: Correspondence Files 1914–55, Reel 10:0323.

27. Mary McLeod Bethune letter to Ruth Scott, April 9, 1951, LOC-MS Division, Mary McLeod Bethune Papers, Part 2: Correspondence Files 1914–55, Reel 10: 0325–26.

28. Invitation to Ferebee Bon Voyage Party, NPS, NABWH, Records of the NCNW, Series 6, Box 1, Folder 8.

29. "NCNW Honors Prexy with 'Bon Voyage' Fete," *Atlanta Daily World*, March 16, 1951.

30. Mary McLeod Bethune letter to Ruth Scott, April 9, 1951.

31. Ferebee Annual Message, Minutes of NCNW Annual Convention, October 25–27, 1951, 5, NPS, NABWH, Records of the NCNW, Series 2, Folder 58.

32. "Honor President of National Council of Negro Women . . . ," *New York Amsterdam News*, March 17, 1951; invitation to Bon Voyage Party.

33. Dorothy Ferebee, "Echoes from Our President Abroad," *Telefact* 9.3 (1951): 3, NABWH, NCNW Collection, Series 13, Box 2, Folder 34.

34. "Dr. Ferebee Attends Meet for Women in Greece," *Atlanta Daily World*, April 6, 1951.

35. Resolutions Adopted by the International Council of Women at Triennial Meeting, Athens, March–April 1951, NPS, NABWH, Records of the NCNW, Series 6, Box 1, Folder 9.

36. Cliff Mackay, "The Week's News in Tabloid . . . Personalities in the News," Baltimore *Afro-American*, March 17, 1951.

37. Ferebee letter to Jeanetta Welch Brown, May 9, 1951, NPS, NABWH, Records of the NCNW, Series 6, Box 1, Folder 9.
38. Jeanetta Welch Brown letter to Ferebee, May 1, 1951, NPS, NABWH, Records of the NCNW, Series 6, Box 1, Folder 9; Marion H. Jackson, for the Executive Board, letter to Ada B. Jackson, April 24, 1951, NPS, NABWH, Records of the NCNW, Series 6, Box 1, Folder 8; U.S. House of Representatives, Committee on Un-American Activities, 82nd Cong., 1st Sess., Report on the Communist "Peace" Offensive: A Campaign to Disarm and Defeat the United States, April 1, 1951.
39. Jeanetta Welch Brown letter to Ferebee, May 1, 1951.
40. Jeanetta Welch Brown letter to Ferebee, May 1, 1951.
41. "Executive Committee Meets at Council House," *Telefact* 9.3 (1951): 1, NABWH, NCNW Collection, Series 13, Box 2, Folder 34.
42. Marion H. Jackson for the Executive Board, NCNW, letter to Vivian Carter Mason, April 23, 1951, NPS, NABWH, Records of the NCNW, Series 6, Box 1, Folder 8. Marion H. Jackson for the Executive Board, NCNW, letter to Ada B. Jackson, April 24, 1951.
43. Jeanetta Welch Brown letter to Ferebee, May 1, 1951.
44. Jeanetta Welch Brown letter to Ferebee, May 1, 1951.
45. Minutes of the Executive Committee Meeting, June 9, 1951, NPS, NABWH, Records of the NCNW, Series 3, Box 1, Folder 29.
46. Testimony of Dorothy Ferebee, Executive Sessions of the Senate Permanent Subcommittee on Investigations of the Committee on Government Operations, vol. 2, 1st Sess., 83rd Cong., 1953 (made public January 2003), 1291, 1299–300.
47. Testimony of Dorothy Ferebee, 1299–302.
48. Testimony of Dorothy Ferebee, 1299–303.
49. Todd Boulding Ferebee interview with the author.
50. Ferebee letter to President Harry S. Truman, July 19, 1951, Official File, Truman Papers, Harry S. Truman Presidential Library and Museum, Independence MO.
51. Matthew J. Connelly letter to Ferebee (addressed "My dear Miss Ferebee"), July 24, 1951, Official File, Truman Papers, Harry S. Truman Presidential Library and Museum.
52. Ferebee letter to council presidents, outlining "Nine-Point Program of the National Council of Negro Women," January 23, 1950, NPS, NABWH, Records of the NCNW, Series 6, Box 1, Folder 1.
53. "White House Conference on Children and Youth Held in Washington, DC," *Telefact* 8.12 (1950): 2; NPS, NABWH, Records of the NCNW, Series 13, Box 2, Folder 36.
54. Prepared Testimony of Dorothy Boulding Ferebee before Senate Rules Committee, October 18, 1951, NABWH, NCNW Collection, Series 2, Folder 60.
55. Prepared Testimony of Dorothy Boulding Ferebee before Senate Rules Committee, October 18, 1951.

56. Dorothy Ferebee Testimony prepared for the Senate Subcommittee on Health of the Senate Committee on Labor and Public Welfare, March 13, 1952, MSRC-HU, Ferebee Papers, Box 183-10, Folder 19; "National Council of Negro Women . . . 'Strengthening the Forces of Freedom: Statement by Dr. Dorothy B. Ferebee . . . ," *Atlanta Daily World*, April 10, 1952.

57. Dorothy Ferebee, "Women Looking Forward," column, written September 20, 1950, NPS, NABWH, Records of the NCNW, Series 7, Box 14, Folder 8.

58. Ferebee telegram to President Harry Truman, December 31, 1951, NPS, NABWH, Records of the NCNW, Series 6, Folder 12.

59. Ferebee letter to "Executive Committee Member," March 14, 1950, NPS, NABWH, Records of the NCNW, Series 6, Box 1, Folder 2.

60. Ferebee letter to "Executive Committee Member," March 14, 1950.

61. "National Council of Negro Women to Conduct Mid-century Register of Women," *Telefact* 8.2–3 (1950): 1.

62. Margaret Truman letter to Jeanetta Welch Brown, December 6, 1950, NPS, NABWH, Records of the NCNW, Series 6, Box 1, Folder 6.

63. "You Are Invited to Attend," *Telefact* 9.2 (1951): 7, NPS, NABWH, Records of the NCNW, Series 13, Box 2, Folder 37; "Caribbean Cruise," *Telefact*, May–June 1952, NPS, NABWH, Records of the NCNW, Series 13, Box 2, Folder 38; Arabella Denniston letter to Mary McLeod Bethune, August 12, 1952, LOC-MS Division, Mary McLeod Bethune Papers, Part 2: Correspondence Files 1914–55, Reel 3:0796.

64. "Barkley, Alben William (1877–1956)," http://www.bioguide.congress.gov/scripts /biodisplay.pl?index=b000145, accessed January 25, 2015; "Alben Barkley with His Wife Jane Rucker Hadley," http://www.corbisimages.com/stock-photo/rights-man aged/u11282811iNP/alben-barkley-with-his-wife-jane-rucker, accessed March 3, 2014.

65. Mary McLeod Bethune letter to Ruth Scott, April 9, 1951, LOC-MS Division, Mary McLeod Bethune Papers: Part 2: Correspondence Files, 1914–55, Reel 10:0326.

66. Adam Clayton Powell Jr. draft letter to "Dear Friend," April 24, 1951, NPS, NABWH, Records of the NCNW, Series 7, Box 14, Folder 5.

67. Karen Chilton, *Hazel Scott: The Pioneering Journey of a Jazz Pianist from Café Society to Hollywood to HUAC* (Ann Arbor: University of Michigan Press, 2008), 49, 52, 62, 68, 72, 140–41.

68. Chilton, *Hazel Scott*, 143–48.

69. "Josephine Baker Biography," Biography Channel, http://www.biography.com /people/Josephine-baker-9195959?, accessed March 11, 2014.

70. Alice A. Dunnigan, "DC Soda Fountain Manager Refuses to Serve Josephine Baker: Manager Says Segregation Policy Will Be Practiced as Long as It Was the Social Pattern in DC," *Kansas City Plain Dealer*, July 13, 1951.

71. Jeanetta Welch Brown letter to Ferebee and attached "Report of the Josephine Baker Concert," July 8, 1951, 1, to Ferebee, NPS, NABWH, Records of the NCNW, Series 7, Box 1, Folder 9.

72. Contract between Sam Schulyer, manager for Josephine Baker, and the NCNW, June 8, 1951, NPS, NABWH, Records of the NCNW, Series 7, Box 1, Folder 9.

73. Adam Clayton Powell Jr. draft letter to "My Dear Friend," April 24, 1951.

74. "Report of the Josephine Baker Concert," 2–3.

75. Ferebee letter to President Truman, June 22, 1951, NPS, NABWH, Records of the NCNW, Series 7, Box 1, Folder 9.

76. Ferebee letter to Maj. Robert Barrett, DC Metropolitan Police Department, June 25, 1951, NPS, NABWH, Records of the NCNW, Series 7, Box 1, Folder 9.

77. Memo re: "Reception for Josephine Baker, Order of the Day," NPS, NABWH, Records of the NCNW, Series 7, Box 1, Folder 9.

78. "Josephine Baker Wardrobe Envy of All Women: Affair at Armory Monday Night Expected to Be a Sellout," *Washington Gaily News*, June 30, 1951.

79. "Jo Baker Coming Here on July 2," Baltimore *Afro-American*, June 23, 1951.

80. "At the Armory: Josie Baker Glamorizes Cement Barn," *Washington Post*, July 3, 1951.

81. Arabella Denniston letter to Mary McLeod Bethune, September 15, 1951, LOC-MS Division, Mary McLeod Bethune Papers, Part 2: Correspondence Files 1914–955, Reel 3:0777–78.

82. Arabella Denniston letter to Mary McLeod Bethune, May 5, 1952, LOC-MS Division, Mary McLeod Bethune Papers, Part 2: Correspondence Files 1914–55, Reel 3:0789–90.

83. Minutes of the NCNW Annual Convention, 9.

84. Handwritten tally of votes at the NCNW 1951 Annual Convention, NPS, NABWH, Records of the NCNW, Series 2, Folder 62.

85. A series of letters from Ferebee to these colleges and/or their responses, all written during the summer of 1951, are on file at MSRC-HU, Ferebee Papers, Box 183-7, Folder 2.

86. "American Women Praise Germany," *Reno Evening Gazette*, December 11, 1952.

87. Ferebee recipe, "New England Suet Pudding & Hard Sauce," in *Historical Cookbook of the American Negro* (Washington DC: National Council of Negro Women, 1958), 133, NPS, NABWH, Records of the NCNW, Series 13, Box 1, Folder 2.

88. Arabella Denniston letter to Mary McLeod Bethune, February 21, 1952, Library of Congress, Mary McLeod Bethune Papers, Part 2: Correspondence Files 1914–55, Reel 3:0785–86.

89. Reading glasses prescription for Ferebee, September 9, 1929, courtesy of Dorothy Ruth Ferebee.

90. Hazel Garland, "NCNW Slates First Biennial Meeting: New Officers Will Be Elected Nov. 12 to 14," *Pittsburgh Courier*, November 7, 1953.

91. Arabella Denniston letter to Mary McLeod Bethune, January 26, 1953; LOC-MS Division, Mary McLeod Bethune Papers, Part 2: Correspondence Files 1914–55, Reel 3:0814–15.

92. Ferebee letter to President Dwight D. Eisenhower, October 14, 1953, NPS, NABWH, Records of the NCNW, Series 2, Folder 63.

93. Hazel Garland, "Vivian Carter Mason NCNW President: Former Vice Prexy Elected in Close Race," *Pittsburgh Courier*, November 21, 1953; Ferebee memo to National Officers, National Committee Chairmen, Heads of Affiliate Organizations, Local Council Presidents and Junior Council Presidents, October 22, 1953, NPS, NABWH, Records of the NCNW, Series 2, Folder 63.

94. Arabella Denniston letter to Mary McLeod Bethune, January 26, 1953.

95. Robert M. Ratcliffe, "Behind the Headlines: Turkey and Stuffings . . . ," *Pittsburgh Courier*, November 28, 1953.

96. Ratcliffe, "Behind the Headlines,"

97. Vivian Carter Mason letter to Ferebee, November 25, 1953, NABWH, NCNW Collection, Section 6, Folder 18; "A Brief History of the Edward S. Harkness Eye Institute," http://www.columbiaeye.org/about-us/the-harkness-s-eye-institute, accessed March 17, 2014.

19. A BAD BITTER PILL

1. Diane McWhorter, *Carry Me Home: Birmingham, Alabama. The Climactic Battle of the Civil Rights Revolution* (New York: Simon & Schuster/Touchstone, 2002), 94, 113.

2. Claude Thurston Ferebee II Military Records, NARA. National Military Personnel Records Center, St. Louis MO, FOIA request by the author.

3. Ruth Scott letter to Mary McLeod Bethune, undated, LOC-MS Division, Mary McLeod Bethune Papers, Part 2: Correspondence Files 1914–55, Reel 10:0391.

4. Gwendolyn M. Floyd, "Right around Us," *Arkansas State Press*, May 16, 1952.

5. Dorothy Ferebee, "Women's Role, and Her Responsibility to Herself, Her Home and Her Community," speech prepared for the annual dinner meeting at the Fort Wayne IN, YWCA, February 10, 1961, Ferebee Papers, MSRC-HU, Box 183-9.

6. Meeting of the National Board of the YWCA, October 10–15, 1960, Sophia Smith Collection, Smith College, Northampton MA, YWCA of the U.S.A. Records, 1860–2002 MS 324, Reel 7.

7. "Full Schedule Set for Y.W.C.A. Week," *New York Times*, April 20, 1961; "YWCA Will Honor Dr. D. B. Ferebee," (Worchester MA) *Evening Gazette*, May 27, 1970.

8. White House press release, January 10, 1962, John F. Kennedy Presidential Library and Museum, Boston, Departments and Agencies, President's Official Files, JFKPOF-079-001.

9. "Kennedy Names Group to Fight World Hunger," *Boston Globe*, May 7, 1961; George McGovern memo to President Kennedy, February 11, 1961, John F. Kennedy

Presidential Library and Museum, Departments and Agencies, Food for Peace Project, 1961, President's Office Files, JFKPOF-078-026.

10. Thomasina W. Norford, "The Women Meet with President," *New York Amsterdam News*, July 20, 1963.

11. Charles A. Horsky memorandum for the President, July 9, 1963, "Notes for Meeting with Women at 4:00 p.m., July 9, 1963," John F. Kennedy Presidential Library and Museum, Civil Rights: General, July 1963: 9–14, Series 8, President's Office Files, JFKPOF 097-005.

12. Meeting with Representatives of Women's Organizations to Discuss Civil Rights, John F. Kennedy Presidential Library and Museum, White House Photos, Robert Knudsen, JFKWHP-1963-07-09-B.

13. L. B. Nichols memorandum to Mr. Tolson, "Mrs. W. T. Mason National Council of Negro Women," February 20, 1956, FBI File No. 100-348501-30, FOIA request by the author.

14. M. A. Jones memorandum to Mr. Nichols, "National Council of Negro Women, Inc. Representatives to See the Director February 28, 1956," February 27, 1956, FBI File No. 100-347501-33.

15. M. A. Jones memorandum to Mr. Nichols, "Mrs. W. T. Mason National Council of Negro Women, Inc. (NCNW), February 17, 1956, FBI File No. 100-348501-20/19.

16. L. B. Nichols memorandum to Mr. Tolson [untitled], February 29, 1956, FBI File No. 100-348501.

17. Ethel Payne, "Dorothy Height New NCNW Head," *Chicago Daily Defender*, November 12, 1957.

18. "Getting Personal: Personal and Pleasant," (Cleveland OH) *Call and Post*, March 1, 1958.

19. "NCNW Presented 'Historic Pen,'" *Atlanta Daily World*, July 31, 1958.

20. Constitution of the National Council of Negro Women, Inc., November 9, 1966, NPS, NABWH, Records of the NCNW, Series 1, Box 1, Folder 3.

21. Elaine H. Smith, "Historic Resource Study: Mary McLeod Bethune and the National Council of Negro Women, Pursuing a True and Unfettered Democracy," Report for the Mary McLeod Bethune Council House National Historic Site, September 2003, 289.

22. Payne, "Dorothy Height New NCNW Head"; Margalit Fox, "Dorothy Height, Largely Unsung Giant of Civil Rights Era, Dies at 98," *New York Times*, April 20, 2010.

23. U.S. Internal Revenue Service Form 990, 2008 Tax Return of Organization Exempt from Income Tax, National Council of Negro Women, October 1, 2008–September 30, 2009, 7.

24. IRS Form 990, 2008 NCNW Tax Return, 1.

25. Susan Goodwillie Stedman interview with the author.

26. Fox, "Dorothy Height, Largely Unsung Giant of Civil Rights Era."

27. Joyce A. Hanson, *Mary McLeod Bethune and Black Women's Political Activism* (Columbia: University of Missouri Press, 2003), 1.

28. Harry McAlpin, "50 Negro Leaders at FDR Inaugural," *Chicago Defender*, January 27, 1945; Fox, "Dorothy Height, Largely Unsung Giant of Civil Rights Era."

29. Bio, "Patricia Roberts Harris Biography (1924–1985)," http://www.biography .com/people/patricia-roberts-harris-205630, accessed February 10, 2014.

30. "Obama Breaks Down in Tears at Funeral of 'Godmother' of American Civil Rights Movement, Dorothy Height," *Mail Online*, April 30, 2010, http://www .dailymail.co.uk/news/article-1269836/Obamas-tears-Dorothy-Heights-funeral-washington.html, accessed February 1, 2014; Julie Pace, "Dorothy Height's Funeral: Obama Honors 'Godmother' of Civil Rights Movement," *Huffington Post*, April 29, 2010, http://www.huffingtonpost.com/2010/04/29/dorothy-height-funeral-ob_n_556747.html, accessed February 1, 2014.

31. Pace, "Dorothy Height's Funeral."

32. Susan Goodwillie Stedman interview with the author.

33. McWhorter, *Carry Me Home*, 561.

34. McWhorter, *Carry Me Home*, 238.

35. Polly Cowan Oral History Interview with Dorothy Height, March 28, 1975, National Park Service, Mary McLeod Bethune Council House NHS, National Archives for Black Women's History, Polly Spiegel Cowan Papers, Series 6, Folder 13, Side 1.

36. Susan Goodwillie Stedman interview with the author.

37. Polly Cowan interview with Dorothy Height.

38. Debbie Z. Harwell, "Wednesdays in Mississippi: Uniting Women across Regional and Racial Lines, Summer 1964," *Journal of Southern History* 76.3 (2010): 624.

39. Dorothy Height, *Open Wide the Freedom Gates: A Memoir* (New York: Public Affairs, 2003), 157.

40. Douglas Martin, "James Forman Dies at 76: Was Pioneer in Civil Rights," *New York Times*, January 12, 2005.

41. McWhorter, *Carry Me Home*, 489.

42. PBS, "Prathia Hall," *This Far by Faith*, http://www.pbs.org/thisfarbyfaith/people /prathia_hall.html, accessed February 3, 2014; Something Within: For Thinking Women of Faith, "Remembering Prathia (1940–2002)," http://www.something within.com/blog/?p=312, accessed February 10, 2014.

43. Bruce Gordon, "Field Report," Selma, Alabama, November 9, 1963, 1, James Forman Papers, LOC-MS Division, Box 22, Folder 8.

44. Colia Lafayette "Field Report," April 5, 1963, LOC-MS Division, James Forman Papers, Box 22, Folder 7.

45. Colia LaFayette, "Field Report."

46. Polly Cowan interview with Dorothy Height, Side 2.

47. Margalit Fox, "Jim Clark, Sheriff Who Enforced Segregation, Dies at 84," *New York Times*, June 7, 2007.

48. Fox, "Jim Clark"; Height, *Open Wide the Freedom Gates*, 157.

49. Polly Cowan, unpublished memoir, chapter 1, p. 15, n.d., NPS-NABWH, Polly Spiegel Cowan Papers, Series 1, Box 1, Folder 8.

50. Through a Freedom of Information Act request to the FBI filed by the author in May 2011, the bureau released documents (File No. 157-HQ-6-61) relating to the October 1963 SNCC voter registration campaign in Selma.

51. "Racial Situation, State of Alabama, Selma, Alabama," FBI Memorandum, Mobile AL, October 1, 1963, 5, 157-HQ-6-61, Section 5.

52. "Leaders Urge Big Turnout in Selma," *Birmingham News*, October 6, 1963; Special Agent in Charge, Mobile AL, teletype to Director, FBI, October 4, 1963, 157-HQ-6-61, Section 5.

53. "Leaders Urge Big Turnout in Selma."

54. Harwell, "Wednesdays in Mississippi," 624–25; Special Agent in charge, Mobile AL, teletype to Director, October 4, 1963, 157-HQ-6-61, Section 5; Polly Cowan interview with Dorothy Height, Sides 1 and 2.

55. Cowan, unpublished memoir, chapter 1, p. 12.

56. "Leaders Urge Big Turnout in Selma"; "Foreman [*sic*] Demands Release of Dick Gregory's Wife," *Atlanta Daily World*, October 6, 1963.

57. Harwell, "Wednesdays in Mississippi," 624; Cowan, unpublished memoir, chapter 1, p. 12.

58. Cowan, unpublished memoir, chapter 1, p. 12.

59. Height, *Open Wide the Freedom Gates*, 158.

60. Special Agent in Charge, Mobile AL, teletype to Director, FBI, October 4, 1963.

61. Cowan, unpublished memoir, chapter 1, pp. 13, 20.

62. Cowan, unpublished memoir, chapter 1, p. 13.

63. Cowan, unpublished memoir, chapter 1, p. 16.

64. "Weather Reports throughout the Nation," *New York Times*, October 5, 1963.

65. Special Agent in Charge, Mobile AL, teletype to Director, FBI, October 5, 1963, 157-HQ-6-61, Section 5.

66. Megan McShea, Hannah Rosen, and Wendy Shay, "Overview of the Moses Moon Collection, 1963–64," Moses Moon Audiotapes Collection, Archives Center, Smithsonian Institution, National Museum of American History, AC0556; Judy Collins, *Suite Judy Blue Eyes: My Life in Music* (New York: Crown Archetype, 2011), 66.

67. James Forman, First Baptist Church, Selma AL, October 4, 1963, Moses Moon Audiotapes Collection, Archives Center, Smithsonian Institution, National Museum of American History, AC0556, Box 9, Tape 5 SE 1.2, N47.

68. Dorothy Height, First Baptist Church, Selma AL, October 4, 1963, Moses Moon Audiotapes Collection, AC0556, Box 9, Tape 5 SE 1.2, N47.

69. Forman, Moses Moon Audiotapes Collection.

70. Dorothy Ferebee, First Baptist Church, Selma AL, October 4, 1963, Moses Moon Audiotapes Collection, AC0556, Box 9, Tape 5 SE, 1.2, N47.
71. Dick Gregory, Moses Moon Audiotapes Collection, AC0556, Box 9, Tape 5 SE 1.3, N48.
72. Forman, Moses Moon Audiotapes Collection.
73. Height, *Open Wide the Freedom Gates*, 160.
74. Polly Cowan interview with Dorothy Height, Side 2.
75. Polly Cowan interview with Dorothy Height, Side 2.
76. Height, *Open Wide the Freedom Gates*, 160.
77. Voting Rights Act, 1965, http://www.ourdocuments.gov/doc.php?flash= true&doc=100, accessed February 16, 2014.

20. A CITIZEN CONCERNED WITH INTERNATIONAL AFFAIRS
1. Mrs. Oscar M. Ruebhausen, "Report to the Annual Meeting: Women's Africa Committee," May 23, 1960, Women's Africa Committee Records, 1958–78, MS 318, Sophia Smith Collection, Smith College, Northampton MA.
2. Harriet Stix, "African Women Told How to Get Own Way," *New York Herald Tribune*, October 19, 1960.
3. "Friends of Ghana Collect Brown Dolls for Accra Kids," (Baltimore) *Afro-American*, December 9, 1961.
4. Ferebee Africa Diary, "Monrovia," July 13, 1960, MSRC-HU, Ferebee Papers, 183-2, Folder 2.
5. State Department Itinerary for Ferebee, June 20–28, 1964 (with Ferebee's notations about her clothing), MSRC-HU, Ferebee Papers, Box 183-2, Folder 4.
6. Ferebee's Africa Diary, "Ghana," July 14, 1960.
7. Ferebee Africa Diary, "Ghana." July 7, 1960.
8. Dorothy Ferebee, "Africa, the Continent of the Hour," *Simmons Review* 43.2 (1961): 28.
9. Ferebee Africa Diary, "Ghana," July 16, 1960.
10. Ferebee Africa Diary, "So. Rhodesia," Salisbury, July 7, 1960. This is an error in the diary. Dorothy was apparently there on August 7, 1960, based on other entries.
11. Ferebee, Africa Diary, "Left for Kano," August 6, 1960.
12. Statement of Dr. Dorothy Ferebee, American Association of University Women, Washington DC, Foreign Assistance Act of 1962, Senate Committee on Foreign Relations, 87th Cong., 2nd Sess., S-2996, April 5–18, 1962, 452, 454.
13. Ferebee travel schedule estimated from a collection of her speeches during that period that list the dates and locations, Ferebee Papers, MSRC-HU, Box 183-10.
14. "Mrs. Dorothy B. Ferebee," personnel folder U.S. Department of State.
15. "For State Department: She'll Doctor to Prevent Disease," *Washington Post*, April 14, 1964.

16. Florence Paige Boulding, Certificate of Death No. 59-9168, District of Columbia, Department of Health.

17. Todd Boulding Ferebee email to the author, April 11, 2014.

18. "Dr. Ferebee Is Honored," *Washington Post, Times Herald*, May 14, 1964.

19. Dorothy Ferebee, "Toward Better Health for American Personnel on Foreign Duty: Report on an Assignment in South America and Africa for the U.S. Department of State, April through August, 1964," April 1965, Part II, 2; Travel Diary, State Department Trip, May 18, 1964, MSRC-HU, Ferebee Papers, Box 183-2, Folder 4.

20. Ferebee letter to Dr. Lewis K. Woodward, April 1965, submitting "Toward Better Health" report and the report at Part I, 2 & Itinerary, n.p.

21. Dr. Harold G. Beeson letter to Dr. Carl C. Nydell, April 30, 1994, Ferebee personnel file, U.S. Department of State.

22. Ferebee, "Toward Better Health," Part I, 2–3.

23. Ferebee, "Toward Better Health," Part II, 3, Part I, "The Assignment," Part III, 1, 2–6.

24. Ferebee, "Toward Better Health," Part I, "The Assignment," "Medical Facilities Visited" [attachment to Ferebee's itinerary].

25. Simeon Booker, "From the Notebook," *Jet*, June 8, 1961, 11.

26. Booker, "From the Notebook," 11; "UN Women, World Conferences on Women: World Conference of the International Women's Year—Mexico City, (19 June to 2 July 1975)," http://www.unwomen.org/womenwatch/daw/beijing/mexico.html, accessed January 10, 2015; Trescott, "Making a Practice of Persistence."

27. Various Ferebee Travel Diaries, MSRC-HU, Ferebee Papers, Box 183-1, Folders 6–10, Box 183-2, Folders 1–6.

28. Ferebee letter to Harriet [Gordon Ellis, president Alumnae Association of Simmons College], June 16, 1959, Simmons College Archives.

29. White House Luncheon Guest List, Tuesday, October 24, 1967 at one o'clock; Bess Abell memorandum for the President, October 24, 1967, Lyndon Baines Johnson Presidential Library and Museum, Austin TX.

30. Menu, October 24, 1967, White House Luncheon, Lyndon Baines Johnson Presidential Library and Museum.

31. Matthew B. Coffey memorandum to John W. Macy Jr., August 17, 1967, "DC Council Candidates (Negroes)," Lyndon Baines Johnson Presidential Library and Museum.

32. Ferebee letter to the President, April 29, 1967, and Matthew B. Coffey memorandum to John W. Macy Jr., Lyndon Baines Johnson Presidential Library and Museum.

33. "Guest at Third White House Lunch for Doers," *Washington Post, Times Herald*, April 3, 1968.

34. "Biographical Data, Ferebee, Dorothy Boulding," August 22, 1967, Lyndon Baines Johnson Presidential Library and Museum.

35. Ferebee Bargain and Sale Deed for 114–15 176th Street, Queens NY, Office of the City Register, Queens County, Deed Book 7022:697.

36. Ferebee Oral History, 5.

37. Ferebee Application for Employment, Ferebee Personnel Folder, U.S. Department of State.

38. "Dr. Dorothy Ferebee Discusses Nations of Africa at AAUW Founders' Day Meet," *Hagerstown* [MD] *Morning Herald*, February 19, 1962.

39. Heather Munro Prescott, *Student Bodies: The Influence of Student Health Services in American Society and Medicine* (Ann Arbor: University of Michigan Press, 2007), 2–3, 83–84.

40. Deed, George M. Chandler to Dorothy Boulding Ferebee, September 2, 1957, Washington DC, Deed Book 10927:193.

41. Todd Boulding Ferebee interview with the author; Ferebee business card, MSRC-HU, Ferebee Papers, Box 183-1, Folder 1.

42. Deed of Trust, Ferebee and Bank of Columbia, No. 02296, January 19, 1979.

43. Ben W. Gilbert and the Staff of the *Washington Post, Ten Blocks from the White House: The Anatomy of the Washington Riots of 1968* (New York: Praeger, 1968), 3.

44. Dorothy Ruth Ferebee interview with the author.

45. Hampton Sides, *Hellhound on His Trail: The Stalking of Martin Luther King Jr. and the International Hunt for His Assassin* (New York: Doubleday, 2010), 208; Benjamin Shore, retired Washington correspondent for Copley Newspapers, email to the author, May 2, 2014.

46. "The City's Turmoil: The Night It Began," *Washington Post, Times Herald*, April 14, 1968.

47. Todd Boulding Ferebee email to the author, June 12, 2009.

48. Manning Marable, *Malcolm X: A Life of Reinvention* (New York: Viking Press 2011), 295.

49. Dorothy Ferebee, "Open Letter to Wilkins," *Muhammad Speaks*, November 8, 1963.

50. *Dr. Dorothy Boulding Ferebee v. Muhammad Speaks Newspaper & Samuel Hammitt*, Civil Action No. 609-64 (Washington DC, March 11, 1964).

51. *Dr. Dorothy Boulding Ferebee v. Muhammad Speaks Newspaper & Samuel Hammitt*, No. 609-64, Case Action Sheet.

52. *Dr. Dorothy Boulding Ferebee v. Muhammad Speaks Newspaper & Samuel Hammitt*, No. 609-64, Pretrial Proceedings, November 9, 1966.

53. *Dr. Dorothy Boulding Ferebee v. Muhammad Speaks Newspaper & Samuel Hammitt*, No 609-64, Verdict and Judgment of Inquisition, January 3, 1967.

54. "Dorothy Boulding Ferebee, MD," citation read by Dean K. Albert Harden at retirement ceremony, June 4, 1968, courtesy of HU Archives.

55. Bulletin of Tufts University, School of Medicine, 1968–69, 44.

56. Rachel Mack, communications coordinator, American College Health Association, email to the author, November 21, 2011; "Edgar Hitchcock Award to

Dorothy B. Ferebee, M.D.," *Journal of the American College Health Association* 20.1 (1971): 61.

57. "Dorothy (Boulding) Ferebee, '20: The First Alumnae Achievement Award Winner," *Simmons Review* 41.4 (1959): 22.

58. Letter from Harriette Gordon Ellis to Ferebee, April 11, 1959, Simmons College Archives.

59. Letter from Ferebee to Harriette Gordon Ellis, April 15, 1959, Simmons College Archives.

60. "Dorothy Ferebee, '20: The First Alumnae Achievement Award Winner," *Simmons Review*: 23.

61. "Review of the Classes," *Simmons Review* 68.4 (1986): 21n4.

62. "Simmons First Ferebee Scholars Arrive," *Simmons Now* 17.3 (1988): 1.

63. "Dorothy Boulding Ferebee, M'24, an Eminent Alumna," *Tufts Medical Alumni Bulletin* 27.1 (1968): 10–11.

64. Esther Peterson, "A Suggested Speech on the Occasion of the Appreciation Dinner Honoring Dr. Dorothy B. Ferebee," Sheraton Park Hotel, Washington DC, November 1, 1965, Schlesinger Library, Radcliffe College, Esther Peterson File MC 450, Series III, No. 787, 9; Program for Ferebee Appreciation Dinner.

65. Todd Ferebee email to the author, May 4, 2014.

66. Carolyn Lewis, "Hard Work Can Topple the Barriers," *Washington Post*, November 1, 1965.

67. J. Y. Smith, "Dr. Dorothy Ferebee Dies: Fought for Rights of Women, Blacks," *Washington Post*, September 16, 1980.

68. "Mrs. Martin Luther King, Jr.; Dr. Mildred Mitchell-Bateman; the Hon. Shirley Chisholm; Miss Elma Lewis; Dr. Dorothy B. Ferebee," *Vogue*, May 1969, 168, 173.

69. Allene Talmey, *Vogue* associate editor, letter to Ferebee, February 5, 1969, MSRC-HU, Ferebee Papers, Box 183-7, Folder 9.

70. Ferebee letter to "Miss Tally [sic]," n.d., MSRC-HU, Ferebee Papers, Box 183-7, Folder 9

21. WOMAN POWER

1. Office of Women's Policy and Initiatives, "DC Commission for Women," http://www.owpi.dc.gov/page/dc-commission-women, accessed April 28, 2014.

2. Mayor Walter E. Washington letter to Ferebee, February 29, 1968, MSRC-HU, Ferebee Papers, Box 183-7, Folder 12.

3. Mrs. Henry Gichner, chairman DC Commission on the Status of Women 1967–68, letter to Mayor Walter E. Washington, February 18, 1969, Ferebee Papers, Box 183-8, Folder 14.

4. Ferebee letter to Mayor Washington, April 24, 1969, Ferebee Papers, Box 183-7, Folder 12; National Abortion Federation, History of Abortion, https://www.prochoice.org/about_abortion/history-abortion.html, accessed May 1, 2014.

5. Ferebee letter to the editor, *Washington Post*, November 19, 1969, Ferebee Papers, Box 183-7, Folder 15.

6. Ferebee résumé, Ferebee Papers, Box 183-1, Folder 3.

7. Dorothy Ferebee, "Call for More Policewomen," letter to the editor, *Washington Post*, March 27, 1969; Dorothy Ferebee, "Equality for Women," letter to the editor, *Washington Post*, December 3, 1971.

8. Louise Lague, "District to Study Its Lost Women," (Washington DC) *Daily News*, November 2, 1971.

9. Richard Boulding letter to Ferebee, October 8, 1960, Ferebee Papers.

10. Benjamin Richard Boulding Jr., Certificate of Death, Commonwealth of Virginia, Department of Health, Division of Vital Records, No. 80-005983.

11. Ruffin Paige Boulding, Medical Examiner's Certificate of Death, North Carolina Department of Human Resources, Division of Health Services, No. 18153.

12. Julia Wyche Boulding, Certificate of Death, North Carolina State Board of Health, Office of Vital Statistics, No. 10342.

13. Kathleen McClain, "History of Mecklenburg's Black Lawyers Comes from Fascination with 'Olden Days,'" *Charlotte Observer*, April 20, 1997; Marion A. Ellis and Howard E. Covington Jr., *An Independent Profession: A Centennial History of the Mecklenburg County Bar* (Davidson NC: Lorimer Press, 2012), 78–79.

14. Ruffin Boulding letter to Richard Boulding, November 15, 1963, courtesy of Dorothy Ruth Ferebee.

15. Ruffin Boulding letter to Ferebee, August 12, 1958, courtesy of Dorothy Ruth Ferebee.

16. Carolyn Wyche Martin Wilson interview with the author.

17. Wallace McKelvey, "Egg Harbor Township's Morris Beach Community Gave Black Professionals a Resort to Call Their Own," *Press of Atlantic City.com*, February 19, 2012, www.pressofAtlanticCity.com; Atlantic County Deed Book 1098:419–21.

18. Atlantic County Deed Book 1296: 19–21; Atlantic County, Deed Book 3739:41–45.

19. Peter A. Shelton interview with the author.

20. Certificate of Sale for Unpaid Municipal Liens, No. 13-01104, Block 9308, Lot 5, Ferebee, Todd, et als. [sic], Township of Egg Harbor, County of Atlantic, December 18, 2013. Early foreclosure actions were initiated on the other lots in Morris Beach owned by the family; see *Clayton v. Todd B. Ferebee, et al.*, Dkt. No., F-005304-12, New Jersey Superior Court, Atlantic County, Chancery Division, April 3, 2012.

21. American Foreign Service Association letter to Ferebee, July 10, 1967, Ferebee Papers, Box 183-2, Folder 11.

22. Ruth Scott, Social Security Death Index, www.ancestry.com, accessed November 8, 2011.

23. Jim Nicholson, "Obituary: Teacher, Community Activist Ruth Scott," *Philadelphia Daily News*, June 27, 1985.

24. "Eighty-One Sorors Attend Fifth Annual Conference," *Chicago Defender*, June 8, 1935.
25. Ruth A. Scott, "Life's Blood in Mississippi . . . An Account of the 1940 Mississippi Health Clinic," *Ivy Leaf*, September 1940, 5; Scott, Social Security Death Index.
26. "Scouting for Black Girls Topic for Atlanta Meet," *Frederick* (MD) *News*, March 11, 1970.
27. Amy Finnerty, "Saluting a Centennial: The Girl Scouts' Success in America Merits Attention—As Does Their Founder's Colorful Life," *Wall Street Journal*, February 11–12, 2012.
28. "Racial/Ethnic Membership," GSUSA 2012 Annual Report, 10–11, courtesy Girl Scouts of the USA.
29. "Tribute to Dr. Dorothy B. Ferebee," October 23, 1980, courtesy Girl Scouts of the USA.
30. Memorandum from Mrs. Douglas H. MacNeil, President, and Miss Louise A. Wood, National Executive Director, January 8, 1970, courtesy Girl Scouts of the USA.
31. Memorandum from MacNeil and Wood, January 8, 1970.
32. Mrs. Douglas H. MacNeil, president and Louise A. Wood, national executive director, Girls Scouts of the USA draft letter to supporters, January 28, 1970, courtesy Girl Scouts of the USA.
33. Jean Tyson, "Black Girl Scouts Open Two-Day Conference Here," *Atlanta Journal*, March 13, 1970.
34. Helen J. Claytor letter to Ferebee, February 21, 1973; Ferebee letter to Mrs. Robert W. Claytor, March 5, 1973, MSRC-HU, Ferebee Papers.
35. Mayor Walter E. Washington letter to Ferebee, May 9, 1974, and Mayor Walter E. Washington letter to Ferebee, July 28, 1977, both from Ferebee Papers, Box 183-7, Folder 12.
36. Jesse Mae Brown, "Huge California Delegation Attends Unveiling of Bethune Memorial Monument," *Los Angeles Sentinel*, August 1, 1974; National Park Service, "Lincoln Park," http://www.nps.gov/cahi/historyculture/cahi_lincoln.htm, accessed May 4, 2014.
37. "Mary McLeod Bethune Memorial Dedication—July 10–12, 1974, Washington, DC," Event Flyer, NPS, NABWH, Records of the NCNW, Series 8, Box 7, Folder 6.
38. Brown, "Huge California Delegation."
39. Bethune Memorial Dedication Event Flyer; Hollie I. West, "Paying Homage," *Washington Post*, July 11, 1974.
40. Brown, "Huge California Delegation."
41. Dorothy Ruth Ferebee interview with the author.
42. Todd Boulding Ferebee email to the author, May 1, 2014.
43. Lisa Ferebee interview with the author.
44. John Beckley interview with the author.

45. Ferebee Oral History, 18.

46. Todd Boulding Ferebee interview with the author.

47. William Johnson interview with the author.

48. Ferebee handwritten notes on back of NYU acceptance letter, Ferebee Papers, Box 183-2, Folder 8; "Melvin R. Laird, Health Care and Education Legacy, a Statesman in Medicine," http://www.lairdcenter.org/melvinlaird/?page=health legacy, accessed May 7, 2014.

49. Todd Boulding Ferebee interview with the author.

50. Todd Boulding Ferebee email to the author, May 4, 2014; National Building Museum, http://www.nbm.org/about-us/about-the-museum/our-historic-building.html, accessed May 7, 2014.

51. Todd Boulding Ferebee email to the author, May 10, 2014.

52. Carol Phillips Ferebee, Personal Qualifications Statement, part of government job application, NARA, National Civil Personnel Records Center.

53. Todd Boulding Ferebee email to the author, May 4, 2014.

54. Ferebee, Claude Thurston II, New York Dental License No. 026768, January 17, 1967, NYSED.gov, Office of the Professions, Verification Searches, http://nysed.gov/coms/op001/opsc2a?profcd=50&plicno=026768&namechk=fer, accessed August 6, 2013.

55. Todd Boulding Ferebee email to the author, January 10, 2014.

56. Claude T. Ferebee II, Government of the District of Columbia Personnel Action, July 28, 1970, December 3, 1981; Serge F. Kovaleski, "Lorton's Final Lockdown: Last Inmates Leave as 91-Year-old Facility Completes a Difficult Four-Year Closure," Washingtonpost.com, http://www.washingtonpost.com/ac2/wp-dyn/a55478-2001nov19?language=printer, accessed March 20, 2012.

57. Todd Boulding Ferebee interview with the author.

58. John Beckley interview with the author.

59. William Johnson interview with the author.

60. John Russell Eberhardt III interview with the author.

61. Todd Boulding interview with the author.

62. Marion Barry interview with the author.

63. William Johnson interview with the author.

64. Charlene Drew Jarvis interview with the author.

65. Charlene Drew Jarvis interview; Margo Pinson interview with the author.

66. Joy Jones, Registrar, Tilton School, interview with the author.

67. Meg Rand, Tilton School, email to the author, April 14, 2014.

68. Todd Boulding Ferebee email to the author, April 25, 2014.

22. I SHOULD NOT BE HERE BUT I HAD TO COME

1. Barbara K. Phillips, "An Alpha Kappa Alpha Tribute to Soror Dorothy Boulding Ferebee," *Ivy Leaf*, 57.3 (Fall 1980): 4.

2. Rick Randall, "Sudden Death of Noted Health Authority after Being Honored Stuns Community," *Capitol Spotlight*, September 18, 1980.

3. Edward D. Sargent, "Youth Day for Anacostia: 'Good Vibes' All Around," *Washington Post*, September 11, 1980.

4. Phillips, "Alpha Kappa Alpha Tribute."

5. Gerry Widdicombe, "The Fall and Rise of Downtown D.C.," *Urbanist*, no. 488 (January 2010), http://www.spur.org/publications/article/2010-01-10/fall-and-rise -downtown-dc, accessed May 13, 2014.

6. Todd Boulding Ferebee interview with the author; Todd Boulding Ferebee email to the author, May 10, 2014.

7. Ferebee speech, November 12, 1979 for "Black Women: An Historical Perspective," at the First National Scholarly Research Conference on Black Women, November 12–13, 1979, Washington DC, NPS, NABWH.

8. Isabelle Shelton and Jacqueline Trescott, "First Inaugural in 100 Years," *Washington Evening Star-News*, January 4, 1974.

9. Ferebee November 12, 1979 speech.

10. Todd Boulding Ferebee interview with the author.

11. Lisa Ferebee email to the author, May 18, 2014.

12. Dorothy Ruth Ferebee email to the author, May 25, 2014.

13. Sgt. Brent Kearney interview with the author.

14. Lisa Ferebee interview with the author.

15. Todd Boulding Ferebee email to the author, May 22, 2014.

16. Lisa Ferebee email to the author, May 16, 2012.

17. Lisa Ferebee interview with the author.

18. Todd Boulding Ferebee email, May 22, 2014.

19. Todd Boulding Ferebee interview with the author; The History Makers, "Education Makers: Carl Edwin Anderson," http://www.thehistorymakers.com/biography /carl-edwin-anderson-43, accessed May 22, 2014.

20. Todd Boulding Ferebee interview with the author.

21. Todd Boulding Ferebee email to the author, May 22, 2014.

22. Dorothy Ruth Ferebee interview with the author; Lisa Ferebee interview with the author.

23. Todd Boulding Ferebee email to the author, September 15, 2008.

24. Lisa Ferebee email to the author, August 13, 2009.

25. Dorothy B. Ferebee, Certificate of Death, No. 80-006041, District of Columbia, Department of Health.

26. "The Weather," *Washington Post*, September 15, 1980.

27. Todd Boulding Ferebee email to the author, September 15, 2008.

28. Martin Schram, "President Voices Optimism, Muskie Wary on Hostages," *Washington Post*, September 16, 1980.

29. Margaret B. McK. Black letter to Aurelia R. Brooks, September 23, 1980, courtesy of Aurelia Brooks.

30. Margaret B. McK. Black letter to Aurelia R. Brooks.

31. Todd Boulding Ferebee email to the author, March 20, 2014.

32. Horace G. Dawson Jr., "The Legacy of Patricia Roberts Harris at Howard University," HUArchivesNet, May 4, 2000, http://www.huarchivesnet.howard.edu/0005huanet/harris1.htm, accessed January 7, 2015.

33. Program for Funeral Services, Dorothy Bolding [sic] Ferebee, MD, September 20, 1980, 11:00 a.m., Andrew Rankin Memorial Chapel, Howard University; Todd Boulding Ferebee email to the author, March 20, 2014.

34. Lisa Ferebee email to the author, April 8, 2014.

35. Margaret B. McK. Black letter to Aurelia R. Brooks; Todd Ferebee email to the author, March 20, 2014.

36. Margaret B. McK. Black letter to Aurelia R. Brooks.

37. Todd Boulding Ferebee interview with the author

38. Lisa Ferebee email to the author, December 12, 2008.

39. Lisa Ferebee email to the author, September 14, 2011, and interview with the author.

40. *In re: Estate of Dorothy B. Ferebee*, No. 2165-80, Superior Court of the District of Columbia, Probate Division, Order, February 13, 1981 granting Claude Thurston Ferebee II leave to resign as administrator of his mother's estate.

41. *In re: Estate of Dorothy B. Ferebee*, No. 2165-80, Petition for Letters of Administration, December 4, 1980.

42. *Pioneer Bank and Trust v. Estate of Dorothy B. Ferebee*, Civ. Action No. 7417-81, Superior Court of the District of Columbia, Civil Division, complaint, May 18, 1981.

43. Todd Boulding Ferebee email to the author, April 10, 2014.

44. Claude T. Ferebee II, Government of the District of Columbia Personnel Action, December 3, 1981.

45. "Obituary: Ferebee, Claude," *Washington Post*, October 23, 1981.

46. Todd Boulding Ferebee email to the author, May 21, 2014.

47. Andrew E. Jenkins III letter to Board of Education of the District of Columbia, "Renaming Friendship Educational Center and Washington Highland Elementary School," March 22, 1989, and Report of the Committee of the Whole of the Board of Education of the District of Columbia, June 20, 1990, 2–3, both in Charles Sumner School Museum and Archives, Washington DC, "Marion C. Hope, First Director of Southeast Neighborhood House," *Washington Post*, September 6, 1974.

48. Yolanda Woodlee, "For Barry, a Crisis around Every Corner: From Capitol Hill to Neighborhood School, Mayor Finds Trouble," *Washington Post*, February 24,

1995; DeNeen L. Brown, "Bid Renewed to Privatize DC Schools: Superintendent Wants Board to Hire Firm to Run 11 Facilities," *Washington Post*, June 28, 1995.

49. Gretchen Lacharite, "Control Board Summons Smith: 13 Schools Fall Short of Safety, Judge Says," *Washington Times*, August 10, 1996.

50. Rachel L. Swarns, "A Human Bridge to the Have-Nots in Washington," *New York Times*, May 16, 2009.

51. School Scorecard 2012–13, "Ferebee-Hope Elementary School (Closing July 2013)," District of Columbia Public Schools Bulletin, http://www.profiles.dcps.dc.gov /pdf/ferebee-hope2012.pdf, accessed January 7, 2015.

52. Cultural Tourism, DC, "Dorothy Boulding Ferebee Residence," http://www .culturaltourismdc.org/things-to-do-see/dorothy-boulding-ferebee-residence, accessed January 24, 2013.

53. "County Police Mourn the Loss of One of Their Own: 25-Year-Veteran Officer Is Killed in Motorcycle Accident," Montgomery County, MD, Department of Police, Office of Media Services, press release, August 29, 2000.

54. Laurence Jones interview with the author.

55. Margo Pinson interview with the author.

56. Lisa Ferebee interview with the author.

57. Todd Boulding Ferebee and Dorothy Ruth Ferebee interviews with the author.

58. Todd Boulding Ferebee interview with the author.

59. Todd Boulding Ferebee email to the author, April 25, 2014.

60. Todd Boulding Ferebee interview with the author.

61. Dorothy Ruth Ferebee email to the author, May 25, 2014.

62. Obituary: "Claude T. Ferebee," *Norfolk Virginian-Pilot*, August 7, 1996.

63. Bargain and Sale Deed, Claude Ferebee and Hazel Ferebee to John Joseph and Merrysil Joseph, Westchester County, Deed Book, Town of Greenburgh, Liber 10625:83, May 28, 1993; Lisa Ferebee email to the author, July 14, 2011.

64. Lisa Ferebee interview with the author.

65. Lisa Ferebee email to the author, July 14, 2011.

66. Lisa Ferebee email to the author, July 14, 2011.

67. Obituary: "Hazel J. Ferebee," *Selma Times-Journal*, September 26, 2007; Power of Attorney, Claude T. Ferebee to Hazel J. Ferebee, May 27, 1993, Westchester County Court, Liber 208: 117.

68. Calvary Cemetery, Norfolk, Interment Files, "Charles S. Ferebee," April 26, 1956, Nannie J. Ferebee, May 17, 1961.

69. Obituary: "Constance F. Jones," *Virginian-Pilot*, November 22, 1997; Laurence Jones interview with the author.

70. Obituary: "Maxine F. Burrell," *Virginian-Pilot*, September 24, 1998.

71. Dorothy Ruth Ferebee email to the author, May 25, 2014; Lisa Ferebee interview with the author.

EPILOGUE

1. Lisa Ferebee emails to the author, January 15 and 30, 2014; Dorothy Ruth Ferebee interview with the author.

2. Dorothy Ferebee, Certificate of Death. No. 80-006041, Government of the District of Columbia, Department of Health.

3. "Cemetery Clean-up Due: History and Underbrush Heavily Cloak Mt. Olive," (Norfolk) *New Journal and Guide*, July 21, 1962.

4. "Cemetery Clean-up Due"; "Norfolk Atty. Dies; Practiced 47 Years," (Norfolk) *New Journal and Guide*, June 22, 1963.

5. "Backed by Civil Groups: Mount Olive Cemetery's Annual Clean Up May 15," (Norfolk) *New Journal and Guide*, April 17, 1971; "Hawthorne Club to Clean-up Cemetery: Underbrush Again Target at Historical Mt. Olive," (Norfolk) *New Journal and Guide*, August 8, 1972; "Mt. Olive Cemetery Clean-up Planned: Cemetery Eye Sores to Be Healed," (Norfolk) *New Journal and Guide*, July 19, 1975.

6. "Mount Hope Cemetery," promotional brochure, 1961, courtesy Mount Hope Cemetery, Hastings-on-Hudson NY.

7. Invoice from Mount Hope Cemetery to author, March 17, 2014.

8. Laurence Jones interview with the author.

BIBLIOGRAPHY

ARCHIVAL SOURCES

A. C. Long Health Sciences Library, Columbia University Medical Center

Amistad Research Center, Tulane University

    Heslip-Ruffin Family Papers

Bancroft Library, University of California at Berkeley

    Ida L. Jackson Oral History

    Ida L. Jackson Papers

Beinecke Rare Book and Manuscript Library, Yale University

    Walter Francis White and Poppy Cannon Papers

Bobst Library, New York University

    Records of the Associated Colleges of Upper New York (ACUNY)

Benjamin Feinberg Library, Plattsburgh State University College

    Champlain College Collection

Charles Sumner School Museum and Archives

Franklin D. Roosevelt Presidential Library and Museum, Hyde Park NY

Gelman Library, George Washington University

    Friendship House Association Records

Girl Scouts of the USA

Hampton University Museum and Archives

Harry S. Truman Presidential Library and Museum, Independence MO

Howard University Archives

John F. Kennedy Presidential Library and Museum, Boston MA

Library of Congress, Manuscript Division

    James Forman Papers

    Mary McLeod Bethune Microfilm Collection

    Montgomery Family Papers, 1872–1938

    NAACP Collection

    U.S. Army, 93rd Infantry Division Collection

Lyndon Baines Johnson Library and Museum, Austin TX

Mississippi State University Libraries
    Allen Eugene Cox Papers
Moorland-Spingarn Research Center, Howard University
    Alpha Kappa Alpha Collection
    Dorothy Boulding Ferebee Papers
    George Freeman Bragg Papers
    Marian Anderson—DAR Controversy Collection
    Ruffin Family Papers
National Museum of American History, Smithsonian Institution
    Moses Moon Audiotape Collection
National Park Service, Mary McLeod Bethune Council House National Historic
    Site, National Archives of Black Women's History
    Madeline Kountze Dugger Garnett Kelley Papers
    Pauline Spiegel Cowan Papers
    Records of the National Council of Negro Women
Richard Nixon Presidential Library and Museum, Yorba Linda CA
Schlesinger Library on the History of Women in America, Radcliffe Institute, Har-
    vard University
    Dorothy Boulding Ferebee Oral History, Black Women's Oral History
        Project
    Edith Spurlock Sampson Papers
    Esther Peterson Papers
Schomburg Center for Research in Black Culture, New York Public Library
    Melva L. Price Papers
    New York World's Fair Negro Week Records, 1940
    St. Philip's Episcopal Church Records
    Wilhelmina F. Adams Papers
Shields Library, University of California at Davis
    E. M. Lashley, "Glimpses into the Life of a Great Mississippian and a Majestic
    American Educator, 1926–1976." Manuscript, 1977.
Sophia Smith Collection, Smith College
    Florence Rose Papers
    International Council of Women Records
    Margaret Sanger Papers
    Mary Ritter Beard Papers
    YMCA of the U.S.A. Records, 1860–2002

PUBLISHED SOURCES

Anderson, Marian. *My Lord, What a Morning.* New York: Viking, 1956.
Austin, Sharon D. Wright. *The Transformation of Plantation Politics.* Albany: State
    University of New York Press, 2006.

Baker, Jean H. *Margaret Sanger: A Life of Passion*. New York: Hill and Wang, 2011.

Banks, Henry H. *A Century of Excellence: The History of Tufts University School of Medicine, 1893–1993*. Boston: Tufts University Press, 1993.

Barry, John M. *Rising Tide: The Great Mississippi Flood of 1927 and How It Changed America*. New York: Touchstone, 1998.

Bartlett, Cynthia Chalmers. *Images of America: Beacon Hill*. Charleston SC: Arcadia, 1996.

Bateson, Mary Catherine. *Composing a Life*. New York: Grove Press, 1989.

Bearse, Austin. *Reminiscences of Fugitive-Slave Law Days in Boston*. Boston: Warren Richardson, 1880.

Bernard, Emily. *Carl Van Vechten and the Harlem Renaissance*. New Haven CT: Yale University Press, 2012.

Bolton, Charles C. *The Hardest Deal of All: The Battle over School Integration in Mississippi, 1870–1980*. Jackson: University Press of Mississippi, 2007.

Bordewich, Fergus M. *Washington: The Making of the American Capital*. New York: Amistad, 2008.

Brinkley, David. *Washington Goes to War*. New York: Knopf, 1988.

Brown, Ellen F., and John Wiley Jr. *Margaret Mitchell's "Gone with the Wind": A Bestseller's Odyssey from Atlanta to Hollywood*. Lanham MD: Taylor Trade, 2011.

Bundles, A'Lelia. *On Her Own Ground: The Life and Times of Madam C. J. Walker*. New York: Scribner, 2001.

Campbell, Stanley W. *The Slave Catchers: Enforcement of the Fugitive Slave Law: 1850–1860*. New York: Norton, 1972.

Carter, Robert L. *A Matter of Law: A Memoir of Struggle in the Cause of Equal Rights*. New York: New Press, 2005.

Chilton, Karen. *Hazel Scott: The Pioneering Journey of a Jazz Pianist from Cafe Society to Hollywood to HUAC*. Ann Arbor: University of Michigan Press, 2008.

Clarke, Thurston. *JFK's Last Hundred Days: The Transformation of a Man and the Emergence of a Great President*. New York: Penguin, 2013.

Cobb, W. Montague. "A Short History of Freedmen's Hospital." *Journal of the National Medical Association* 54.3 (1962): 271–87.

———. "William Alonza Warfield, M.D., 1866–1951." *Journal of the National Medical Association* 44.3 (1952): 206–19.

Collins, Judy. *Suite Judy Blue Eyes: My Life in Music*. New York: Crown Archetype, 2011.

Cookson, Peter W., Jr., and Caroline Hodges Persell. *Preparing for Power: America's Elite Boarding Schools*. New York: Basic Books, 1985.

Cooney, Terry A. *Balancing Acts: American Thought and Culture in the 1930's*. New York: Twayne, 1995.

Crosby, Molly Caldwell. *The American Plague: The Untold Story of Yellow Fever, the Epidemic That Shaped Our History*. New York: Berkeley Books, 2006.

Dailey, Jane. *Before Jim Crow: The Politics of Race in Post Emancipation Virginia.* Chapel Hill: University of North Carolina Press, 2000.

Dallas, Jerry W. "The Delta and Providence Farms: A Mississippi Experiment in Cooperative Farming and Racial Cooperation, 1936–1956." *Mississippi Quarterly* 4.3 (1987): 283–308.

Dong, Zhenghai. "From Postbellum Plantation to Modern Agribusiness: A History of the Delta and Pine Land Company." PhD diss., Purdue University, 1993.

DuBois, W. E. B. "The Talented Tenth." September 1903. http://www.teachingameri canhistory.org/library/index.asp?document=174. Accessed September 14, 2013.

Dummett, Clifton O. "The Negro in Dental Education: A Review of Important Occurrences." *Phylon Quarterly* 20.4th quarter (1959): 379–88.

Dyja, Thomas. *Walter White: The Dilemma of Black Identity in America.* Chicago: Ivan R. Dee, 2008.

Ervin, Elsie Ann. "Dr. Ded (Dr. Rosier Davis Dedwylder 1883–1948)." Unpublished manuscript. Delta State Teachers College, 1951.

Farwell, Byron. *Over There: The United States in the Great War 1917–1918.* New York: Norton, 1999.

Flexner, Alexander. "Medical Education in the United States and Canada: A Report to the Carnegie Foundation for the Advancement of Teaching." 1910. http://www.archive.carnegiefoundation.org/pdfs/elibrary/Carnegie_Flexner_Report.pdf. Accessed January 26, 2015.

Foner, Eric. *Freedom's Lawmakers: A Directory of Black Office Holders during Reconstruction.* New York: Oxford University Press, 1993.

Forrest, William S. *The Great Pestilence in Virginia: An Historical Account of the Origin, General Character, and Ravages of Yellow Fever in Norfolk and Portsmouth in 1855. . . .* New York: Derby & Jackson, 1856.

Franklin, Buck Colbert. *My Life and an Era: The Autobiography of Buck Colbert Franklin,* edited by John Hope Franklin, and John Whittington Franklin. Baton Rouge: Louisiana State University Press, 1997.

Franklin, John Hope. *From Slavery to Freedom: A History of Negro Americans.* 4th ed. New York: Knopf, 1974.

Frazier, E. Franklin. *Black Bourgeoisie.* New York: Free Press Paperbacks, 1997.

Fried, Richard M. *Nightmare in Red: The McCarthy Era in Perspective.* New York: Oxford University Press, 1990.

Gamble, Vanessa Northington. *Making a Place for Ourselves: The Black Hospital Movement 1920–1945.* New York: Oxford University Press, 1995.

———, ed. *Germs Have No Color Line: Black and American Medicine 1900–1940 (Medical Care in the United States).* New York: Garland Publishing, 1989.

Gara, Larry. *The Liberty Line: The Legend of the Underground Railroad.* Lexington: University of Kentucky Press, 1961.

Gerlernter, David. *1939: The Lost World of the Fair.* New York: Free Press, 1995.

Gibson, Truman K., Jr., with Steve Huntley. *Knocking Down Barriers: My Fight for Black America*. Evanston IL: Northwestern University Press, 2005.

Giddings, Paula J. *Ida: A Sword among Lions. Ida B. Wells and the Campaign against Lynching*. New York: Amistad, 2008.

Gilbert, Ben W., and the staff of the Washington Post. *Ten Blocks from the White House: Anatomy of the Washington Riots of 1968*. New York: Praeger Publishers, 1968.

Gill, Jonathan. *Harlem: The Four Hundred Year History from Dutch Village to Capital of Black America*. New York: Grove Press, 2011.

Gitlin, Todd. *The Sixties: Years of Hope, Days of Rage*. New York: Bantam Books, 1989.

Goodwin, Doris Kearns. *No Ordinary Time: Franklin and Eleanor Roosevelt. The Home Front in World War II*. New York: Simon & Schuster, 1994.

Graham, Lawrence Otis. *Our Kind of People: Inside America's Black Upper Class*. New York: Harper Collins, 1999.

Green, Constance McLaughlin. *The Secret City: A History of Race Relations in the Nation's Capital*. Princeton NJ: Princeton University Press, 1967.

Greenburg, Cheryl Lynn. *Or Does It Explode? Black Harlem in the Great Depression*. New York: Oxford University Press, 1991.

Greenhouse, Linda, and Reva B. Siegel. *Before "Roe v. Wade": Voices That Shaped the Abortion Debate before the Supreme Court's Ruling*. New York: Kaplan, 2010.

Grover, Kathryn, and Janine V. da Silva. "Historic Resource Study." National Park Service, Boston African American National Historic Site, December 31, 2002. http://www.cr.nps.gov/history/online_books/bost/hrs.pdf. Accessed January 26, 2015.

Hamilton, Charles V. *Adam Clayton Powell, Jr.: The Political Biography of an American Dilemma*. New York: Atheneum, 1991.

Hamilton, Sally Atwood, ed. *Lift Thine Eyes: The Landscape, the Buildings, the Heritage of Northfield Mount Hermon School*. Mount Hermon MA: Northfield Mount Hermon, 2010.

Hanson, Joyce A. *Mary McLeod Bethune and Black Women's Political Activism*. Columbia: University of Missouri Press, 2003.

Harwell, Debbie Z. "Wednesdays in Mississippi: Uniting Women across Regional and Racial Lines, Summer 1964." *Journal of Southern History* 76 (2010): 617–54.

Height, Dorothy. *Open Wide the Freedom Gates: A Memoir*. New York: Public Affairs, 2003.

Holt, Rackham. *Mary McLeod Bethune: A Biography*. Garden City NY: Doubleday, 1964.

Hucles, Michael. "Many Voices, Similar Concerns: Traditional Methods of African-American Political Activity in Norfolk, Virginia, 1865–1875." *Virginia Magazine of History and Biography* 100.4 (1992): 543–66.

Jackson, Luther Porter. *Negro Office-Holders in Virginia, 1865–1895*. Norfolk VA: Guide Quality Press, 1945.

Jackson, Maurice Elizabeth. "Mound Bayou—A Study in Social Development." Master's thesis, University of Alabama, 1937.

Jaffe, Harry S., and Tom Sherwood. *Dream City: Race, Power and the Decline of Washington DC*. New York: Simon & Schuster, 1994.

Jefferson, Robert F. *Fighting for Hope: African American Troops of the 93rd Infantry Division in World War II and Postwar America*. Baltimore MD: Johns Hopkins University Press, 2008.

———. "Making the Men of the 93rd: African American Servicemen in the Years of the Great Depression and the Second World War, 1935–1947." PhD diss., University of Michigan, 1995.

Johnson, Charles S. *The Negro in American Civilization: A Study of Negro Life and Race Relations in the Light of Social Research*. New York: Henry Holt, 1930.

Johnson, F. Ernest. "The American Seminar." *Religious Education* 22.8 (1927): 867–69.

Johnston, James Hugo, Jr. "The Participation of Negroes in the Government of Virginia from 1877 to 1888." *Journal of Negro History* 14.3 (1929): 251–71.

Kaplan, Carla. *Miss Anne in Harlem: The White Women of the Black Renaissance*. New York: HarperCollins, 2013.

Kaplan, Laura. *The Story of Jane: The Legendary Underground Feminist Abortion Service*. New York: Pantheon Books, 1995.

Kearney, James R. *Anna Eleanor Roosevelt: The Evolution of a Reformer*. Boston: Houghton Mifflin, 1968.

Keiler, Allan. *Marian Anderson: A Singer's Journey*. New York: Lisa Drew/Scribner, 2000.

Kershaw, Ian. *Hitler, 1936–1945: Nemesis*. New York: Norton, 2000.

King, Gilbert. *Devil in the Grove: Thurgood Marshall, the Groveland Boys and the Dawn of a New America*. New York: Harper Perennial, 2012.

King, Mary. *Freedom Song: A Personal Story of the 1960's Civil Rights Movement*. New York: William Morrow, 1987.

Klara, Robert. *The Hidden White House: Harry Truman and the Reconstruction of America's Most Famous Residence*. New York: St. Martin's Press, 2013.

Lederman, Georges Gilbert. "Disease in History: The Influence of Yellow Fever and Malaria on Black Slavery in South Carolina during the Seventeenth and Early Eighteenth Centuries." Senior thesis, Brown University, 1979.

Lewis, David Levering. *District of Columbia: A Bicentennial History*. New York: Norton, 1976.

———. *When Harlem Was in Vogue*. New York: Knopf, 1981.

Lewis, Earl. *In Their Own Interests: Race, Class and Power in Twentieth-Century Norfolk, Virginia*. Berkeley: University of California Press, 1991.

Li-Marcus, Moying. *Beacon Hill: The Life and Times of a Neighborhood.* Boston: Northeastern University Press, 2002.

Lisio, Donald B. "A Blunder Becomes a Catastrophe: Hoover, the Legion and the Bonus Army." *Wisconsin Magazine of History* 51 (Autumn 1967): 37–50.

Locke, Alain. *The New Negro: An Interpretation.* New York: Albert and Charles Boni, 1923.

Logan, Rayford W. *Howard University: The First Hundred Years, 1867–1967.* New York: New York University Press, 1969.

Marable, Manning. *Malcolm X: A Life of Reinvention.* New York: Viking, 2011.

Mark, Kenneth L. *Delayed by Fire: Being the Early History of Simmons College.* Concord NH: Rumford Press, 1945.

Marmorstein, Gary. *The Label: The Story of Columbia Records.* New York: Thunder's Mouth Press, 2007.

Mauro, James. *Twilight at the World of Tomorrow.* New York: Ballantine Books, 2010.

McCabe, Katie, and Dovey Roundtree. *Justice Older than the Law: The Life of Dovey Johnson Roundtree.* Jackson: University Press of Mississippi, 2009.

McCann, Carole R. *Birth Control Politics in the United States, 1916–1945.* Ithaca NY: Cornell University Press, 1994.

McCord, Theodore. "John Page of Rosewell: Reason, Religion, and Republican Government from the Perspective of a Virginia Planter, 1743–1808." PhD diss., American University, 1991.

McCullough, David. *Truman.* New York: Simon & Schuster, 1992.

McKinney, Richard. *Mordecai: The Man and His Message. The Story of Mordecai Wyatt Johnson.* Washington DC: Howard University Press, 1997.

McWhirter, Cameron. *Red Summer: The Summer of 1919 and the Awakening of Black America.* New York: Henry Holt, 2011.

McWhorter, Diane. *Carry Me Home: Birmingham, Alabama. The Climactic Battle of the Civil Rights Revolution.* New York: Simon & Schuster/Touchstone, 2002.

Messer, Ellen, and Kathryn E. May. *Back Rooms: Voices from the Illegal Abortion Era.* New York: St. Martin's Press, 1988.

Moore, James T. "Black Militancy in Readjuster Virginia, 1879–1883." *Journal of Southern History* 41 (May 1975): 167–86.

Moran, Ella Payne. "A Project Conducted in Mississippi: Alpha Kappa Alpha Sorority Health Project, Mississippi 1935–1942." Unpublished manuscript. Howard University, 1942.

More, Ellen S. *Restoring the Balance: Women Physicians and the Profession of Medicine 1850–1995.* Cambridge MA: Harvard University Press, 1995.

Morris, James McGrath. *Pulitzer: A Life in Politics, Print and Power.* New York: Harper Collins, 2010.

Nagorski, Andrew. *Hitlerland: American Eyewitnesses to the Nazi Rise to Power.* New York: Simon & Schuster, 2012.

Newby, Cassandra L. "The World Was All before Them: A Study of the Black Community in Norfolk, Virginia, 1861–1884." PhD diss., College of William and Mary, 1992.

Osgood, Kenneth A. "Hearts and Minds: The Unconventional Cold War." *Journal of Cold War Studies* (Spring 2002): 85–107.

Paige, T. F. *Twenty-Two Years of Freedom.* Norfolk VA: Thos. F. Paige, 1885.

Parker, Marjorie H. *Alpha Kappa Alpha through the Years 1908–1988.* Chicago: Mobium Press, 1990.

Persico, Joseph E. *Franklin and Lucy: President Roosevelt, Mrs. Rutherfurd, and the Other Remarkable Women in His Life.* New York: Random House, 2008.

Petchesky, Rosalind P. *Abortion and Woman's Choice: The State, Sexuality, and Reproductive Freedom.* Boston: Northeastern University Press, 1990.

Phillips, Cabell. *New York Times Chronicle of American Life: From the Crash to the Blitz, 1929–1939.* Toronto: Macmillan, 1969.

Prescott, Heather Munro. *Student Bodies: The Influence of Student Health Services in American Society and Medicine.* Ann Arbor: University of Michigan Press, 2007.

Reich, Cary. *The Life of Nelson Rockefeller: Worlds to Conquer, 1908–1958.* New York: Doubleday, 1996.

Sanger, Alexander. *Beyond Choice: Reproductive Freedom in the 21st Century.* New York: Public Affairs, 2004.

Savage, Barbara Dianne. *Your Spirits Walk Beside Us: The Politics of Black Religion.* Cambridge MA: Belknap Press of Harvard University Press, 2008.

Shaw, Stephanie J. *What a Woman Ought to Be and to Do: Black Professional Women during the Jim Crow Era.* Chicago: University of Chicago Press, 1996.

Siebert, Wilbur Henry. *The Underground Railroad in Massachusetts.* Worcester MA: American Antiquarian Society, 1936.

Simmons, Dovie Marie, and Olivia L. Martin. *Down Behind the Sun: The Story of Arenia Conelia Mallory.* Memphis TN: Riverside Press, 1983.

Smart, Fred Andrew. *The Builders of Tilton School: A Centennial Record.* Concord NH: Privately published, 1945.

Smith, Elaine H. "Historic Resource Study: Mary McLeod Bethune and the National Council of Negro Women, Pursuing a True and Unfettered Democracy." Report for the Mary McLeod Bethune Council House National Historic Site, September 2003.

Smith, Fred C. "Agrarian Experimentation and Failure in Depression Mississippi: New Deal and Socialism, the Tupelo Homesteads and the Delta and Providence Cooperative Farms." Master's thesis, Mississippi State University, 2002.

———. "The Delta Cooperative Farm and the Death of a Vision." *Journal of Mississippi History* 71.3 (2009): 235–74.

———. *Trouble in Goshen: Plain Folk, Roosevelt, Jesus and Marx in the Great Depression South*. Jackson: University Press of Mississippi, 2014.

Smith, Susan L. *Sick and Tired of Being Sick and Tired: Black Women's Health Activism in America, 1890–1950*. Philadelphia: University of Pennsylvania Press, 1995.

Spencer, Samuel R., Jr. *Booker T. Washington and the Negro's Place in American Life*. Boston: Little, Brown, 1955.

Still, William. *The Underground Railroad: A Record of Facts, Authentic Narratives, Letters & Etc.* . . . Chicago: Johnson, 1970.

Stone, Irving, ed. *There Was a Light: Autobiography of a University. Berkeley: 1868–1968*. Garden City NY: Doubleday, 1970.

Stowe, Harriet Beecher. *Uncle Tom's Cabin*. Boston: St. James Press, 1854.

Talbot, Edith Armstrong. *Samuel Chapman Armstrong: A Biographical Study*. New York: Doubleday, Page, 1904.

Tate, Merze. Dorothy Ferebee Oral History Interview. December 28 and 31, 1979, in *Black Women Oral History Project*, edited by Ruth Edmonds Hill. Schlesinger Library on the History of Women in America. https://www.radcliffe.harvard.edu/schlesinger-library/collection/black-women-oral-history-project.

Taylor, Anne-Marie. *Young Charles Sumner and the Legacy of the American Enlightenment, 1811–1851*. Amherst: University of Massachusetts Press, 2001.

Terrell, Mary Church. *A Colored Woman in a White World*. Washington DC: Ransdell, 1940.

Thompson, Julius Eric. *Lynchings in Mississippi: A History, 1865–1965*. Jefferson NC: McFarland, 2007.

Trento, Susan. *The Power House: Robert Keith Gray and the Selling of Access and Influence in Washington*. New York: St. Martin's Press, 1992.

Tucker, Anjulet. "Get the Learnin' but Don't Lose the Burnin': The Socio-Cultural and Religious Politics of Education in a Black Pentecostal College." PhD diss., Emory University, 2009.

Unger, Irwin, and Debi Unger. *Postwar America: The United States since 1945*. New York: St. Martin's Press, 1990.

Van Vechten, Carl. *Nigger Heaven*. 1930. New York: Knopf, 1973.

Ward, Geoffrey C. *Unforgivable Blackness: The Rise and Fall of Jack Johnson*. New York: Knopf, 2004.

Ward, Thomas J. *Black Physicians in the Jim Crow South*. Fayetteville: University of Arkansas Press, 2003.

———. "Medical Missionaries of the Delta: Dr. Dorothy Ferebee and the Mississippi Health Project, 1935–1941." *Journal of Mississippi History* 63.3 (2001): 189–203.

Washington, Booker T. *Up from Slavery: An Autobiography*. Garden City NY: Doubleday, 1901.

Watkins, T. H. *The Great Depression: America in the 1930s*. Boston: Little, Brown, 1993.

White, Deborah Gray. *Too Heavy a Load: Black Women in Defense of Themselves, 1894–1994*. New York: Norton, 1999.

White, Walter. *A Man Called White*. New York: Viking, 1948.

———. *Rope and Faggot: A Biography of Judge Lynch*. Notre Dame IN: University of Notre Dame Press, 2001.

Williams, Michael Vinson. *Medgar Evers: Mississippi Martyr*. Fayetteville: University of Arkansas Press, 2011.

Williams, Wirt, ed., *History of Bolivar County, Mississippi*. Jackson: Mississippi Delta Chapter, Daughters of the American Revolution, 1948.

Wilson, Beverly, ed. *The Selected Letters of Charles Sumner (1830–1859)*. Vol. 1. Boston: Northeastern University Press, 1990.

Wilson, Sondra Kathryn. *Meet Me at the Theresa: The Story of Harlem's Most Famous Hotel*. New York: Atria Books, 2004.

Winchell, Meghan K. *Good Girls, Good Food, Good Fun: The Story of USO Hostesses during World War II*. Chapel Hill: University of North Carolina Press, 2008.

Woodward, C. Vann. *The Strange Career of Jim Crow*. New York: Oxford University Press, 1966.

INDEX

abolitionists, 8, 33, 78, 140

abortion, as possible reason for Dorothy (Dolly) Ferebee Jr.'s death, 169–72, 182

abortion rights, Dorothy's support for, xxi, 169–72, 182, 223–24

Aframerican Woman's Journal (NCNW), 155, 157

Africa, Dorothy's visits to, 211–13

African American Institute, 211

African Americans: in 1920s Norfolk VA, 34; Benjamin Boulding's fundraising for, 11; Bethune's campaigning for, 152; Claude Ferebee as military role model, 112; Dorothy's race-based hospital internship rejections, 21; Dorothy's Settlement House for children, xviii; Dr. Vaughn on life in Holmes County, 58; Harlem NY culture, 33; Madam C. J. Walker House for women, 134; military discrimination, 121–22; Mississippi illiteracy, poverty, 1, 2; segregation in Washington DC, 26; Southern voting restrictions, 2; support for Franklin Roosevelt, 99; suspicions about birth control, 129; *Vogue* spread of achieving women, May, 1969, 221–22; Washington DC as Mecca for, 26, 218; White on memoirs by, xxi. *See also* Alpha Kappa Alpha (AKA) sorority; civil rights movement; Jim Crow South; National Council of Negro Women

"Africa: The Continent of the Hour" article (D. Ferebee), 212

Afro-American, Baltimore newspaper, 41, 42, 47, 89

Alabama Department of Public Safety, 205

Alexander, Virginia, 104

Alpha Kappa Alpha (AKA) sorority: 1908 founding, 54; 1941 summer clinic, 107; 1950 regional meeting, 183; Boyd's co-founding of, 53; complaints about Dorothy, 107–8; Dorothy's leadership, xix, 20, 98, 100; Dorothy's letters to sorority sisters, 55, 77–78, 216; Epsilon Chapter, Tufts University, 54; fiftieth anniversary celebration, 226; funding for health project, 98; Ida Jackson's leadership, 50–51, 126; "Improving the Social Status of the Race" talk, 60–61; *Ivy Leaf* magazine, 61, 63, 72, 74, 91, 95, 235; letters from Dorothy to, 55, 77–78; Mississippi Health Project legacy concerns, 95; Non-Partisan Council, 89–90, 153, 155; planning for Mississippi Health Project, 53–54; Providence Cooperative Farm proposal, 126–27; public speaking at conferences, 24; sorors' reaction to health project, 56; sorors' trip to Mississippi, 62; sponsorship of Mississippi Health Project, xviii, 3, 59; Whitby's leadership, 127; Xi Omega Chapter, 54, 71, 77, 89–90

consultancy work, for U.S. Department of State, 213–15
contraception. *See* birth control
Cornely, Paul, 101, 130, 147, 217, 240
"Cotton Field Clinic" article (Ratcliff), 103–4
Cowan, Polly, 206–7
Crisis, NAACP magazine, 41
Crocker, Emma, 10, 12, 13, 14, 45
Crusade for Freedom, 176
Cumberland Street Colored School (Norfolk VA), 13

Daughters of the American Revolution (DAR), 96, 97
DC Commission on Human Rights, 228
Dean, Buddy, 232
deaths: of Benjamin Richard Boulding, 224; of Benjamin Richard Boulding Jr., 224; of Carol Phillips Ferebee, 245; of Claude Ferebee II, 218, 242, 245, 248; of Claude Thurston Ferebee, 244; of Dorothy (Dolly) Ferebee Jr., xxi, 138, 147, 166, 167–68, 169, 170–74, 184; of Dorothy, xx, 63, 234–35, 239–43, 246; of Florence Paige Boulding, 10, 13, 214, 224, 247
Dedwylder, Rosier Davis, 93, 107; letter of welcome to Dorothy, 78–79; support of Mississippi Health Project, 4–5, 79, 81–82, 83
Delano, Sara, 151
Delta and Pine Land Plantation (Bolivar County), 68, 78, 84
Delta Cooperative Farm: founding of, 92; as health project location, 93; integration of whites and blacks, 85; planning stage by AKA, 126; visit by Katharine Gardner, 103
Democratic Republic of the Congo, 212
Dies, Martin, 97, 154
diet of farmworkers, 1–2, 96–97, 102
diphtheria, 58, 79, 82, 83
Distinguished Achievement Award (Simmons College), 220–21

Division of Negro Service (Planned Parenthood), 129
divorce of Dorothy and Claude Ferebee, xx, xxi, 90; Dorothy's filing for divorce in Chicago, 175; Dorothy's version of events, 118, 175–76; extramarital affair of Claude, 109–14, 115–20, 178; newspaper reports about, 176–77; Sampson's legal services, 175; settlement agreement, 176
Donowa, Arnold, 37, 46, 48
Douglass, Frederick, 26, 141
Drew, Charles, 141
Du Bois, Shirley Graham, 211–13
Du Bois, W. E. B.: Dorothy's *Crisis* article pitch, 41; founding of NAACP, 6; Negro Advisory Council participation, 130; Talented Tenth description, xxii, 6–7
Dugger, Madeline Mabray Kountze, 109–11; extramarital affair with Claude Ferebee, 109–14, 115–20, 178; letter to Nannie Ferebee, 116–17
dysentery, 2, 55

Eberhardt, J. Russell, III, 137, 140, 179, 231
Eddy, Sherwood, 85, 92, 93
education of Claude Thurston Ferebee, 33–34, 36–37; boarding schools, 141, 145–46; Champlain College, 140, 163–66; Howard Dental School, 229–30
education of Dorothy Ferebee: Cumberland Street Colored School, 13; Girls' High, Boston, 14–15; Simmons College, 15, 16–17, 135, 212, 220; Tufts College Medical School, xxi, 17–19; yearbook staff activities, 17, 19, 20
education of Dorothy (Dolly) Ferebee Jr.: boarding schools, 142–44, 146; Champlain College, 163–66, 168, 169, 172, 231
Edward C. Hitchcock Award (1971), 220
Eisenhower, Dwight D., 53, 196, 201
Eisenhower, Mamie, xix, 196, 203
Epsilon Chapter of AKA (Tufts University), 54

achievement of tax-exempt status, 202; anger at DAR, 96; Bethune's leadership of, 105, 148; black women's employment issue, 153; Brown's resignation, 185; Committee on Family Planning, 104, 128; concerts hosted by, 193–95; Dorothy's German goodwill tour, 184–89, 191; Dorothy's leadership, xix, xxi, 104–5, 130, 161–62, 166, 171, 174, 190–91; Dorothy's trip to Greece, 184–85, 187; Edith Sampson's loan to, 157–58; Eleanor Roosevelt's support for, 150, 151, 152; ending of Dorothy's two terms, 196–97; endorsement of contraception, 128; FBI negativity towards, 153–54, 201; financial aid from Dorothy, 200–201; financial issues, 184, 186, 189, 195; fundraising activities, 130–31; Height's leadership, 156, 201–3; HUAC accusations against, 188–89; implosion of, 188; Intercultural Committee, 185; International Night events, 159–60, 196; interracial tea-hosting event, 192–93; NAACP membership, 155; negative press for, 157, 184–85, 186; origin of, 73, 90; speeches by Dorothy, 24; stance against racial inequality, 90; support for women in the military, 155; UN Conference representation, 131–32

National Negro Advisory Council, 129–30
National Negro Business League, 11
National Negro Congress, 101
National Negro Health Movement, 58
National Negro Health Week, 101
National Youth Administration, 73, 149, 151, 160
Nation of Islam, 219
NCNW. *See* National Council of Negro Women
Negro Health Week, 41, 101
Nehru, Jawaharlal, 135
New Deal programs (Roosevelt), 5, 73, 90, 92, 149, 151
New Frontier initiatives (Kennedy), 199

New Journal and Guide newspaper, 47, 162, 247
New York Times, 5, 72, 202, 205
Nickens, Portia, 91
Nixon, Patricia, xix, 228
Nixon, Richard, 79, 228
Non-Partisan Lobby for Economic and Democratic Rights (AKA), 89–90, 153, 155
Northfield/Mount Hermon School, 142–46, 163, 172, 173

Obama, Barack, xxii, 203
Obama, Michelle, 242
obituary of Dorothy Ferebee, xx, xxiii
Open Wide the Freedom Gates (Height), 204
Osborne, Mary D., 58

Paige, Joseph, 247
Paige, Leslie, 247
Paige, Lillie, 247
Paige, Richard Gault Leslie "R. G. L.," xx, 7–8, 9, 224, 238, 246, 247
Paige, Thomas, 7
Paige cemetery (Norfolk, Virginia), 246–47
Pandit, V. L., 135
Parker, Barrington, Jr., xxii, 79
Parker, Marjorie Holloman, xxii, 70
Parks, Rosa, xvii, 198
Patterson, Frederick D., 60
Payne, Ella, 63, 69, 97, 102, 103
pellagra, 2, 94
Penn, Irving, xix–xx, 222
Pennsylvania Institute of Negro Health, 104
People's Republic of China, 219
Perkins, Frances, 59–60
Peterson, Esther, 211, 221
Phillips, Barbara, 235
Phillips, Carrie, 179
Phillips, Vaughn, 178–79
Phillips, W. Franklin, 177
Pierson, Richard N., 130
Pinson, Margo, 232
Pittsburgh Courier articles, 183, 196, 197
Planned Parenthood, 104, 128, 129–30